THE COLLECTORS ENCYCLOPEDIA OF

DOLLS and COLLECTIBLES

The current values in this book should be used only as a guide. They are not intended to set prices, which vary from one section of the country to another. Auction prices as well as dealer prices vary greatly and are affected by condition as well as demand. Neither the Author nor the Publisher assumes responsibility for any losses that might be incurred as a result of consulting this guide.

Additional copies of this book may be ordered from:

Collector Books
P.O. Box 3009
Paducah, KY 42001

@ $19.95. Add $2.00 each for postage and handling.

THE COLLECTORS ENCYCLOPEDIA OF

DOLLS and COLLECTIBLES

By Sibyl DeWein
and
Joan Ashabraner

Edited by
Annemarie Dunzelmann

COLLECTOR BOOKS
A Division of Schroeder Publishing Co., Inc.

ACKNOWLEDGMENTS

This book could not have been written without the generous cooperation of Mattel, Inc. Information about the early dolls and the company's history was tremendously helpful. We are especially indebted to Beverly Stennett, Judy Carell and Ellen Wahl for their courteous cooperation.

We want to thank the following people for the following reasons:

Norris Whittaker, David Glick, Joe Butler Gaines, Larry Brechbuhl, Nancy Byrd, Annie Greenwell and Nell Gilkey provided us with vital research material.

Patricia and Dwight Smith were especially helpful with advice, information and encouragement. And they introduced us to Bill Schroeder, the publisher!

Richard McFalls, Sunday Editor of the Clarksville Leaf-Chronicle (Tennessee's oldest Newspaper), offered advice and information about editorial procedures. Gerald L. Tenney, Instructor of Photography at Austin Peay State University, and Loy Duncan did their best to teach us photographic procedures.

Kristen Johnson, Teresa Stefko and Bill St. John searched European toy stores for dolls, related items and research material. Trudy Banks, Beulah Caswell, Bernice Lieb and Joan Pinney sent us dolls and information from Canada.

Helma Denninger, Erhard Herdt, Wilhelm Hofman, Carl Kaublough and Christine Riedrich sent us dolls, related items and research material from Germany. John R. Ashley and Vivien King sent information from England.

Over the years the following friends added one or more pieces to the Barbie puzzle: Olga Ashurst, Jan Bacon, Kathy Bennett, Shirley Berry, Marjorie Buxton, Hazel Carney, Jane Causey, Laura Choquette, Marie Cluster, Mary Cole, Alice Craig, Marie Ernst, Bobbie Espinosa, Esther Frederick, Burnie Freeman, Dawn Forbes, Maria Gaia, Beverly Gardner, Helen Gaydarik, Geraldine Gray, Chris Harris, Ellie Haynes, Sharon Hazel, Betty Herning, Fern Hotzel, Phyllis Houston, Ruth Hutton, Maxine Jamnick, Janice Kaderly, Dixie Kennett, Mirium Knox, Bernice Lieb, Ruth Lane, Margaret Magner, Glenn Mandeville, Margie Marion, Benita Martin, Melanie Martin, Carol McCall, Connie McDonald, Frazia McDonald, Mike McDonald, Doris McElfresh, Debbie Muller, Matilda Nagel, Angela Nickerson, Paul Nielsen, Grace Otto, Jean Patterson, Vickey Ann Paulson, Shirley Puertzer, Cathy Radice, Norma Rivorie, Jo Robison, Barbara Ann Rogers, Mae St. John, Sigrid Sanders, Ilse Scott, Virginia Sherrad, Carolyn Simpson, Sarah Sink, Virginia Slade, Beth Stanfill, Betty Tait, Faye Von Dracek, Mary Walsten, Emily Weakley, Paula Weakley, Phyllis Weakley and Stella Wolfenbarger.

We are especially grateful to our husbands, Harold DeWein and Philip Ashabraner. Without them, this Book would not have been possible.

INTRODUCTION

Doll collecting is one of the most popular hobbies in the country. It is a hobby enjoyed by both women and men, young and old. The type of doll collected varies from the costly antique to the newest doll on the toy store shelf.

One of the most rapidly growing group of doll collectors is the Barbie collector. As more and more collectors become interested in the Barbie doll, the need for a really comprehensive book on the subject becomes more urgent.

For the past 18 years the Barbie doll has been the most widely publicized doll ever created, but surprisingly little has been written about the doll for the collector's benefit. It is because of this that we decided to publish this book.

We hope that the information we have gained from years of intensive research will be of value to the long time collector as well as to the new collector. The more knowledge a person has of his hobby, the more he enjoys it.

Some of the terms we use in the book should be defined. By "booklet" we mean the small fashion publication packaged with the dolls, clothes and other items. Over the years these varied in size from 2-7/8" x 3-7/8" up to 3-1/2" x 6-1/4". (In the United States booklets were discontinued after 1973. They were still being published in Europe at least through 1975.)

By "catalogue" we mean the larger publications (about 8½" x 11") that Mattel furnishes retail merchants. The catalogue features all of the Mattel toys, not just the Barbie doll.

We use the term 'Barbie doll' as the name of a specific doll; we refer to the 'Barbie collection' when we intend to refer to more than the Barbie doll. All of the doll names in this book are registered trademarks of Mattel, Inc.

We would like to offer a word of advice to the new Barbie collector about used dolls found at flea markets and yard sales. If they are inexpensive, buy them! If they are unusually expensive, and if you are not sure about them, a little caution is advisable.

During play, children often swapped doll heads and bodies. Sometime these are easy to spot—a Barbie head on a Skipper body, for example—but other changes can be harder to detect. Only an expert can spot a #4 head on a #5 body. So be sure of the doll before you pay a big price for it.

Occasionally a doll will surface that does not quite fit a specific model. Most of these are transitional dolls. A good example of a transitional doll is the Barbie with the pale white torso and head (No. 3's) with the tan arms and legs (No. 4's). Another example is the hard hollow Pats. Pend. torso (No. 5) with the softer tan arms and legs (No. 4's).

These two examples are easy to understand—parts from one model being used on the following model. But another doll not so easy to understans is the one with the No. 1 body with a head from the No. 3 doll.

CONTENTS

I. The Barbie Era Begins

In 1959 a new doll reached toy store shelves. This was a long limbed, shapely doll, 11½ inches tall, named Barbie. After a slow start, the doll suddenly began selling like no other doll in history. Barbie is now the most successful and the most famous doll ever created.

Although created and marketed as a play doll for children, Barbie has now become the "darling" of adult doll collectors, not only in the United States, but also in foreign countries.

Just what—or who—is this Barbie doll? Barbie and her doll friends are responsible for making Mattel, Inc., the world's largest toy company. To date they have brought Mattel sales of over a billion dollars.

In 1945 Ruth and Elliott Handler and a friend, Harold Matson, founded Mattel—MATT for Matson and EL for Elliott. At the beginning the company made mostly picture frames. Then Elliott Handler began using the scraps from the frames to make doll furniture. This was the beginning of the toy business.

The company gradually grew. After a few years Mr. Matson left the company because of ill health. Elliott Handler remained as creator of new toys with Mrs. Handler in charge of marketing them.

In 1955 Mrs. Handler took a daring gamble. She used a large part of the company's funds to advertise their toys by sponsoring a 15 minute segment of a new children's television show called "The Mickey Mouse Club," a Walt Disney production. This experience helped to make Mattel the most effective advertiser in the toy industry.

The company kept growing. In 1958 they patented a new type of doll—a fashion doll. The Handler's daughter was indirectly responsible for this particular choice of doll. Over the years Mrs. Handler had noticed that her young daughter rarely ever played with dolls of her own age group. Instead she preferred the teenage paper dolls with fashions and accessories. She used the dolls to create play situations involving teenage activities.

This gave Mrs. Handler an idea. Why not create a well-made doll with a teen-age figure with a wardrobe of suitable, pretty clothes. The Mattel product planners went to work and did just that.

The doll was named Barbie after the Handler's daughter. The doll's first showing was at the 1959 New York Toy Show. The toy buyers, predominately male, were more impressed by a new Mattel gun that fired rubber bullets than they were with Barbie.

In spite of this unspectacular beginning, by 1960 the popularity of the doll was well established and the orders started pouring in. It took several years to catch up with the demand.

During 1960 the decision was made to create a boy friend for Barbie. He was named Ken after the Handler's son.

These dolls were so popular that over the years many other dolls have been added to the line. Along with the dolls have come clothes, accessories, houses, shops, animals, cases, trunks, cars, boats, planes and so on.

Although no longer being published, for many years (from September 1961 through July 1972) Barbie had her own magazine. At one time the Barbie Fan Club was the second largest girls' organization in the country—only the Girl Scouts being larger.

In 1974 a survey showed that ninety percent of all the girls in the Untied States between the ages of 5-11 owned one or more Barbie dolls. To date over 92 million dolls have been sold. More than 6 million dolls are sold every year.

Barbie has certainly become a household word! Songs have been sung about her, columnists have written about her and television shows have done skits about her.

And all over the country uncounted numbers of adult doll collectors are searching toy stores, flea markets and yard sales for Barbie, the world's most famous doll!

II. Barbie Year by Year (1957-1976)

1957—1958

During 1957 and 1958 the Barbie doll was designed and tested by the product designers at Mattel in California. In 1958 the doll was patented.

1959

The first Barbie was sold in 1959. Made of flesh-toned vinyl plastic, she was a long-limbed, shapely doll, 11½ inches tall. She had movable head, arms and legs and was dressed in a black and white striped jersey swimsuit, sunglasses, high heeled shoes and "gold" hoop earrings. Her stock number was 850.

She had rooted hair made of a soft, silky Saran material styled in a ponytail with curly bangs, either blonde or brunette. Blondes outnumbered the brunettes two to one. She had bright red lips and nails, heavy eyeliner and *pointed* eyebrows (not curved like the later dolls). Her eyes had *white irises* (not blue) with a slightly Oriental appearance. She had a heavy, partially solid torso marked: Barbie TM/ Pats. Pend./©MCMLVIII/by/Mattel/Inc..

She had metal cylinders in both legs with openings in the feet. These openings, or holes in the feet and legs, fit down on a pedestal stand with two prongs.

Most of these first dolls are now a pale ivory color. A few are sickly white! But ivory or sickly white,these old dolls are scarce and are highly prized by those lucky enough to own one.

The metal cylinders in the legs and feet proved to be a costly and an unnecessary part of the original Barbie doll. Also, the first type of stand was not completely satisfactory. As a result, the second type of Barbie and the second type of posing stand were produced.

This doll was just like the first one except she no longer had the metal cyliners in her legs and feet, and a few of the dolls wore pearl earrings instead of the gold hoops.

The prongs on the original posing stand were eliminated and a specially shaped wire was added at the back of the disc. Both types of posing stands are extremely rare.

First Barbie posing stand. Prongs on stand fit cylinders in doll's feet and legs. (Courtesy Marjorie Buxton)

First Barbie (850). White irises. Pointed eyebrows. Pale skin. (Ashabraner collection)

First Barbie. Metal cylinders in feet and legs with openings in feet. These fit prongs of first posing stand. (Ashabraner collection)

First Barbie (850) complete. Notice hole in bottom of shoe to fit posing stand.

Second Barbie (850) complete. Same as first except no holes in feet. (Ashabraner collection)

1960

The second Barbie, introduced last year, was still on the market in 1960.

—:—

During the early part of the year the third type of Barbie was introduced. This doll had *blue irises* and *curved eyebrows.* A few of these dolls had brown eyeliner instead of the usual blue. Otherwise, the dolls were about the same as the second Barbie. They, too, are now ivory or sickly white.

Later in the year a different type of vinyl plastic formula was used. These dolls have not turned white but have retained their original tan-toned color. Collectors consider these dolls the fourth type of Barbie.

These 1960 dolls wore the striped swimsuit, sunglasses and high heeled shoes, and the second type of stand came with them. Some dolls wore pearl earrings and some wore the gold hoops.

—:—

It was during 1960 that Mattel decided to create a boy friend for Barbie. He was designed, patented and given the name Ken.

Third Barbie (850) complete. Same markings as preceding doll. This should show the second booklet with Barbie only on the cover.

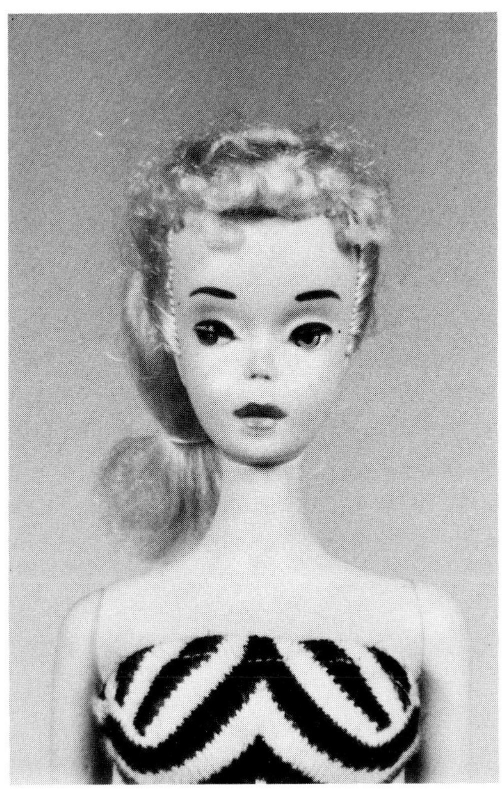

Third Barbie (850). Now has blue irises and curved eyebrows. This doll has brown eyeliner; others have blue. Same pale skin.

Fourth Barbie (850). Now has tan skin. Blue eyeliner. Rest same as third doll.

1961

During the early part of 1961 the tan toned Barbie from 1960 was still on the market.

—:—

Ken was introduced in 1961. He was 12 inches tall, had short flocked hair (collectors call him "fuzzy headed"), blue eyes, movable head, arms and legs. His hard plastic, hollow torso was marked: Ken® /Pats. Pend./©MCMLX/by/Mattel,/Inc.

He was dressed in bathing trunks and sandals. The trunks were red with a white stripe up the side, and the sandals were brown and red.

Most of the dolls were packaged with a yellow towel and a black wire stand, but the first dolls on the market did not have a towel.

Dolls have been found with blond, brunette and brown hair colors. #750 was his stock number.

—:—

A new type of body was made for Barbie this year. Although the same size and with the same Pats. Pend. markings as the first four, the new torso was made of hard plastic and was hollow inside (similar to Ken's).

Most of the these dolls had hard plastic arms and legs. A few have been found with the older, rubbery-feeling arms and legs. Perhaps Mattel had some of these older limbs on hand and decided to use them up on the new model.

Some of the dolls had new firmer textured Saran hair. Some had the old soft hair. A few had a combination of both the firm and the soft.

Most of the dolls continued to have the ponytail with curly bangs hair-do, but a few were made with a new hair style—a bubble cut. Both styles of hair came in assorted colors.

Bright red was still being used for lips and nails. The dolls were still dressed in high heeled shoes and the striped jersey swimsuit (most were black and white but a few may have been in different colors). Some dolls of 1961 still had sunglasses and pearl earrings replaced the gold hoops. Most of the dolls had new black wire stands similar to Ken's, but a few had the old pedestal type.

—:—

New in 1961 were the special arm tags identifying the dolls as the only Genuine Barbie or the only Genuine Ken.

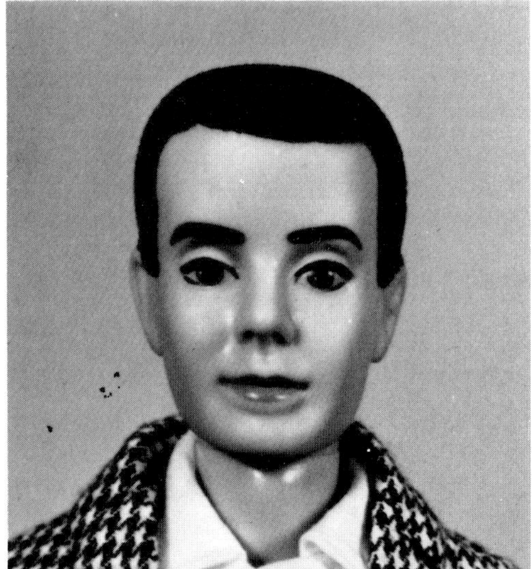

First Ken (750). Flocked hair.

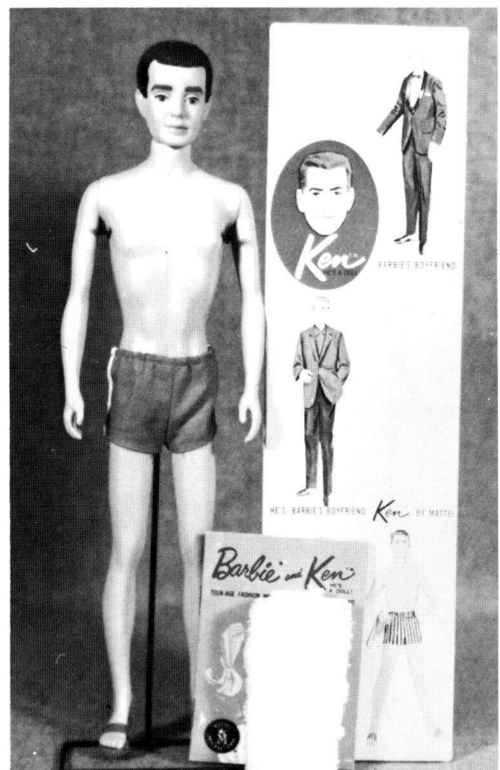

First Ken (750) complete. Flocked hair. See text for complete description.

1961 ponytail Barbie (850). Soft hair with new firmer textured bangs. Same bright red lips and nails. Doll pictured has pale blonde hair.

1961 ponytail Barbie (850) complete.

New in 1961 were Barbies with bubble cut hair (850). Same bright red lips and nails. Same markings.

1961 bubble cut Barbie (850). Doll pictured has bright titian hair.

1961 ponytail Barbie (850) with new firmer textured hair. Doll pictured has bright titian hair.

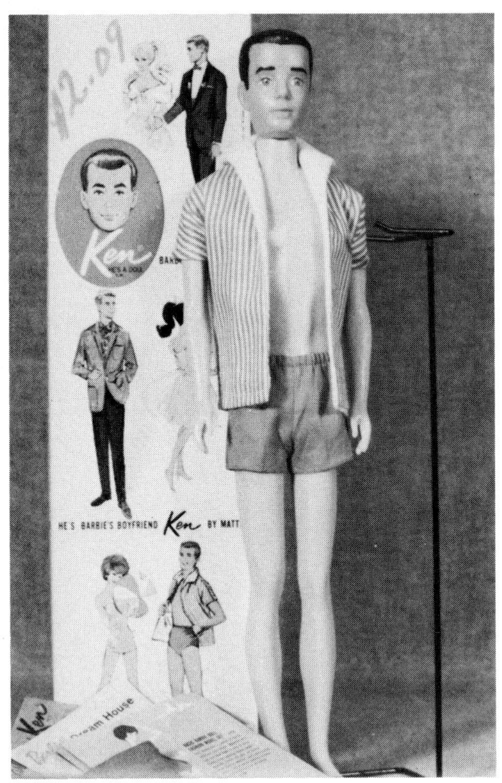

1962 Ken (750) complete. New painted hair. Same markings.

In 1962 the ponytail Barbie continued to be made, but the new bubble cut, introduced the year before, was in greater supply.

The hard, hollow Pats. Pend. bodies were still being used, but the dolls were dressed in a new red jersey swimsuit, high heeled shoes and pearl earrings. Black wire stands were included.

Lip and nail colors varied from pale pink to bright red.

—:—

Ken underwent a few changes this year—a new head mold and new painted crew-cut hair in blond or brunet.

He was still on the same Pats. Pend. body. He came dressed in red trunks, a red and white striped beach jacket and sandals.

This first jacket had a stitched-on white terrycloth collar and lining. Most of the trunks were made of smooth poplin material, but a few were made of cotton jersey. Black wire stands were included.

—:—

The first type of Ken was still on the market during the early part of 1962.

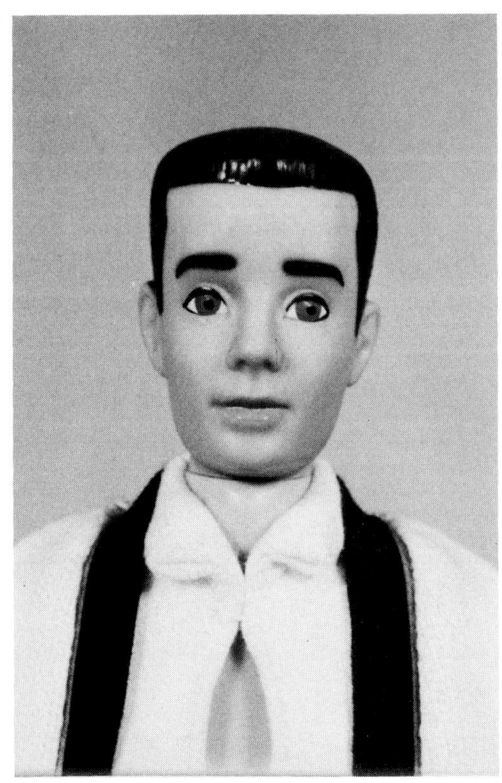

1962 Ken (750) with new painted hair.

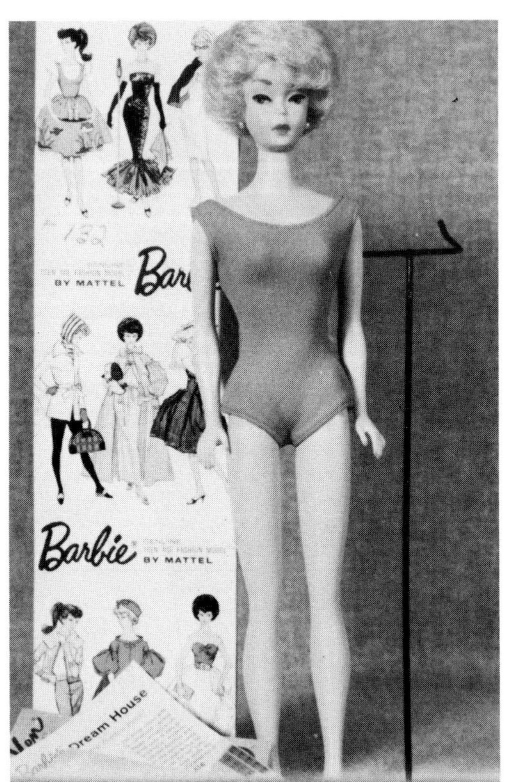

1962 bubble cut Barbie (850) complete. New red swimsuit. Lip and nail colors varied. Same markings.

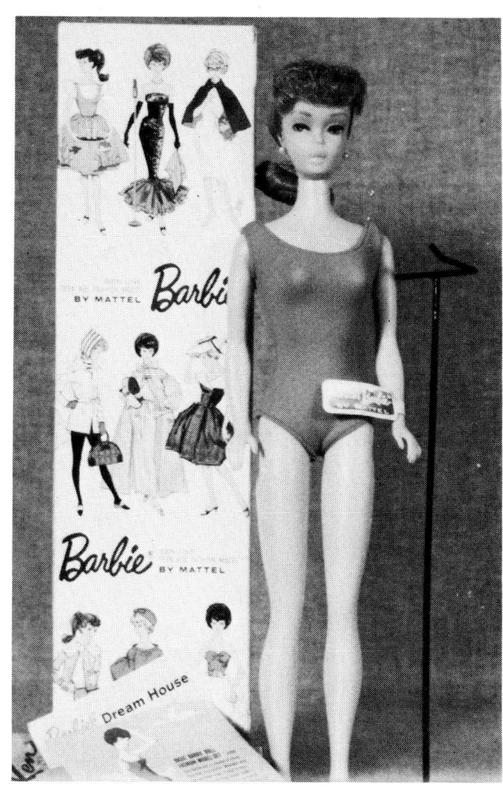

1962 ponytail Barbie (850) complete. New red swimsuit. New undated box. Same markings.

1962 ponytail Barbie (850). Firmer hair and bangs. Pink lips and nails. Red swimsuit. Same markings.

1962 bubble cut Barbie (850). Bright red lips and nails. Red swimsuit. Same markings.

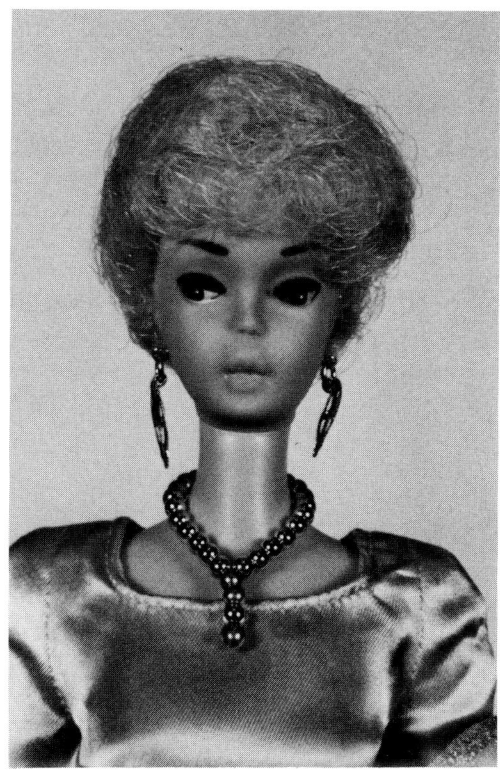

1962 bubble cut Barbie (850). Pale pink lips and nails.

Barbie's girl friend, freckle faced, blue eyed Midge (#860) was marketed this year. She was the same size as Barbie and was dressed in a two-piece swimsuit in assorted colors. Her rooted Saran hair was either sunny blonde, brunette or titian. The blonde doll's suit was of two shades of blue, the brunette's was red and pink and the titian's was orange and chartreuse. High heeled shoes and a black wire stand were included.

Midge was on a slightly taller body with new markings: Midge TM/ ©1962/Barbie® / ©1958/by/Mattel, Inc..

—:—

Most Barbies had the bubble cut hair style this year, but some ponytails with curly bangs were still being produced. Both came dressed in the red swimsuit, high heeled shoes and pearl earrings. Black wire stands were included.

Both dolls were on the same body as Midge with the same markings.

—:—

Late in 1963 a super sophisticated new Barbie was introduced. This was a "Fashion Queen" Barbie (#870). She had a molded head with a blue band and three wigs on a wig stand—a blonde bubble-on-a-bubble, brunette page boy and titian side part flip.

She wore a one-piece gold and white striped swimsuit and beach bandana, pearl earrings and high heeled shoes. A black wire stand was included. Her body had the Midge/ Barbie markings.

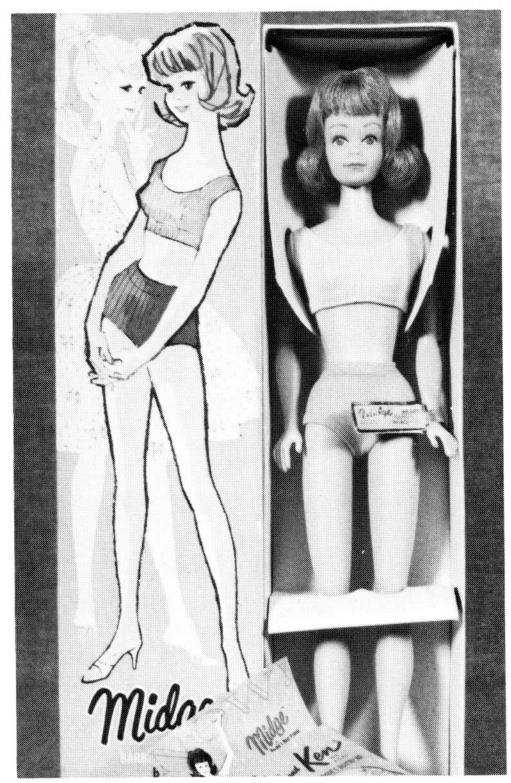

1963 Midge (860) complete. See text for new markings.

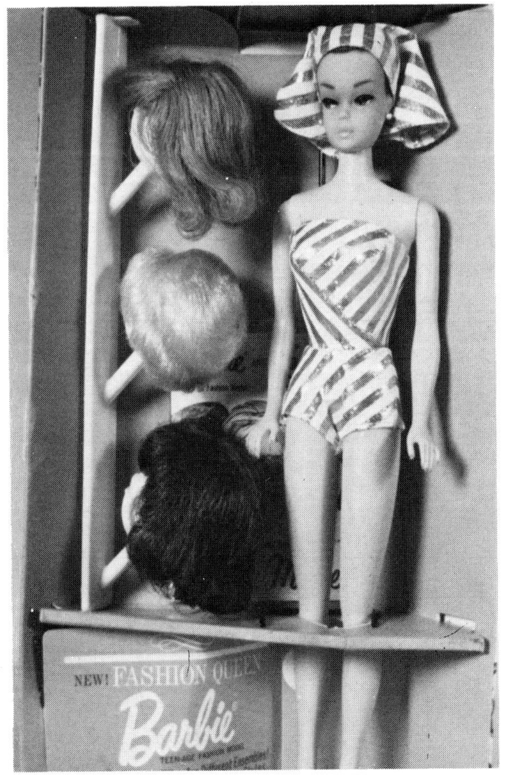

1963 Fashion Queen Barbie (870) complete. Has the new Midge/Barbie markings.

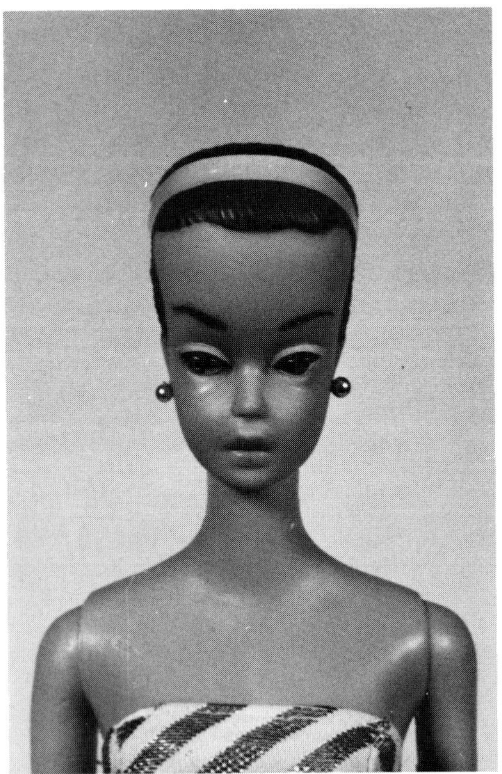

1963 Fashion Queen Barbie (870). First girl doll to have a molded hair-do. (Courtesy Rosemary Rogers)

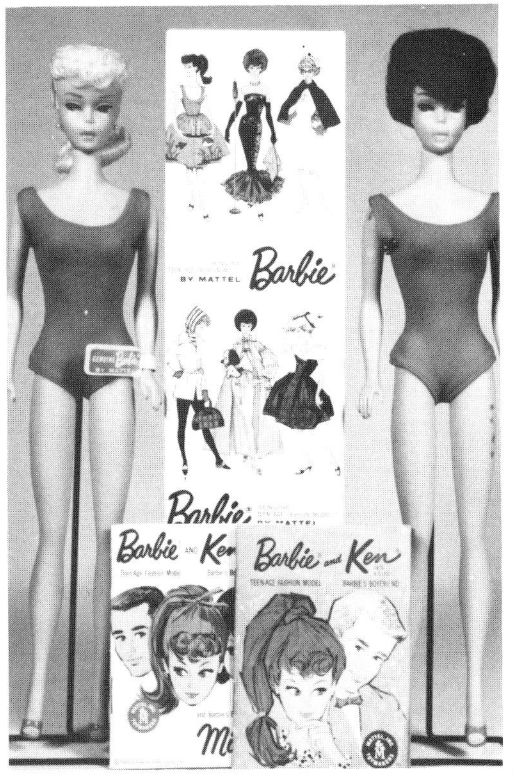

1963 ponytail and bubble cut Barbies (850) complete. New Midge/Barbie markings. Boxes now dated ©1962.

1963 ponytail Barbie (850).

1963 Midge (860). Came in three hair colors. (Courtesy Barbara Craig)

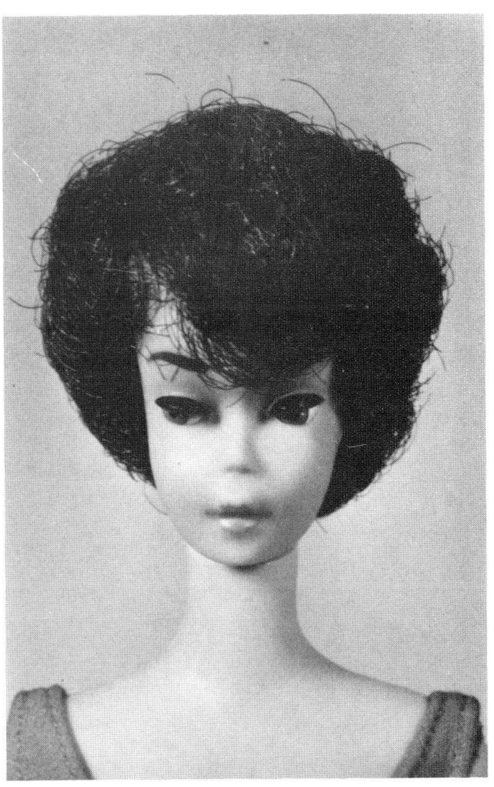

1963 bubble cut Barbie (850). Has the Midge/ Barbie markings.

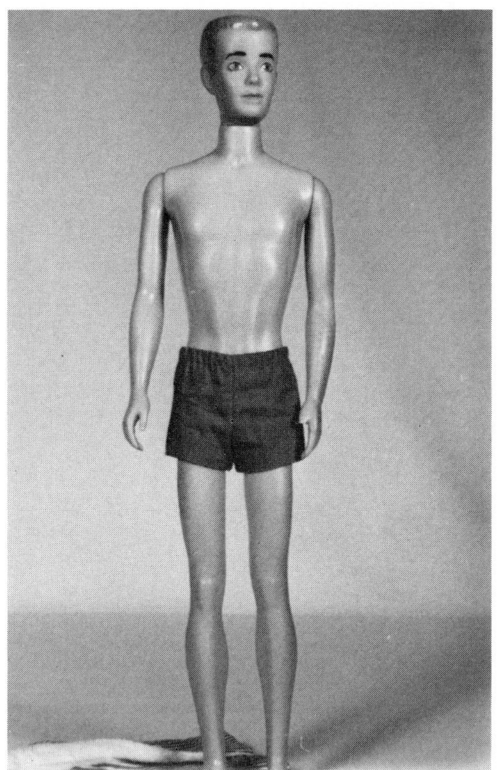

1963 Ken (750). 1/4" shorter than preceding dolls. Pronounced kneecaps. New markings.

Now for a different, unusual kind of Ken doll—unusual because of his height and unusual because of his construction.

This Ken was 1/4 inch shorter than the rest of the early dolls. His legs fit loosely where they join the torso. His arms were slightly shorter and fatter, and his kneecaps were more pronounced. He could be made to stand alone much easier than the other dolls.

The hard plastic material used for his torso had a slightly different quality, a different "feel" to it. All of the dolls have a flaw on the back right edge of the torso where the right leg joins. In some dolls this flaw is more pronounced. In a few it is barely discernable. This probably depends on the length of time the mold had been in use. The newer the mold, the more pronounced the flaw.

His torso had new markings: Ken®/©1960/by/Mattel, Inc./Hawthorne/Calif., U.S.A. He had the painted crew-cut hair in blond or brunet, and his clothes and stand were similar to those of last year.

—:—

Also in 1963 a darling soft vinyl baby doll was introduced. The doll came in a package called "Barbie Baby Sits" (#953). About 3 inches tall, it had painted blonde hair, blue eyes and was jointed at the neck, shoulders and hips.

In the set there was a pink and white striped apron for Barbie, her school books in a strap, eyeglasses, clock, bottle of soda, box of pretzels, phone list and telephone.

For the baby there was a bassinet with a lace-edged liner, pillow, blanket, nursing bottle, two diapers and a sacque.

1963 "Barbie Baby-sits" set (953). Baby has blond painted hair.

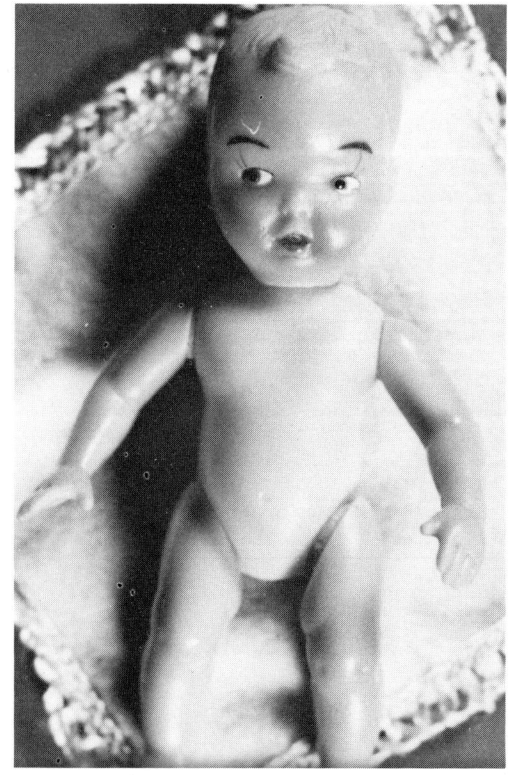

Close-up of baby from "Barbie Baby-sits" set. No markings. (Photo by Richard McFalls)

1964

The next Ken on the market looked the same and was the same height as the 1962 crew-cut doll. He also had the same type of body but with different markings. ©1960/by/Mattel, Inc./Hawthorne/Calif., U.S.A.

This Ken was dressed like the 1962 doll with one exception. The white terry cloth collar and lining were no longer stitched in. Now they were bonded onto the red and white striped jacket material.

Barbie's ponytail hair-do underwent a style change in 1964. The curly bangs were omitted. Some of the hair was brushed from the left side of the forehead across to the right side, then back to the rear. To collectors this style has become known as the Swirl Ponytail (#0850).

The first issue of these dolls had the same markings as the 1963 dolls. Later issues had the word "patented" added. A few dolls have been found on the hard, hollow Pats. Pend. bodies. It seems unlikely that Mattel would have had any leftover Pats. Pend. bodies as late as 1964. So most likely, somewhere along the line, someone switched heads and bodies on these dolls.

In addition to the new style ponytail Barbie, the bubble cut (#0850) and the regular ponytail (#0850) were also available. All three dolls wore the red swimsuit, pearl earrings and high heeled shoes. Black wire stands were included.

Midge (#0860) and Fashion Queen Barbie (#0870) were still available in 1964.

All four dolls were on the Midge/Barbie bodies with the addition of the word "patented" as a last line.

The "Barbie Baby Sits" baby (#0953) was also available but with a few minor differences. The baby's hair was thicker and a brighter shade of yellow. The design of the bassinet cover was slightly different.

A new item on the market this year was Barbie's Wig Wardrobe (#0871). This had a molded Barbie head with a blue headband, three wigs and a wig stand. The wig styles were bubble-on-bubble, side part flip and page boy. They came in shades of blonde, titian and brunette.

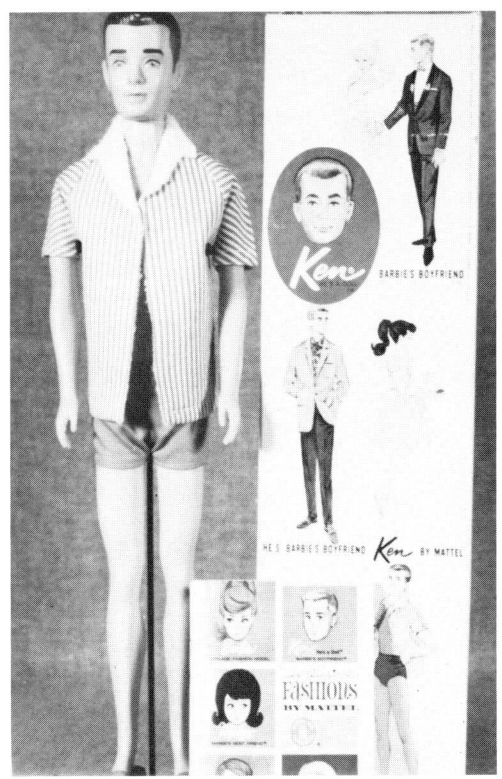

1964 Ken (0750) complete. New markings. Now same height as first dolls.

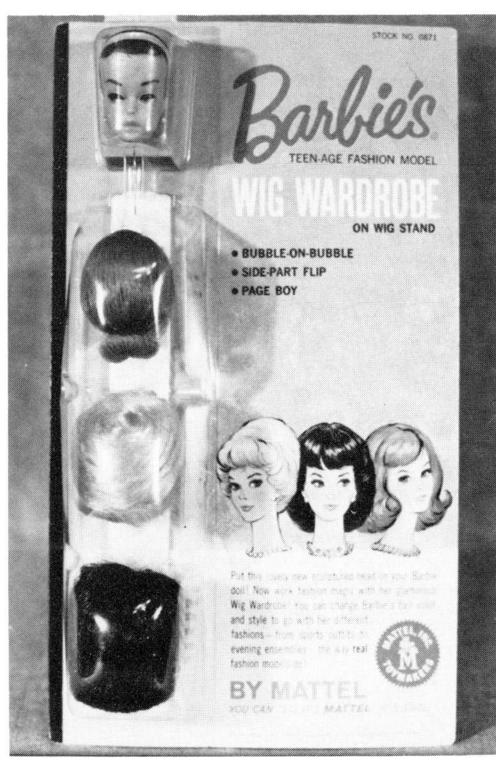

1964 Barbie's Wig Wardrobe (0871). Head similar to Fashion Queen's.

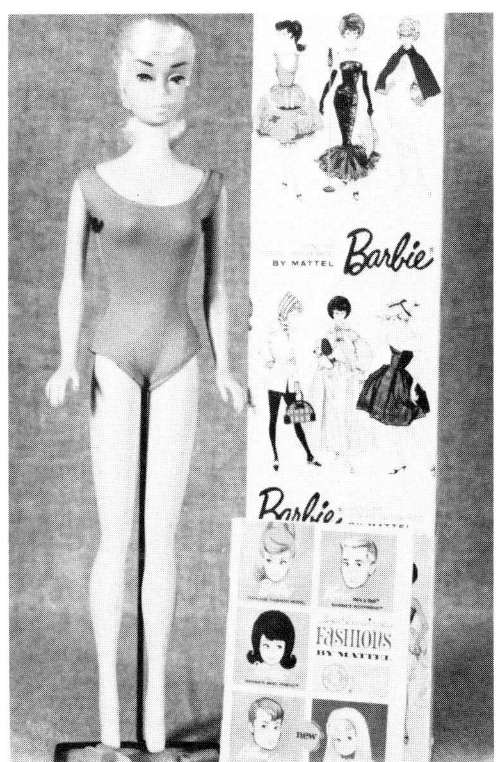

1964—New type of ponytail Barbie (0850) complete. See text for two types of markings.

Three new dolls were introduced this year—actually two new dolls and a new type of Barbie doll.

First there was Allan (#1000), Ken's buddy. He had the same body and the same markings as the 1964 Ken: ©1960/by/Mattel, Inc./Hawthorne/Calif., U.S.A.

He had molded red hair and brown eyes. He wore blue trunks, a multi-colored striped jacket and blue and tan sandals.

Next came Barbie's little blue eyed sister, Skipper (#0950). She was 9¼ inches tall, made of vinyl plastic with movable arms, legs and head. She wore a "brass" headband on her long straight hair, either blonde, brunette or titian. She was dressed in a one-piece red and white swimsuit and red shoes. A comb, brush and black wire stand were included.

Her markings were : Skipper/©1963/Mattel, Inc.

—:—

The big introduction in 1964 was "Miss Barbie." This doll was a real innovation in the Mattel fashion doll line. She was the first doll with life-like bendable knees and the only doll with eyes that would open and close.

She had a molded head with an orange band and three wigs on a wig stand. The wigs were in three different styles and in various shades of blonde, brunette and titian.

She was dressed in a one-piece pink swimsuit with matching cap, and high heeled shoes. Included was a lawn swing and planter and a new gold colored wire stand.

Although the Miss Barbie body was the same size as the other Barbie bodies, it had a different neck knob. This type of neck was necessary because of the special construction of the Miss Barbie head.

The back of the head is marked: ©M.I.. The torso is marked with intaglio lettering: ©1958/Mattel, Inc./U.S. Patented/U.S. Pat. Pend.

1964 "Miss Barbie" (1060) complete. First doll with bendable knees. Open and close eyes.

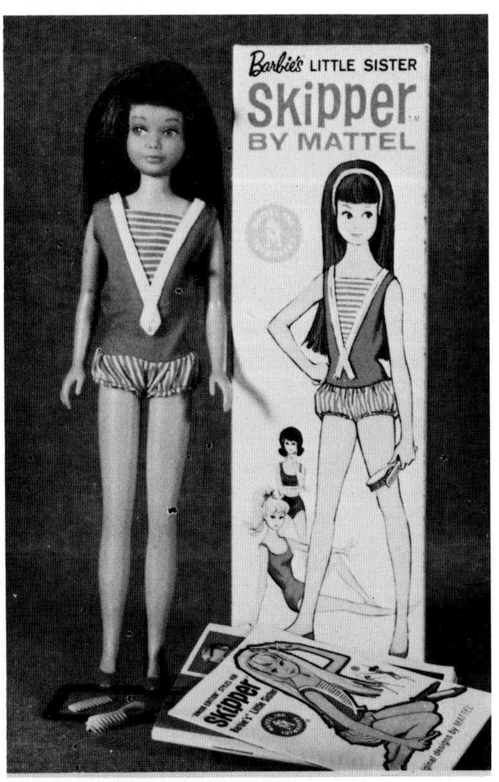

1964 Skipper (0950). Straight legs. Hair came in three colors. Tan toned skin.

1964 Allan (1000) complete. Straight legs. Red painted hair.

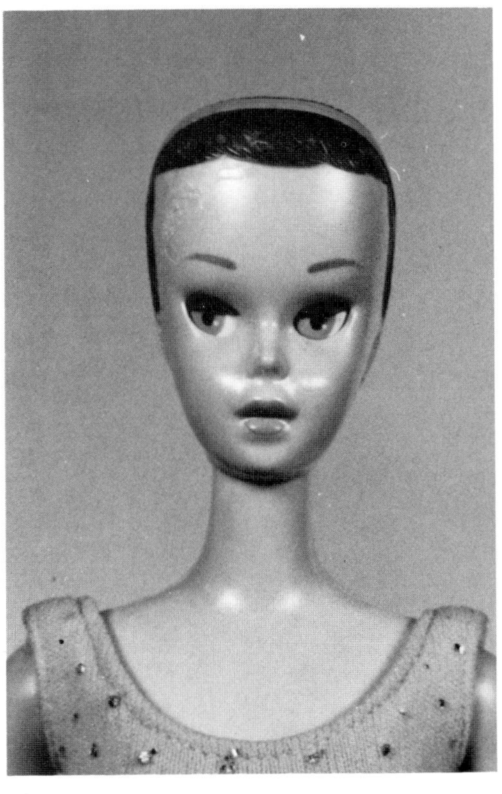
"Miss Barbie" (1060). Flaw on head caused by wig left on too long.

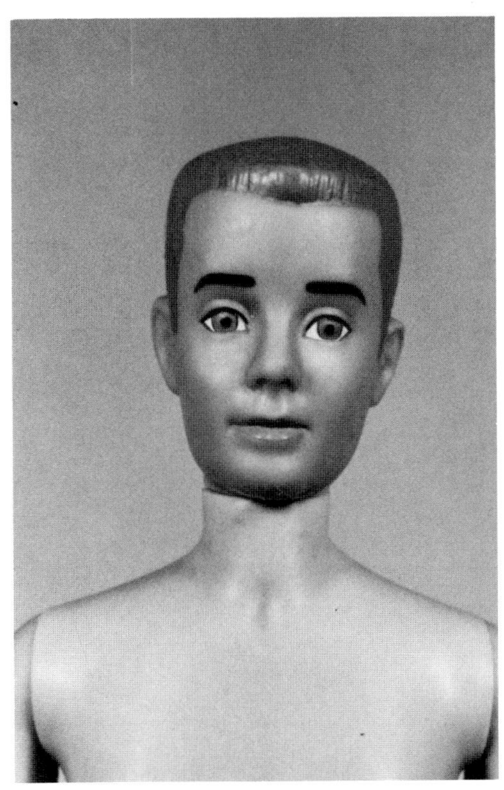
1964 Ken (0750). New markings same as Allan's.

1964 "Swirl" ponytail Barbie (0850). Hair recombed in back.

1964 Skipper (0950). Original red and white swimsuit.

Skipper got two new friends this year—Skooter (#1040) and Ricky(#1090). Ricky had painted red hair and straight legs. He wore blue shorts, multi-colored striped jacket and sandals.

Skooter had freckles, brown eyes, a double ponytail hair-do and straight legs. She wore a two-piece red and white swimsuit. Her hair colors were blonde, brunette and red. Comb and brush were included.

Both dolls were 9¼ inches tall and both were marked: ©1963/Mattel, Inc.. Ricky's wire stand was black and Skooter's was gold-colored.

—:—

Skipper (#0950) was still available, but now her markings were the same as the ones shown above for Ricky and Skooter. She now had the gold-colored stand.

—:—

Barbie's Wig Wardrobe (#0871) was still on the market in 1965. In addition there was a new Midge Wig Wardrobe (#1009) available. This set contained a molded Midge head, three wigs (Double Ponytail, Swirl 'n Curl and Topknot Pouf) in shades of titian, blonde and brunette, and a wig stand.

This Midge set was not shown in the fashion booklets but it was featured in the 1965 Mattel toy catalogue.

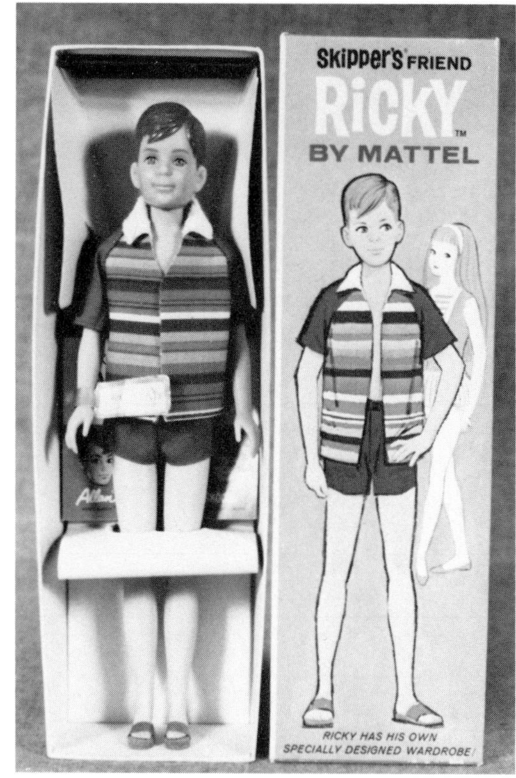

1965 Ricky (1090). Straight legs, tan toned skin, red hair and freckles.

1965 Skooter (1040).

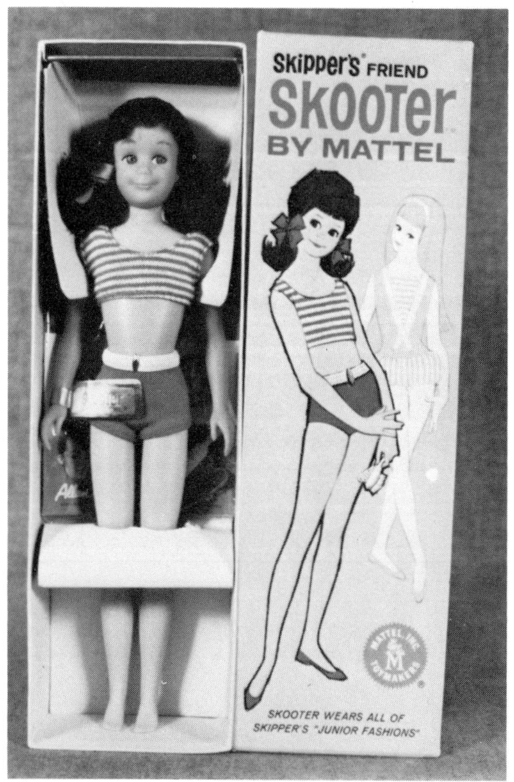

1965 Straight leg Skooter (1040). Tan toned skin, freckles and brown eyes. Red and white swimsuit.

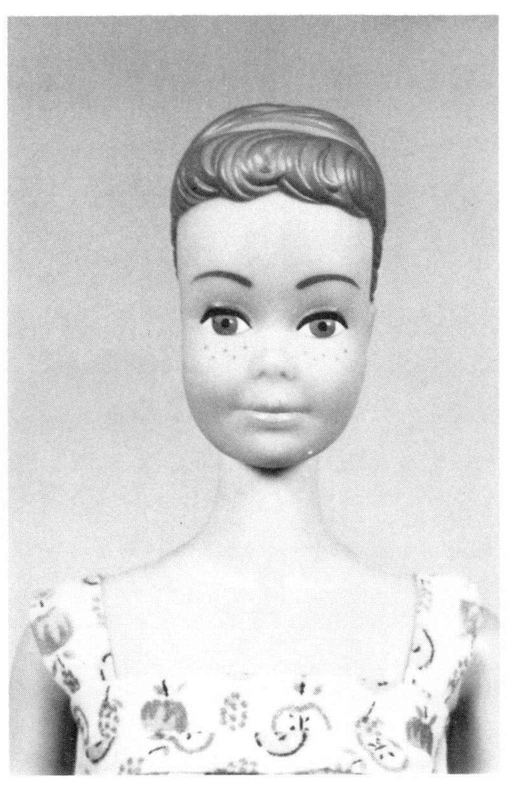

1965—Molded Midge head from Midge's Wig Wardrobe (1009). Orange band on head.

"Double Ponytail" wig from Midge's Wig Wardrobe set. Titian.

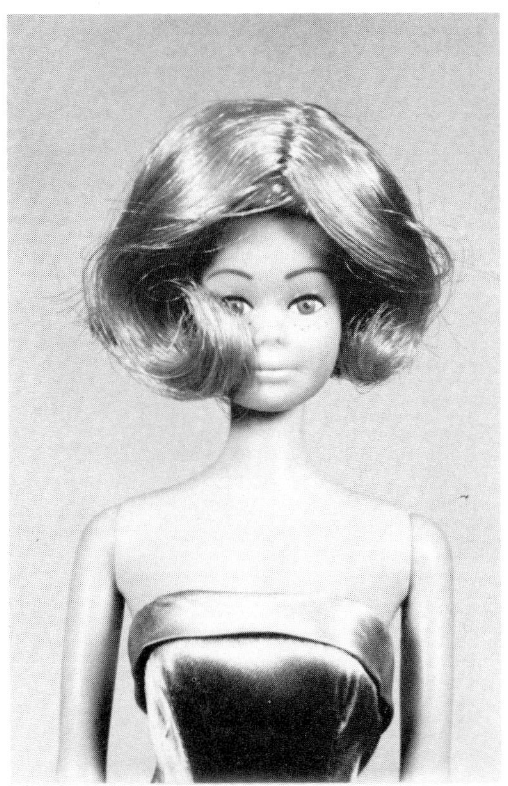

"Swirl 'N Curl" wig from Midge's Wig Wardrobe set. Blonde.

"Topknot Pouf" wig from Midge's Wig Wardrobe" set. Brunette.

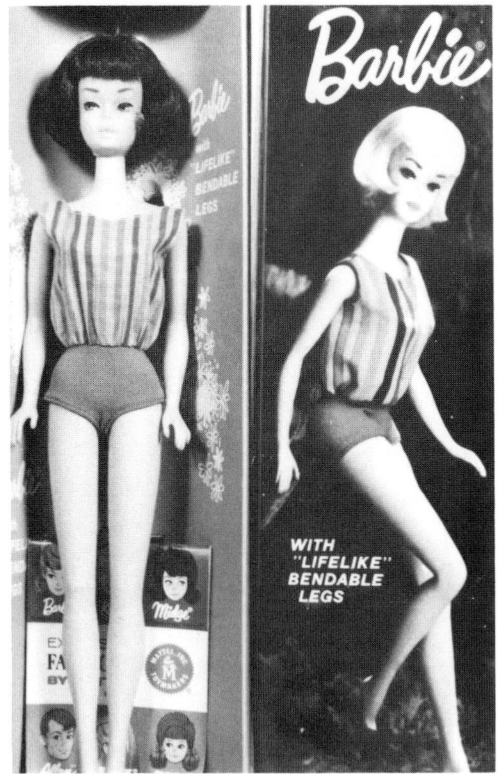

1965 bendable leg Barbie (1070) complete. See text for complete description.

"Legs" was the big news in 1965. Barbie (#1070), Ken (#1020), Midge (#1080), Allan (#1010) and Skipper (#1030) all had "lifelike" bendable knees.

Ken, Allan and Skipper had the same hair style, but Barbie and Midge had new styles. Midge had a short bouffant with bangs and a ribbon band on her head.

Most of the Barbies had a classic American Girl style. Although quite rare, there were two other styles—a bubble cut and a medium long side-part flip.

Allan and Ken had the same markings as the 1964 dolls. Skipper had the same as the 1965 straight leg doll. Barbie's and Midge's markings were the same as Miss Barbie's of 1964.

Ken wore red trunks and a blue jacket marked with the letter "K." Allan's trunks were blue and his red jacket was marked with an "A." Both wore sandals.

Skipper wore a one-piece blue suit with red and white trim. Midge wore a one-piece multi-colored striped suit. Barbie's new one-piece suit had a solid blue bottom with a multi-colored striped top.

Black wire stands were still used for the boy dolls. The girl dolls had the new gold colored ones. A comb and brush came with Skipper.

#4035 Color 'N Curl set. Molded Barbie head and molded Midge head. 4 wigs. (Some accessories missing).

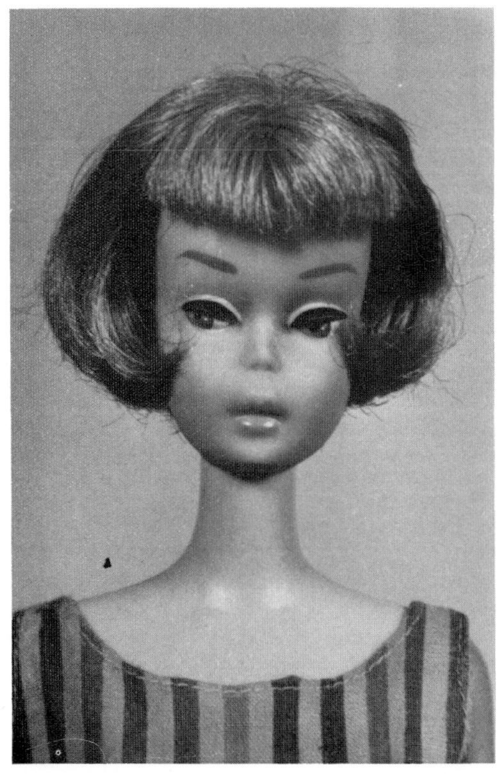

Close-up of 1965 bendable leg Barbie (1060). Most dolls had this hair style.

#4038 Color 'N Curl set. Molded Barbie head. 2 wigs. (Some accessories missing).

1965 bendable leg Ken (1020) complete. Red trunks, blue jacket.

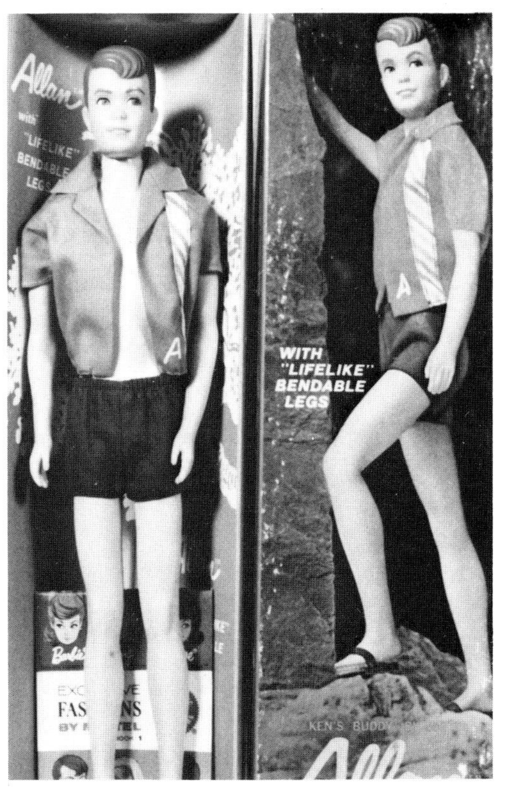

1965 bendable leg Allan (1010) complete. Blue trunks, red jacket.

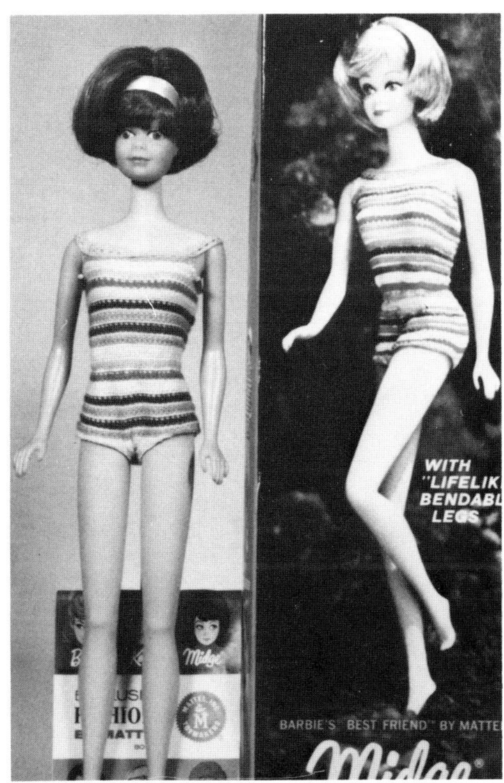

1965 bendable leg Midge (1080) complete. Doll pictured has rare brownette hair color.

Close-up of bendable leg Midge. Doll pictured has blonde hair.

In 1965 two new hair fashion sets were introduced. These were called Color 'N Curl sets. The first set (#4035) contained two molded heads—one Barbie and one Midge head. It also contained a battery powered hair dryer, 4 wigs in four different colors, rollers and curlers, comb, brush, pins, refillable activator solutions, wig stand, hair spray and an instruction booklet.

The second set (#4038) had one Barbie head, two wigs, wig stand, solutions, rollers, pins, comb, brush and trims.

In both sets the wig colors were:
Gold——changed to Lilac
Redhead——changed to Brownie
Topaz——changed to Brunette
Flame——changed to Carrot Top

—:—

The straight leg Barbie (both ponytail and bubble cut), Midge, Ken and Allan were still on the market with the same markings as the 1964 dolls.

—:—

This year there was an interesting change in the "Barbie Baby Sits" (#0953) set. The baby was the same, but the accessories were different.

The "baby sitter" items were omitted—the apron, box of pretzels, bottle of pop, clock, eyeglasses, school books with strap, phone and phone book.

The following were added: long baby dress, cap, wrapper with hood, formula recipe and a baby sitter's manual.

—:—

Miss Barbie (#1060) and Fashion Queen Barbie (#0870) were still available through mail-order catalogues until August or September of 1965. A few of the Miss Barbie markings had raised letters instead of the usual intaglio.

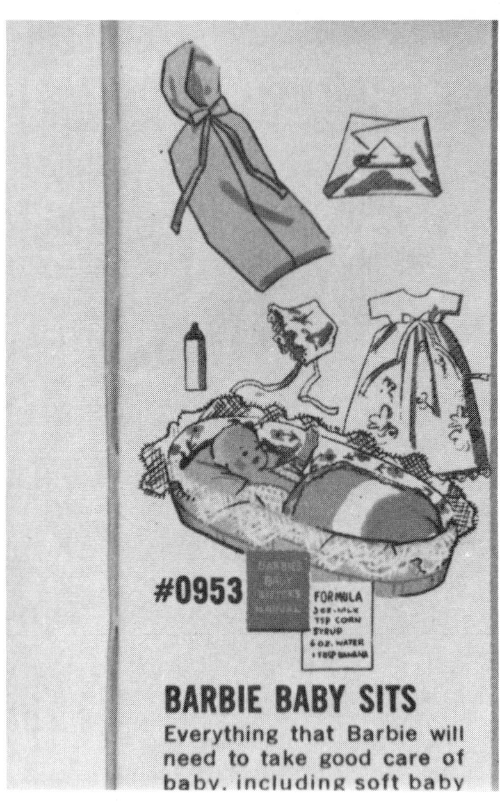

1965 "Barbie Baby-sits" set. "Sitter" items omitted and a layette added.

1965 bendable leg Skipper (1030) complete. Tan toned skin. Navy blue with red and white trim swimsuit.

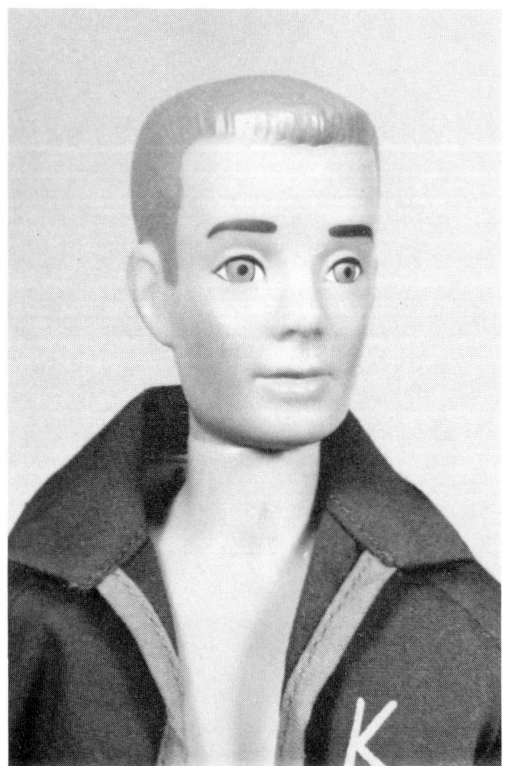

Second issue bendable leg Ken (1020) with painted cheeks.

1966

1966 saw the introduction of a doll whose hair and costume colors could be changed—Barbie Color Magic (#1150).

The doll had lifelike bendable legs and long straight, specially treated, rooted hair in two basic hair colors—Midnight or Golden Blonde. By applying color changer solution, Midnight changed to Ruby Red and Golden Blonde changed to Scarlet Flame. Colors could be changed back and forth, over and over again.

The doll wore a one-piece diamond pattern swimsuit and matching headband in blue, green, yellow and fluorescent red. By applying color changer solution, the green diamond changed to purple and the yellow to red. This doll had no posing stand.

The doll came in a see-into hard plastic box, 12" x 5" x 2", that could be converted into a clothes closet. Included was a hair styling set with instructions for many different hair-dos.

The first issue of this doll had the same intaglio markings as Miss Barbie, ©1958/Mattel, Inc/U.S. Patented/U.S. Pat. Pend., and with two additional lines of raised lettering: Made in/Japan. In later issues the words remained the same but all lettering was raised.

Fashion booklets dated ©1965 showed sketches of the Barbie Color Magic doll dressed in the diamond pattern suit, and two booklets (Francie only and Tutti only on covers) showed the doll dressed in a floral print suit. All of these dolls were sketched with long curly hair and bangs.

The floral suit was never on the market. The curly hair and bangs hair-do was probably shown as an example of one way the regular hair could be re-styled, for no doll with this hair-do was ever on the market.

1966 Color Magic Barbie (1150). Container converts to clothes closet.

—:—

Still available this year was #4038, Barbie's Color 'N Curl set. In addition a new set was introduced—#4039, Barbie's Color 'N Curl set. This set contained a molded Barbie head with a blue head band, 4 wigs that could be color-changed, color changer solution, rollers, pins, comb, brush, and instruction booklet. Also included in this set was a battery powered hair dryer and a wig stand.

—:—

This year Skooter came with lifelike bendable legs (#1120) and dressed in a new two-piece swimsuit—navy shorts with a red and white polka dot top. Comb and brush were included.

The first of these bendable leg Skooters were made of the old greyish tan tone vinyl material. Later in the year they were made of the new pink material.

This new pink material was also used for bendable leg Skipper (#1030), straight leg Skipper (#950), straight leg Ricky (#1090) and straight leg Skooter (#1040).

All of these dolls have the same markings as the 1965 dolls. Ricky's wire stand was black, Skipper and Skooter's was gold.

—:—

Sometime during 1966 Allan was discontinued by Mattel. However, both types (#1000 and #1010) were available through mail-order catalogues until August or September 1966.

1966 Bendable leg Skooter (1120). First issue had old tan toned skin. Later issues had pink skin. Blue shorts, red and white top.

This year Francie was introduced as Barbie's cousin. Not quite as shapely as Barbie, she was 11¼ inches tall, and she was the first of the line to have rooted eyelashes.

The first Francie on the market (#1130, bendable legs) was made of the old greyish tan tone material. She was dressed in a one-piece patterned swimsuit with a teal blue background.

Later dolls had the new pink skin, and they came dressed in a one-piece swimsuit with a white background top and a solid green bottom section. This swimsuit was not shown in the booklets or the Mattel catalogue, but it was shown in one of the mail-order catalogues.

Later in the year another Francie was presented. #1140 had straight legs, pink skin and painted eyelashes. She was dressed in a two-piece red and white swimsuit. All dolls had wire stands. Hair colors were blonde or brunette.

These 1966 Francies were marked: ©1965/Mattel, Inc./ U.S. Patented/U.S. Pat. Pend./Made in Japan. On some dolls the third line read "U.S. Pat'd."

1966 Straight leg Francie (1140). Pink skin, brown eyes and painted eyelashes. Red and white suit. (Notice that the actual doll's hair differs slightly from the hair pictured on the box).

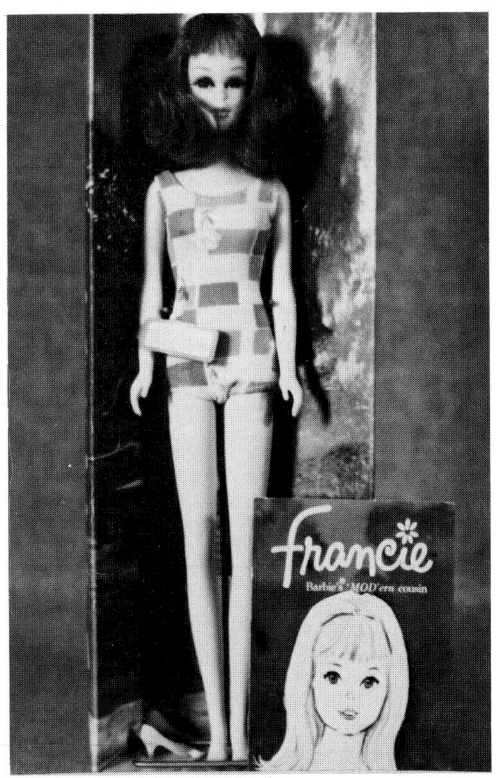

1966 Bendable leg Francie (1130). First doll to have rooted eyelashes. First issue with greyish tan skin. Aqua background swimsuit.

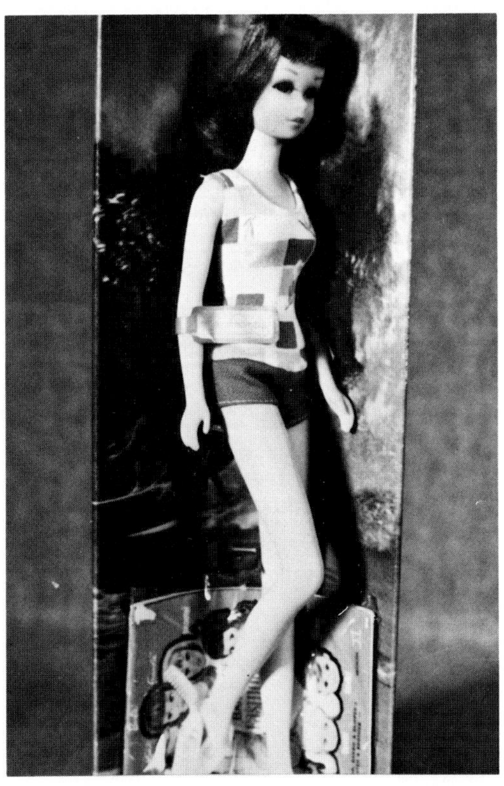

1966 Bendable leg Francie (1130). Later issue with pink skin. White background suit with solid green bottom.

Color Magic Barbie (1150). See text for markings.

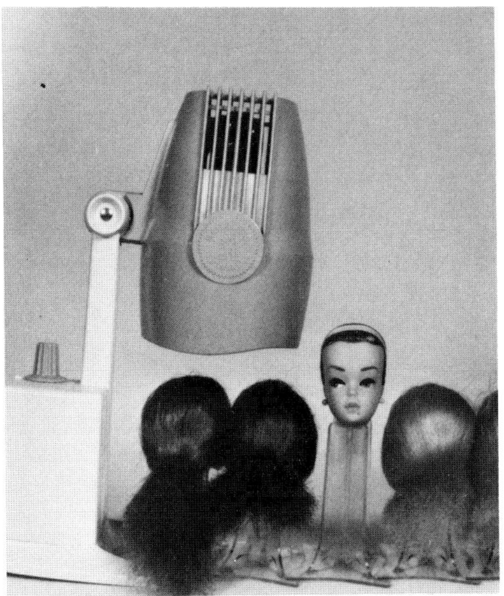

Barbie's Color 'N Curl set #4039 of 1966. One molded Barbie head, four wigs. (Some accessories missing.)

1966—Second issue bendable leg Francie (1130). Blonde or brunette hair, rooted eyelashes.

1966—Straight leg Francie (1140). Painted eyelashes. Blonde or brunette hair.

Barbie's Wig Wardrobe (# 0871) was still on the market in 1966. Barbie, Ken and Midge were still available in both straight and bendable leg versions. All markings were the same as 1965 except the words "Made In Japan" were added to bendable leg Barbie (#1070) and bendable leg Midge (#1080). During the first part of the year these markings were similar to the Color Magic markings. Later all lettering was of the raised type.

The straight leg Barbie (#0850) still came with either the ponytail or the bubble cut hair style.

—:—

Tutti and Todd, Barbie's little twin sister and brother, joined the group in 1966. Both were about 6¼ inches tall and were fully poseable.

Tutti (#3550) was dressed in a red and white checked gingham sunsuit and hat with white trim. She had long straight blonde or brunette hair, parted on the left side with bangs, and a pink ribbon band on her head. Her eyes were blue.

—:—

Now for another one of those mystery dolls. In Mattel's official historical listings, for 1966 they list #3550 Tutti and #3580 Todd. Years of research have uncovered only two other references to a #3580 Todd.

In late 1972 or early 1973 a large Barbie collection was offered for sale. A new-in-box #3580 Todd was one of the dolls listed. The seller was contacted, but she could not remember any details about the doll—how he was dressed, the box he was in, etc., but she was very positive that the stock number on her list was correct.

The only other reference was from a collector who *thinks* that at one time she had a Todd whose stock number was 3580. Since she did not save the box he came in, she cannot be absolutely sure.

A #3580 Todd was not shown in any booklet nor in the 1966 Mattel Toy Catalogue. The only Todd shown was the one with Tutti in "Sundae Treat" (#3556), one of the Tutti Play-Settings sets. This Todd was dressed in blue shorts and socks, white shirt and shoes and a red and white striped Eton jacket.

The Tutti from this set was dressed in a matching dress of red and white stripe with navy and white trim. She had long titian hair with a blue ribbon bow.

Todd had titian hair and brown eyes. Todd was the first male doll to have rooted hair.

—:—

A Tutti and Todd, like the Sundae Treat dolls, were offered in the 1966 Sears' and Wards' Christmas catalogues. These came in small brown boxes without a stock number. The same two dolls also came in a Tutti and Todd Playhouse, a Sears' exclusive.

Nowhere was there a #3580 Todd offered for sale.

—:—

In addition to the "Sundae Treat" there were four other Play-Settings on the market in 1966. They were:

#3552——"Walkin' My Dolly"

#3553——"Night-Night, Sleep Tight"

#3554——"Me and My Dog"

#3555——"Melody in Pink"

In each setting, Tutti had a different hair style, different hair color and different clothing. (See page 167 for a complete description.)

All Tuttis and Todds were marked: ©1965/Mattel, Inc./ Japan.

—:—

Mail-order catalogues (good until August or September, 1966) still offered the "Barbie Baby Sits" set (#0953) and the #4035 Color 'N Curl set.

1966 Tutti (3550). Barbie's little sister. Jointed only at neck but completely poseable. Blonde or brunette hair.

1966—Tutti and Todd "Sundae Treat" (3556). Both dolls have titian hair. (Todd's haircut courtesy Harold DeWein)

1966 Todd and Tutti (no stock number). Came in a small brown box from Sears and Montgomery Ward. Similar to "Sundae Treat" dolls.

1966 Tutti's "Walkin' My Dolly" set (3552). Blonde hair. Baby doll has red painted hair, blue hair bow.

1966 Tutti's "Night-Night, Sleep-Tight" set (3553). Reddish hair.

1966 Tutti's "Me And My Dog" (3554). Dark brown hair. White dog. (Gift from Janice Kaderly)

1966 Tutti's "Melody In Pink" (3555). Pale blonde hair.

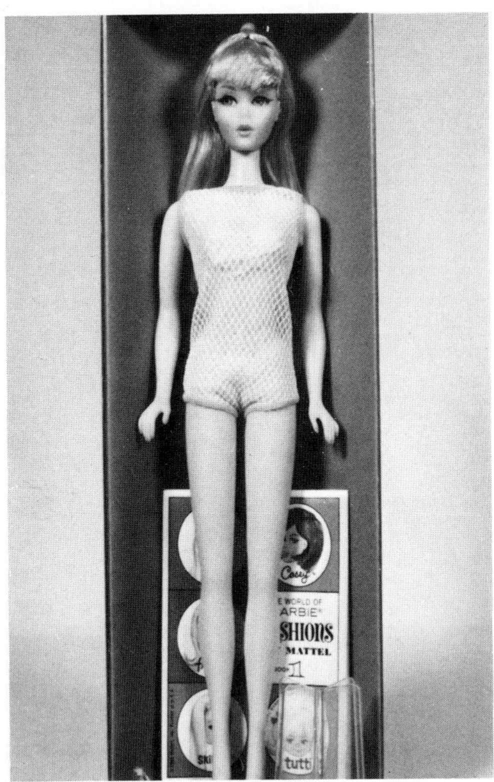

1967 Twist 'N Turn Barbie (1160). New head mold, makeup and hair style.

1967

The big news of 1967 was the "twist 'n turn" waist—and Barbie's new "facelift"! Since teenage makeup and hair styles had changed drastically since 1958, Mattel felt that Barbie should have a more modern appearance. Therefore, a new head was designed for her.

The twist and turn waist was a major technological change, making the dolls more poseable than ever before.

In May there was an official Mattel Trade-In program to introduce the new Twist 'N Turn Barbie. One could trade in an old doll, plus $1.50, and get one of the new dolls. 1,250,000 old dolls were traded during the month of May alone. These were given to charity.

The stock number for the Trade-In doll was #1162. #1160 was the stock number for the regular Twist Barbie.

The twist Barbie had long straight hair with bangs in four colors. The catalogue lists these colors as Summer Sand, Chocolate Bon-Bon, Go Go Co-Co and Sun Kissed. She had rooted eyelashes, pink skin and bendable knees. She was marked: ©1966/Mattel, Inc./U.S. Patented/U.S. Pat. Pend. /Made In/Japan. (Some of the Trade-In dolls had "Made In Japan" on one line.) This doll was dressed in a salmon vinyl bikini with a white net cover-suit.

Included was a new type of posing stand—a clear plastic type. When turned upside down, it could be used as a seat.

—:—

Also in 1967 a standard (straight leg) Barbie (#1190) was on the market. This doll had the same head mold and hair-do as the twist Barbie above, and there were four different hair colors available.

The doll had painted eyelashes and pink skin and was marked: Midge T.M./©1962/Barbie®/©1958/by/Mattel, Inc./Patented. She wore a two-piece pink swimsuit. The shorts were trimmed with a white plastic flower on the left side.

1967 Trade-in Barbie (1162). Promotional doll to introduce the new twist waist.

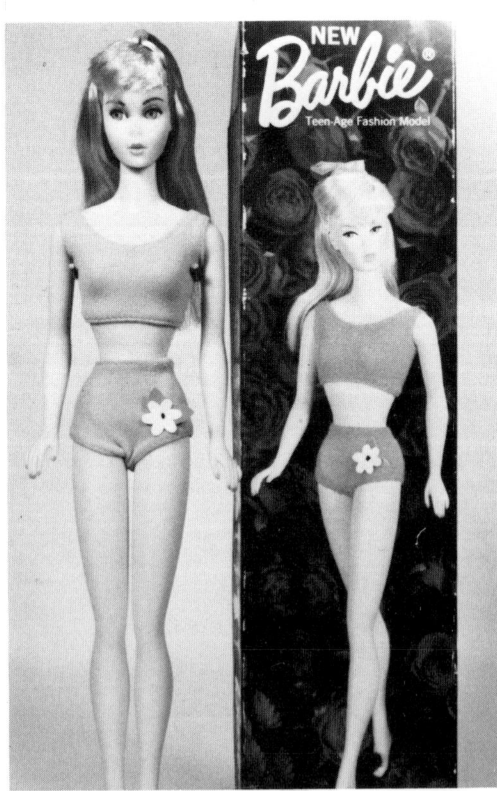

1967 new standard Barbie (1190). Painted eyelashes. Hair-do similar to #1160.

Display Casey—#1768 "Waltz in Velvet."

Francie (1122)—#3451 "Midi Duet."

Francie (1130)—#1295—375 "Prom Pinks."

Ken in "Night Scene." Francie in "Two for the Ball."

1961 Barbie—#983 "Enchanted Evening."

Kelley and #7180 "Ganz festlich" from Germany.

A rare type bend leg Barbie in "Midnight Blue." (Courtesy Janice Kaderly)

"Rise 'N Shine" Francie set. Skipper in #7220 Best Buy.

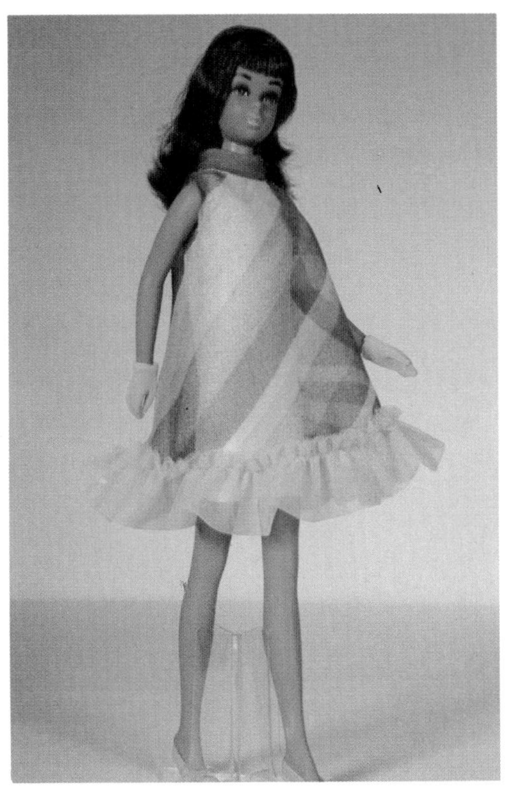

Francie (1100) in #1207 "Floating —In."

Brownette bend leg Barbie in "The Lace Caper."

1964 Barbie in "Solo in the Spotlight."

Deluxe Quick Curl Skipper (9428).

Allan in "Touchdown!". Ken in "Play Ball!"

Skipper in "Velvet 'N Lace." Skooter in "Lots of Lace."

1970 re-issued Skipper and "Dog Show" set.

Living Barbie in "Country Music," a Fashion 'N Sounds outfit.

Re-issued Tutti in #7968 "Hubsch und praktisch" from Germany.

Midge in "Cheerleader," 1964.

Twiggy in 1973 Get-Ups 'N Go outfit.

1970 Twist Barbie in "Poodle Doodles," a Put—ons & Pets set.

1971 Twist Barbie in "Kitty Kapers," a Put-ons & Pets set.

1969 Twist Barbie in "Hot Togs," a Put-ons & Pets set.

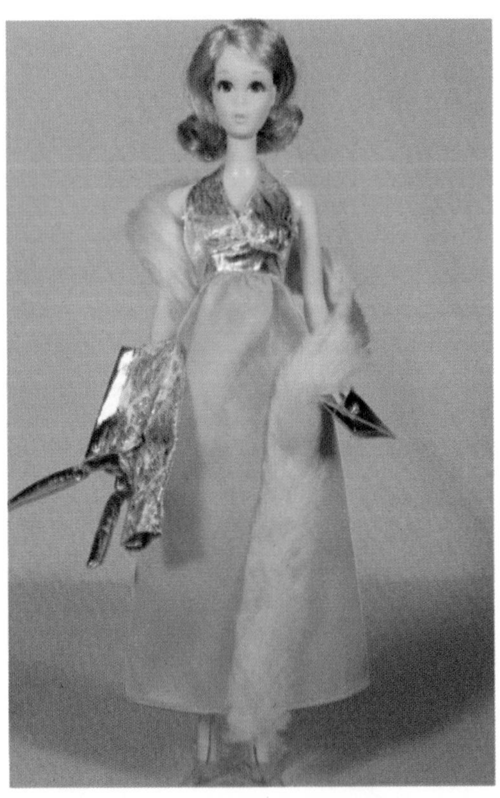

Walking Jamie in #7843 Get-ups 'N Go outfit.

Barbie wearing rare #1616 "Campus Sweetheart." (Courtesy Janice Kaderly)

Living Fluff wearing #3473 "Lullaby Lime." Tutti wearing #3616 "Pink P.J.'s." The beds are #4011 Skipper and Skooter bunk beds, 1965-1967.

1968 to 1971 Talking Christies with four different shades of hair and skin tones.

#1100 Francie. First issue with rust colored eyes and hair that turns red. Second issue with brown eyes and hair that retains the brown color.

Ken in rare "Business Appointment." (Gift from Harold John DeWein)

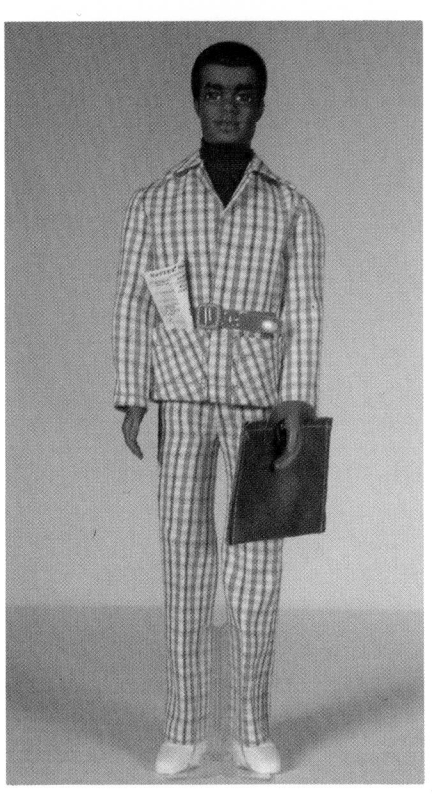

Curtis in #9167 Get-Ups 'N Go suit of 1976.

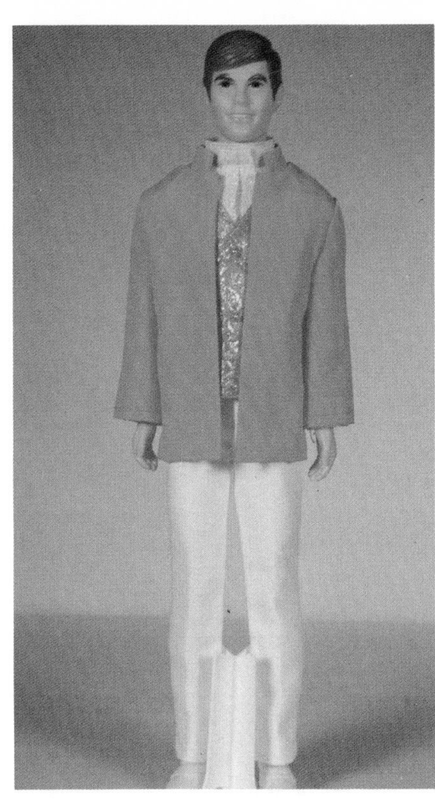

Ken (1124) in #1431 "Guruvy Formal" of 1969.

A "Dressed Doll" box with the doll—Barbie in "American Airlines Stewardess." (Ashabraner collection)

Quick Curl Miss America wearing "Majestic Blue," a 1972 costume.

Francie (#1170) now had a twist waist, as well as bendable legs, rooted eyelashes and pink skin. She was dressed in a one-piece suit with solid pink bottom and a multi-colored striped top. Hair colors were blonde or brunette. She was marked: ©1966/Mattel, Inc./U.S. Patented/U.S. Pat. Pend. /Made In/Japan.

—:—

A new type of Francie doll, Colored Francie (#1100), was made this year. She also had a twist waist, bendable knees and rooted eyelashes. She had medium brown skin, rust brown eyes, dark brown hair, and the same markings as the above Francie. Her multi-colored two-piece suit with a transparent overlay was unusual and attractive.

This doll did not sell well so Mattel produced only a limited number of them. It is now one of the most sought after dolls ever produced by Mattel.

—:—

Another new doll this year was Casey (#1180). She was the same size as Francie and had the same markings as the #1170 above. She had a twist waist, bendable knees, rooted eyelashes, molded teeth and pink skin. Her blonde or brunette hair was short, straight and parted on the left side. (See Chapter VII for one or two exceptions)

She wore a one-piece swimsuit with a gold lame bottom section and a gold and white check top. She had a dangling gold earring in her left ear.

All three dolls had the new clear plastic posing stand.

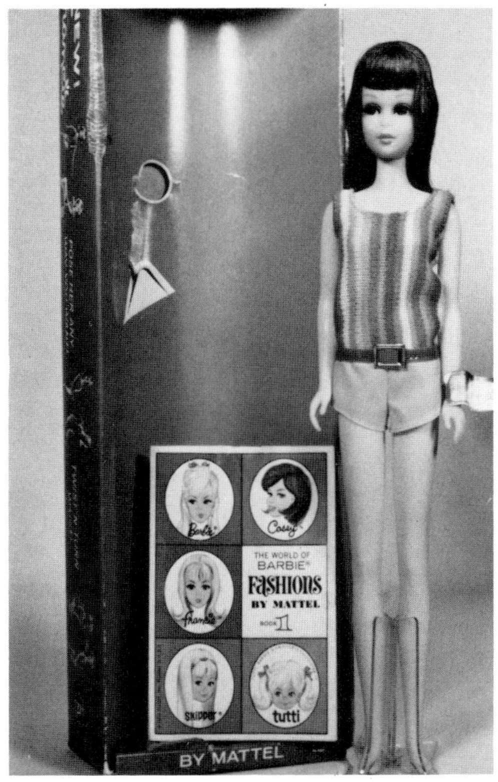

1967 Francie with twist waist (1170) complete. Rooted eyelashes. Blonde or brunette hair.

1967 Colored Francie (1100). The first black doll in the line.

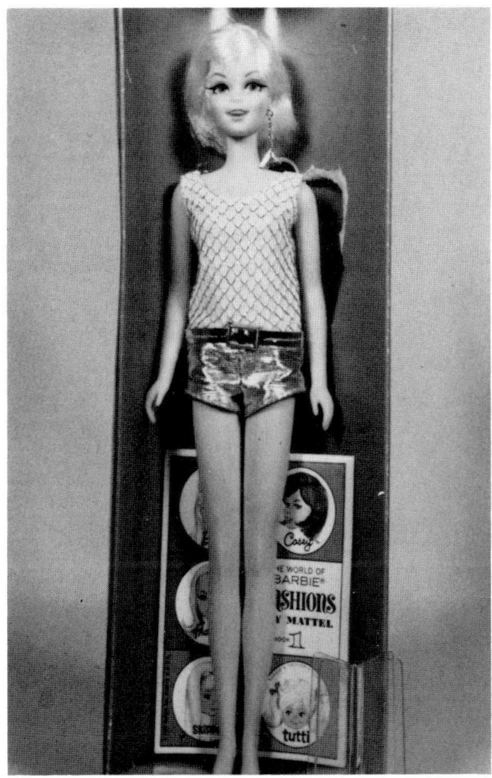

1967 Casey (1180). Blonde or brunette hair. Earring in left ear.

1967 Todd (3590). Titian hair. Brown eyes. One-piece body and limbs fully poseable.

Two new Tutti Play-Settings were added this year. They were "Cookin' Goodies" (#3559) and "Swing-A-Ling" (#3560). All five sets from 1966 were still available.

Mattel lists new stock numbers and new sizes for Tutti and Todd in 1967—Tutti #3580, Todd #3590 and 7 5/8 inches tall. This size was incorrect. The dolls remained about 6¼ inches tall but there was a change in their stock numbers. At least there was a change in Tutti's. If Todd was ever numbered 3580, which is questionable, then he, too, got a new number in 1967.

Todd (#3590), pictured in the catalogue but not in the booklets, was on the market this year. He was dressed in red, white and blue checked pants and cap, blue short sleeved shirt, blue socks and red shoes. He had titian hair and brown eyes and was marked: ©1965/Mattel, Inc./Japan.

Early in the year Tutti was shown in a new dress but with the old stock number 3550. The dress had a solid rose colored waist and a floral print skirt.

Later in the year she was shown in the same dress but with a new stock number, 3580.

The 1967 Mattel catalogue shows the #3580 Tutti wearing the dress shown here, but the catalogue states that half of the dolls wore a second style of dress—the reverse of this one. It was not until the © 1968 booklet (1969 market) that this reversed style was actually shown.

—:—

Another new doll this year was Chris (#3570), Tutti's friend. She was the same size as Tutti, made from the Tutti head mold, had brown eyes and came with either brunette or blonde hair. Her markings were the same as Tutti's: ©1965/Mattel, Inc./Japan. She wore a multi-colored print dress, and she had a green barrette and two green bows in her long straight hair with straight bangs.

1967 Tutti's "Cookin' Goodies" (3559). Black hair.

1967 Tutti's "Swing-A-Ling" (3560). Blonde hair.

1967 Chris (3570). Brown eyes. Blonde or brunette hair.

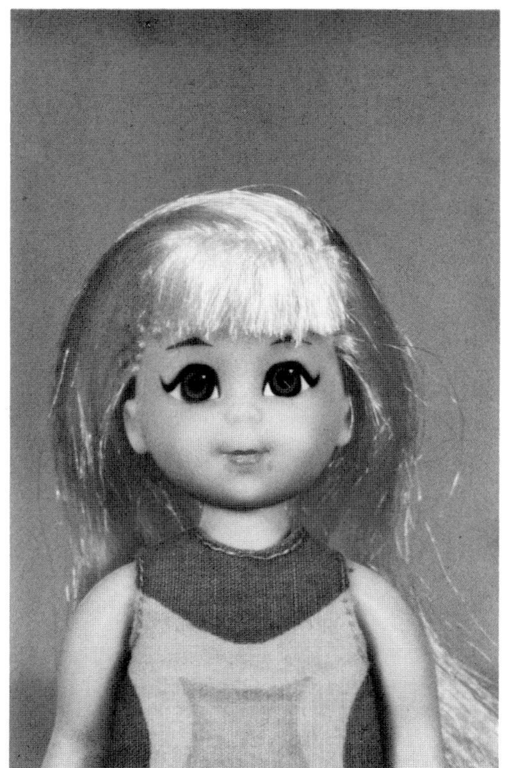
Close-up of Chris (3570) with blonde hair. Original green hair ribbons and barrette missing.

1967 Tutti dolls. First doll is #3550 in new dress. Second is #3580 in the new dress. Blonde or brunette hair.

Close-up of Todd (3590). Brown eyes. Titian hair.

Twiggy (#1185), the first doll copied from a real personality (the well-known English model), was presented in the latter part of the year. She had a twist waist and bendable knees and was the same size as Francie. She wore a blue, yellow and green striped mini dress, panties and yellow boots.

Her short, pale blonde hair and exaggerated eye make-up made her appear different from Casey, even though the same head mold was used for both dolls. She had rooted upper eyelashes and painted lower lashes. Her markings were: ©1966/Mattel, Inc./U.S. Patented/U.S. Pat. Pend./ Made In/Japan.

Another item offered this year was Barbie Hair Fair (#4042). This set contained a Barbie head with short blonde or brunette hair, a wig, three hair pieces and several hair trim accessories. The full wig came in three colors; the other hair pieces in only blonde or brunette.

—:—

Color Magic Barbie (#1150) was on the market this year in a new box, an open-faced cardboard type. This doll had the same words in the markings but now all letters were raised.

—:—

This year bendable leg Skipper (#1030) also came in a new open-faced cardboard box. The rest was the same as 1966.

—:—

The 1967 Mattel Catalogue lists the following as still available:

(0850) Barbie
(0750) Ken
(0860) Midge
(0950) Skipper
(1030) Skipper
(1090) Ricky
(1140) Francie
(1130) Francie
(1040) Skooter
(4039) Color 'N Curl

—:—

The following were still available through mail-order catalogues: bendable leg Ken, bendable leg Barbie, bendable leg Midge, #0871 Wig Wardrobe, bendable leg Skooter and the Sundae Treat Tutti and Todd alone in a small brown box.

1967—Twiggy (1185). First doll copied from a real personality. (Gift from Ginger Kendrick)

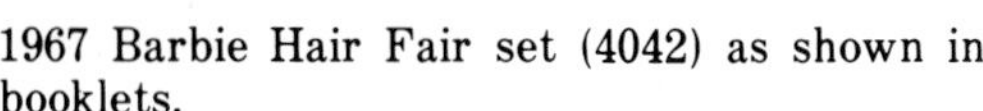

1967 Barbie Hair Fair set (4042) as shown in booklets.

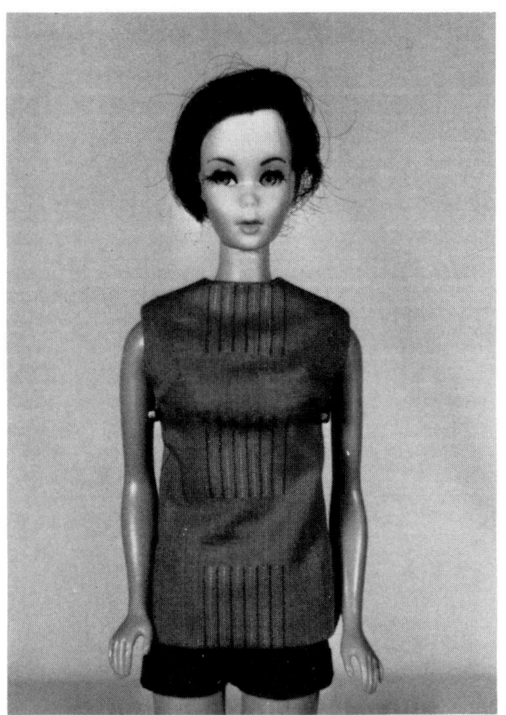

Head from Barbie Hair Fair set (4042). Badly worn—most of bangs missing.

Twiggy (1185) and Casey (1180). Made from the same head mold. Twiggy has shorter hair and heavier eye makeup. Notice Twiggy's lower painted lashes.

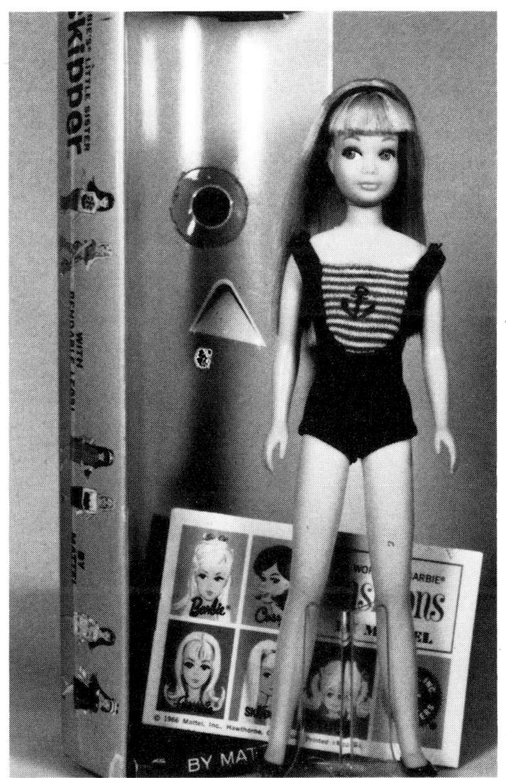

In 1967 bendable leg Skipper (1030) came in an open-faced cardboard box. These are very rare. (Ashabraner collection)

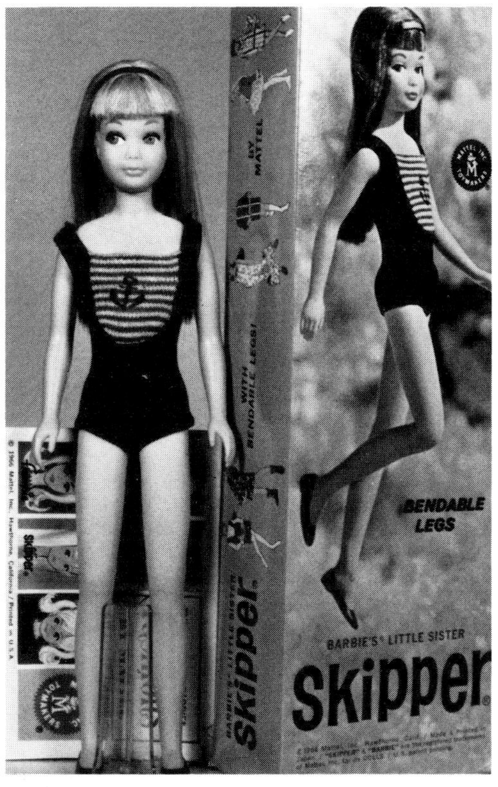

This shows back of rare open-faced Skipper box (1030). (Ashabraner collection)

1968

They Talk!! That was the big news in 1968. Barbie talked in English (1115) and in Spanish (8348).

Two new Barbie friends, Stacey and Christie, were introduced this year, and both were talking dolls.

Stacey (1125) spoke with a British accent. She was dressed in a two-piece, multi-colored striped swimsuit. She had blue eyes and molded teeth. Her long straight hair, in blonde or titian, was drawn to the left side in back and tied with a green ribbon.

Christie (1126), a black doll, wore a green knit top over rose shorts. She had light brown skin, dark brown curly hair, parted on the side, and dark brown eyes.

Talking Barbie wore a rose knit top over rose shorts. Her long hair, in four colors, was drawn to the right side, then twisted and trimmed with three rose colored ribbons. The first talking Barbies mentioned Stacey in their speech. All three dolls had the same markings: ©1967/Mattel, Inc./U.S. & Foreign/Pats. Pend./Mexico. Also all three dolls had rooted eyelashes and bendable knees.

These first talking dolls came in a small clear plastic box. The plastic posing stand, introduced in 1967, was included. By placing the box top on the posing stand, a colorful seat could be made. Barbie's was pink and lavender, Christie's orange and yellow and Stacey's was two shades of green.

Prior to 1968 all dolls, except Miss Barbie, had been made in Japan. These first talking dolls were made in Mexico. The Barbie-size dolls, made in Japan, had divided fingers. These new Talking dolls, except Spanish Talking Barbie, had newly shaped hands—long, slender undivided fingers. Collectors refer to hands of this type as the "Mexico" hands. The first Spanish Talking Barbie had the old type hands. Her wrist tag was marked "Made in U.S.A." but her hip had the Mexico markings.

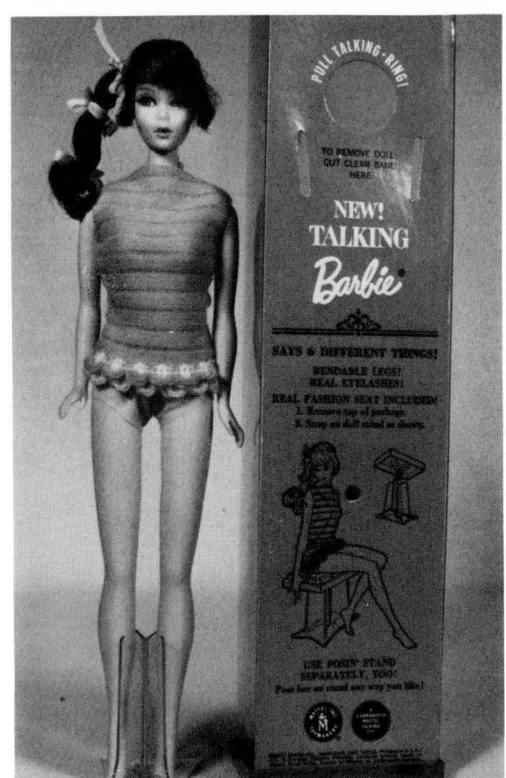

1968 Talking Barbie (1115). New undivided fingers. This pictures back of hard plastic box doll came in.

1968 Spanish Talking Barbie (8348). Pink swimsuit and hair ribbons (same as regular Barbie.).

Closer view of Spanish Talking Barbie. Wrist tag says "Made in U.S.A." Notice the original divided fingers.

Close-up of Talking Barbie (1115). Came in many shades of hair.

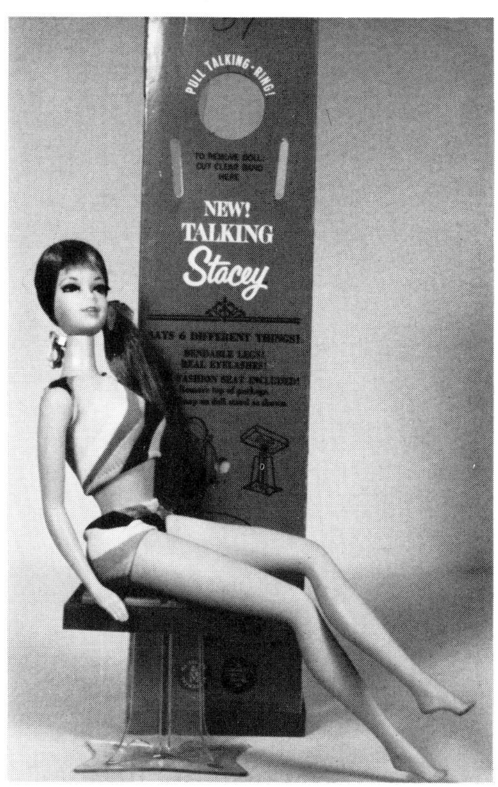

1968 Talking Stacey (1125). Posing stand and box top make a seat.

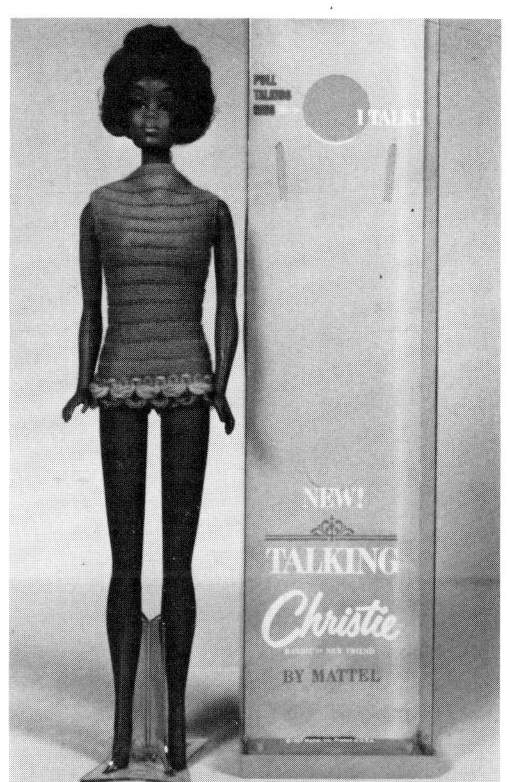

1968 Talking Christie (1126). Green top over rose shorts.

Close-up of Talking Christie (1126). This first Christie had dull brown hair.

This year two new Twist 'n Turn dolls were presented.

Stacey (1165) was dressed in a one-piece red swimsuit with button trim. Her long straight hair, titian or blonde, was drawn back and tied with a ribbon. She had blue eyes, molded teeth, rooted eyelashes and bendable knees. Her markings were: ©1966/Mattel, Inc./U.S. Patented/U.S. Pat. Pend./Made in/Japan.

Skipper (1105) wore a one-piece swimsuit. The suit was blue with a pink and blue striped waist. She had the same long hair style as the former dolls, but now blue elastic replaced the "brass" headband. All of the first Twist Skippers were marked: ©1967 Mattel, Inc./U.S. Pat'd./U.S. Pats. Pend./Made in Japan. Late in the year the dolls were made in Taiwan and so marked.

—:—

Twist 'n Turn Casey (1180), Francie (1170) and Barbie (1160) were still on the market this year. Casey and Francie were the same but Barbie was available in a new swimsuit—a checked top in shades of pink and green over pink shorts. During the early part of the year, the 1967 suit was still being used.

—:—

"Family Affair," a television show of the era, featured an adorable little girl named "Buffy" and her doll, "Mrs. Beasley." (Buffy was played by Anissa Jones.)

In 1968 Mattel introduced Buffy and Mrs. Beasley dolls (3577) based upon these television personalities. Buffy was the same size as Tutti and had the same markings. She had freckles, blue eyes and blonde hair in a "puppy-ears" style tied with red ribbons.

Her dress had a red skirt with a red and white polka dot waist. She wore red shoes and white socks. Mrs. Beasley wore granny glasses and a blue and white polka dot outfit trimmed in yellow.

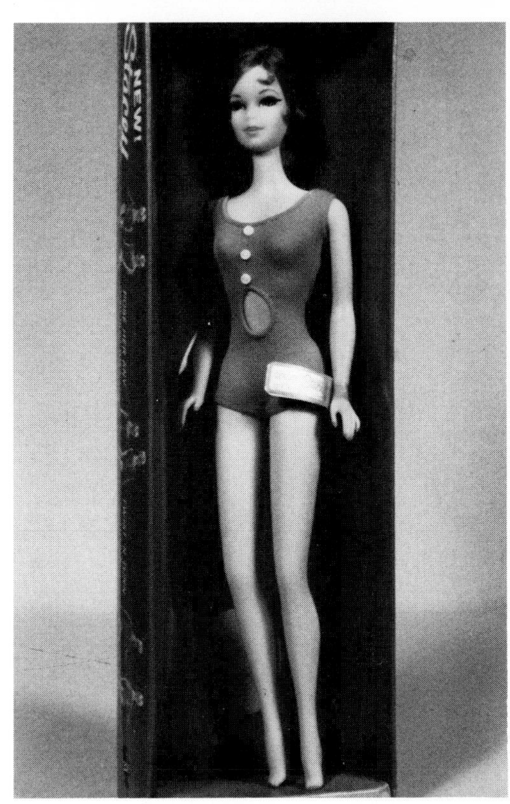

1968 Twist 'N Turn Stacey (1165). Hair either blonde or titian. Molded teeth. Red swimsuit.

1968 Twist 'N Turn Skipper (1105). Swimsuit is solid blue and blue and pink stripes. The first dolls were made in Japan.

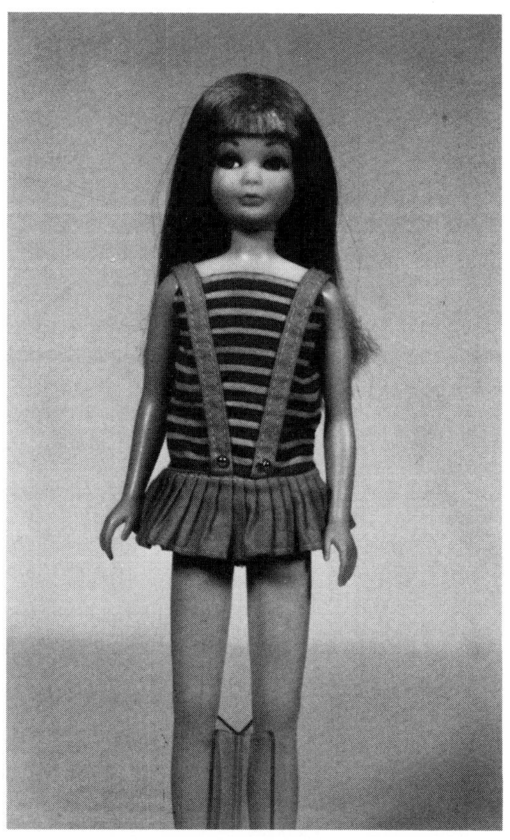

Late in 1968 the twist Skipper (1105) was made in Taiwan. Notice the swimsuit material is slightly different from the first one.

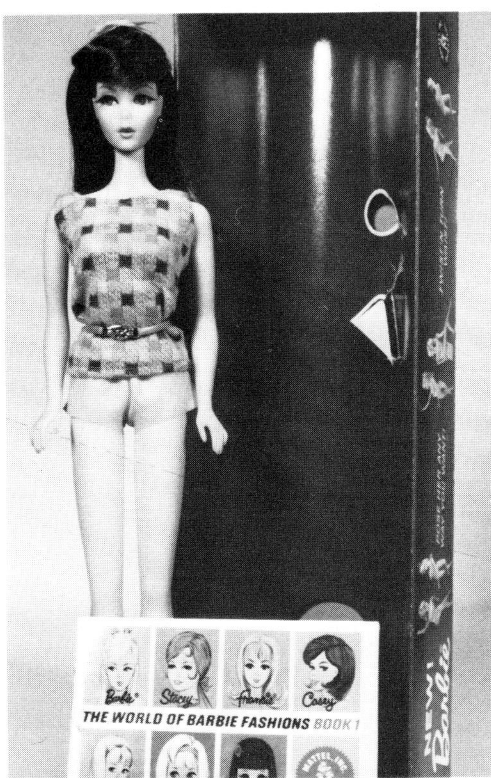

In 1968 Twist 'N Turn Barbie (1160) came in a new swimsuit. Same hair style.

This year Colored Francie (1100) had darker brown eyes and the material used for her hair was different. It did not turn reddish like the first type did. The rest of the doll remained the same.

—:—

The following dolls were still available:

#1185 — Twiggy
0950 — Skipper, straight legs
1190 — Barbie, standard
1170 — Francie, twist
1140 — Francie, straight legs
1180 — Casey
3580 — Tutti
3570 — Chris
4042 — Hair Fair set
All 7 Tutti Play-Settings.

—:—

Mattel did not list a Ken for 1968.

—:—

Mail order catalogues (good until August or September, 1968) still offered a bendable leg Skipper (1030), straight leg Skooter (1040) and a 0750 Ken in a gift set.

1968—Buffy and Mrs. Beasley (3577). Based on characters from "Family Affair," a television show of the era.

Close-up of Buffy (3577). In the T.V. show Buffy was played by Anissa Jones.

In 1969 two new personality dolls joined the Barbie group—Julia, the popular T.V. nurse (played by Diahann Carroll) and Truly Scrumptious from the movie, "Chitty Chitty Bang Bang."

Talking Julia (1128) was dressed in a gold and silver jumpsuit. She had light brown skin, brown eyes, rooted eyelashes and short straight dark brown hair. Twist Julia (1127) had the same hair and skin. She wore a two-piece white nurse's uniform.

Both dolls had bendable knees and both were made from the Christie head mold. The talking doll had the "Mexico" hands. The twist doll's hands were made from the original Barbie mold, but the fingers were not cut completely through as the originals were.

Truly Scrumptious came in a talking version (1107) that had bendable legs. She also came in a standard straight leg version (1108). The Francie head mold was used for both dolls and both had blue eyes and rooted eyelashes. Their blonde hair was brushed straight back from the forehead and held in place with a rubber band.

Both dolls wore lovely old-fashioned dresses and fancy hats. The talking doll's dress was made of pink and rose satin and black net. The other doll's dress was made of pale pink net over pale pink taffeta.

The talking doll had the "Mexico hands" and the standard doll had the original Barbie type hands. The talking doll was marked: ©1967/Mattel, Inc./U.S. & Foreign/Pats. Pend./Mexico. The standard doll had the Midge/Barbie markings.

1969—Talking Truly Scrumptious (1107). Based upon a character in the movie, "Chitty Chitty Bang Bang." Bendable legs.

1969—Straight leg Truly Scrumptious (1108). Head same as #1107. Original divided fingers.

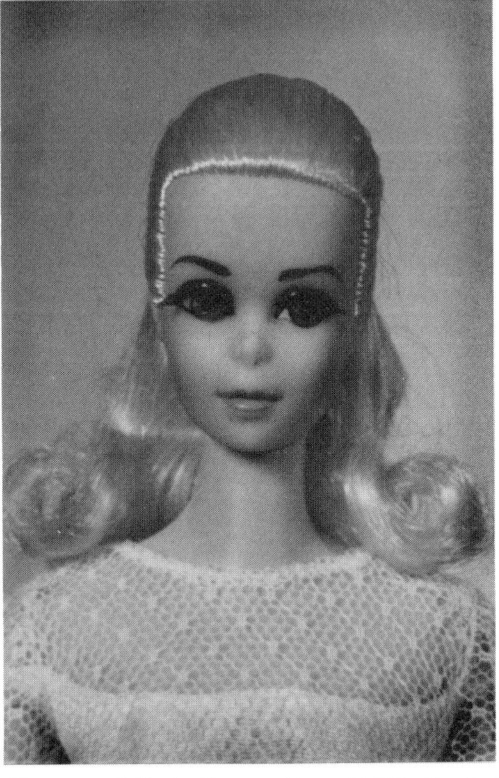

Close-up of Truly Scrumptious #1108. Rooted eyelashes. Blonde hair.

1969—Twist 'N Turn Julia (1127). Based upon the T.V. show, "Julia." Julia was played by Diahann Carroll.

1969—Talking Julia (1128). Both versions of Julia made from the Christie head mold.

After a year's absence, Ken was back in 1969 in a completely new version. He had a new head mold, a huskier body, pinker skin, bendable knees and he could talk. His new Edwardian hair style was in a medium shade of brown.

Talking Ken (1111) was dressed in a solid red jacket and shorts. He was marked: ©1968/Mattel, Inc./U.S. & For. Pat'd./Other Pat's/Pending/Mexico.

There may have been a Spanish version (8372) of this first talking Ken, but this is only speculation since to the present time none of these have been found.

—:—

Later in the year another new doll joined the growing list of Barbie friends. This was Talking P.J. (1113). Made from the Midge head mold, she had bendable legs, brown eyes, rooted eyelashes and long straight blonde hair with bangs. Her hair was divided into two sections, and each section was decorated with strands of beads. She had the "Mexico hands."

She wore a long sleeved, orangy floral tricot mini dress, red shoes, panties and sunglasses. Her markings were: ©1967/Mattel, Inc./U.S. & Foreign/Pats. Pend./Mexico.

—:—

This year a new Hair Fair (4043) was available. The hair pieces differed slightly from the older set, but the head remained the same.

The 4042 set was still available through mail order catalogues until August or September 1969.

—:—

This year was the first time Tutti (3580) was pictured in the booklets and catalogues wearing the dress with the print top and solid rose skirt. (The dress was described as being available in the 1967 catalogues.)

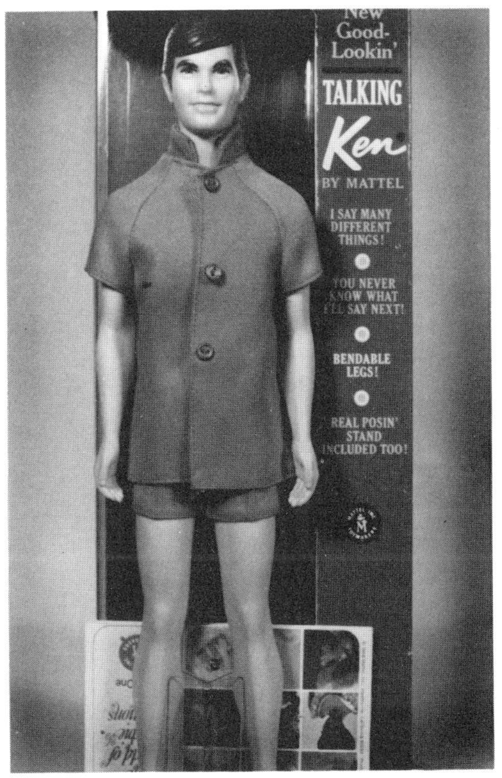

1969—Talking Ken (1111). All new doll. Pink skin, bendable knees, brown painted Edwardian hair style. Red jacket and trunks.

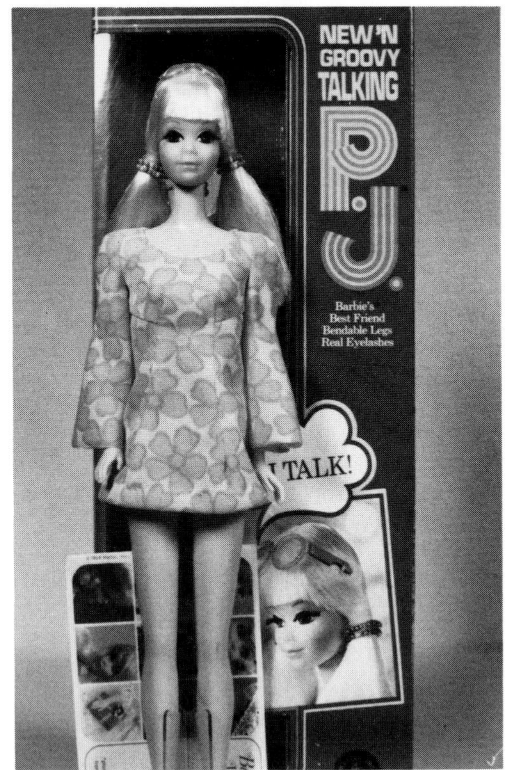

1969—Talking P.J. (1113). Made from the Midge head mold. Blonde hair.

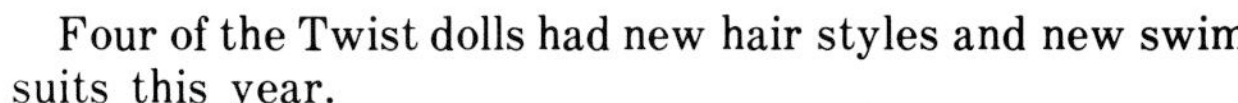

Four of the Twist dolls had new hair styles and new swimsuits this year.

Barbie (1160) had a long flip hair-do. She wore a one-piece, multi-colored diagonal striped suit. The stripes crossed forming a diamond pattern.

Francie (1170) had a short flip hair style. She wore a pink one-piece swimsuit with a solid top and striped bottom.

Stacey (1165) had short turned-up hair. She wore a one-piece psychedelic print swimsuit. (The catalogues and booklets showed a two-piece suit that was never on the market.)

Skipper (1105) had two long curls and bangs. She wore a red and orange checked cotton suit. (The catalogues and booklets showed a fuzzy knit-like suit that was never on the market. The doll used in the picture also had the old-style long straight hair-do.)

Talking Barbie (1115), Spanish Talking Barbie (8348), Talking Christie (1126) and Talking Stacey (1125) were still on the market. Christie and Stacey were the same as last year, except they were packaged differently. They, and the two Barbies, were in a cardboard box with a clear plastic "window." Spanish Barbie now had the "Mexico" hands.

During the first part of the year Talking Barbie (1115) had the same clothes, same hair-do and the same neck rim markings (Japan) as last year. During the later part of the year the neck rim was marked "Hong Kong," but the doll had the same side-twist hair style and the same markings. The first of these wore the 1968 outfit. Later ones wore a new outfit—a reddish two-piece vinyl swimsuit with a jacket trimmed in the reddish vinyl.

Standard Barbie (1190), Twist Casey (1180) and Buffy and Mrs. Beasley (3577) were still on the market and the same as last year.

The 1968 Sears catalogue (good until Fall of 1969) offered a Chris (3570) for sale. Todd (3590) was listed in the 1969 Spiegel catalogue.

1969—New Barbie Hair Fair set (4043). Head still has the short rooted hair but the hair pieces are different from the old set, #4042.

1969—Tutti (3580). Dress has a rose colored skirt and a print top. Blonde or brunette hair.

1969—Twist 'N Turn Barbie (1160). New long flip hair-do. New striped swimsuit.

Close-up of 1969 Twist Barbie. (A great favorite with collectors)

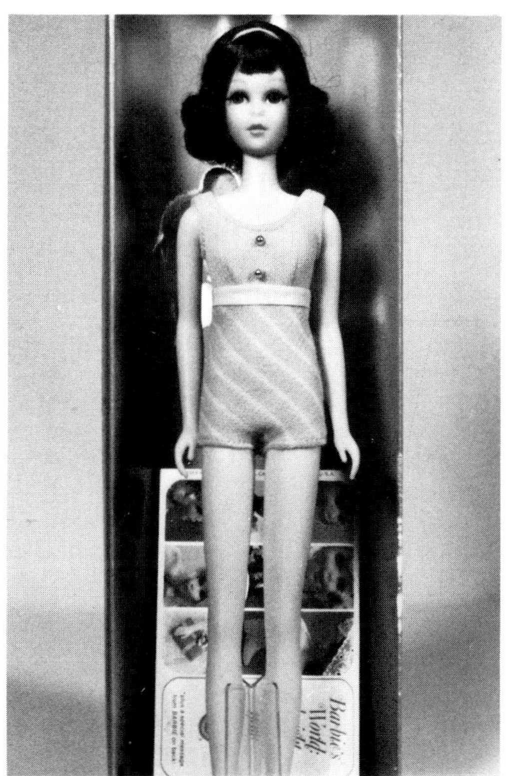

1969—New Twist 'N Turn Francie (1170). New short flip hair style. New swimsuit has pink top and a pink and yellow striped bottom.

1969—Close-up of Twist Francie (1170).

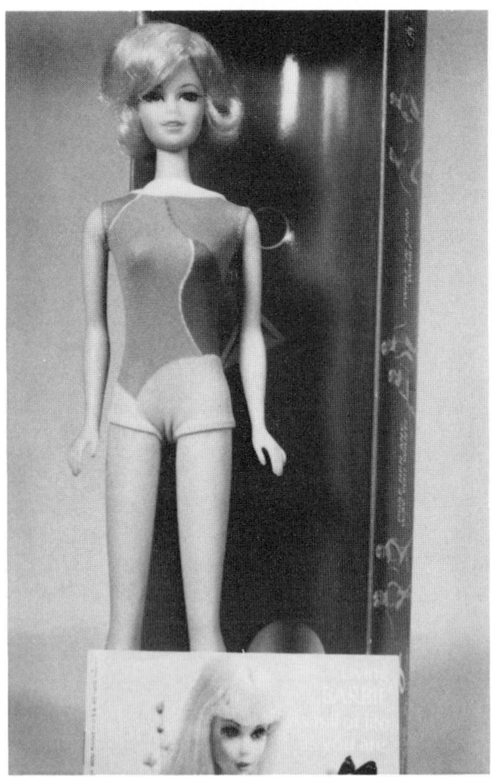

1969—New Twist 'N Turn Stacey (1165). New short hair-do. New psychedelic print swimsuit. First issue came in the old box shown here.

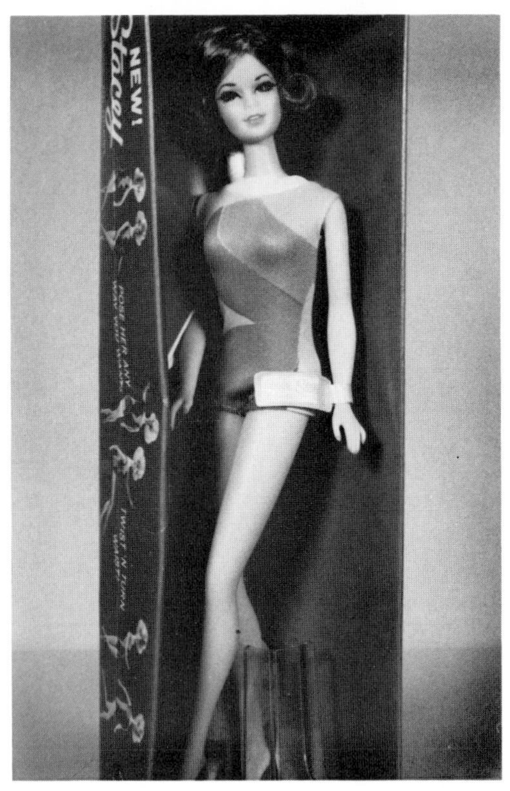

1969—Second issue of the new Twist Stacey came in the new box shown here.

Close-up of the 1969 Twist Stacey (1165).

1969—New Twist 'N Turn Skipper (1105). New two-curl hair style. New swimsuit of orange, red and purple check top and solid orange bottom.

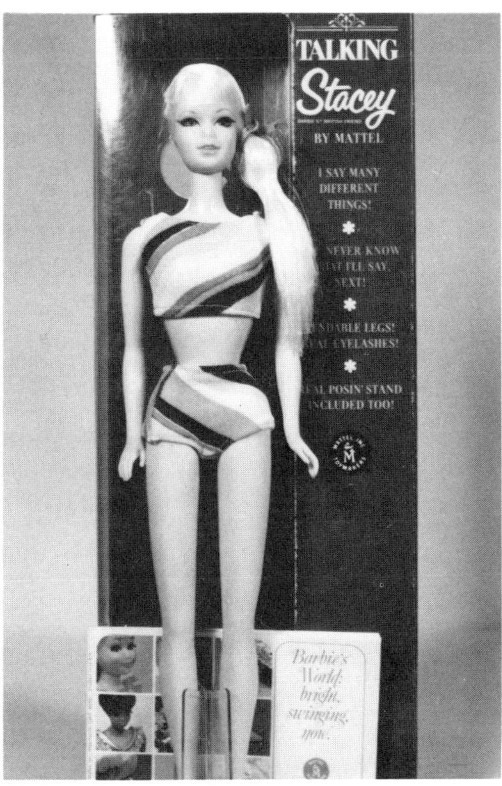

1969—Talking Stacey (1125) in a new "window" box. Rest about the same as 1968.

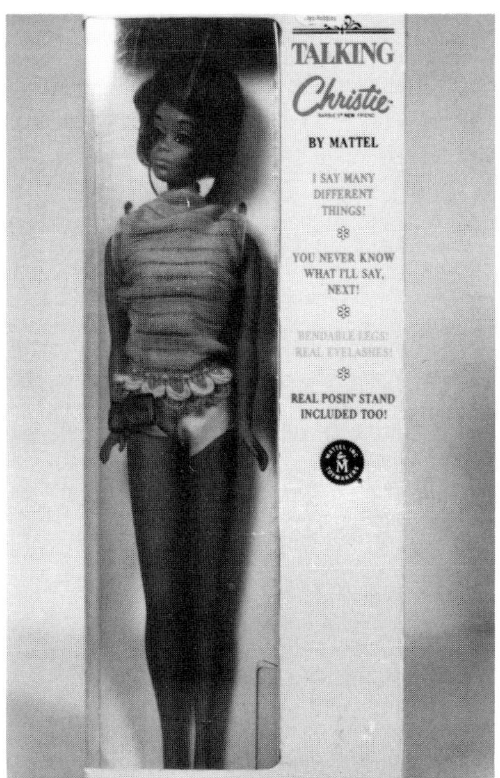

1969—Talking Christie in a new "window" box. Some dolls' hair turned a strange shade of red.

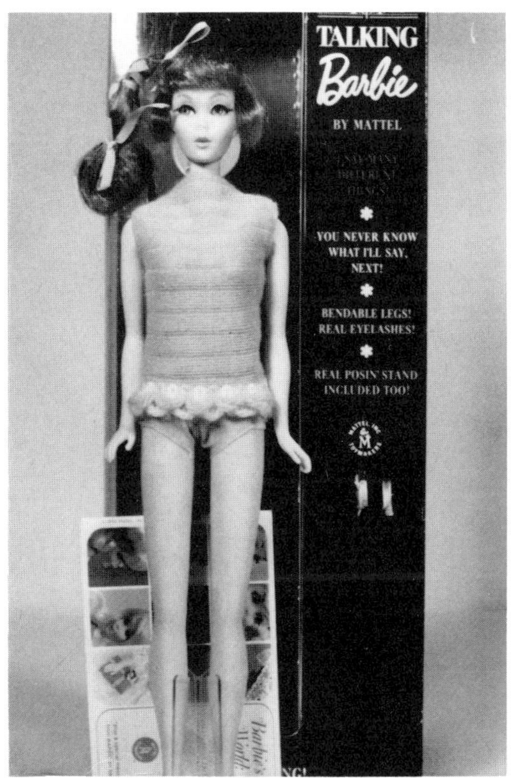

1969—Talking Barbie (1115) in a new "window" box. During most of the year the doll was about the same as 1968. (Gift from Lillie Herning)

During later 1969 Talking Barbie (1115) had the same hair style but new neck rim markings (Hong Kong instead of Japan). First issue wore the old swimsuit. Second issue wore a new swimsuit. Pictured here is the second issue.

1970

The biggest news of 1970 was unpleasant. A fire destroyed the Mattel factory in Mexico.

—:—

This year Barbie and Skipper were more poseable than ever. Known as Living Barbie (1116) and Living Skipper (1117) they had swivel waists, necks, arms, hands and legs and bendable elbows and knees. Barbie also had bendable ankles.

Both had new hair styles. Barbie had medium length straight hair with straight bangs in shades of blonde, titian and brunette. Skipper had blonde hair with curled ends. The hair was divided into two sections and tied with rose colored ribbons. Both dolls had rooted eyelashes. Barbie was marked: ©1968 Mattel, Inc./U.S. & For. Pat'd./Other Pats. Pend./Taiwan. Skipper's markings were: ©1969 Mattel, Inc./Taiwan/U.S. & For. Patd./Other Pats. Pend./Patd. in Canada 1967.

Barbie was dressed in a gold and silver lame swimsuit with an orange net hooded jacket. Skipper wore a one-piece green, blue and rose tricot swimsuit.

Mattel used a Trade-In special (1147) to introduce the Living Skipper. The doll could be acquired for $1.99 and any old doll. The old dolls were donated to charity.

The 1970 and 1971 Sears Christmas catalogues offered an exclusive Mattel Gift Set called "Action Accents" (1585). This set featured a Living Barbie plus sports clothing and gear. The doll was made in Japan, not Taiwan, and was so marked. This was the doll pictured in the 1970 Japanese Barbie booklet. See Chapter III for details.

1970—Living Barbie (1116). The most poseable doll to date. Several hair shades.

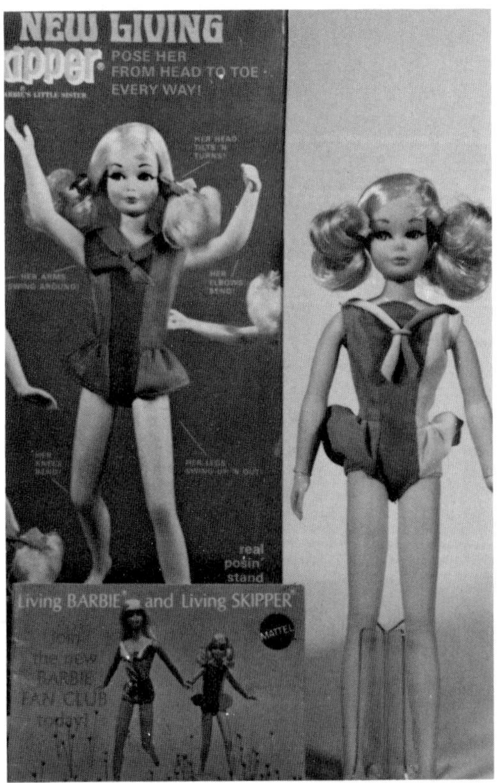

1970—Living Skipper (1117). Blonde hair. (Gift from Jan Bacon)

1970—Trade-in Skipper (1147). Promotional doll to introduce the new "living" line of dolls.

Little Theatre Costumes—"Barbie Arabian Nights" and "Ken Arabian Nights."

Little Theatre Costumes—"Cinderella" and "The Prince."

Little Theatre Costume—"Red Riding Hood and the Wolf."

Little Theatre Costumes—"King Arthur" and "Guinevere."

Travel Costumes—"Barbie in Switzerland" and "Ken in Switzerland."

Travel Costumes—"Barbie in Holland" and "Ken in Holland."

Travel Costumes—"Ken in Hawaii" and "Barbie in Hawaii."

Travel Costumes—"Ken in Mexico" and "Barbie in Mexico."

Travel Costume—"Barbie in Japan."

This is "Becky," the doll that was never put on the market. The Casey head mold was used for this sample doll.

A poster showing early clothes, including Barbie's first fish.

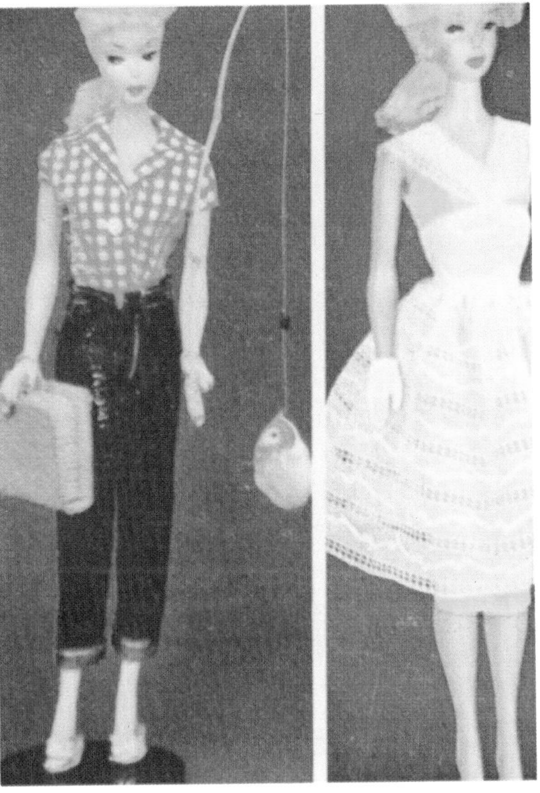

An enlargement of the fish from the poster.

Living Barbie wearing 1974 Sears' exclusive "Red Gown."

Barbie (1070) wearing #7932, a Fashion Original of 1975.

Jamie wearing 1975 Sears' exclusive "Pink Gown."

Bendable Midge wearing "Senior Prom." (Gift from Dixie Kennett)

#7377 Carla from Germany, 1976.

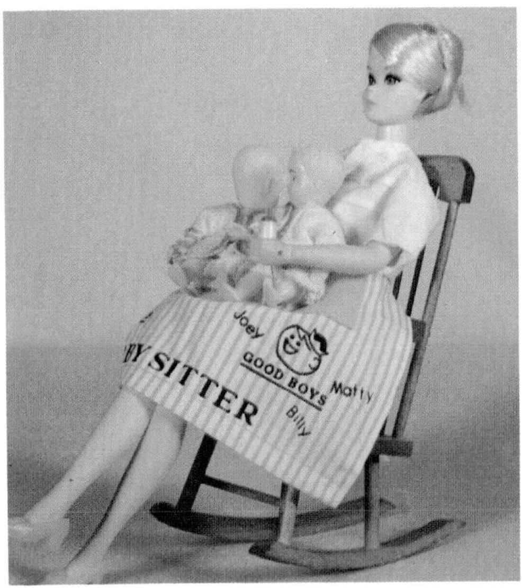

"Barbie Baby-sits" babies with two shades of hair.

Color Magic Barbie wearing "Blue Royalty" of 1970.

Flocked hair Ken with unusually thick eye liner. (Ashabraner collection)

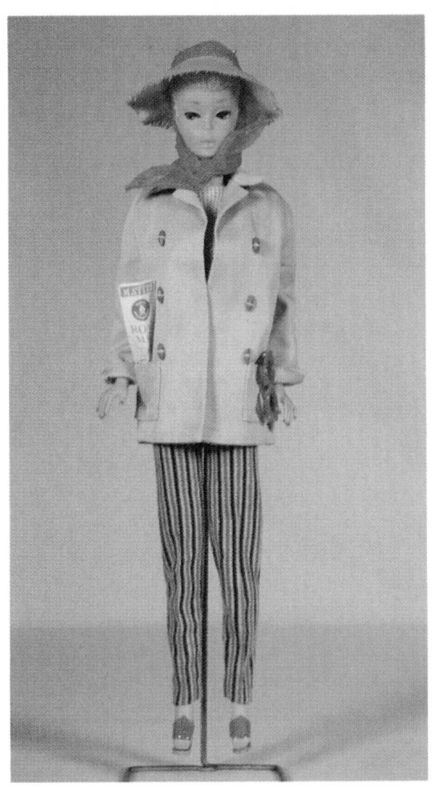

"Swirl" ponytail Barbie in #985 "Open Road."

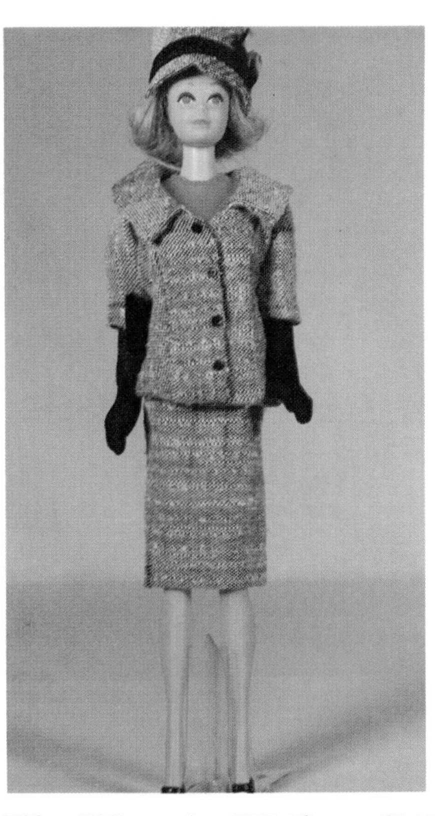

Midge (860) wearing #954 "Career Girl."

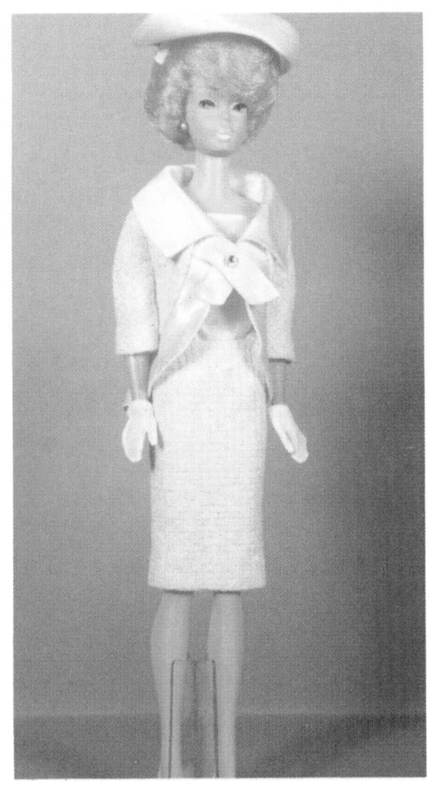

A 1964 Barbie wearing #1656 "Fashion Luncheon."

1974 and 1975 Todd clothes from Germany.

Tutti wearing #8504 "Schneeflockchen" from Germany.

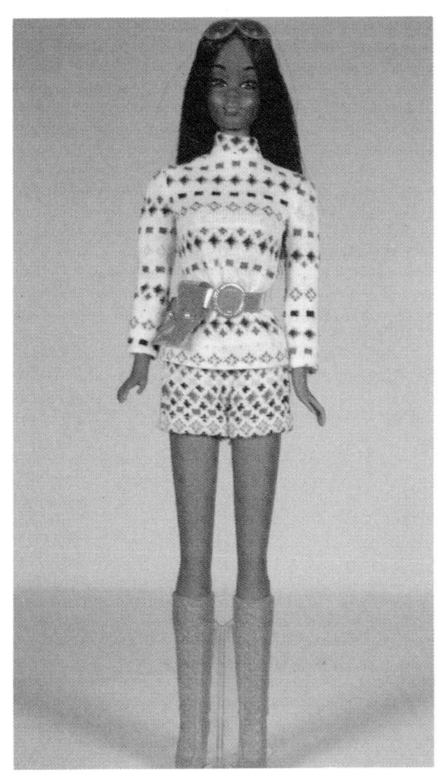
Malibu Christie wearing #3481 "The Short Set" of 1972.

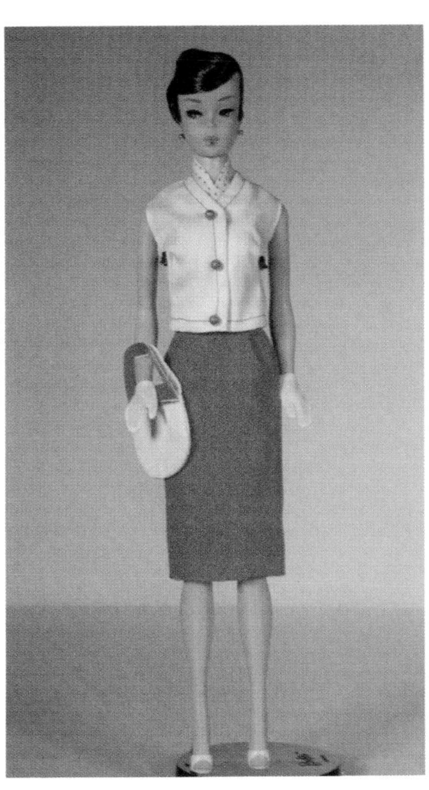
"Swirl" ponytail Barbie in #1604 "Crisp 'N Cool."

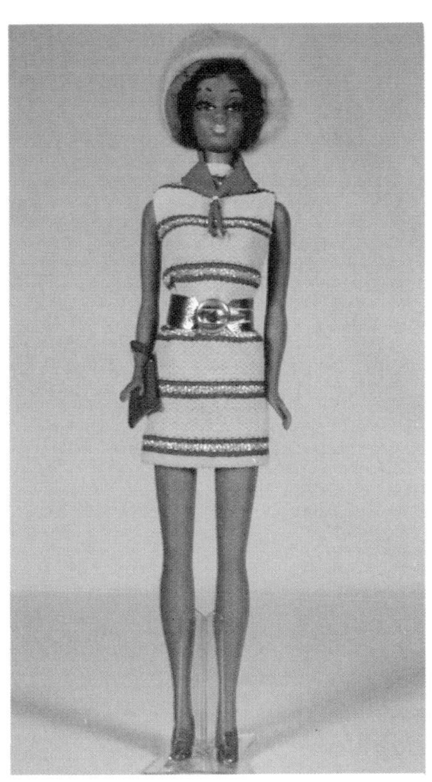
Talking Christie wearing #1452 "Now Knit" of 1970.

Rare silver haired Miss Barbie in "Sophisticated Lady."

Twist Stacey wearing Julia's "Pink Fantasy."

Bendable leg Barbie in #1799 "Maxi 'N Mini."

Walk Lively Miss America (3194-9991), a Kellogg Company offer of 1972.

Quick Curl Barbie in #7934, a Fashion Original of 1975.

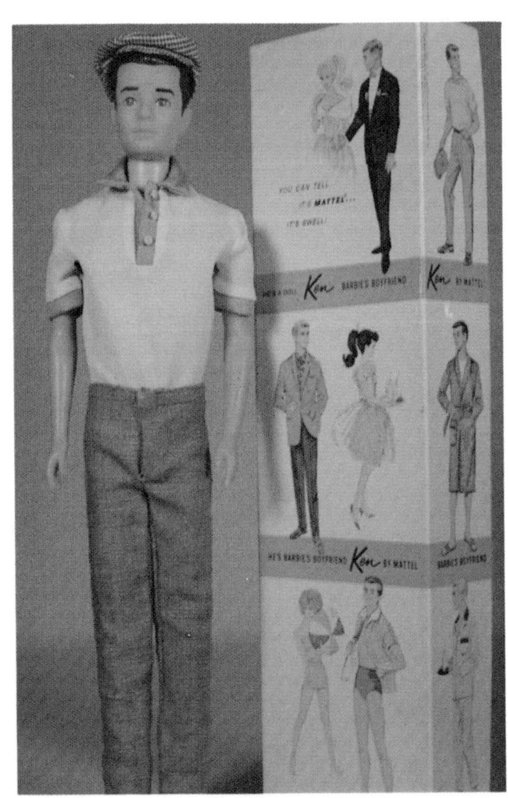

A "Dressed Doll" box with doll—Ken in "Holiday." (Ashabraner collection)

Close-up of 1970 Living Barbie (1116). Wore a gold and silver swimsuit.

Close-up of 1970 Living Skipper (1117). Two shades of blonde hair were available.

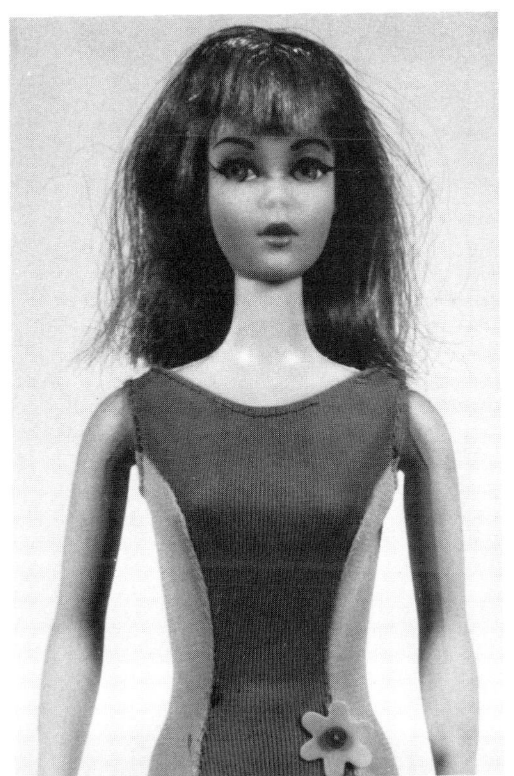

Most Living Barbies were made in Taiwan. This is a rare one made in Japan. Swimsuit is orange and blue.

1970 Japanese Barbie booklet. The rare Living Barbie is shown on cover. (Gift from Viki Lyn Paulson)

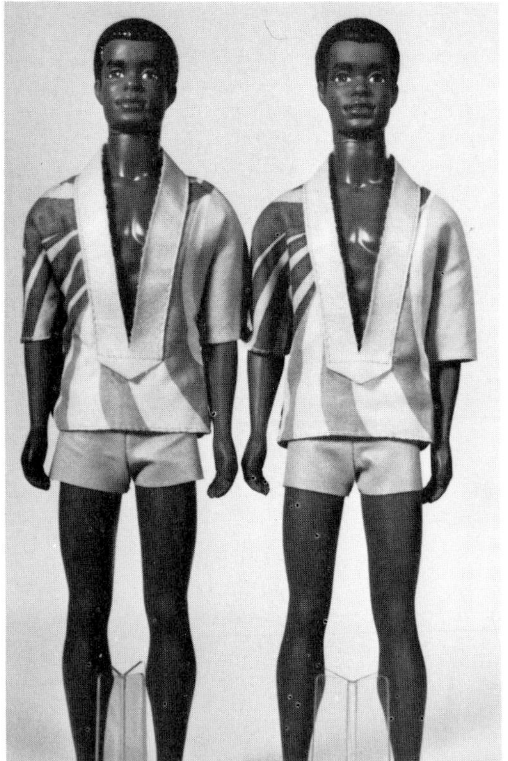

1970—Talking Brad (1114). The first black male doll. First issue made in Mexico. Second issue made in Hong Kong.

There was a new black doll on the market in 1970—Talking Brad (1114), the same size doll as Ken.

He had dark brown skin, brown eyes and painted black hair. He was dressed in a brightly colored Afro style shirt and shorts.

The first dolls were made in Mexico and were marked: ©1968/Mattel, Inc./U.S. & For. Pat'd./Other Pats./Pending/Mexico. Later in the year the dolls were made in Hong Kong and were so marked. The heads of both were marked: ©1969 Mattel, Inc.

—:—

Talking Christie (1126) had new clothes this year—clothes that matched Brad's. The rest of the doll was about the same as last year.

—:—

This year Mattel made Walking Jamie (1132) for Sears. The Barbie head mold was used for her head. She had brown eyes, rooted eyelashes and bendable knees. Her hair, either blonde, brunette or titian, was styled in a medium length flip.

She wore a mini dress, panties, boots and a head scarf. The dress was made from a knit-like fabric in yellow with orange and purple checks. The scarf was purple and the boots were orange.

There was a press-plate on her back. When pressed, this caused her head, arms and legs to move, giving the impression of walking. Markings were: ©1967 Mattel, Inc./U.S. Patented/Pat'd. Canada 1967/Other Pats. Pend./Japan.

1970—Talking Christie (1126). New clothes that match Brad's. New pink box.

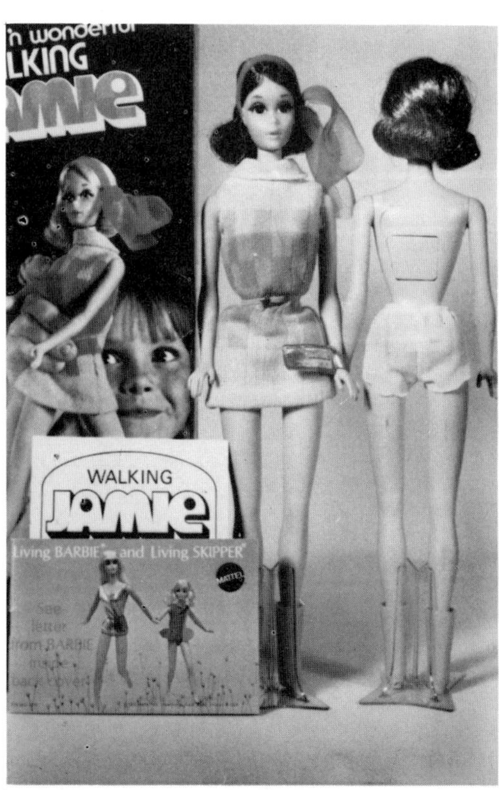

1970—Walking Jamie (1132). Made for Sears. Notice press plate on back. Blonde, brunette or titian.

Two new Francies were introduced this year.

Francie Hair Happenin's (1122) was a twist doll with bendable knees. She had short blonde hair with bangs and four extra blonde hair pieces. She wore a blue mini dress with white lace trim. Her markings were: ©1966/Mattel, Inc./U.S. Patented/U.S. Pat. Pend./Made In/Japan.

Francie With Growin' Pretty Hair (1129) had a new innovative hair style. By pulling a certain way, a section of her hair could be lengthened or shortened. There were no extra hair pieces with this doll and the only hair color was blonde. She had bendable knees and was dressed in a short pink satin and net party dress.

The first issue of this doll had arms and hands made from the original Barbie mold with the divided fingers. She was marked: ©1966/Mattel, Inc./U.S. Pat. Other/Pats. Pend./ Pat. Canada/1967/Japan.

—:—

This year three new dolls the same size as Tutti were sold. Called "Pretty Pairs," each doll held either a doll or a teddy bear.

1133—Lori 'N Rori (a blonde doll holding a brown teddy bear)

1134—Nan 'N Fran (a black doll holding a black toy doll)

1135—Angie 'N Tangie (a brunette doll holding a blonde toy doll)

These dolls were not 5" tall as stated in the booklets. They were about 6" or 6¼" tall. (The toys being held were about 3" to 3½" tall.)

1970—Francie Hair Happenin's (1122). Short blonde hair with bangs. Four hair pieces.

Close-up of Walking Jamie. Made from the Barbie head mold. Brown eyes.

1970 Francie With Growin' Pretty Hair (1129). First issue had arms and hands made from original Barbie molds. No hair pieces.

1970—Lori 'N Rori (1133). Blonde doll holding brown Teddy bear.

There were two new twist dolls in 1970—P.J. (1118) and Christie (1119).

P.J. looked the same as talking P.J. from 1969. She wore a one-piece pink swimsuit and sunglasses.

Christie had dark reddish brown curly hair with a part. She had light brown skin, brown eyes and bendable knees. She wore a one-piece pink and yellow tricot swimsuit.

Both dolls had hands made from the original Barbie mold but Christie's fingers were not cut completely through. Both were marked: ©1966/Mattel, Inc./U.S. Patented/U.S. Pat. Pend./Made In/Japan.

—:—

Five of the twist dolls wore new suits this year, but all five had the same hair style and the same markings as the 1969 dolls.

Skipper (1105) wore an orange colored vinyl jacket over a two-piece swimsuit.

Francie (1170) was in a two-piece suit—a side closing floral top over rose shorts.

Julia (1127) was dressed in a one-piece nurse's white uniform and cap. Some dolls were dressed the same as 1969.

Stacey (1165) wore a one-piece blue and rose floral print swimsuit during the later part of the year. During the first part of the year she was dressed the same as last year.

Barbie (1160) was dressed in a one-piece rose and white figured swimsuit.

1970—Nan 'N Fran (1134). Black doll holding small black doll.

1970—Angie 'N Tangie (1135). A brunette doll holding a small blonde doll.

1970—Twist 'N Turn P.J. (1118). Made from the Midge head mold.

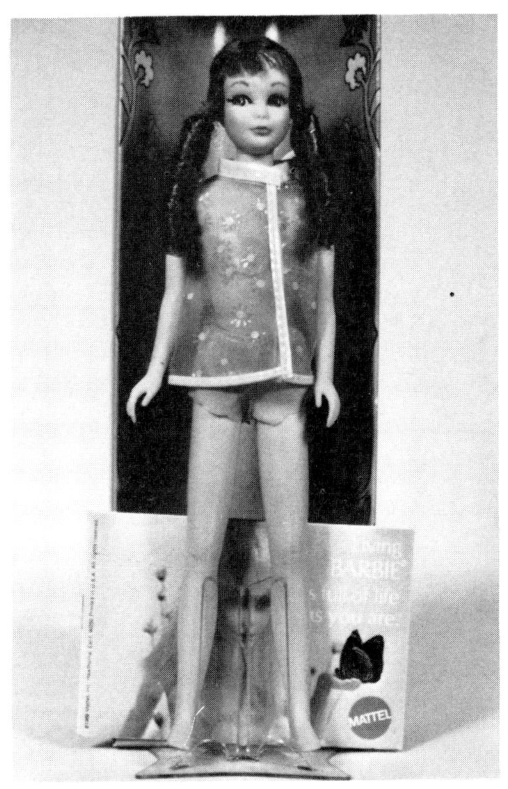

1970—Twist Skipper in a new swimsuit. Same hair style. Same stock number, 1105.

1970—Twist 'N Turn Christie (1119). Pink and yellow swimsuit.

1970 Twist Francie (1170) in new swimsuit. The doll pictured has brown hair.

1970—Twist Barbie (1160) in a new swimsuit. Deep rose with white design.

1970 Twist Julia (1127) wore a new one-piece white nurse's uniform.

1970—Twist Stacey (1165). Early part of year she had new shorter hair, old swimsuit.

1970—Twist Stacey (1165). During later part of year she wore a new swimsuit, rose and blue floral design.

Close-up of the 1970 Twist Julia.

New this year were bendable leg Ken (1124) and bendable leg Brad (1142).

Ken wore a yellow tricot shirt and multi-colored print shorts. Brad wore a reddish orange tricot shirt and multi-colored print shorts.

Brad's skin was slightly darker while Ken seemed about the same. Both still had molded and painted hair—Brad's was black, Ken's was medium brown. Brad was marked: ©1968/Mattel, Inc./U.S. & For. Pat'd/Other Pats./Pending/Hong Kong. Ken's markings were: ©1968/Mattel, Inc./U.S. & For. Pat'd/Other Pats./Pending/Mexico.

—:—

The following dolls were still available:

#4043 — Hair Fair
3580 — Tutti
1128 — Talking Julia
1180 — Twist Casey
1113 — Talking P.J.
3577 — Buffy & Mrs. Beasley

—:—

The 1969 Spiegel catalogue (good until Fall of 1970) offered a Todd (3590) for sale.

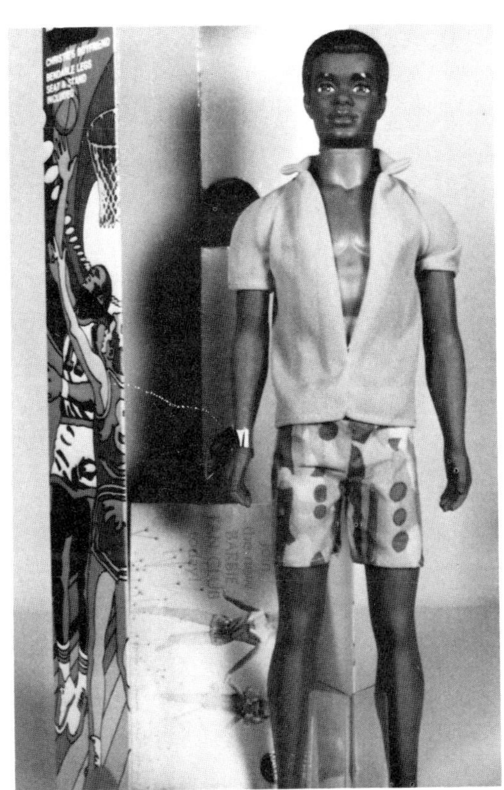

1970—Bendable leg Brad (1142). Head similar to talking doll's.

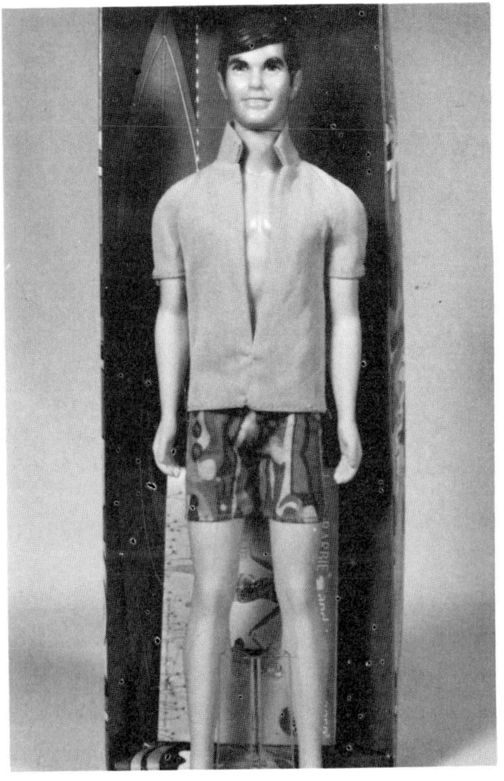

1970—Bendable leg Ken (1124). Brown painted hair.

This year Talking Ken (1111) and Spanish Talking Ken (8372) wore a new outfit—a blue jacket with orange trim and orange shorts. The rest was the same as 1969.

—:—

Late in 1970 Talking Stacey (1125) was on the market in a new one-piece blue and silver swimsuit, new box and new markings: ©1967/Mattel, Inc./U.S. & Foreign/Pats. Pend./ Hong Kong. She had paler eyes and thinner bangs but the same hair style.

During the earlier part of the year the doll from 1969 was still on the market.

—:—

In 1970 the straight leg Skipper was reissued. She had the same swimsuit and the same hair-do as the old Skipper, but her skin was pinker. The box she came in had newer clothes pictured but the same stock number as the old doll (0950). She was marked: ©1963/Mattel, Inc.

—:—

Now straight leg Barbie (1190) was dressed in a one-piece rose and green tricot swimsuit. (The booklet stated that this doll had real eyelashes. This was an error; her lashes were painted instead.) She was in a new box with a new plastic posing stand but her markings remained the same.

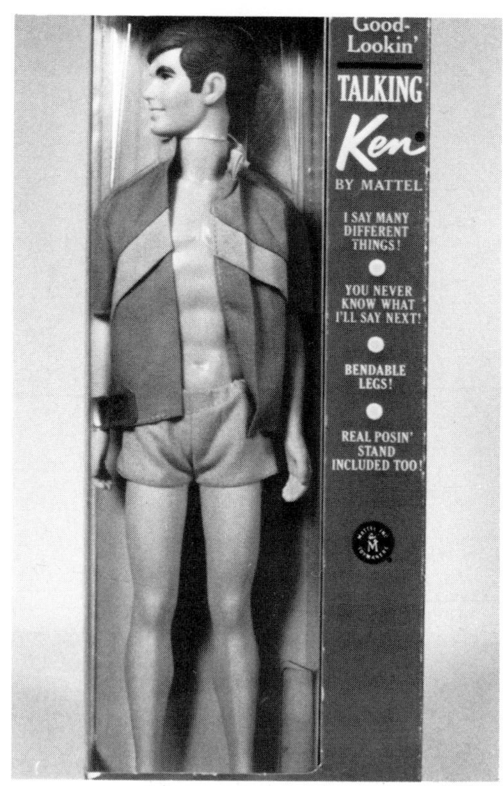

The 1970 Talking Ken (1111) in new blue and orange outfit. Rest same as 1969.

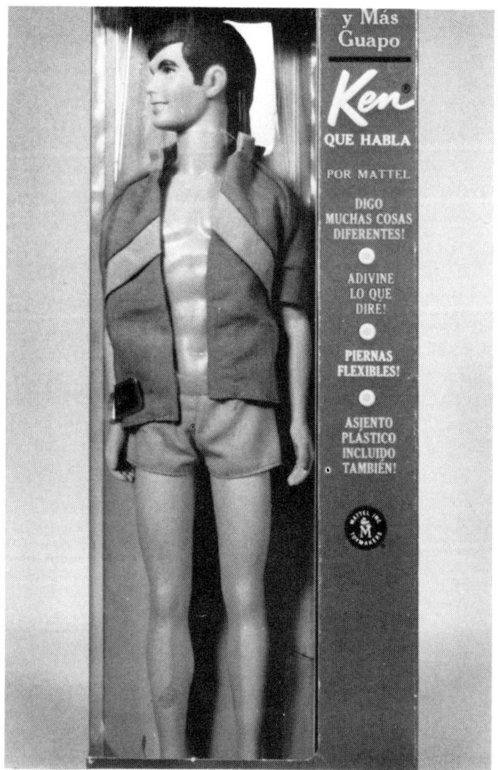

1970—Spanish Talking Ken (8372). Same clothes as #1111 Ken.

Late in 1970 Talking Stacey (1125) had new box, new blue and silver swimsuit and new markings.

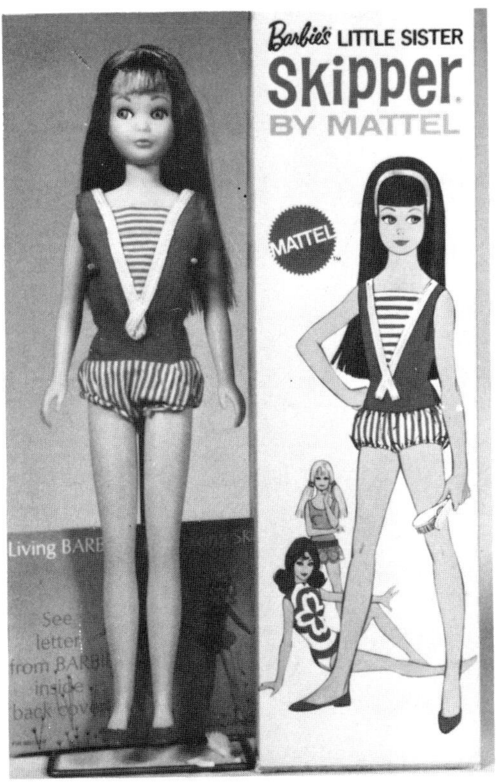

In 1970 Mattel re-issued straight leg Skipper. Pinker skin. Different box.

This shows the sides of the re-issued Skipper box. 1969 and 1970 fashions are featured.

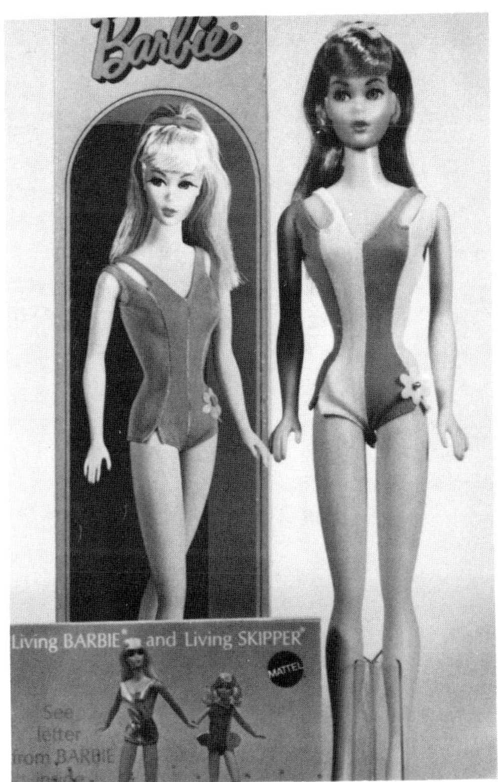

1970—Standard Barbie (1190). New swimsuit. New box. Same doll. Same painted eyelashes.

1970—Standard Barbie Box (1190). Strip of paper on box covers the words "Real Eyelashes." Doll pictured has rooted eyelashes. Actual doll had painted eyelashes.

Talking Barbie (1115) had a new hair-do this year. The hair was parted on the left side with three spit curls and curls on the back of the neck.

She wore the two-piece reddish vinyl swimsuit and the net jacket that was on the market late in 1969.

The first of these dolls had the old talking tape, the one that mentioned Stacey. Later a new tape was used. This new tape mentioned P.J. instead of Stacey. Early dolls had the same markings as last year. Late in the year they were marked: ©1967/Mattel Inc./U.S. & Foreign/Pats. Pend./ Hong Kong.

Spanish Talking Barbie (8348) also had the new hair style and the same clothes as the regular Talking Barbie.

—:—

This year two unusually interesting Barbies were produced. These were Talking Barbie (1115) and Spanish Talking Barbie (8348) with the same hair style and clothes as the dolls described above. The regular Barbie was made in Mexico and the Spanish Barbie was made in Hong Kong. What made these dolls different were their head molds. *A Stacey head mold was used.*

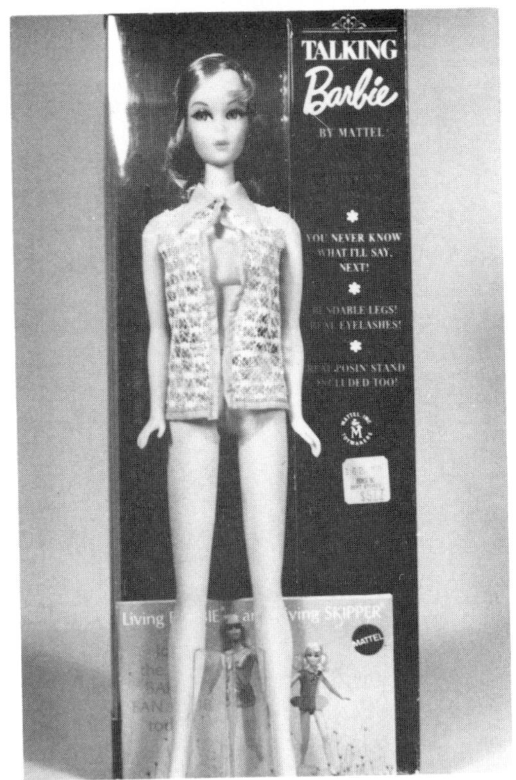

1970—Talking Barbie (1115). New hair-do. Clothes introduced late in 1969. Made in Mexico.

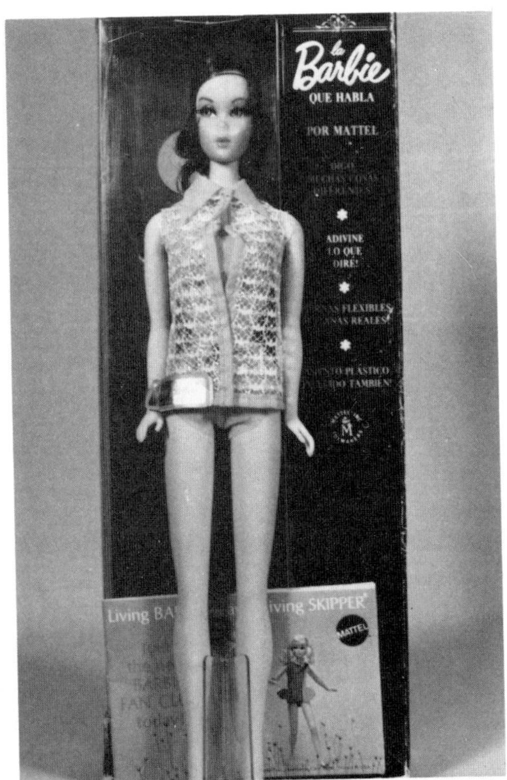

1970—Spanish Talking Barbie (8348). Made in Mexico. Similar to regular Barbie.

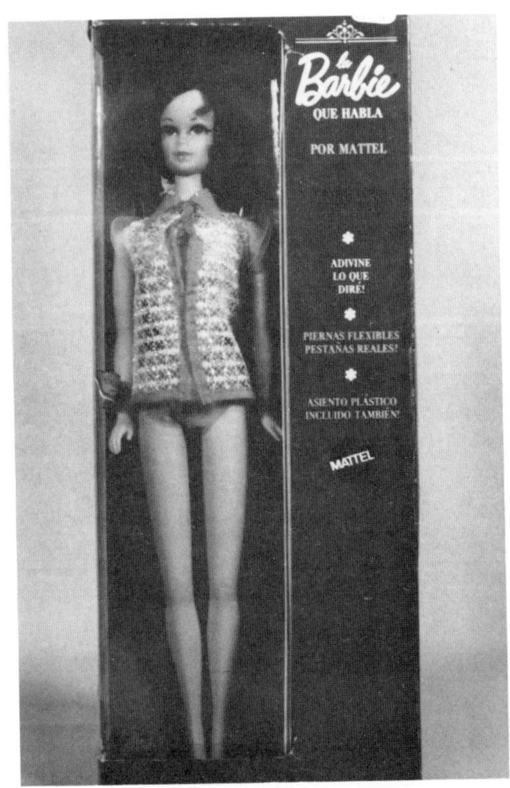

1970—Spanish Talking Barbie (8348). Head made from the Stacey mold. Made in Hong Kong.

1970—Talking Barbie (1115). Head made from the Stacey mold. Made in Mexico. New box.

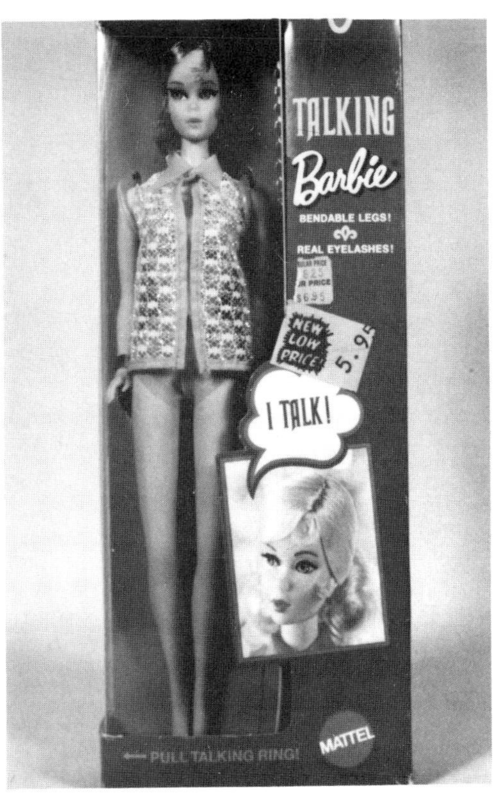

1970—Talking Barbie (1115). Made in Hong Kong. (Gift from Kathy DeWein)

Close-up of Talking Barbie made from the Stacey head mold.

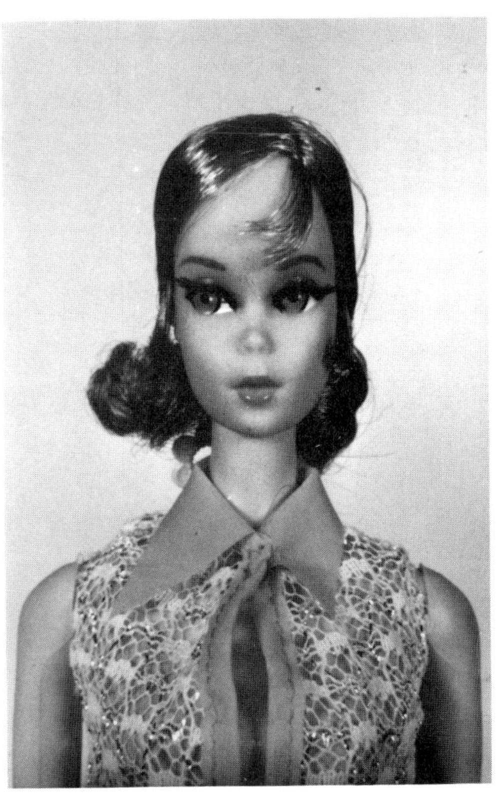

Close-up of the Talking Barbie made from the Barbie mold to show the difference.

Until 1971 Barbie's eyes looked to the right. Beginning in 1971 they looked straight ahead.

—:—

In 1971 Barbie, Ken and P.J. were more active than ever before. Presented on a motorized stage they were:

#1152 — Live Action Barbie on Stage
1172 — Live Action Ken on Stage
1153 — Live Action P.J. on Stage

Included in each set were a 7" two-sided 45 RPM record and a microphone. In addition the P.J. set had a guitar with strap.

Barbie, Ken, P.J. and Christie were also presented on a Touch 'N Go stand. These were:

#1155 — Live Action Barbie
1159 — Live Action Ken
1156 — Live Action P.J.
1175 — Live Action Christie

All of the Live Action dolls were dressed in wild mod clothing with fringe trim. Ken had the same hair style but the three girl dolls had new hair-dos.

Barbie had long blonde hair, parted near the center without bangs. P.J. had long blonde hair with a small strip of braided hair on each side of her head. Gold beads encircled the braids. Christie had long straight black hair. The Midge head mold was used for this Christie.

All of the girl dolls had rooted eyelashes, bend knees, ankles and elbows, and swivel waist, neck, arms and legs (similar to Living Barbie except for a different looser waist construction). Ken had bendable knees and a loosely jointed waist section.

The girl dolls were marked: ©1968 Mattel, Inc./U.S. & Foreign Patented/Patented in Canada 1967/Other Patents Pending/Taiwan. Ken's markings were: ©1968/Mattel, Inc./Taiwan/U.S. & For. Pat'd./Patented in/Canada 1967/ Other Pats./Pending. Head marked: ©1968 Mattel, Inc..

1971—Live Action Barbie On Stage (1152). Light blue stage.

1971—Live Action P.J. On Stage (1153). Pink stage.

1971—Live Action Ken On Stage (1172) Medium blue stage.

1971—Live Action Barbie (1155). Touch 'N Go posing stand.

1971—Live Action Ken (1159).

1971—Live Action P.J. (1156). Head still made from the Midge mold.

1971—Live Action Christie (1175). Her head also made from the Midge mold.

1971—Barbie With Growin' Pretty Hair (1144). See text for complete description.

New this year were dolls with suntan skin called Malibu dolls—Ken (1088), Barbie (1067), Francie (1068) and Skipper (1069).

All of the girl dolls had painted eyelashes, bendable knees, twist waist, long straight blonde hair with a pair of sunglasses on their heads. Ken had bendable knees and yellow painted hair.

The dolls were in a new bubble type package. Included in this package was a beach towel but no posing stand.

Barbie, made from the Stacey head mold, wore a one-piece blue swimsuit with a yellow towel. She had the original divided fingers and was marked: ©1966/Mattel, Inc./U.S. Patented/U.S. Pat. Pend./Made in/Japan.

Francie was made from the Casey head mold. This Francie had blue eyes instead of the usual brown. She wore a one-piece swimsuit with a rose waist and red bottom. Her towel was orange and she had the same markings as Barbie.

Skipper wore a two-piece orange swimsuit with a dark blue towel. She was marked: ©1967 Mattel, Inc./U.S. Pat'd/U.S. Pats. Pend./Made in Japan.

Ken was dressed in orange/red trunks with a medium blue towel. His markings were: ©1968/Mattel, Inc./U.S. & For. Pat'd/Other Pat's/Pending/Hong Kong.

Barbie Hair Happenin's (1174) was a new doll in 1971. She came with three extra hair pieces to match her short titian hair. She had the new centered eyes, bendable knees and the old divided fingers.

She wore a dress that had a white tricot waist and a rose colored tricot skirt with attached white panties, a wide black belt and black shoes. Her markings were: ©1966/Mattel, Inc./U.S. Patented/U.S. Pat. Pend./Made in/Japan.

Since Mattel made this doll as a Department Store special, she was not pictured in the 1971 booklet. The doll is extremely hard to find. Fortunate indeed is the collector who has one!

This year there was a Barbie with Growin' Pretty Hair (1144). Her blonde hair "grew" in the same manner as the Francie doll of 1970. She had two extra hair pieces and the new centered eyes and rooted eyelashes. She wore a short pink satin party dress with a point in the front hemline. She had bend knees, the "Mexico" hands and was marked: ©1967 Mattel, Inc./U.S. Patented/Other Patents Pending/Patented in Canada 1967/Taiwan.

1971—Barbie Hair Happenin's (1174). Limited Edition Department Store Special. Rare.

Close-up of Barbie Hair Happenin's (1174). Titian hair, no bangs. Centered eyes.

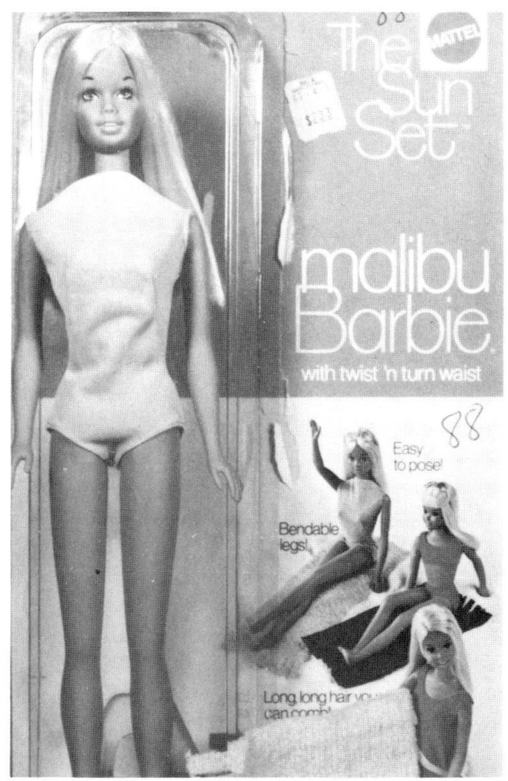

1971—Malibu Barbie (1067). Suntan skin. Original divided fingers. Made in Japan. Painted eyelashes.

1971—Malibu Ken (1088). Made in Hong Kong.

1971—Malibu Francie (1068). Made from the Casey head mold. Painted eyelashes.

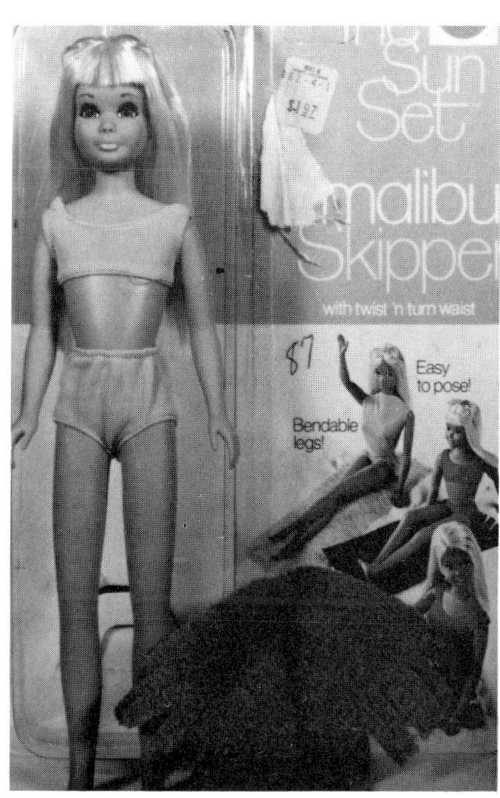

1971—Malibu Skipper (1069). Painted eyelashes.

Skipper got a new friend this year—Living Fluff (1143). She was dressed in a one-piece suit that had a yellow, orange and green striped top and a solid orange bottom. She had brown eyes, rooted eyelashes and her blonde hair was tied in two ponytails, one on each side of her head. Included was a round plastic posing stand and a yellow skateboard. She was marked: ©1969 Mattel, Inc./Taiwan/U.S. & For. Patd./ Other Pats. Pend./Patd. In Canada 1967.

—:—

Francie with Growin' Pretty Hair had a new stock number this year—#1074. She came in a new box and had two extra hair pieces included. She wore the same dress as the old #1129 and had the same markings. The old #1129 doll was also available during 1971. Now the #1129 had arms and hands made from the same mold as Talking Barbie—long slender undivided fingers. So did the #1074 doll.

—:—

Francie Hair Happenin's (1122) was still on the market in 1971. This doll had paler lip color, but the rest of the doll was about the same as last year.

—:—

In 1971 standard Barbie (1190) wore the same swimsuit as 1970 and had the same markings, but she had the new centered eyes. This doll, plus a Barbie outfit was available through a Chef Boy-ar-dee promotional offer.

1971—Living Fluff (1143). Same construction as Living Skipper.

1971—Francie With Growin' Pretty Hair (1074). New box, new number. Two extra hair pieces. Arms and hands made from the Barbie "Mexico" molds.

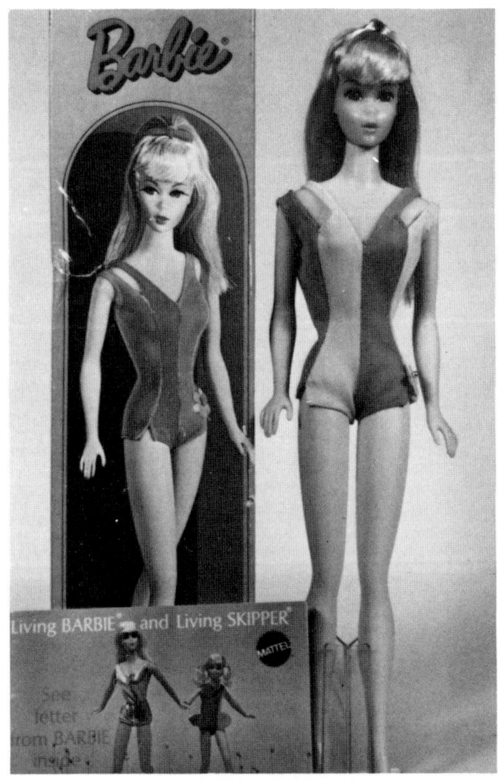

1971—Standard Barbie (1190). Notice that the sticker has been deleted from the box. Doll has new centered eyes.

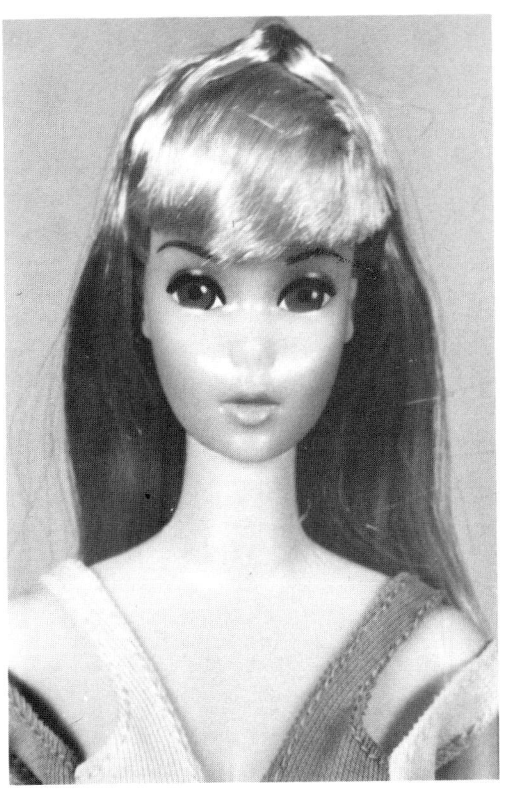

Close-up of the 1971 Standard Barbie (1190). Centered eyes.

Close-up of Living Fluff (1143). Brown eyes. Blonde hair.

Close-up of the 1971 Twist Francie (1170). New hair style.

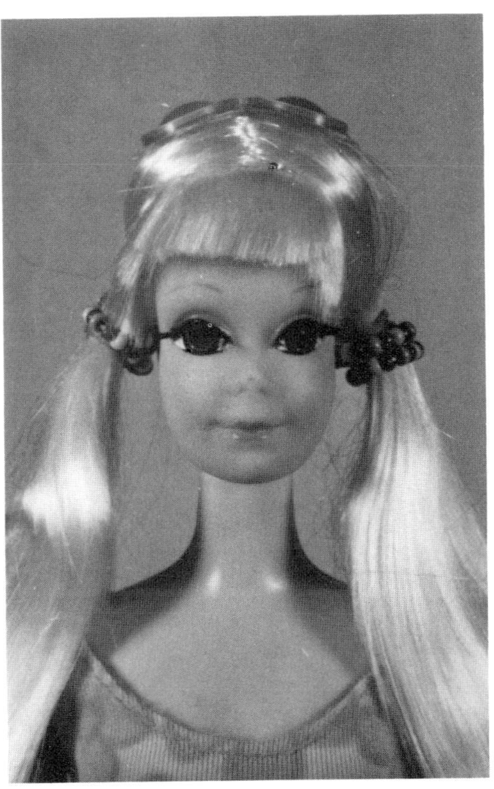

Close-up of Talking P.J. (1113) now being made in Hong Kong.

This year Talking Barbie (1115) had the new straight-facing eyes. She was dressed in a new two-piece white swimsuit with a gold midi coat. She was made in Hong Kong.

She had the same hair style as last year, rooted eyelashes and bend knees. Some of the dolls had a hard plastic head.

Spanish Talking Barbie (8348) was still on the market in 1971 and was the same as 1970.

—:—

Talking P.J. (1113) was dressed the same as last year but she had new markings in 1971: ©1967/Mattel, Inc./U.S. & Foreign/Pats. Pend./Hong Kong.

—:—

This year twist Barbie (1160) had the new centered eyes but the same hair style as last year. She was dressed in a new swimsuit, a brightly colored striped tricot.

Twist Francie (1170) wore a new short orange colored pleated dress with white trim. She also had a new hair-do this year. Shoulder length with flip ends, it was brushed straight back from the forehead and held in place with an orange band.

—:—

The following were still available and the same as last year:

#1127 — twist Julia	1119 — twist Christie
1124 — bend leg Ken	1105 — twist Skipper
1132 — Walking Jamie	0950 — straight leg Skipper
1118 — twist P.J.	3580 — Tutti

—:—

Stacey, both twist (1165) and Talking (1125), was still available through mail-order catalogues until August or September of 1971.

1971—Talking Barbie (1115). New clothes. White bikini, gold coat. Made in Hong Kong. New centered eyes.

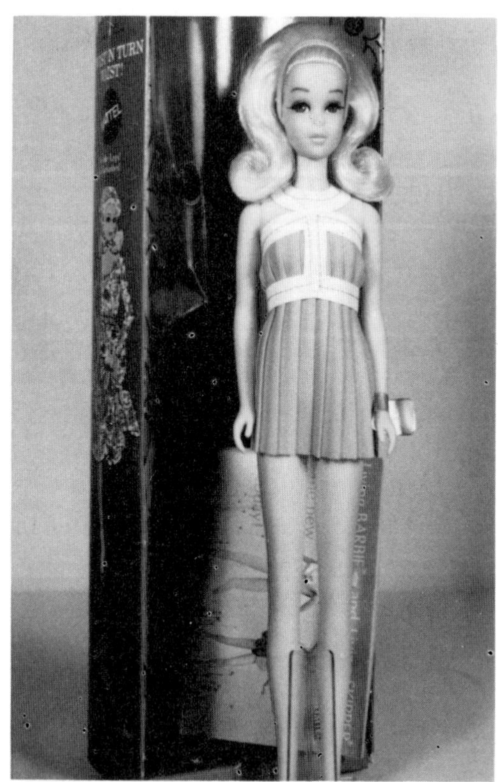
1971—Twist 'N Turn Francie (1170). New orange mini dress. New hair in blonde or brunette.

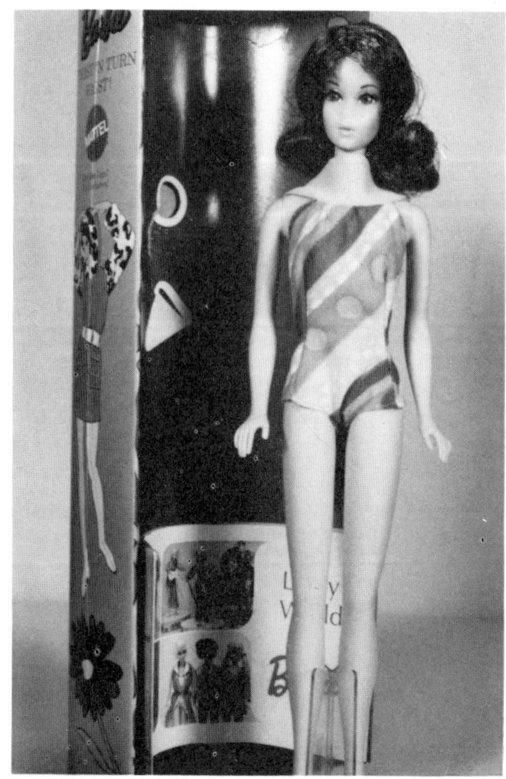
1971—Twist 'N Turn Barbie (1160). New swimsuit. New centered eyes.

1971—Talking Christie (1126). New darker skin. New modified afro hair-do.

This year Talking Christie (1126) was dressed in the same suit as last year, but now her skin was darker. She had a new hair-do—a modified Afro—and new markings: ©1967/Mattel, Inc./U.S. & Foreign/Pats. Pend./Hong Kong.

—:—

Talking Julia (1128) also had the new modified Afro hair style and darker skin and the same new markings as Christie. She wore the same outfit as last year.

—:—

In 1971 Living Barbie (1116) and Living Skipper (1117) wore new clothes.

Skipper wore a new two-piece yellow swimsuit. Barbie wore a two-piece pink, raspberry and red dotted outfit. Barbie had the new centered eyes. Both had a new round plastic posing stand, and Skipper had a new reddish skateboard included. Their markings remained the same.

The #1585 Sears set containing the Living Barbie made in Japan was still on the market.

—:—

This year there was a new Hair Fair set (4044) on the market. The head had the eyes facing straight ahead; the rest of the set was similar to the #4043 set of 1970.

—:—

Both Talking Brad (1114) and bendable leg Brad (1142) were dressed the same as last year, but this year they had slightly darker skin. Talking Brad had the same markings as the second doll of 1970: ©1969/Mattel, Inc./U.S. & For. Pat'd./Other Pats./Pending/Hong Kong.

—:—

Talking Ken (1111) had new markings in 1971: ©1968/Mattel, Inc./U.S. & For. Pat'd./Other Pat's./Pending/Hong Kong. The rest was about the same as 1970.

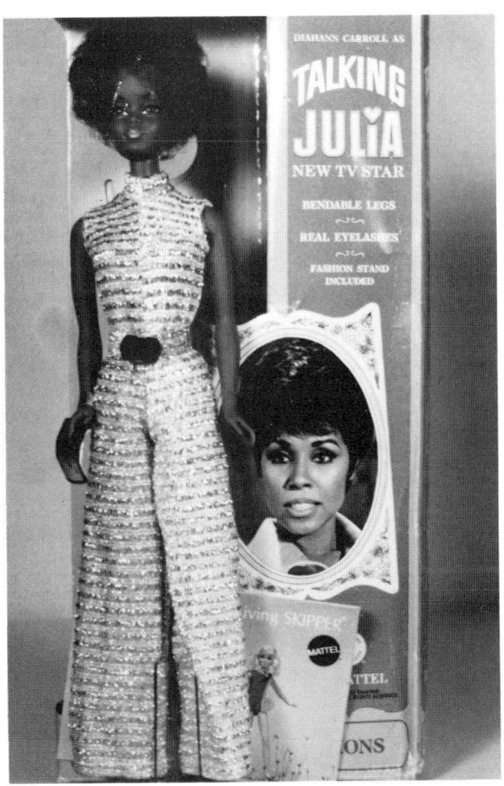

1971—Talking Julia (1128). New darker skin. New modified afro hair style.

1971—Barbie Hair Fair (4044). New number. New packaging. New centered eyes.

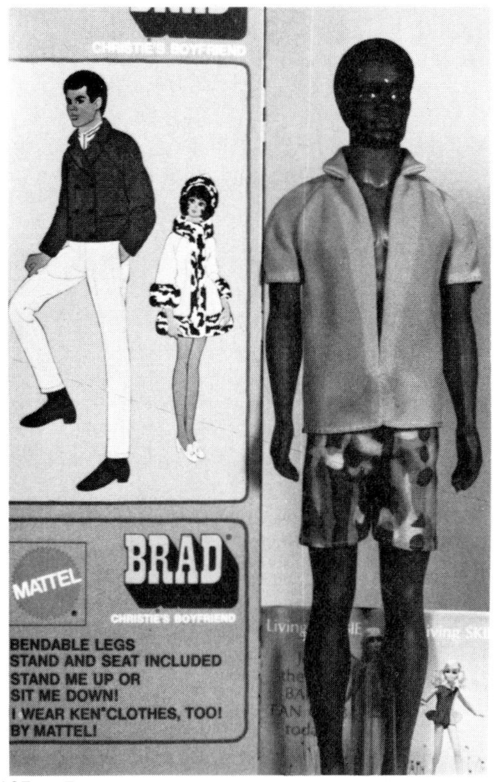

1971—Bendable leg Brad (1142). Darker skin.

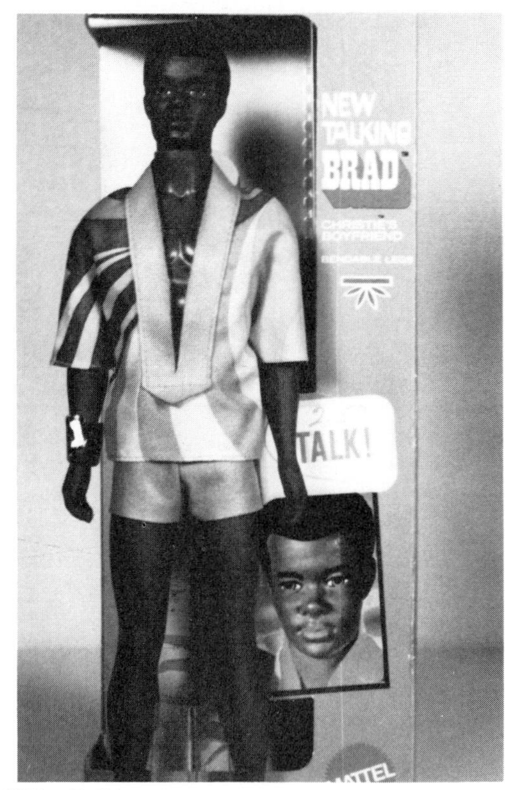

1971—Talking Brad (1114). Darker skin.

1971—Living Barbie (1116). New centered eyes. New clothes. New box. (Gift from Cathy Radice)

1971—Living Skipper (1117). New yellow play-suit. Skateboard and stand. New box.

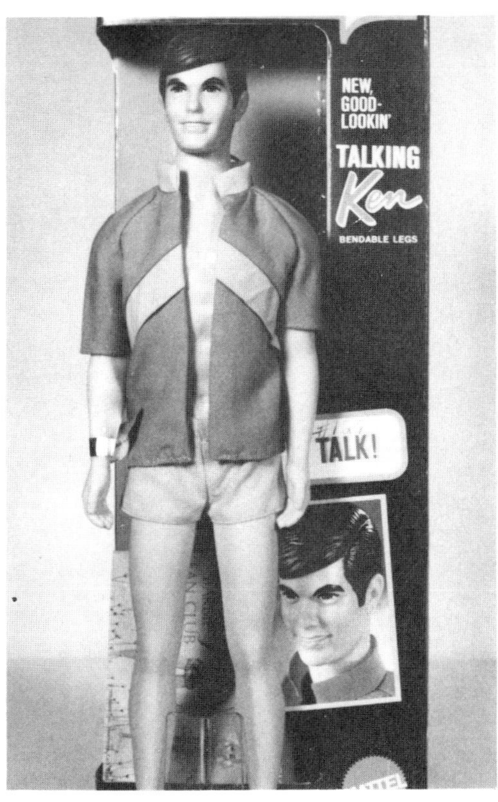

1971—Talking Ken (1111). Now being made in Hong Kong. New box. (Gift from Harold DeWein III)

Close-up of 1971 Talking Julia showing a slightly different hair-do.

Close-up of 1971 Live Action P.J. Made from the Midge mold.

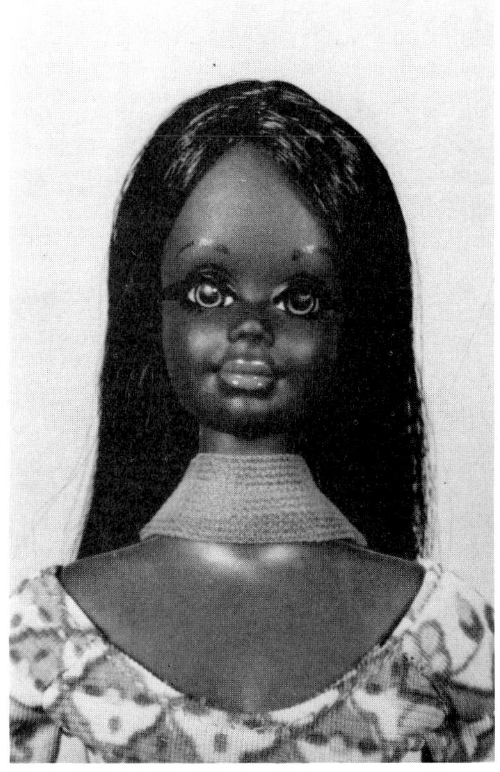

Close-up of Live Action Christie of 1971. Also made from the Midge mold.

1972

There were no fashion booklets for 1972—the first time this had happened.

—:—

In 1972 Barbie and her friends became still more active. The dolls, on "Walk 'N Turn" stands, were called Walk Lively dolls. There were four of them—Barbie (1182), Ken (1184), Steffie (1183) and Miss America (3200).

These dolls had special arms that moved and head that turned as their legs moved back and forth. They also had bendable knees.

The girl dolls had rooted eyelashes and were marked: ©1967 Mattel, Inc./U.S. Pat. Pend./Taiwan.

Walk Lively Barbie wore red pants and top with a tan suede double belt, red shoes and a yellow shoulder bag.

She had long blonde hair, turned under on the ends. The Walk Lively head was similar to the Live Action head but there were distinguishing differences. The Walk Lively hair was a lighter shade of blonde, and the eyelashes were shorter and less exaggerated. Her eyebrows were slightly thinner and further apart, and her eyeliner was slightly lighter.

Walk Lively Ken came in a dark blue short sleeved shirt, brown and blue plaid pants and brown shoes.

His hair was molded and painted brown. He was marked: ©1968 Mattel, Inc./U.S. Pat. Pend./Taiwan. Back of head was marked: ©1968 Mattel, Inc.

Walk Lively Steffie had long brunette hair with flip ends, brown eyes and wore a rose, black and white figured jumpsuit. She had the same markings as Walk Lively Barbie.

Steffie, 11½ inches tall, was one of the new dolls introduced this year.

The fourth Walk Lively doll was also a new introduction—Miss America. She had medium length brunette hair and blue eyes and the same markings as Barbie. She was made from the Steffie head mold.

She wore an evening gown with a white filmy skirt and gold lame top, white shoes, a filigreed crown of "silver" and a red cape trimmed in imitation ermine.

Her Royal wardrobe included a scepter, a bouquet of red roses and her "Miss America" ribbon.

Miss America's Walk 'N Turn stand was white; the rest were tan colored.

—:—

In addition to the regular Walk Lively Miss America (3200), there was an identical doll (minus the Walk 'N Turn stand) available from the Kellogg Company.

Laurie Lee Schaefer, Miss America of 1972, promoted this special offer. This doll (stock no. 3194-9991)was available for two Kellogg's Corn Flakes box tops and three dollars in cash.

—:—

This year Malibu P.J. (1187) joined the Sun Set. She was dressed in a one-piece lavender swimsuit. Sunglasses and a green beach towel were included.

Her blonde hair was still tied in two sections but she no longer had bangs. A new mold was used for her head: the Steffie head mold was used. She was marked: ©1966/Mattel, Inc./U.S. Patented/Other Pats. Pend./Made In/Japan.

It is interesting that Steiffie, Miss America and Malibu P.J. were all made from the same head mold. Informed collectors consider this the "Steffie" mold.

1972—Walk Lively Barbie (1182). Pale blonde hair.

1972—Walk Lively Ken (1184). See text for description.

1972—Walk Lively Steffie (1183). Brown eyes. Brunette hair.

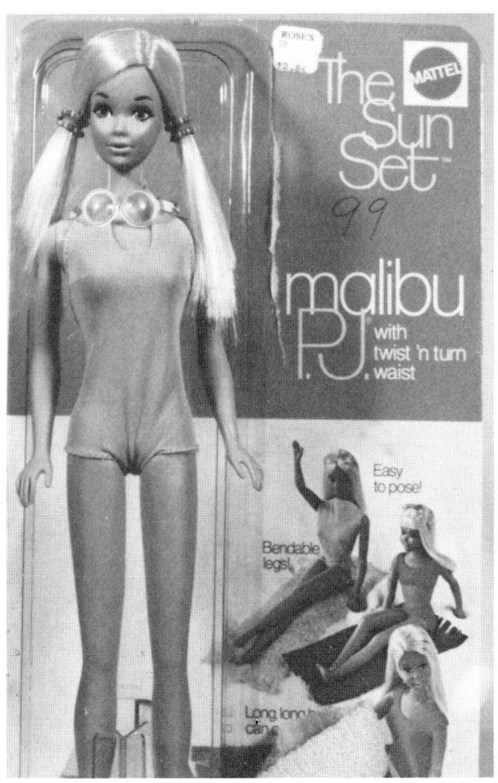

1972—Malibu P.J. (1187). Made from the Steffie head mold. Suntan skin. No longer has bangs. Painted eyelashes.

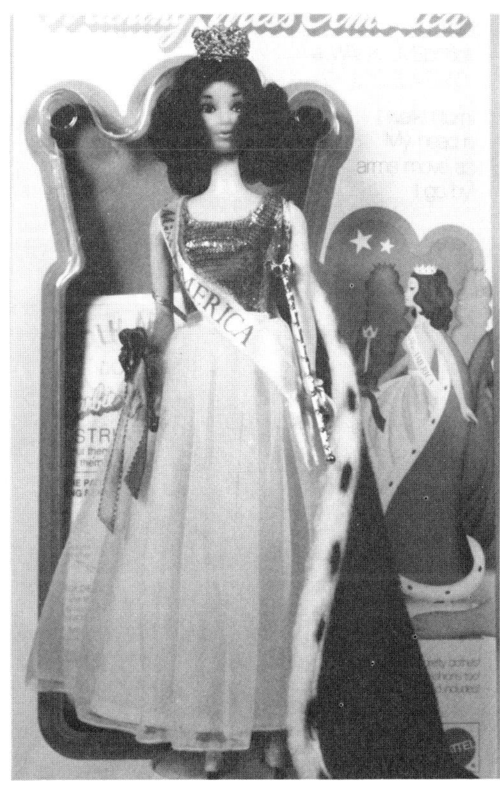

1972—Walking Miss America (3200)—a Walk Lively doll.

Close-up of the 1972 Walk Lively Miss America. Made from the Steffie head mold. Blue eyes.

The most interesting innovation in 1972 was a new type of hand—a hand that could open and close and hold items.

Dolls with this type of hand were called "Busy" dolls. There were four of them. In addition, three of the four dolls were also made as Talking Busy dolls.

All dolls had bendable knees and bendable elbows. (This was the first time a Ken doll had the bendable elbows.) The three female Busy dolls also had twist waists and painted eyelashes. The two female Talking Busy dolls had rooted eyelashes.

Busy Barbie (3311) had long straight blonde hair parted on the right with a "gold" barrette on the left side. She wore a blue denim top with attached panties and a long patchwork print skirt. She was marked: ©1966/Mattel, Inc./U.S. & Foreign/Patented/Other Pat's/Pending/Made in/U.S.A.

Busy Steffie (3312) had long brunette hair and blue eyes. She wore a long dress in 3 different pieces of fabric—a dark print, a light print and solid green. She had the same markings as Busy Barbie.

Busy Francie (3313) wore blue jeans and a green tank top. Her blonde hair was drawn to the back and tied with a ribbon. She was marked: ©1966/Mattel, Inc./Hong Kong/U.S. & Foreign/Patented/Other Pat's/Pending.

Busy Ken (3314) wore jeans and a red tank top. He had brown hair and was marked: ©1968/Mattel, Inc./U.S. & For. Pat'd./Other Pat's/Pending/Hong Kong.

Talking Busy Barbie (1195) had short blonde hair with bangs. She wore blue bibbed hot pants with an attached rose blouse, rose hat, green belt and green boots. She was marked: ©1967/Mattel, Inc./U.S. & Foreign/Pats. Pend./Hong Kong.

Talking Busy Steffie (1186) had the same markings as Barbie. She had shoulder length blonde hair with curly ends and bangs and blue eyes. She wore blue hot pants with attached pink and white checked blouse, pink and white checked leggings, a black and white checked hat and belt and white shoes.

Talking Busy Ken (1196) had brown hair and wore red pants and a red and blue shirt. He was marked: ©1968/Mattel, Inc./U.S. & For. Pat'd./Other Pat's/Pending/Hong Kong.

A record player, travel case, serving set, T.V. and telephone came with all seven dolls.

The first issue of Busy Barbie and Busy Steffie were marked "Made in U.S.A." The second issue of both (in 1973) were made in Hong Kong; so were all the other Busy and Talking Busy dolls.

1972—Busy Steffie (3312). Same hands as Barbie. Blue eyes. First issue made in U.S.A. Painted eyelashes.

1972—Busy Barbie (3311). New hands that open and close. First issue made in U.S.A. Painted eyelashes.

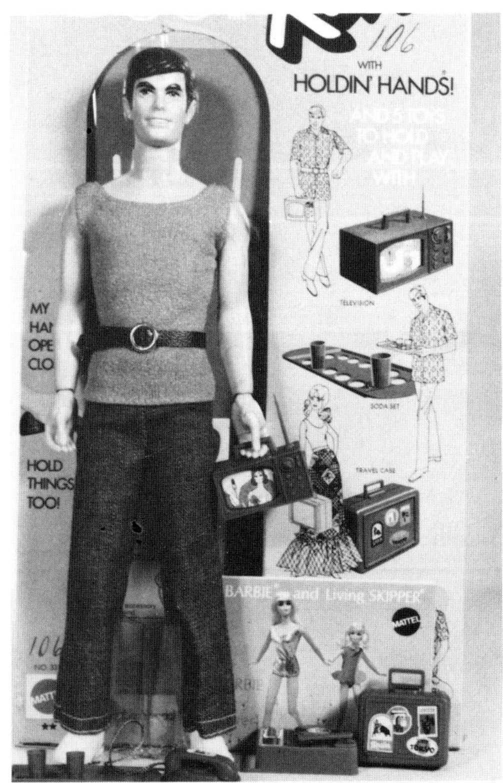

1972—Busy Ken (3314). The first male doll with bendable elbows.

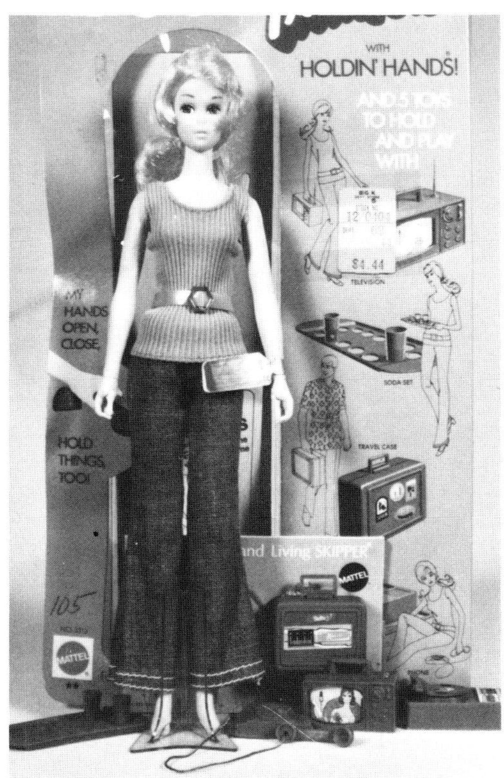

1972—Busy Francie (3313). Blonde hair. Brown eyes. Painted eyelashes.

1972—Talking Busy Steffie (1186). Blonde hair. Blue eyes. Rooted eyelashes.

1972—Talking Busy Barbie (1195). Blonde hair. Rooted eyelashes.

1972—Talking Busy Ken (1196). Notice hand construction.

A new type of Skipper was introduced in 1972—A Pose 'N Play Skipper (1179). She had "swinging-free" arms that allowed her many activities on the Swing-A-Rounder Gym that was included in the set. The rest of her construction was similar to Living Skipper's.

Her new hair-do featured bangs and "puppy ears" tied with blue ribbon. She wore a blue and white checked, with solid blue, one-piece playsuit. Most dolls had light titian hair. In 1975 a few were found with blonde hair. She was marked: ©1969 Mattel, Inc./Taiwan/U.S. & For. Patd./Other Pats. Pend./Patd. in Canada 1967.

And Skipper got a new friend in 1972—Tiff (1199). Tiff also had the "swinging-free" arms and the same markings as Skipper. Her head was made from the Fluff mold.

She had medium long straight titian hair, parted in the center, and she had brown eyes. She wore blue jeans, a sleeveless white top and white with red trim sneakers. A red skateboard was included.

—:—

Growin' Pretty Hair Barbie (1144) was presented in a new dress and a different hair-do in 1972. The four-curl hair piece was now tied with blue ribbon instead of the barrette. The other hair piece was now a long braided strip tied at each end with a blue ribbon.

Her dress was a long one with a red, white and blue print skirt, blue suede waist and attached white panties. Blue shoes and hair accessories were included. She had the same markings and the same hands as 1971.

1972—Skipper and her Swing-A-Rounder Gym (1179). A Pose 'N Play Skipper. New "swinging-free" arms. First dolls had light titian hair. Painted eyelashes.

1972—Pose 'N Play Tiff (1199). Made from the Fluff head mold. Brown eyes. Titian hair. Painted eyelashes.

1972—Barbie With Growin' Pretty Hair (1144). New hair-do. New clothes.

In 1972 Montgomery Ward & Company was one hundred years old. To help celebrate this anniversary, several doll companies reissued famous dolls sold through the years by the Montgomery Ward Company.

Mattel reissued what was supposed to be the first Barbie doll. Actually the reissued Barbie (3210) was more like the Barbie of 1964. She had the tan tone skin, the hard hollow torso, marked: Midge T.M./1962/Barbie®/1958/by/Mattel, Inc./Patented. Her brunette ponytail hair was made from the sturdier, later type of saran material. She also had the blue irises and the curved eyebrows of the later dolls.

—:—

"Forget-Me-Nots" Barbie, #3269, (the same doll as Malibu Barbie #1067) was available this year. This doll came through a promotional offer of the Kellogg Company.

—:—

The following dolls were still available:

#1067 — Malibu Barbie	1128 — Talking Julia
1068 — Malibu Francie	1155 — Live Action Barbie
1069 — Malibu Skipper	1159 — Live Action Ken
1088 — Malibu Ken	1156 — Live Action P.J.
1115 — Talking Barbie	1175 — Live Action Christie
8348 — Spanish Talking Barbie	1119 — Twist Christie
1113 — Talking P.J.	1142 — Bend leg Brad
1126 — Talking Christie	1074 — Francie — Growin Pretty Hair
1114 — Talking Brad	

—:—

A Hair Fair Head was listed in the 1972 Sears' catalogue.

—:—

The following dolls were shown in 1971 mail-order catalogues—good until August or September of 1972: Jamie, Living Barbie, Living Skipper, Living Fluff, Live Action Ken on Stage, Live Action Barbie on Stage, Live Action P.J. on Stage, Francie Hair Happenin's and Sears Living Barbie (Japan) gift set.

1972—Forget-Me-Nots Barbie (3269). A Malibu doll.

1972—Close-up of the Ward's Barbie. Similar to the 1964 Barbie.

1972—Montgomery Ward's anniversary Barbie (3210). Came in brown shipping box or pink store box.

Hair was the big news of 1973. For the first time Ken was made with rooted hair. And some of the girl dolls had a new type of hair that could be curled and styled instantly without water or setting material. Dolls with this hair were called "Quick Curl" dolls.

No longer did any of the dolls have rooted eyelashes; all had painted lashes instead.

—:—

Booklets were back this year but only in limited numbers.

—:—

The new Ken was Mod Hair Ken (4224). He had dark brown hair and bendable knees. Included were four reuseable hair pieces—a beard, sideburns and two moustaches.

He wore a brown and white checked jacket, turtleneck dickey, tan or brown pants and brown shoes. A posing stand was included. Markings were: ©1968/Mattel, Inc./U.S. & For. Pat'd./Other Pat's./Pending/Hong Kong.

Miss America was back this year as a Quick Curl doll (8697). She was dressed the same as the 1972 doll but no longer had the Walk Lively type of body. She had the regular bendable knees and twist waist body and the "Mexico" hands. She still had brunette colored hair and blue eyes. Her markings were: ©1966/Mattel, Inc./U.S. & Foreign/Patented/Other Pat's/Pending/Made In/Taiwan.

—:—

This year there was a new doll on the market—Kelley, a Barbie-size doll.

Quick Curl Kelley (4221) had medium long red hair, brown eyes, "Mexico" hands, bendable knees and twist waist. She was dressed in a long green dress with long sheer white sleeves.

The Steffie head mold was used for Kelley. She had the same markings as Miss America.

Quick Curl Barbie (4220) had blonde hair with decorative beads on each side of her face. She wore a long pink and white checked dress with long sheer white sleeves. She had the same markings as Miss America, bend knees, twist waist and the "Mexico" hands.

Quick Curl Francie (4222) had brunette hair. She wore a long yellow dress with short sleeves. Her arms and hands were made from the Barbie "Mexico" mold. She had bend knees and twist waist. Her markings were: ©1966/Mattel, Inc./Taiwan/U.S.&Foreign/Patented/Other Pat's/Pending.

Quick Curl Skipper (4223) had blonde hair and freckles, bend knees and twist waist. Her dress was long with short sleeves. The sleeves and skirt were blue and white checked, and the waist was solid blue. She was marked: ©1967 Mattel, Inc./U.S. Pat'd./U.S. Pats. Pend./Made in Taiwan.

A brush, comb, curlers, ribbons, rubber bands and bobby pins accompanied all five Quick Curl dolls. All had posing stands and wrist tags. New fashion booklets came with Mod Hair Ken and the five Quick Curl dolls.

—:—

Busy Barbie (3311) and Busy Steffie (3312) were now made in Hong Kong and were so marked. Talking Busy Barbie (1195) had a different voice with slightly different words. She had new markings: ©1967/Mattel, Inc./U.S. & For./Pat'd Pat'd/In Canada/1967 Other/Pat's. Pend./Hong Kong.

1973—Mod Hair Ken (4224). First male doll since Todd to have rooted hair.

1973—Quick Curl Miss America (8697). Brunette hair. New body construction. Painted eyelashes.

1973—Quick Curl Kelley (4221). Made from the Steffie head mold. Brown eyes. Red hair. Painted eyelashes.

1973—Quick Curl Barbie (4220). Painted eyelashes.

1973—Quick Curl Skipper (4223). Freckles. Blonde hair. Painted eyelashes.

1973—Quick Curl Francie (4222). Brunette hair. Painted eyelashes.

There was a new Christie on the market in 1973—a Malibu Christie (7745).

She had long straight black hair, brown eyes, twist waist and bendable knees and the "Mexico" arms and hands. She wore a one-piece red tricot swimsuit and sunglasses. A white beach towel was included. Her markings were: ©1966/Mattel, Inc./U.S. & Foreign/Patented/Other Pats./Pending/Made in/Taiwan.

—:—

Malibu Barbie (1067) and Malibu P.J. (1187) were now made in Taiwan, with the "Mexico" arms and hands. They were marked: ©1966/Mattel, Inc./U.S. & Foreign/Patented/Other Pat's./Pending/Made in/Taiwan.

Malibu Skipper (1069) and Malibu Francie (1068) were now made in Korea. Skipper was marked: ©1967 Mattel, Inc./U.S. Pat'd./U.S. Pats. Pend./Made in Korea. Francie was marked: ©1966/Mattel, Inc./U.S. Patented/U.S. Pat. Pend./Made in/Korea.

—:—

1973 was the year of the "Baggies." "Baggie" is the name collectors gave those dolls marketed in plastic bags!

Apparently after a doll has been discontinued, the left-over dolls are packaged in plastic bags and sold at a reduced price. Possibly some factory error dolls, or dolls returned to the company because of faulty talking mechanisms, were also sold this way.

Talking Barbies, Kens and P.J.s (stamped "non-talking" on the back of the doll) were sold in plastic bags. The regular stock number was used for these dolls.

Also, Live Action Barbies, Kens and P.J.s were available in plastic bags, and they, too, had the regular stock numbers.

Pose 'N Play Skipper was another doll sold in the plastic bag, but this doll was not sold with the Pose 'N Play stock #1179. Instead #1117 was used. This was the stock number of the Living Skipper of 1970.

—:—

A Miss America doll was available again this year from the Kellogg Company. The 1973 Miss America, Terry Anne Meeuwsen, did the promoting.

Some people received a doll like the one in 1972, while others received the new Quick Curl doll. Both dolls had the same stock no.—3194-9991.

—:—

The following dolls were still on the market:

#3314 — Busy Ken	1183 — Walk Lively Steffie
1179 — Pose 'N Play Skipper	1184 — Walk Lively Ken
1182 — Walk Lively Barbie	1088 — Malibu Ken

—:—

During the early part of the year the Montgomery Ward anniversary Barbie (3210) of 1972 was still available.

—:—

The 1973 Sears catalogue listed a Hair Fair Head. 1972 mail-order catalogues (good until August or September of 1973) still listed the following: Live Action Barbie, Live Action Ken, Live Action P.J., Live Action Christie, Pose 'N Play Tiff, Walk Lively Miss America, Barbie With Growin Pretty Hair, Francie With Growin Pretty Hair, Busy Francie, Talking Barbie, Talking Ken, Talking P.J. and Talking Brad.

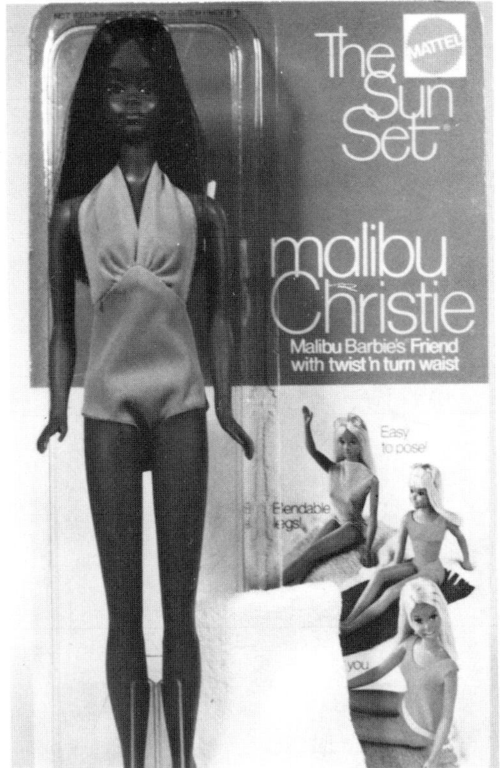

1973—Malibu Christie (7745). First dolls had the "Mexico" hands. Made in Taiwan.

Close-up of the 1973 Quick Curl Kelley (4221). Made from the Steffie head mold.

1973—Two Barbie dolls sold in plastic bags. See text for descriptions.

1973—Two Ken dolls sold in plastic bags. See text for descriptions.

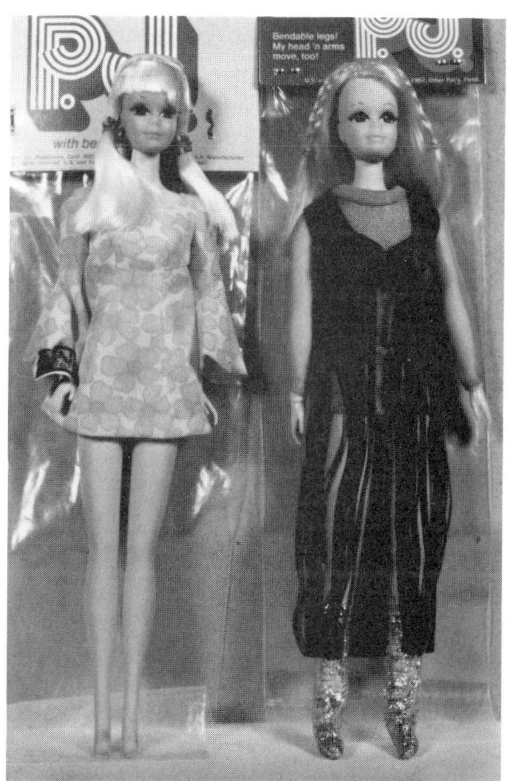

1973—Two P.J. dolls sold in plastic bags. See text for descriptions.

1973—Skipper doll sold in plastic bag. See text for description.

1974

There is something very special about a young lady's sixteenth birthday. And so it was with Barbie's sixteenth birthday in 1974.

An enormous amount of publicity covered this event. Newspapers all over the country printed articles and television coverage was widespread. There were birthday party celebrations in several major cities with celebrities and dignitaries taking part.

To commemorate the event, Mattel introduced a lovely blonde haired doll called "Barbie's Sweet 16" (7796). She had a long shag hair-do with bangs, twist waist and bendable knees.

She was dressed in a long pink and white pin dotted party dress and white shoes. Her markings were: ©1966/Mattel, Inc./U.S. & Foreign/Patented/Other Pat's/Pending/Made in/Taiwan.

A pair of short blue jeans and a yellow tank top were included with the first dolls sold. Since this was a limited special introductory offer, later dolls came without the jeans and top.

Included in both types of Sweet 16 sets were a two-color make-up compact with applicators, brush, comb, and four barrettes with fragrance labels. When these labels were scratched, they released lilac and strawberry fragrances.

There was a coupon on the back of the Sweet 16 package good until May 1, 1975. When this was mailed to Mattel, the sender received a Barbie Charm necklace, packages of sugarless gum, a Barbie iron-on patch and a coupon for a free birthday dinner at a Howard Johnson's. The dinner included a birthday cake, balloons and lollipops. This Howard Johnson's offer was good until June 25, 1975.

1974—Barbie's Sweet 16 (7796). Promotional set to celebrate Barbie's birthday.

1974—Close-up of Barbie's Sweet 16. Blonde hair. Painted eyelashes.

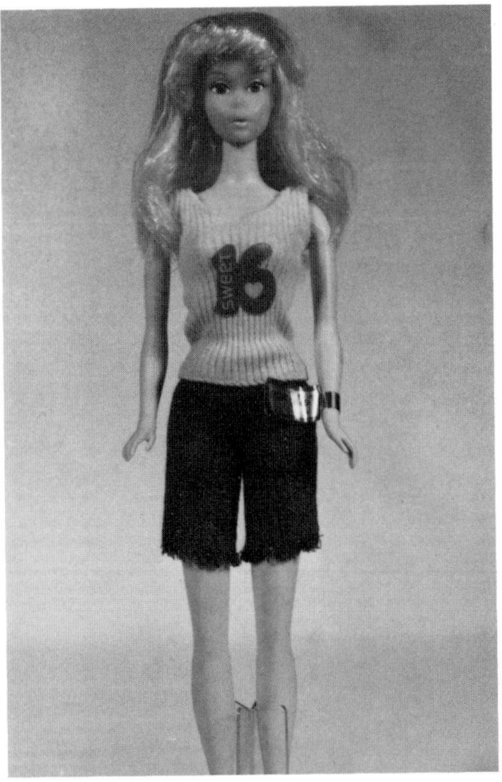

1974—Sweet 16 Barbie wearing free promotional outfit.

Wrist tags were discontinued the last half of 1974.

—:—

In 1974 Mattel introduced the Sports Set—Sun Valley Barbie (7806), Sun Valley Ken (7809), Newport Barbie (7807) and Yellowstone Kelley (7808).

The only really new doll was the Yellowstone Kelley. This Kelley had suntan skin and long straight red hair. She had bendable knees, twist waist and the "Mexico" hands.

She was dressed in a red and white dotted blouse, white shoes, white knee length socks and blue and white striped shorts. Matching slacks were included. A sleeping bag and camping gear came with her. Her markings were: ©1966/ Mattel, Inc./U.S. & Foreign/Patented/Other Pats./Pending/Made in/Taiwan.

The Ken and the two Barbie dolls were the regular Malibu dolls. The Sun Valley dolls were dressed for skiing with ski gear included. Barbie's ski outfit was orange and yellow. Ken's was blue and red.

The Newport doll was dressed for sailing. She wore white slacks and a white sailor blouse trimmed in red. A red and white striped bikini was included; also a small sailboat. Most boats were white with a red sail, but a few had a pink sail instead of a red one.

At least two shades of orange material was used for Barbie's ski suit. There were slight variations in the hair color of all three dolls—Barbie, Ken and Kelley.

The two Barbie dolls had the same markings as Malibu Barbie of 1973. Ken was marked: ©1968/Mattel, Inc./U.S. & For. Patd./Other Pats./Pending/Taiwan.

1974—Yellowstone Kelley (7808). New suntan skin. New long straight hair.

1974—Sun Valley Barbie (7806). Malibu doll dressed for skiing.

1974—Sun Valley Ken (7809). Malibu doll dressed for skiing. Hair color varied from orange to mustard.

1974—Newport Barbie (7807). Malibu doll dressed for sailing.

Several interesting items appeared during 1974. One of the most interesting was a doll, sold in a plastic bag, called "Babs," stock number 7888. However, the doll was a regular Busy Steffie, stock number 3312. (The Busy Steffie was discontinued sometime during 1973.)

Another "Baggie" available this year was a non-talking Talking Ken, dressed in the blue and orange clothes, but the cardboard heading called the doll "Action Ken" #1159. Perhaps this was because the head on this doll was similar to the one used on the Action doll.

A very interesting item this year was the carton some of the Malibu P.J.s came in. It was marked "Malibu Steffie," stock number 1187 (the stock number for Malibu P.J.), but the doll inside was the regular Malibu P.J. Since the Steffie head mold was used to make the Malibu P.J., perhaps that accounts for the printing error on the carton.

—:—

The 1973 Sears Christmas catalogue (good until August 16, 1974) offered a Barbie's Hair Fair set. When ordered in mid 1974, the set was a #4043. Instead of the side-glancing eyes as the first 4043's had, this doll had centered eyes like the 4044 doll had. (Mattel listed the 4043 in 1969 and 1970 and the 4044 in 1971.)

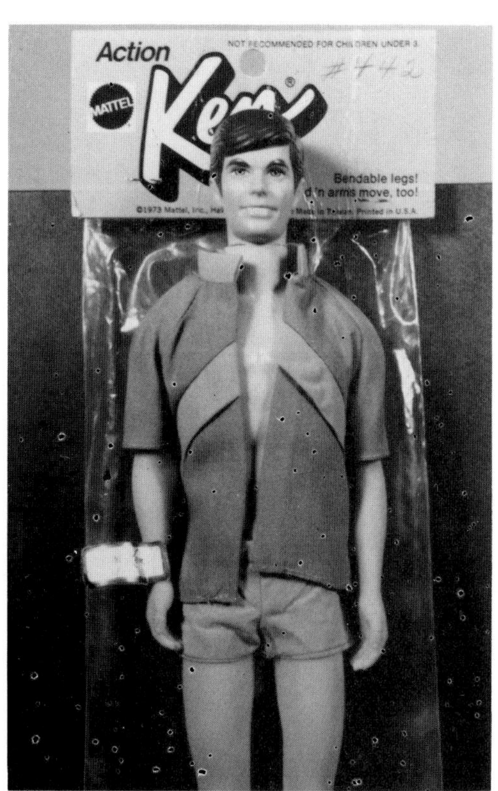

1974—Ken doll sold in a plastic bag. See text for details.

1974—A rare "baggie" doll. See text for details.

1974—Shipping carton with misprint name of doll. Contained Malibu P.J. dolls.

There was a great deal of excitement in the ranks of Barbie collectors in the Fall of 1974. The new Sears Christmas catalogue offered a "Barbie Baby-sits" set for the first time since 1965. A few collectors were disappointed when the baby turned out to be the same baby as the one in the Sunshine Family set, another Mattel product. But most collectors found the little doll delightful, with his wispy blond rooted hair and bright beady eyes!

Except for Miss Barbie back in 1964 with her open and close eyes, this was the only Barbie doll with set-in eyes. All other dolls had painted eyes.

In the set there were a pillow, liner, bib, towel, sunbonnet, sunsuit, christening dress, long flannel night sack, diaper and numerous yellow plastic accessories for the baby. For Barbie there was a phone list and a pink and white checked apron. (A striped apron was pictured in the catalogue but it was not on the market.)

—:—

Still available in 1974 were the Quick Curl dolls—Barbie, Francie, Kelley, Skipper and Miss America.

This year Miss America had new blonde colored hair. There were slight variations in the materials used for her crown, blouse and flowers.

The same Kellogg Company offer was available in 1974. The blonde Quick Curl Miss America (9194-4) was the doll used.

The other Quick Curl dolls were the same as 1973 except for slight variations in hair shades and dress material.

1974—Barbie Hair Fair set (4043). The old #4043 set had side-glancing eyes. This has centered eyes.

1974—Sears' "Barbie Baby-sits" set (7882). Blonde hair. Blue eyes.

1974—Quick Curl Miss America (8697). New blonde hair.

All six of the Malibu dolls were still on the market. Ken, Francie and Skipper were about the same as last year. During the first part of the year Barbie, P.J. and Christie were about the same as last year, except some of the P.J.s wore a new green swimsuit.

During the later part of the year Barbie, P.J. and Christie were made in Korea. Christie had new arms and hands made from the regular Francie mold. Barbie and P.J. had arms and hands made from the original Barbie mold. The rest was about the same as 1973.

—:—

Mod Hair Ken was still available. Although dressed in the same type of clothing as before, the type of material and shades of color varied considerably. His hair texture varied also.

—:—

Montgomery Ward listed an exclusive "dressed" Mod Hair Ken (4234) in 1974. The doll wore red trunks with a blue and black tuxedo included in the brown shipping box.

—:—

Some mail-order catalogues (good until Fall, 1974) listed Busy Barbie and Busy Ken for sale.

1974—Malibu P.J. (1187). Wearing rare green swimsuit. "Mexico" hands.

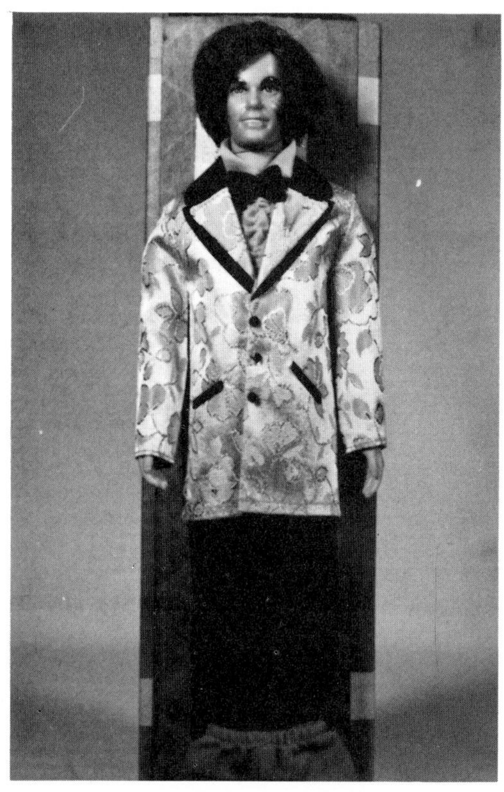

1974—Montgomery Ward's dressed Ken (4234).

1974—Close-up of blonde Quick Curl Miss America (8697).

1974—Close-up of Yellowstone Kelley (7808). Made from the Steffie head mold.

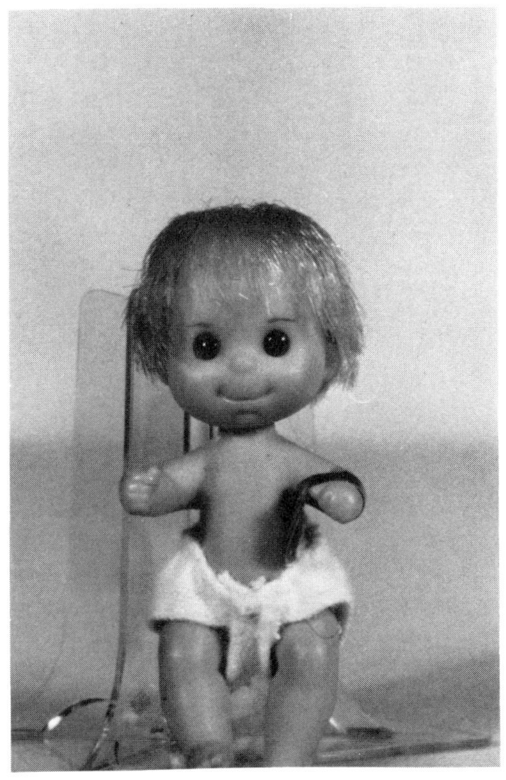

1974—Close-up of baby from Sears' "Barbie Baby-sits" set.

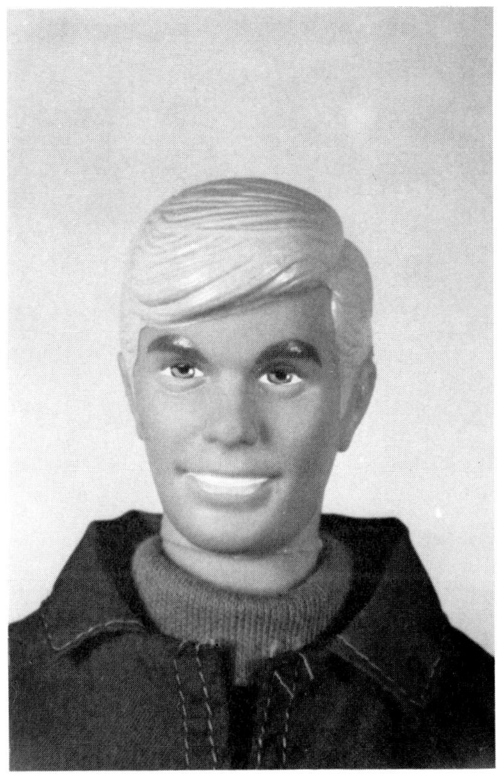

1974—Close-up of Sun Valley Ken (7809). This one has orange hair.

1975 was an exciting year for Barbie collectors. The year got off to a big start in early January with a Gold Medal Barbie (#7233). (A few stores in California presented the doll on December 31, 1974.)

This early Gold Medal Barbie was a promotional doll used to inform the buying public of Mattel's tie-in with the U.S. Olympics Committee for a giant 2-year multi-million dollar advertising spectacular.

The doll was a regular Malibu Barbie dressed in a one-piece red, white and blue swimsuit. Included was a doll-size U.S. Olympic Gold Medal and a child-size Olympic patch, plus a mail-in offer for a special Olympic Record Book, a child-size U.S. Olympic medal and an iron-on shield. This mail-in offer was good until June 30, 1977.

A few weeks later four more Gold Medal dolls reached the market—Barbie Skier (#7264), Barbie Skater (#7262), Ken Skier (#7261) and P.J. Gymnast (#7263).

The dolls were the regular Malibu dolls. Each set was complete with U.S. Olympic-styled sports outfit and gear and a doll-sized U.S. Olympic medal. These dolls had the same mail-in offer as the Gold Medal Barbie.

In addition to the regular appropriate sports gear in each set, the Barbie Skater set included a special skating stand and the P.J. Gymnast set included a balance beam.

—:—

In 1975 Sears had two different exclusive Gold Medal Barbie sets (doll with clothes). One sold through the catalogue and one sold in the stores. It is interesting to note that the set sold through the catalogue (#9042) was made in Taiwan while the one sold in the stores (#9044) was made in Korea.

1975—Gold Medal Barbie (7233). Came in two slightly different boxes.

1975—Barbie Winter Sports set (9042). A Sears' catalogue exclusive.

1975—Barbie and her U.S. Olympic Wardrobe (9044). A Sears' retail store set.

1975—Gold Medal Barbie Skater (7262). A Malibu doll dressed for Olympic skating.

1975—Gold Medal Barbie Skier (7264). A Malibu doll dressed for Olympic skiing.

1975—Gold Medal Ken Skier (7261). A Malibu doll dressed for Olympic skiing.

1975—Gold Medal P.J. Gymnast (7263). A Malibu doll dressed for Olympic gymnastics.

New and interesting dolls this year were the "Action" type called "Free Moving." And the addition of two new black dolls added to the excitement.

In the Free Moving line there were Barbie (#7270), Ken (#7280), P.J. (#7281) and the two new black dolls, Cara (#7283) and Curtis (#7282).

Cara, the same size as Barbie, was made from the Steffie head mold. She had brown eyes and long dark brown hair. Her hair was parted in the center with orange bows on each side.

Curtis, the same size as Ken, was made from the Brad head mold. He had dark brown painted hair and brown eyes.

The Free Moving dolls were specially constructed with a tab on the back. When this tab was pulled out, the doll's waist became completely movable. By rotating the tab, the doll could bend, twist, swing a golf club or tennis racket. When the tab was flat against the back, the doll was fully poseable like a regular bendable knee doll.

The boy dolls were marked: ©1968 Mattel, Inc./Taiwan/ U.S. Patent/Pending, and the three girls were marked: ©1967 Mattel, Inc./Taiwan/U.S. Pat. Pend.

The three girl dolls wore a one-piece play suit. The suit was white with a different colored midriff section—Barbie's was red, Cara's was orange and P.J.'s was green. A long cotton print skirt, in colors that matched the midriff section of the play suit, came with each doll. Also included was a tennis racket, golf club, ball and a pair of white sport shoes.

Barbie (made from the real Barbie head mold) had a new hair-do in a new golden shade of blonde. Her hair, parted on the left side, was long with fluffy ends. Two small special sections of hair were brought together on the right side. These were held in place by a rubber band and a red ribbon bow.

P.J. (made from the Steffie head mold) had long pale blonde hair, parted near the center. The hair was divided into two sections with each section tied by green ribbon. The ends of her hair were slightly curly and fluffy.

Ken and Curtis wore a one-piece short sport suit. Ken's had a solid white bottom with a red and white striped top. Curtis's was white with orange. Both wore white shoes and socks. A golf club, tennis racket and ball were included. Ken had brown painted hair.

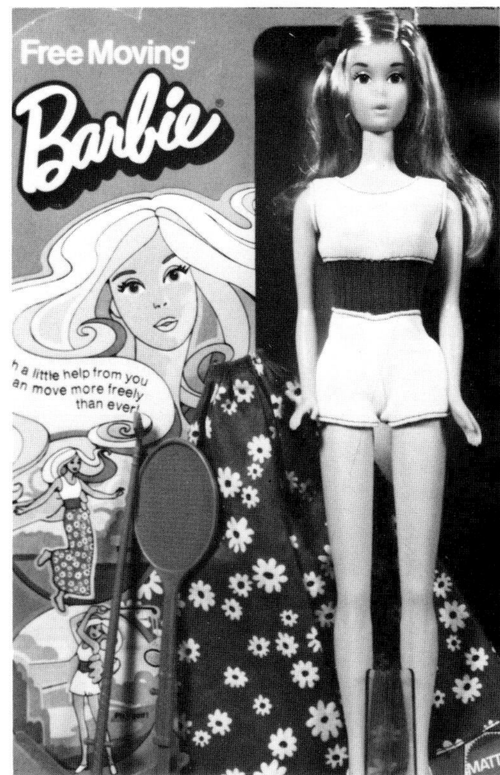

1975—Free Moving Barbie (7270) complete. New construction for a more active doll.

1975—Close-up of Free Moving Barbie. New golden blonde hair-do.

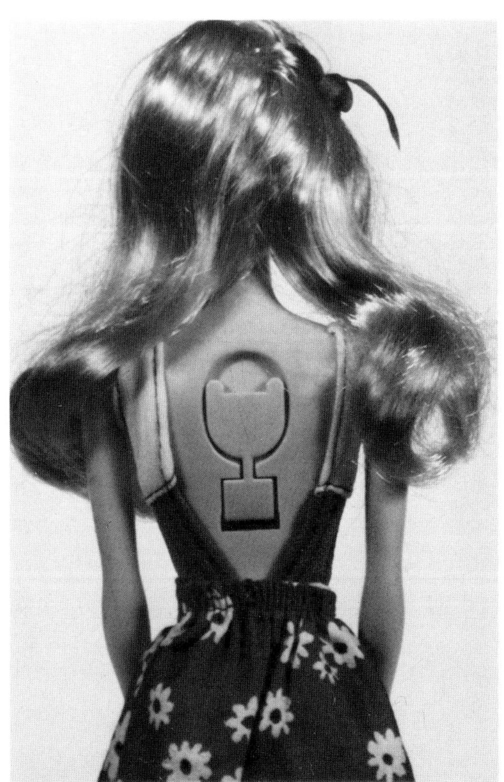
1975—Free Moving Barbie back to show the "Free Mover" tab.

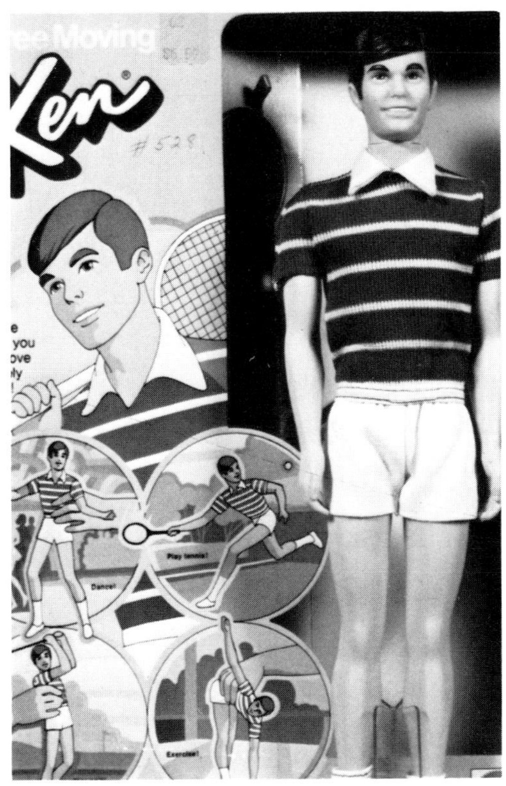

1975—Free Moving Ken (7280). Same back construction as Barbie.

1975—Free Moving P.J. (7281). Same construction as Barbie.

1975—Free Moving Cara (7283). New black doll. Made from the Steffie head mold.

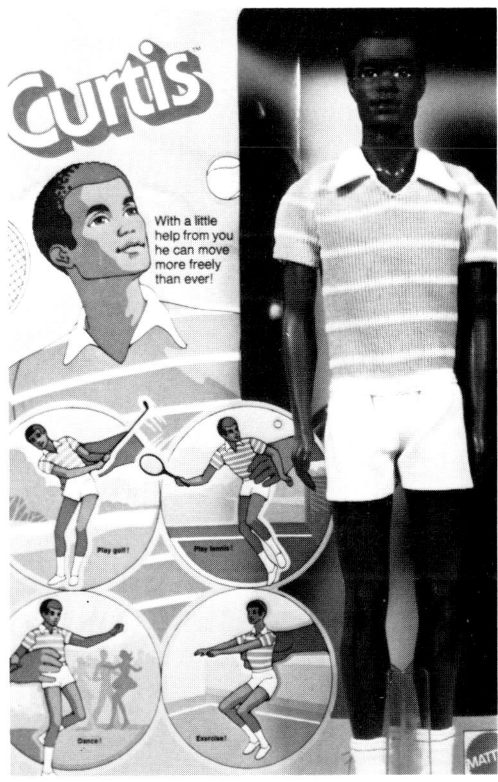

1975—Free Moving Curtis (7282). New black doll. Made from the Brad head mold.

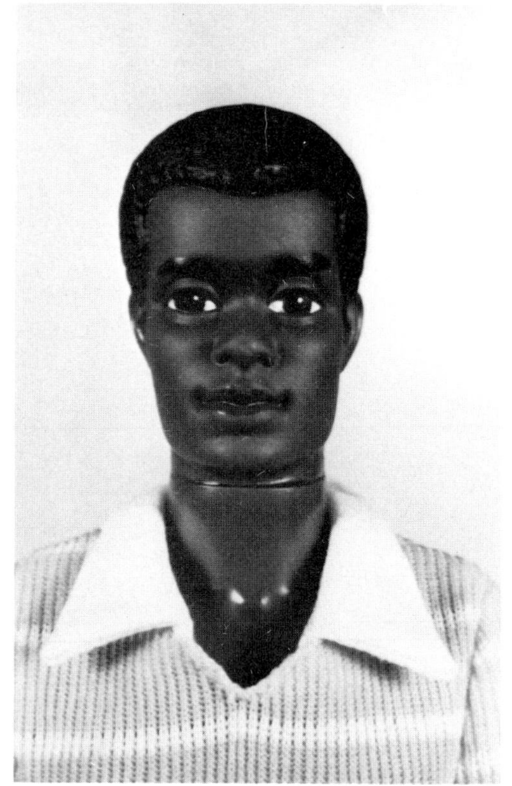

1975—Close-up of Free Moving Curtis (7282). Made from the Brad head mold.

1975—Close-up of Free Moving Cara (7283). Made from the Steffie head mold.

1975—Close-up of Free Moving Ken (7280).

1975—Close-up of Free Moving P.J. (7281). New hair-do. Made from Steffie head mold.

1975—Quick Curl Cara (7291). Made from the Steffie head mold.

Certainly the doll that caused the biggest reaction in 1975 was "Growing Up" Skipper (#7259), two dolls in one. First, she was a cute young girl, 9 inches tall. Then by turning her left arm around, the doll "grew" approximately ¾ of an inch, slimmed at the waist and developed a modest bustline, becoming a curvy teenager. (By turing the arm back around again, she reverted back to a young girl.) Her markings were: ©1967/Mattel, Inc./Hong Kong/U.S. & For. Pat.

Shortly after the doll was introduced at the New York Toy Fair in February, Mattel received a few letters of protest from members of a women's liberation group. A few parents were not enthusiastic either but children (and collectors!) were. Sales for the year were expected to reach one and a half million dolls.

During the year almost every newspaper in the United States had at least one article about the doll that was causing all the fuss.

Skipper had long hair with fluffy ends in either platinum or reddish blonde. There was a red ribbon band on her head. Included was a red body shirt, a blue removable collar, blue scarf, red socks, red flat heeled shoes, white platform sandals and two red and white checked wraparound skirts—one short and one long.

Still available in 1975 were Mod Hair Ken (#4224), Newport Barbie (#7807) and Barbie's Sweet 16 (#7796).

Quick Curl dolls still available were Skipper (#4223), Barbie (#4220), Kelley (#4221) and blonde Miss America (#8697).

Quick Curl Francie (#4222) was dropped from the Mattel Toy Catalogue and a new Quick Curl was added. This was Cara (#7291).

Quick Curl Cara had brown eyes and shoulder length dark brown hair. She was made from the Steffie head mold. She wore a long wraparound skirt in patterned, multi-colored tricot material. Her short blouse of the same material tied in the front and it had long blue sheer sleeves. Her midriff was bare. Markings were: ©1966/Mattel, Inc./U.S. and Foreign/Patented/Other Pat's/Pending/Made In Taiwan.

1975—Growing Up Skipper (7259) complete. See text for description.

1975—Growing Up Skipper (7259). Before and after rotating arm. First issue had long pale blonde hair. Second had shorter golden blonde hair.

1975—Malibu Barbie (1067). New red swimsuit. New white box. Hands made from original Barbie molds but not cut completely through.

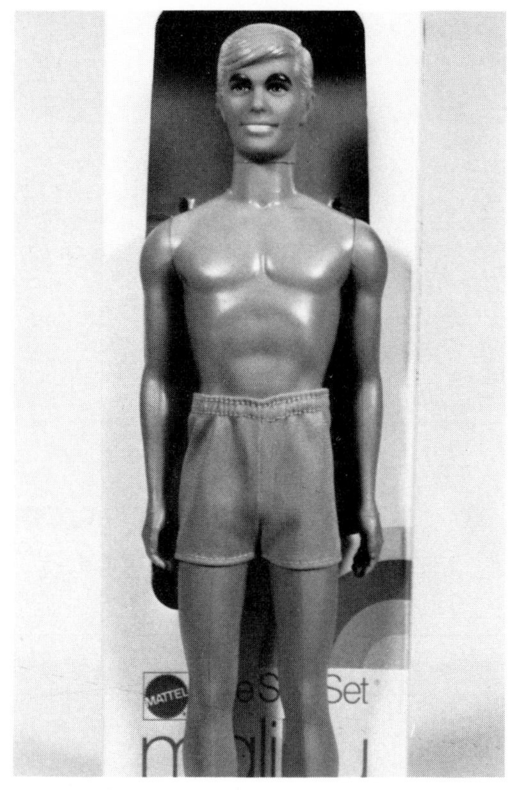

1975—Malibu Ken (1088). New green trunks. New white box. Made in Taiwan.

1975—Malibu Christie (7745). New yellow swimsuit. Hands made from original Barbie mold but not cut completely through.

1975—The other three Malibu dolls in new white boxes. P.J.'s hands same as Barbie's.

All 6 of the Malibu dolls were still available this year but with a few differences. Their stock numbers remained the same but all of them were in a new type of package–a white window type box dated ©1974. Ken was made in Taiwan. The girl dolls were made in Korea. Towels and sunglasses were discontinued.

Skipper, P.J. and Francie wore the same color and style suits as last year, but Christie's suit was now yellow and Ken's trunks were now green. Barbie's suit was not only a different color but also a new style. It was a one-piece red suit with a square neckline.

Late in the year a few of the Malibu dolls were found in the ©1975 shocking pink boxes. See 1976 for a complete description.

—:—

Heretofore "Baggies" (dolls sold in plastic bags) were from Mattel's regular line of dolls. For various reasons they were packaged in the plastic bags and sold at a reduced price. One example is the Talking line of dolls that no longer talked. Another is the Live Action dolls sold without the special stand. Others were leftovers after the line had been discontinued.

But in 1975 there were two "Baggies" that were never a part of the regular line of stock. These were #9000 Casey and #7699 Francie. Both were marked: ©1966/Mattel, Inc./Taiwan.

Both dolls were made from the Francie head mold. They had arms and hands like the Barbie "Mexico mold." Both had pink skin, painted eyelashes, brown eyes, hard shiny straight legs, unjointed waist and long straight hair. Francie's hair was brunette and Casey's was blonde. Both wore a two-piece tricot swimsuit. Francie's was yellow and Casey's was either pink, rose or red.

These dolls were not shown in the 1975 Mattel Toy Catalogue.

—:—

Another doll not shown in the catalogue was Hawaiian Barbie (#7470). On the market in October, this doll was a "Special" sold only in a few stores.

Made from the Steffie head mold, she had suntan skin, twist waist, bendable legs, black painted eyebrows and lashes, brown eyeliner and brown eyes. Her long straight black hair was parted on the left side and she wore a pink flower in her hair. Her markings were: ©1966/Mattel, Inc./ U.S. Patented/U.S. Pat. Pend./Made in/Korea. Her arms and hands were made from the Francie molds.

She wore a multi-colored floral two-piece Bikini swimsuit with a matching long wraparound skirt and lei. A grass skirt, extra pair of panties, ukulele and a sail boat were included in the set.

—:—

Blonde Quick Curl Miss America (#8697) was still available as a Kellogg Co. offer.

—:—

The 1974 Sears catalogue (good until August, 1975) listed Sun Valley Barbie (#7806) and Sun Valley Ken (#7809).

—:—

The Sears "Barbie Baby-Sits" set was still available this year. Stock No. 7882. In some sets the blanket and sacque had a blue background instead of white.

1975—"Baggie" Francie (7699) and "Baggie" Casey (9000). (Found by Maxine Jamnick)

1975—Hawaiian Barbie (7470). A Limited Edition Department Store Special. Arms and hands made from the Francie molds.

Hawaiian Barbie (7470). Made from the Steffie head mold.

"Baggie" Francie (7699). See text for details.

"Baggie" Casey (9000). Made from the Francie head mold.

1975—Quick Curl Cara (7291). Made from the Steffie head mold.

Rare blonde haired "Baggie" Pose 'N Play Skipper found in 1975. The earlier dolls had reddish hair.

The Barbie line got a new Logo in 1976 and packaging now lists assortment numbers as well as stock numbers.

—:—

1976 got off to a nice start with a new promotional doll—Deluxe Quick Curl Barbie (9217). Taped to the side of the box was a Jergen's Barbie Beauty Kit consisting of beauty soap and bubble bath. A free Barbie poster/calendar was also available.

Later Deluxe Quick Curl Barbies had the same stock number but no longer had the free promotional items. Both dolls had medium length blonde hair, twist waist, bend knees, "Mexico" hands and painted eyelashes. Both wore a long blue dress, blue shoes, white fringed stole and white beads. (The promotional brochure showed "pearls.")

Included in the set were a long quick-curl fall attached to a blue ribbon and hair styling equipment and accessories. Markings were: ©1966/Mattel, Inc./U.S. & Foreign/ Patented/Other Pat's/Pending/Made in/Taiwan.

There were two other Deluxe Quick Curl dolls this year—P.J. (9218) and Cara (9220). (See Chapter III for another available in Europe). P.J., made from the Steffie head mold, had blonde hair and brown eyes. She wore a long orange colored dress and shoes. Her extra hair piece was attached to orange ribbon. Cara had dark brown hair and brown eyes. She, too, was made from the Steffie head mold. Her long dress, shoes and hairpiece ribbon were yellow. In all other respects both dolls were the same as Barbie.

1976 Deluxe Quick Curl Barbie (9217). Promotional set with free Jergen's Beauty Kit attached.

1976 Deluxe Quick Curl Cara (9220).

1976 Deluxe Quick Curl P.J. (9218).

1976—Deluxe Quick Curl Barbie (9217).

1976—Deluxe Quick Curl Cara (9220). Made from the Steffie head mold.

1976—Deluxe Quick Curl P.J. (9218). Made from the Steffie head mold.

1976—Ballerina Barbie (9093).

Early in the year a new Ken reached the market. Called Now Look Ken (9342), he had newly styled brown rooted hair and new "feathered" eyebrows. His skin was dark pink and his knees were bendable. He wore a beige jacket and pants, brown shoes and a blue neck scarf. Included were a brown hair brush and decal beard, sideburns and two moustaches. He was marked: ©1968/Mattel, Inc./U.S. & For. Patd./Other Pats/Pending/Taiwan.

Late in the year the doll was different. He had longer hair, pale pink skin and stiff knees. His arms and hands were made of hard plastic. The palms of the hands were turned toward the back instead of the side of the body. This doll was made in Hong Kong and was marked: 1088-0500 3/© Mattel/Inc.1968/Hong Kong.

—:—

Ballerina Barbie (9093) and Ballerina Cara (9528) were beautiful new dolls of 1976. They had specially constructed legs for pirouettes, splits and kicks. Their arms and head were swivel-jointed for graceful posing. The arms and hands were made of hard shiny plastic from newly designed molds. Both were marked: ©Mattel, Inc. 1966/U.S. Patent Pending/Taiwan.

Barbie had pale blonde hair in an unusual ponytail style. Several strands of hair were combed down around her face and then brought to the rear where it became a part of the ponytail. She wore a white tutu with gold trim, a gold crown and white ballet slippers. Included were a white posing stand and a red bouquet.

Cara, made from the Steffie head mold, had a black ponytail hair-do and brown eyes. Her tutu, slippers and stand were pink. Her crown and bouquet were similar to Barbie's.

1976—Ballerina Barbie (9093). White tutu. White posing stand.

1976—Ballerina Cara (9528). Pink tutu. Pink posing stand.

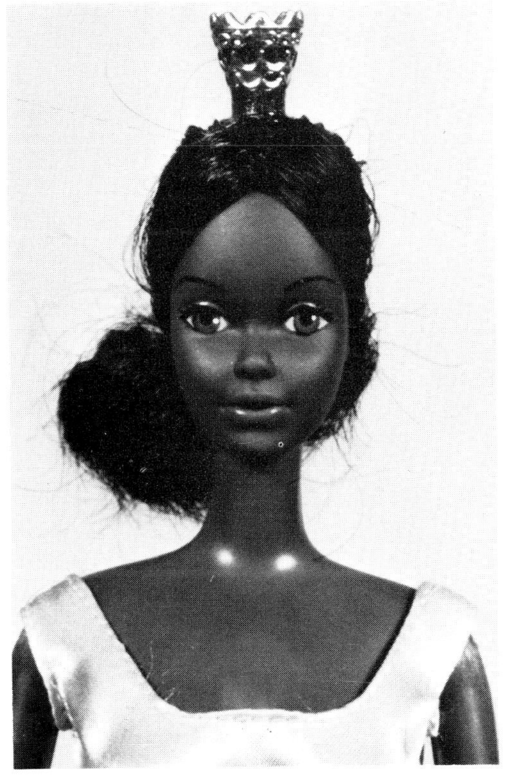

1976—Ballerina Cara. Made from the Steffie head mold.

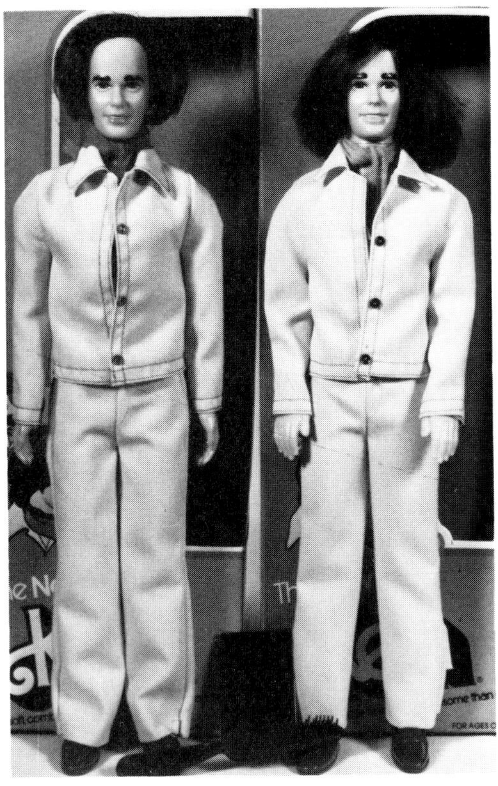

1976—Now Look Ken (9342). First issue made in Taiwan. Second made in Hong Kong.

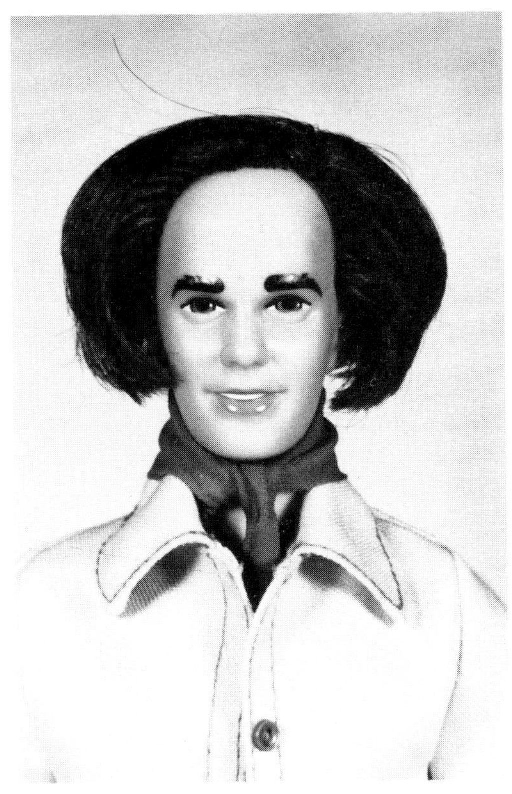

First issue Now Look Ken. Some dolls had a lower hair line than this one.

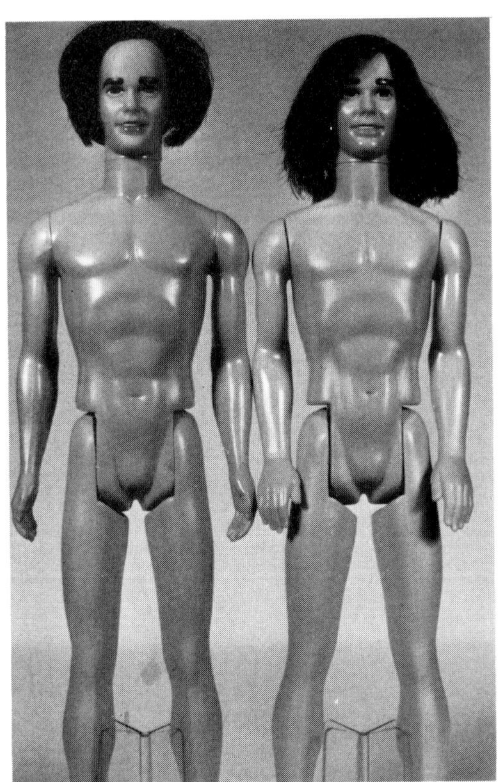

Now Look Kens. Second doll has longer hair, paler skin, wider stance and new arms and hands.

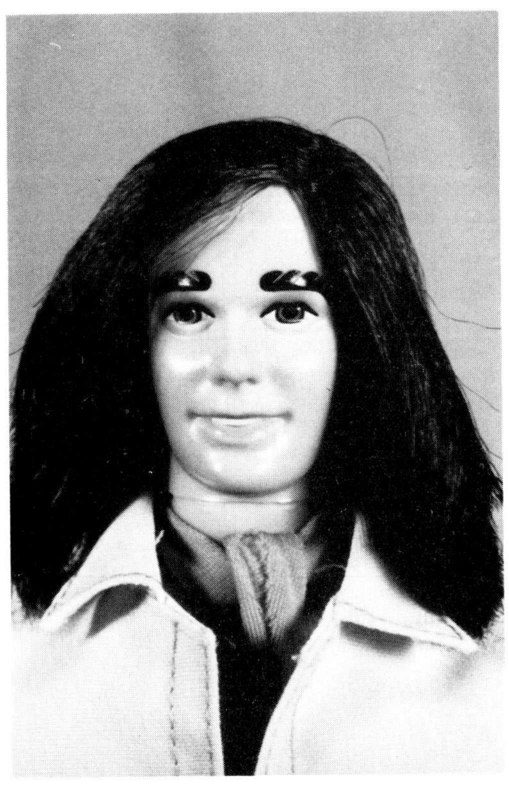

Second issue Now Look Ken.

This year Skipper got a new friend, Growing Up Ginger (9222). Ginger, made from the Skipper head mold, had the same construction as Growing Up Skipper of 1975. She had brunette hair and brown eyes. A blue body suit, two blue and white polka dot skirts (one short, one long), blue flats, white platforms, lavender scarf and lavender collar came with her. She was marked: ©1967/Mattel, Inc./Hong Kong/ U.S. & For. Pat.

Growing Up Skiper (7259) was still on the market. In 1975 the box that she came in had a real doll pictured on it. The 1976 boxes for Skipper and Ginger pictured sketched dolls.

—:—

Hawaiian Barbie (7470) was still available in a few localities in 1976. These dolls had a third type of arm and hand, a hard shiny plastic made from the "Mexico" mold. The rest was about the same as last year.

—:—

This year the Malibu dolls were in new rose colored boxes with the new type of lettering. Francie (1068) was about the same as last year. Skipper (1069) had hard shiny arms and hands with the rest about the same as last year. Barbie (1067), P.J. (1187) and Christie (7745) had new hard shiny plastic arms and hands made from the "Mexico" molds. The rest was about the same as last year.

During the first part of the year Malibu Ken (1088) had the same Taiwan markings as last year. He had orangy blonde hair and a shiny torso. His trunks were thicker and a darker shade of green. Late in the year the doll was being made in Hong Kong and was marked: 1088 0500 3/ © Mattel/ Inc. 1968/Hong Kong. This doll had darker skin than the other Malibu Kens. His arms and hands were similar to Now Look Ken's.

1976—Growing Up Ginger (9222). Same construction as Growing Up Skipper.

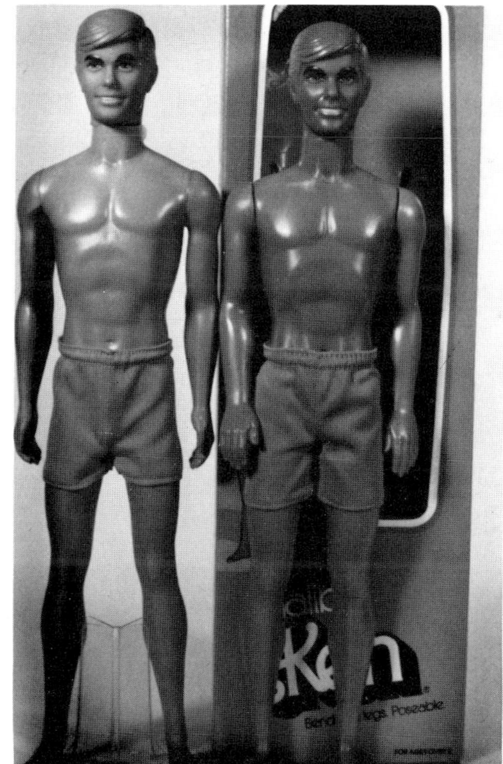

1976 Malibu Kens (1088). First issue made in Taiwan. Second issue made in Hong Kong. Second issue has darker skin and new arm and hand molds. New markings.

1976 Malibu dolls in new rose colored boxes.

One of the year's most interesting dolls was a Barbie found in a plastic bag. The paper heading on the bag called the doll Action Barbie (1155). (#1155) was the stock number of the Live Action Barbie of 1971.)

The doll in the bag was different from any Barbie sold previously in the United States. She was the same doll that had been sold in Europe in 1974, and possibly in 1973, as #8588 Barbie.

She had straight blonde hair tied in two sections (similar to Malibu P.J.'s), hard shiny torso with unjointed waist, bend knees and the "Mexico" arms and hands. She was made from the true Barbie head mold. Her markings were: ©1967 Mattel, Inc./U.S. Patented/Other Patents Pending/Patented in Canada 1967/Taiwan.

—:—

Ballerina Barbie On Tour (9613), a limited edition Department Store Special, was on the market in the Fall of 1976. This was a Set consisting of the regular Ballerina Barbie in the white tutu and two additional outfits, "Snowflake Fairy" and a pink practice set.

—:—

Although not marked "Special" on the box, Beautiful Bride Barbie (9599) was found at the same time and in the same stores as the Special above. This was a new and different Barbie.

She had tan rooted eyelashes, the first doll to have rooted lashes since 1972. Her eyes were greenish and her hair was blonde. The hair was shoulder length with loosely flipped ends. She had bend knees, twist waist and hard shiny arms and hands made from the "Mexico" molds. She was dressed in the 1976 #9419 wedding outfit. Markings were: ©1966/ Mattel, Inc./U.S. Patented/U.S. Pat. Pend./Made in/Korea.

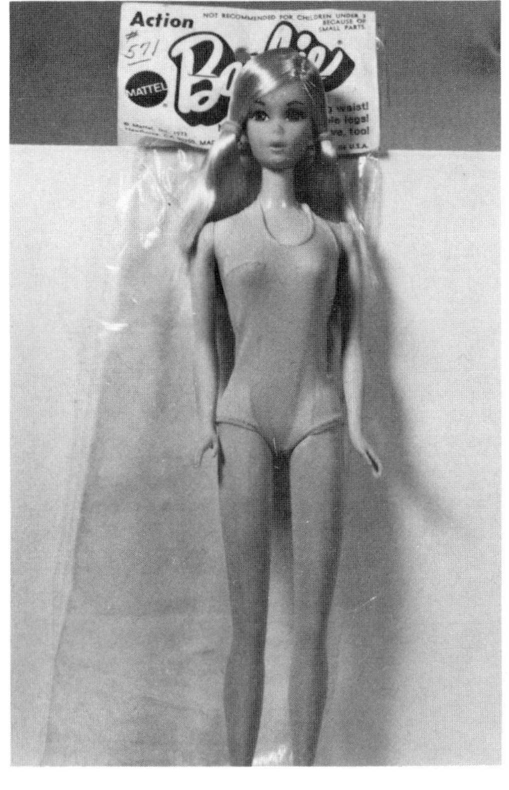

1976 Barbie found in a plastic bag. Doll similar to #8588 Barbie sold in Europe in 1974 and possibly earlier.

1976 Ballerina Barbie On Tour (9613). A Limited Edition Department Store Special.

1976 Beautiful Bride Barbie (9599). Dressed in 1976 #9419 Wedding Gown.

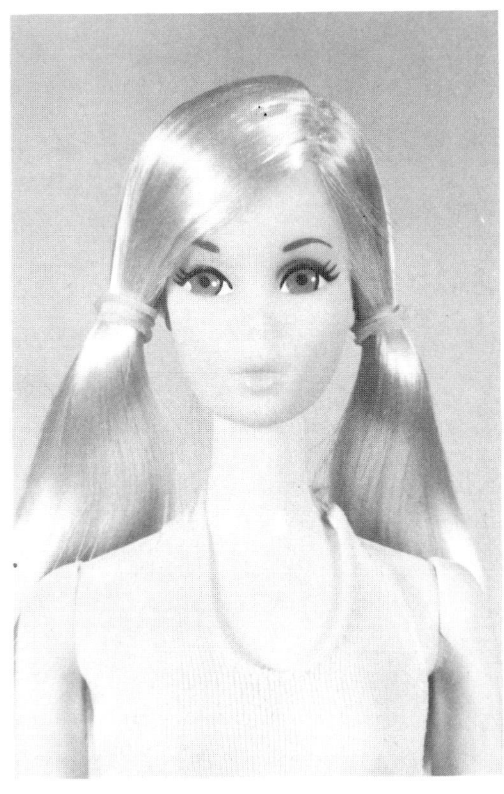

Close up of the "baggie" Barbie found in 1976. Similar to the #8588 Barbie sold in Europe in 1974 and possibly earlier.

1976 Growing Up Ginger (9222). Made from the Skipper head mold.

1976 Beautiful Bride Barbie (9599). Tan rooted eyelashes.

1976 Hawaiian Barbie (7470) with hard shiny "Mexico" arms and hands.

Heretofore, the Sears "Barbie Baby Sits" set (7882), packaged in a small brown shipping box, was available only through the mail order catalogue. In the Fall of 1976 the baby set (same stock number) was available in Sears retail stores. This set was packaged in a new decorated pink box with new pink plastic accessories and a new pink dress for the baby. This same pink set was pictured in the 1976 Sears Christmas catalogue.

—:—

The following dolls were still available and about the same as last year: Gold Medal Barbie Skier (7264), Gold Medal Barbie Skater (7262), Gold Medal P.J. Gymnast (7263), Gold Medal Ken Skier (7261), Quick Curl Miss America (8697), Ward's dressed Mod Hair Ken (4234), baggie Francie (7699) and baggie Casey (9000).

—:—

Available until Fall from mail order catalogues were the following: Quick Curl Barbie (4220), Quick Curl Kelley (4221), Mod Hair Ken (4224), Free Moving Barbie (7270), Free Moving Ken (7280), Free Moving P.J. (7281) and Free Moving Cara (7283).

—:—

This year the 1975 Sears sets, Gold Medal Barbie Winter Sports (9042) and Gold Medal U.S. Olympic Wardrobe (9044), were being sold in a few locations in Discount Department Stores.

—:—

In 1976 a few of the regular Malibu Kens in the green trunks were found in a box marked Funtime Ken (7194). In 1975 and 1976 a Funtime Ken was available in Europe. This European Ken was different from the Malibu doll. He had pink skin and dark brown hair. His trunks were blue.

It is easy to see how such a mix-up could have happened. Both dolls were made in Taiwan. Both boxes look very much alike. To factory workers unfamiliar with English it would be easy to pick up the wrong box.

1976 Sears' "Barbie Baby Sits" set (7882) in new pink packaging. New accessories.

1976 Growing Up Skipper (7259). New sketched illustrated packaging.

1. Regular Malibu Ken.
2. Funtime Ken (7194) from Germany. Pink skin, brown hair.
3. A regular Malibu Ken found in a Funtime box.

III. Barbie in Other Countries

In 1974 Barbie collectors received some startling news. Travelers in England found three Mattel dolls not available in the United States—#8128 Tutti, #8129 Todd and #8130 Chris.

These had been re-issued with new packaging dated ©1973, new stock numbers and new clothes. The old molds had been used but a new type of plastic armature had replaced the old wire type. The originals were made in Japan; the re-issued ones were made in Hong Kong.

The finding of these dolls opened up a new line of inquiry. Were there other dolls available in other countries that were not sold here? Was this something new or had it been going on for years? Hopefully future research will shed more light on the subject. At the present time the following is known.

On March 14, 1968, Elliott Handler spoke to the Newcomen Society in North America. During the talk Mr. Handler stated that Mattel products were sold in over 60 countries. He also stated that 250,000 girls belonged to European Barbie Clubs.

The ©1965 booklets invited girls from Austria, Belgium, Denmark, Finland, France, Germany, Holland, Italy, Norway, Sweden and Switzerland to become members of the International Barbie Club with headquarters in Amsterdam, Holland.

Some of the other places where Barbie Club members lived were Mexico, Canada, Hawaii, Jamaica, Philippines, Puerto Rico, Alaska, Honduras, Zambia, Virgin Islands, Midway Island, Australia, Turkey, Bahamas, Spain, Chile, Japan, Antilles, New Zealand, Hong Kong, Guam, Saudi Arabia, Nicaragua, Peru, Trinidad, Costa Rica, Cyprus, Johannesburg (South Africa), Israel and Brazil.

Over the years Mattel has had factories or subsidiaries in Japan, Canada, Hong Kong, Taiwan, Great Britain, West Germany, Italy, Mexico and Korea.

A Mattel spokesman has stated, "There is no difference in the dolls manufactured for sale in other countries. The packaging is printed in the appropriate language, but the product is the same."

Packaging in Canada usually has both French and English wording. European packaging often has four languages on the same container—English, French, German and Italian.

The following dolls are known to have been on the market in other countries:

Barbie, twist waist [*#8587*]. In 1973 this doll's head was made from the *Stacey* mold. She had brown eyes and long straight titian hair. She wore a one-piece blue swimsuit similar to Malibu Barbie's.Her arms and hands were made from the original Barbie molds.

Barbie, twist waist [#8587]. In 1974 the doll's head was made from the *Steffie* mold. She now had blue eyes and long straight blonde hair. She wore the same blue swimsuit.

In 1975 and 1976 the swimsuit was yellow. The dolls were marked: ©1966/Mattel, Inc./U.S. Patented/U.S. Pat. Pend. /Made in/Korea. These dolls have been found in Europe and in Canada. They have been found with four different arms and hands. These were: the original Barbie mold, the original Barbie mold but the fingers not cut completely through, the regular Francie arm and hand mold and the hard shiny plastic "Mexico" arms and hands of 1976.

Tutti [*8128*]. This doll had long blonde hair and blue eyes. Her dress had a pink yoke with a light print skirt and attached panties. She wore white shoes and a pink hair band. The doll pictured in the booklet and catalogues had light brown hair and wore a yellow dress. None of these have been found so this may have been a sample doll and dress.

Tutti has been available in Europe since 1974. In 1976 she was sold in Canada. The first dolls were not marked but the latest ones are marked: ©1965/Mattel, Inc./Hong Kong.

Todd [*8129*]. Todd had red hair and brown eyes. He wore a blue shirt, red shorts, red cap and white shoes and socks. (The 1974 doll from England wore blue and white striped shorts.) The doll pictured in the booklets and catalogues wore red and blue plaid pants and red shoes.

The first Todds were not marked. The latest ones have the same markings as Tutti. (Recently one brown haired Todd has been found.)

Chris [*#8130*]. The first Chrises had long titian hair and brown eyes. The 1976 doll had medium brown hair. Her print dress had a yellow background with pink and green flowers. She had a barrette and two green bows in her hair. Her shoes were white. The first dolls had no markings. The newest ones have the same markings as Tutti.

The Chris pictured in the booklets and catalogues had blonde hair. She wore a red, white and black striped dress and red shoes. None of these have been found.

In 1973 Chris was available in Germany in the old type of box used in this country in 1967 and 1968. The doll had brown hair. She wore the type of dress that is being used at the present time.

This leads collectors to believe that the Tutti, Todd and Chris dolls were probably available in Europe from their inception up to the present time.

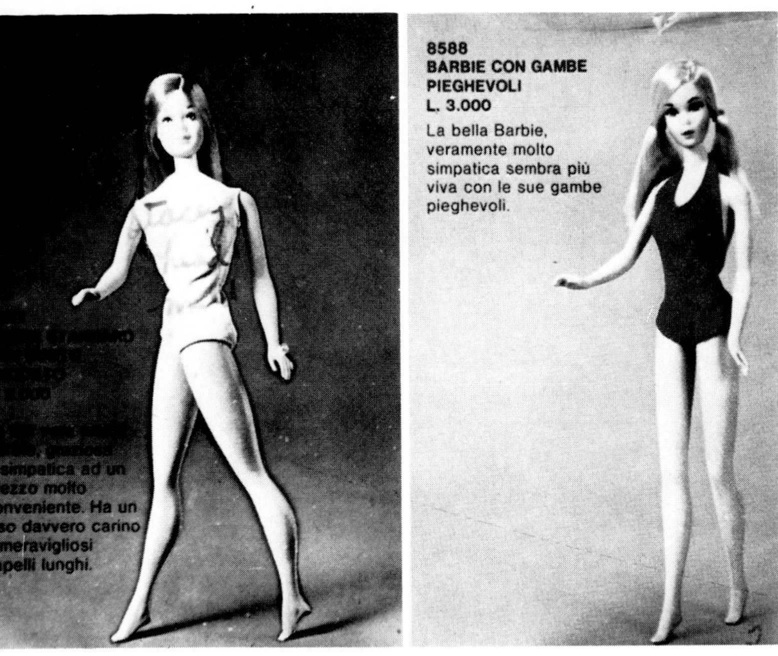

From a 1974 Italian booklet—#8587 Barbie, red hair, brown eyes and made from the Stacey head mold, #8588 Barbie, made from the true Barbie mold.

This shows the #8587 Barbie on display in a German toy store in 1973.

1974—#8587 Barbie from Europe. Blue swimsuit, original Barbie arms and hands. Steffie head mold.

1975—#8587 Barbie from Canada. Yellow swimsuit, original Barbie arms and hands. Steffie head mold.

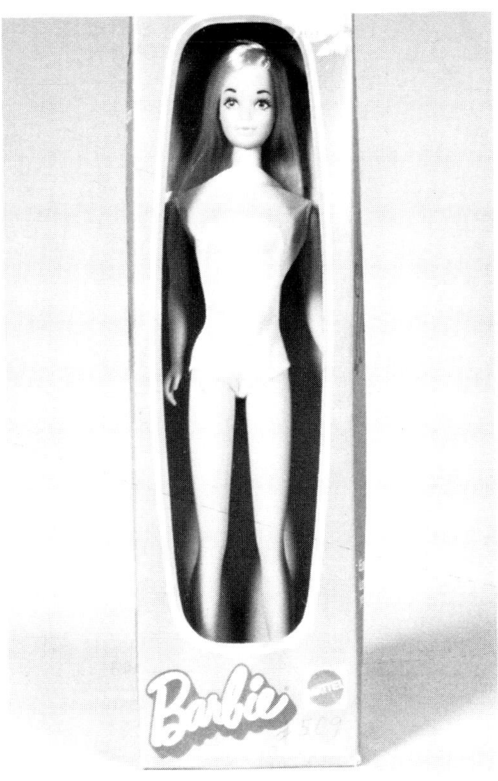

#8587 Barbie from Canada. Arms and hands made from the Francie molds. 1975.

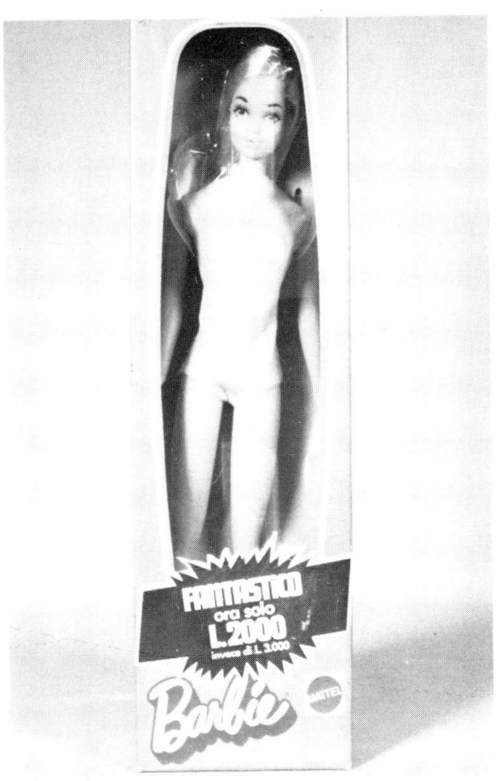

#8587 Barbie from Italy. Arms and hands made from the Francie molds. 1975.

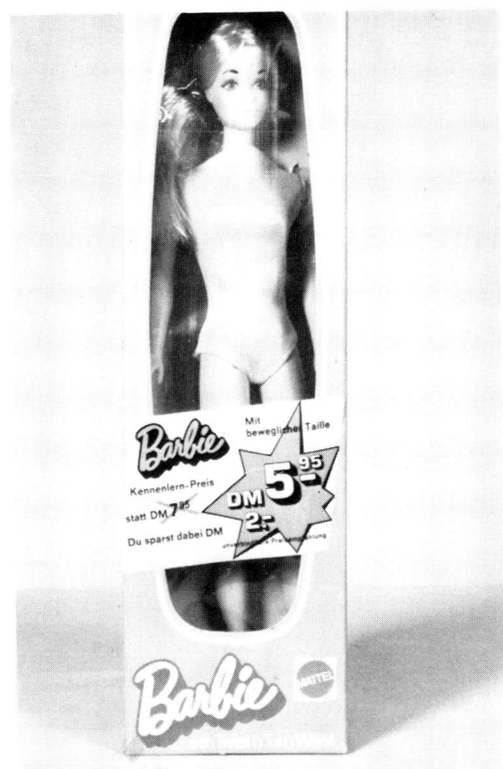

#8587 Barbie from Germany. Arms and hands made from the original Barbie molds but not cut through. 1975.

1976—#8587 Barbie from Canada. Hard shiny arms and hands made from the "Mexico" molds.

Chris from Germany. 1973 and possibly earlier.

#8130 Chris—Re-issued in Europe in 1974.

#8128 Tutti—Re-issued in Europe in 1974.

#8129 Todd—Re-issued in Europe in 1974.

1973—German toy store shelf showing the Chris doll in the old type package.

1975 German catalogue picture of Tutti, Todd and Chris.

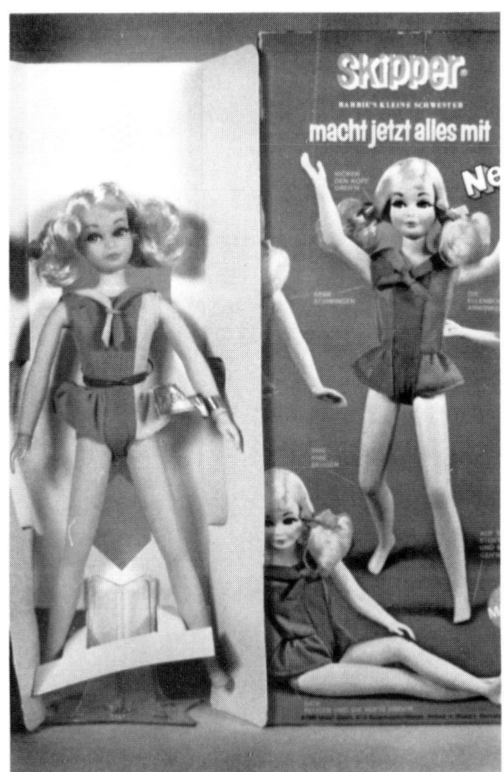

Living Skipper (1117) from Germany. Box made and printed in Germany. Doll made in Taiwan.

Box for the Living Skipper from Germany.

Barbie, bend knee [#8588]. This doll's head was made from the true Barbie mold. She had long blonde hair tied into two sections similar to Malibu P.J.'s. She had a hard shiny torso with unjointed waist, bend knees and the "Mexico" arms and hands. She wore a rose colored swimsuit styled like Malibu P.J.'s. Her markings were: ©1967 Mattel, Inc./U.S. Patented/Other Patents Pending/Patented in Canada 1967/Taiwan.

Skipper, twist waist. In 1973 this Skipper was on the market in Europe. She had long straight blonde or brunette hair and pink skin. Her short playsuit had a red, white and blue print waist with a narrow white pleated skirt.

Skipper, bend knees [#8126]. This Skipper was on the European market in 1974. She had long blonde hair and pink skin. She was dressed in a two-piece navy swimsuit.

Tutti "Swing-A-Ling" set [#7453]. This set was re-issued in Germany in 1975 and was still on the market in 1976. The doll had blonde hair. She wore an orange and yellow dress, orange shoes and head band and white socks.

Tutti "Walkin' My Dolly" set [#7454]. This set was also on the German market. The blonde Tutti wore a red and white checked gingham dress, a white hat and red shoes. The small doll in the buggy was made from the original mold but it was left unpainted.

Tutti "Night-Night, Sleep Tight" set [#7455]. This set was also available in Germany. Tutti had a white ribbon band on her blonde hair. She wore a green nighty and a white robe and scuffs. The white bed was covered with a yellow print spread.

Three new dolls were on the European market in 1975. They were called Funtime dolls. They were still on the market in 1976.

Funtime Barbie [#7192]. This doll, made from the true Barbie head mold, had long blonde hair tied in two sections. She had pink skin, a twist waist and bendable knees. Her arms and hands were made from the Francie molds. She wore a tangerine swimsuit styled like the 1975 Malibu Barbie suit. Her markings were: ©1966/Mattel, Inc./U.S. Patented/U.S. Pat. Pend./Made in/Korea.

Funtime Skipper [#7193]. She had long blonde hair, pink skin, bend knees and a twist waist. Her two-piece swimsuit was yellow. Her markings were: ©1967 Mattel, Inc./U.S. Pat'd/U.S. Pats. Pend./Made in Korea.

Funtime Ken [#7194]. He had pink skin, brown hair, brown eyebrows and bend knees. He wore blue trunks and his markings were: ©1968/Mattel, Inc./U.S. & For. Patd./ Other Pats./Pending/Taiwan.

Late in 1975 Hawaiian Barbie (#7470) was on the market in the United States as a Department Store Special. The same doll was available all year in Europe in all stores that sold toys. The doll from Europe had arms and hands made from the original Barbie mold. Some of the ones in the States had the Francie arms and hands.

The Hawaiian Barbie was sold in Canada in 1976. This doll had hard shiny plastic arms and hands from the "Mexico" molds. This same doll was also on the market in a few localities in the United States. It was also shown in the 1976 German catalogue.

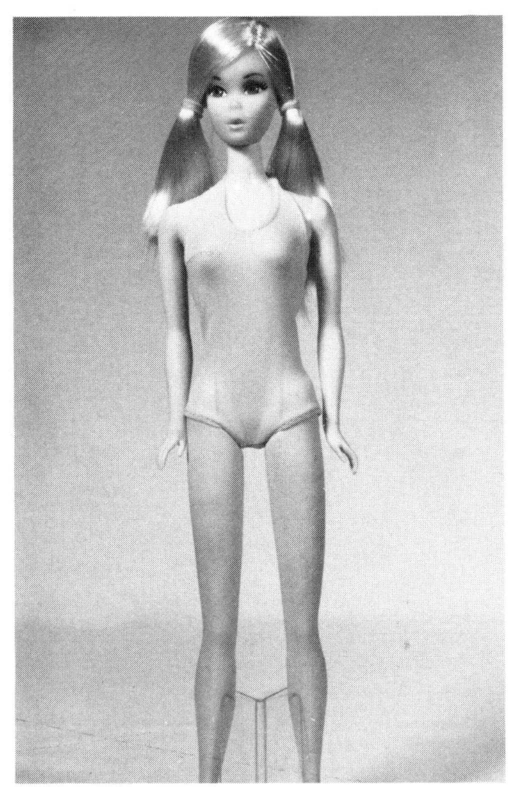

#8588 Barbie—On the market in Europe in 1973. Arms and hands made from the "Mexico" molds.

This 1973 picture of a German toy store shelf shows the Twist Skipper that was not available in U.S.A.

1974—German booklet—#8126 Skipper with bendable knees. Swimsuit is medium blue.

#7453 Swing-A-Ling—Re-issued in Europe in 1975.

#7454 Walkin' My Dolly—Re-issued in Europe in 1975.

#7455 Night-Night, Sleep Tight—Re-issued in Europe in 1975.

1975—#7192 Funtime Barbie from Germany. Arms and hands made from the Francie molds. Pink skin, tangerine swimsuit.

1975—#7193 Funtime Skipper from Germany. Pink skin, yellow swimsuit.

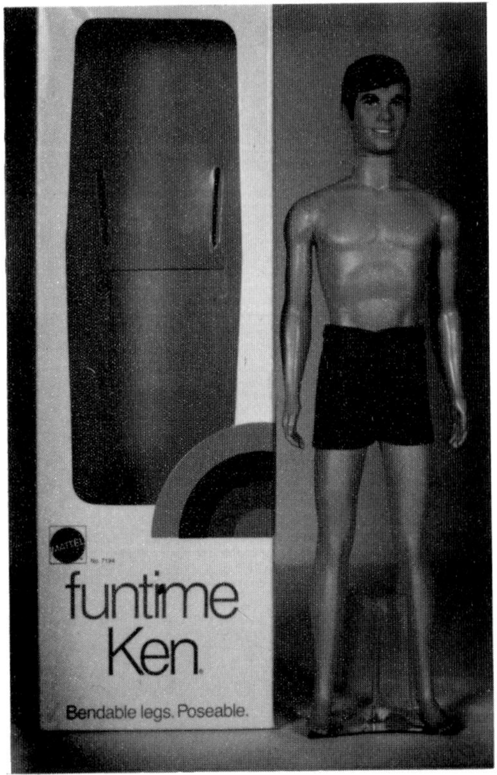

1975—#7194 Funtime Ken from Germany. Pink skin, blue trunks.

1975—#7470 Hawaiian Barbie from Germany. Arms and hands made from original Barbie molds but not cut through.

1973—German toy store shelf—Notice the #8588 Barbie and the Living Barbie (1116) in the box with all-German wording.

1976—#7470 Hawaiian Barbie from Canada. Hard shiny "Mexico" arms and hands.

In 1976 there were four new dolls on the market in Europe. These were:

Barbie [#7382]. This doll had pink skin, straight knees, unjointed waist and the hard shiny plastic "Mexico" arms and hands. Her head was made from the Stacey mold and she had long straight blonde hair. She was dressed in a two-piece blue swimsuit. Her markings were: ©1959/Mattel, Inc./U.S. Patented/U.S. Pat. Pend./Made in/Korea.

Funtime Skooter [#7381]. This Skooter's head was made from the Skipper mold. Her dark red hair was medium length with flip ends. She had blue eyes, pink skin, hard shiny plastic arms and hands, twist waist and bendable knees. Her markings were: ©1967 Mattel, Inc./U.S. Pat'd./U.S. Pats. Pend./Made in Korea.

Carla [#7377]. This was a black Tutti-size doll. She had brown skin, brown eyes and black hair. She had long turned under bangs and a double ponytail tied with white ribbon. Her markings were: ©1965/Mattel, Inc./Hong Kong. She wore an orange dress with white trim and white shoes and socks.

Collectors are in disagreement over her head mold. Some collectors believe that *all* of the 6" dolls were made from the same master molds. These people believe that the variations encountered are due to the length of time the particular mold had been in use. Some collectors believe that Carla was made from a new mold. (Ed. note—We believe that all of the 6" dolls were made from the same master molds.)

Deluxe Quick Curl Skipper [#9428]. This doll had blonde hair, blue eyes, freckles, a twist waist and bend knees. She wore a long pink dress, a fringed white stole, white beads and pink shoes. Included was a long fall attached to pink ribbon and hair styling accessories. Her markings were: ©1967 Mattel, Inc./Taiwan/U.S. Patented/Other Patents Pending.

Dancer (#90-7385). Barbie's horse was re-issued in Europe in 1976. The horse was made from the old Dancer molds but the posing stand was eliminated. The new horse was a lighter shade of brown. A new English sidesaddle was included.

The Dancer molds were used for three more horses sold in Europe in 1976. One was Big Jim's horse and the other two were for Karl May's Cowboy and Indian characters.

The 1974 Italian and German Barbie booklets showed seven Barbie Exclusive outfits that were not sold in the United States. The Italian booklet also showed a child-size Barbie electric iron and a set of Barbie bedroom furniture not available in this country. The German booklet pictured four Todd and twelve Tutti outfits not sold here.

The 1975 Italian Barbie booklet pictured a four-piece set of patio furniture not available here. The German catalogue for 1975 showed four new Tutti and four new Todd outfits. It also pictured eight Tutti and four Todd outfits from the previous year. It also pictured a Tutti case not available here.

The 1975 German catalogue also featured six Barbie Exclusive outfits. Five of these were never sold here. The sixth, a wedding gown (#7176), was on the market here in 1976 in a slightly different version.

The 1976 German catalogue featured six Barbie Exclusive outfits. All but two of these have been found in the United States as Department Store Specials. In addition the wedding outfit was used on Beautiful Bride Barbie (#9599), the Department Store Special.

#8587 Barbie—Twist waist, made from the Steffie head mold.

#8588 Barbie—Bendable knees, made from the Barbie head mold.

#7192 Funtime Barbie—Twist waist, bend knees, pink skin, made from the Barbie mold.

#7382 Barbie—Made from the Stacey head mold. Standard.

1976—#7382 Barbie from Germany. Standard. Made from the Stacey head mold. Blue swimsuit.

1976—#7381 Funtime Skooter. Made from the Skipper head mold. Pink skin, dark red hair, teal blue eyes, blue swimsuit.

1976—#7377 Carla. Tutti's new black friend. Orange colored dress.

1976—#9428 Deluxe Quick Curl Skipper. Pink dress, white stole.

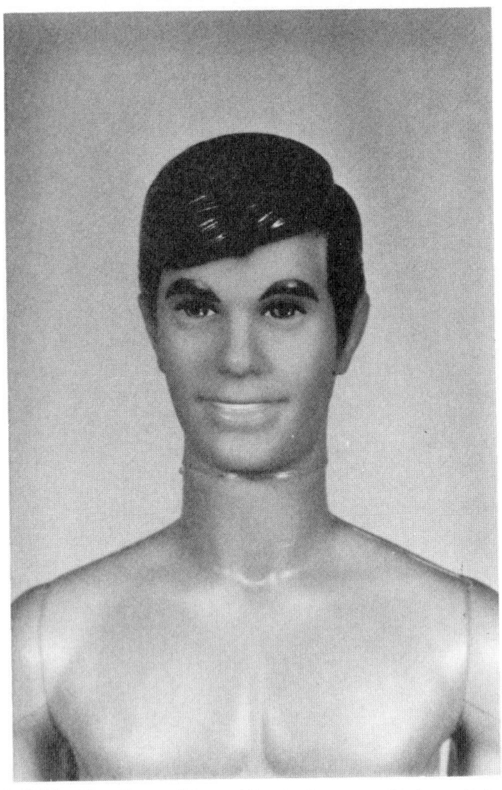

#7194 Funtime Ken—Dark brown hair, pink skin.

#7193 Funtime Skipper—Pink skin, twist waist, bend knees.

#9428 Deluxe Quick Curl Skipper—Twist waist, bend knees.

#7381 Funtime Skooter—Made from the Skipper head mold. First Skooter since 1968.

Walk Lively Barbie from Canada. Different box from U.S.A. Packaged in Canada.

Barbie's Sweet 16 from Canada. Packaged in Canada. Packaging different from U.S.A.

Talking Busy Barbie from Canada. Packaged in Canada in different package from U.S.A.

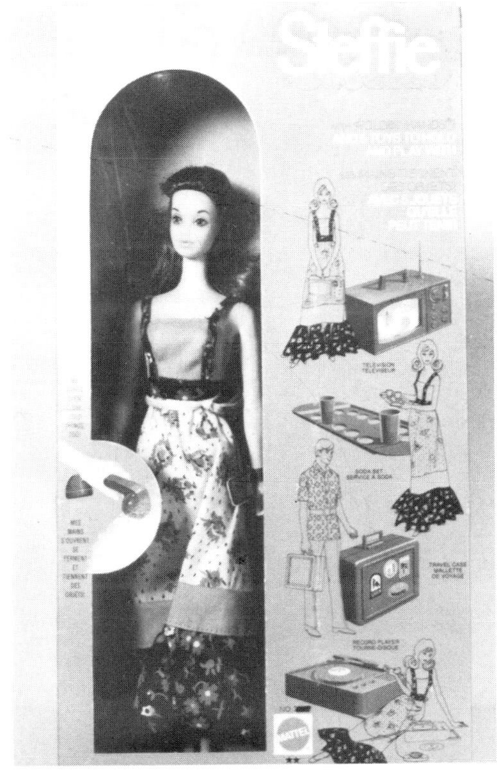

Busy Steffie from Canada. Packaged in Canada in different box from U.S.A. one.

Growing Up Skipper from Canada. Packaged in Canada.

Free Moving Barbie from Canada. Packaged in Canada.

Free Moving P.J. from Canada. Packaged in Canada.

Free Moving Ken from Canada. Packaged in Canada.

Quick Curl Cara from Canada. Packaged in Canada.

1975 Gold Medal Barbie (#7233) from Canada. Different box, coupon offer and medal. Doll has wrist tag. (U.S.A. doll did not have wrist tag.)

COLORATISSIMA LA NUOVA MODA PER BARBIE

I ESTROSI PER BARBIE

PARTY ELEGANTE L. 3.000

MAGLIA L. 3.000

PRIME PIOGGIE L. 3.000

COORD ATO GIOVANE

PELLICCIA SPORTIVA L. 3.500

PRIMI FREDDI L. 3.500

TANTI POIS L. 3.500

These seven outfits were shown in the 1974 Italian and German fashion booklets. They were not available in the U.S.A.

1974 fashion booklet—Germany. (Booklets were discontinued in U.S.A. after 1973.)

1975 fashion booklet—Italian.

1975 fashion booklet—German.

1970 fashion booklet—Japanese. (Gift from Viki Lyn Paulson)

Barbie furniture sold in Europe in 1974. (Not available in U.S.A.)

1973 German toy store display.

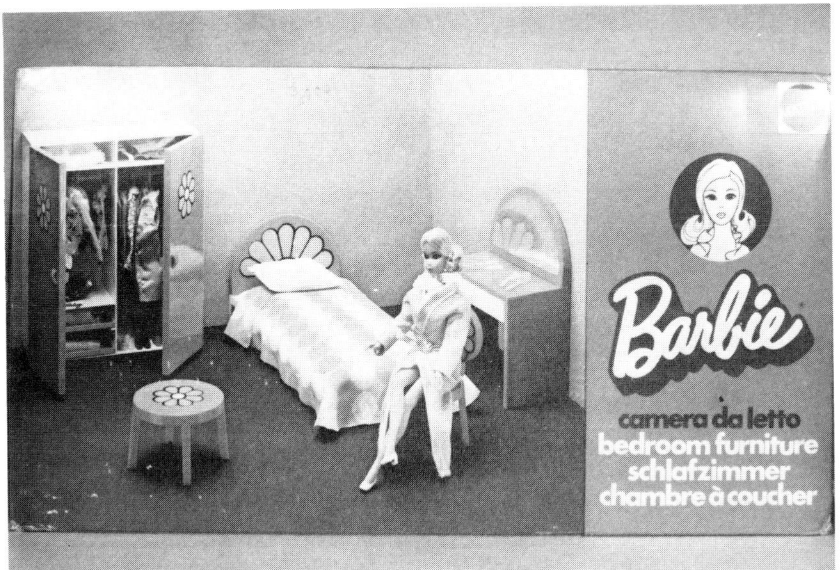

Barbie bedroom furniture found in Europe in 1975. (Gift from Bill St. John). Not available in U.S.A.

Barbie's horse, Dancer (7385), re-issued in Europe in 1976. New English saddle. No posing stand. Different shade of brown.

Another horse made from the Dancer mold. Germany, 1976.

Big Jim's horse, Thunder (90-9400), new in 1976 in Europe. Made from the Dancer molds. Cream colored.

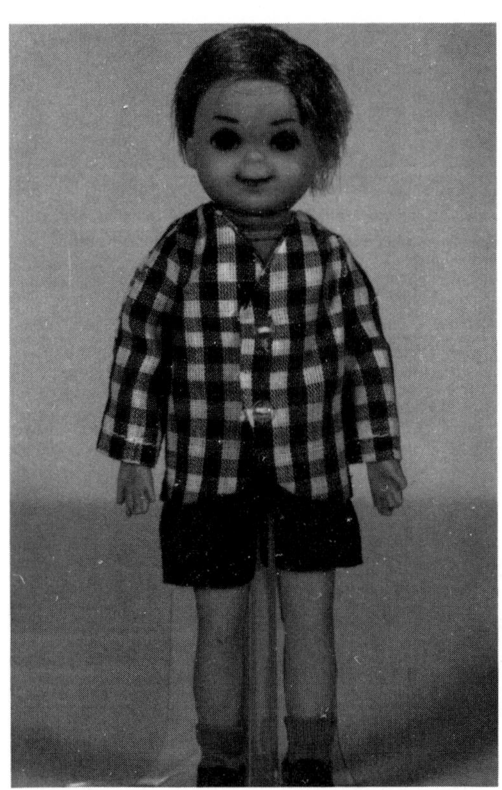

#8597 "Check Mate"—Todd outfit from Germany. Matches Mod Ken's clothes.

#7176 "Hochzeitsglocken"—Germany, 1975. (Slightly different version available in U.S.A. in 1976.)

#7177 "Presseball"—Germany, 1975.

#7178 "Grosse Mode"—Germany, 1975.

#7179 "Jeans Komb. Mode"—Germany, 1975.

#7180 "Ganz festlich"—Germany, 1975.

#7181 "Freizeitmode"—Germany, 1975.

#9419 "Der schonste Tag"—Germany, 1976. (Available in U.S.A. as a Department Store Special. Also worn by Beautiful Bride Barbie, another Dept. Store Special.)

#9420 "Segel—Regatta"—Germany, 1976.

#9421 "Abendkleid"—Germany, 1976. (Available in U.S.A. as a Dept. Store Special.)

#9422 "Cocktail-Party"—Germany, 1976. (Available in U.S.A. as a Dept. Store Special)

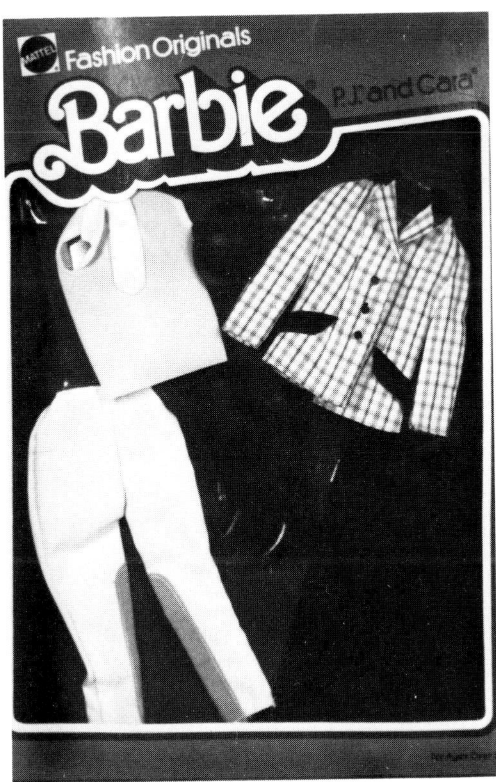

#9423 "Reit-Dress"—Germany, 1976.

#9424 "Chic in Hosen"—Germany, 1976. (Available in U.S.A. as a Dept. Store Special.)

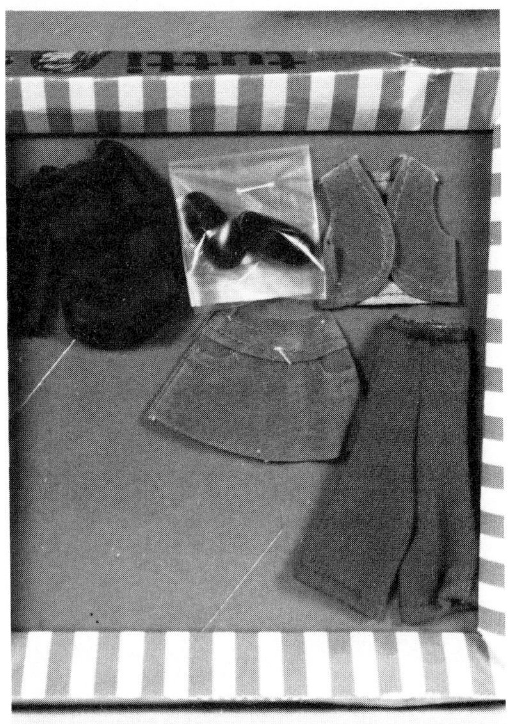

#8502 "Bequem und praktisch." Tutti outfit from Germany.

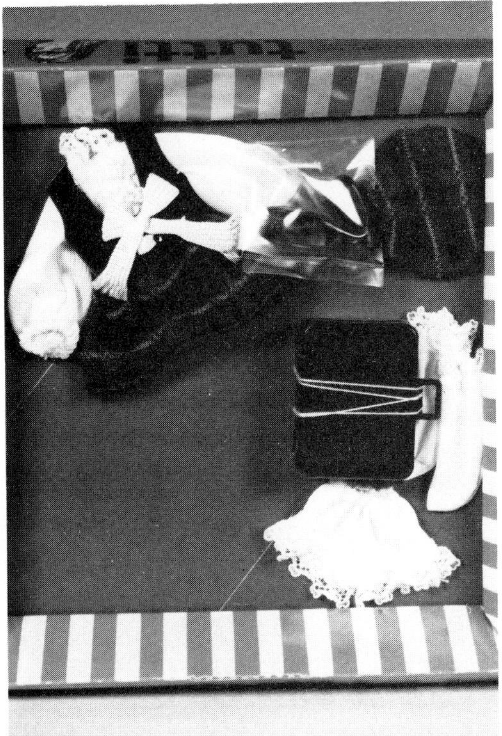

#8503 "Grosse Reise." Tutti outfit from Germany.

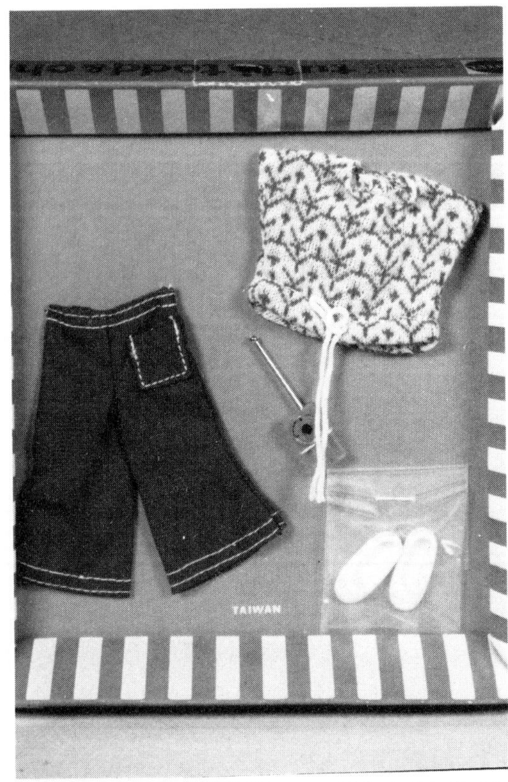

#8592 "Blue Jeans und Ringelpulli." Tutti, Todd and Chris outfit from Germany.

#8594 "Regentropfen." Tutti, Todd and Chris outfit from Germany.

Two versions of #8593 "Bloomin Blue." Tutti and Chris outfit from Germany.

Blond haired Chris wearing #7970 "Gartenfest." Tutti and Chris outfit from Germany.

Titian haired Chris wearing #7969 "Ausflug." Tutti and Chris outfit from Germany.

#7980 "Mein neuer Mantel." On left, red version. The other is maroon.

#7967 "Regenmantel" from Germany.

Three versions of #7982 "Hosenanzug." Tutti and Chris outfit from Germany.

Todd outfits from Germany. Top row—1974: #7984 "Jeans—Anzug," #7985 "Ausflug," #7986 "Hubsch angezogen," #7987 "Sport—Fan." Bottom row—1975: #7974 "Pulli und Hose," #7971 "Fur Kuhle Tage," #7972 "Zum Spielplatz," #7973 "Gut angezogen."

#7478 "Ferienzeit"—Germany, 1976.

#7479 "Zum Spielplatz"—Germany, 1976.

#7480 "Grosse Ferien"—Germany, 1976.

#7481 "Kinder-Geburtstag"—Germany, 1976.

#7482 "Grosse Ferien"—Germany, 1976.

#7483 "Neue Jeansmode"—Germany, 1976.

#7484 "Hubsch zur Schule"—Germany, 1976.

#7485 "Zum Spielplatz"—Germany, 1976.

IV. Dolls on Review

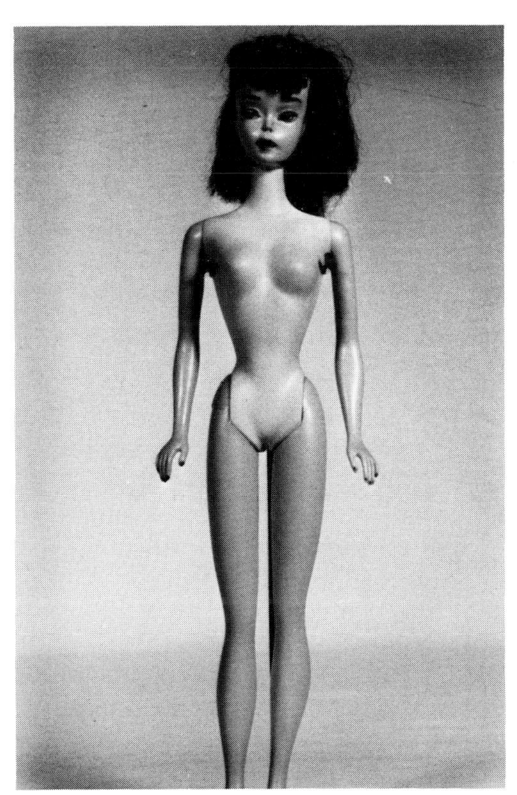

Transitional Barbie—White head and torso (No. 3) and tan limbs (No. 4).

Transitional Kens.
1. No. 2 with No. 1 legs.
2. No. 4 with No. 3 legs.

1960—#3 Barbie with brown eyeliner.

1960—#4 Barbie with blue eyeliner, bright red lips.

1964—Ponytail Barbie with Midge/Barbie patented markings.

1964—Bubble cut Barbie with Midge/Barbie patented markings.

#3580 Tutti. #3550 Tutti had the same hair style.

#3552 Tutti ("Walkin' My Dolly").

#3553 Tutti ("Night-Night, Sleep Tight").

#3554 Tutti ("Me and My Dog").

#3555 Tutti ("Melody in Pink").

#3556 Tutti ("Sundae Treat").

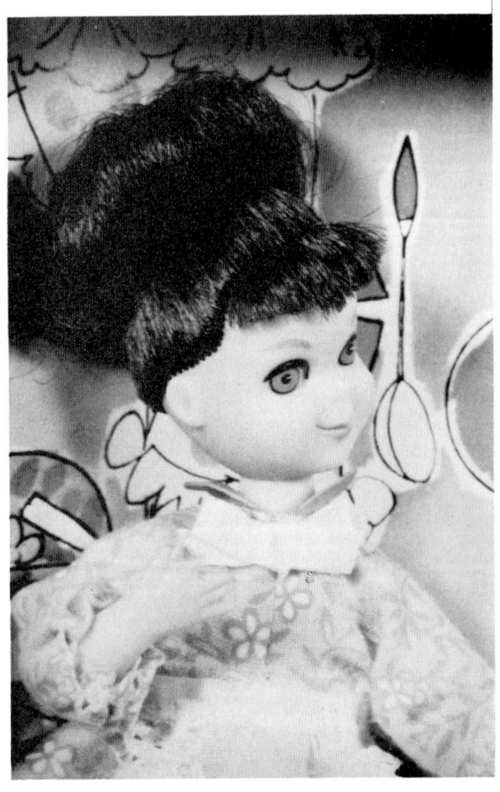

#3559 Tutti ("Cookin Goodies").

#3560 Tutti ("Swing-A-Ling").

#1133 Lori (Pretty Pairs).

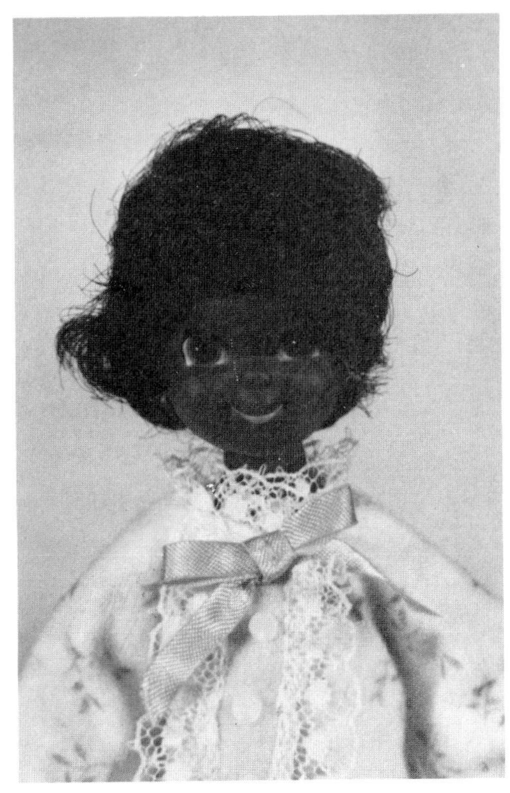

#1134 Nan (Pretty Pairs).

#1135 Angie (Pretty Pairs).

#7377 Carla.

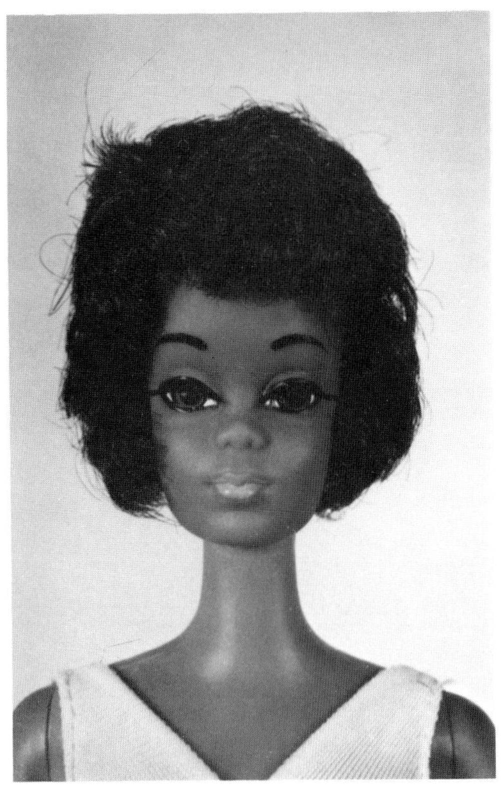

#1119 Twist Christie.

#1126 Talking Christie with bubble cut.

#7745 Malibu Christie.

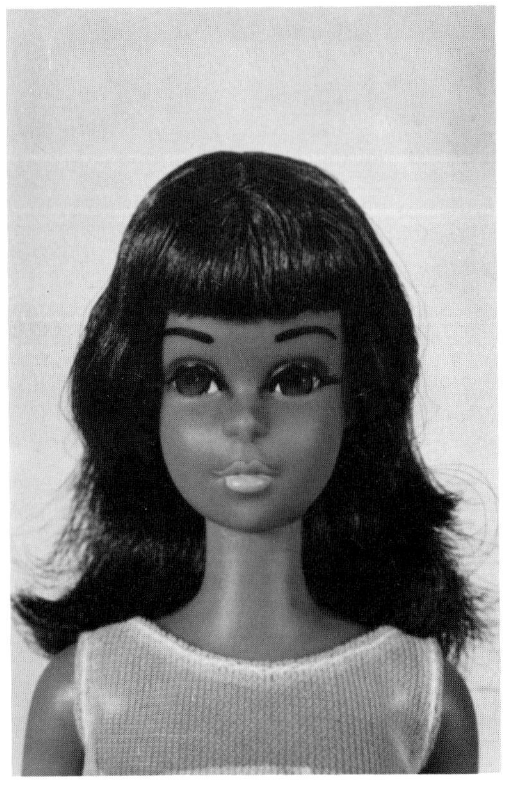

#1100 Colored Francie, the first black doll in the line.

Walk Lively Steffie (1183). Brown eyes.

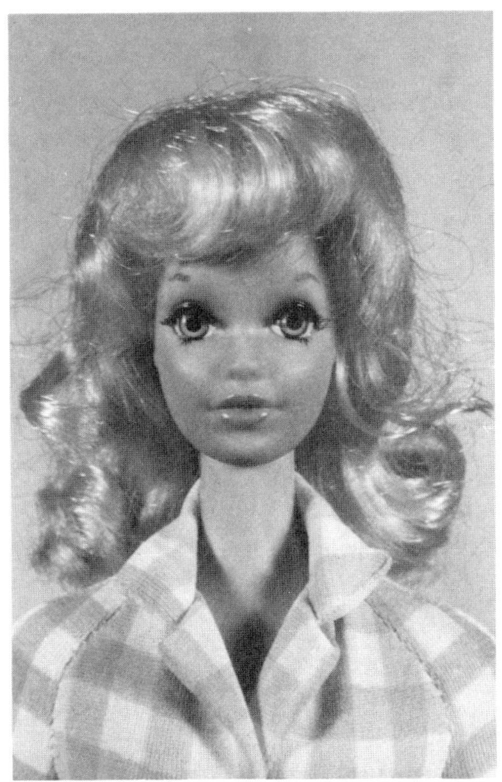

Talking Busy Steffie (1186). Blue eyes.

Busy Steffie (3312). Blue eyes.

Although Steffie was on the market only a short time (1972—1973), her head mold was one of the most popular ever made. It is still being used. The following dolls were made from it:

Miss America	#8587 Barbie
Malibu P.J.	Hawaiian Barbie
Free Moving P.J.	Gold Medal P.J.
Cara	Deluxe Quick Curl P.J.
Kelley	

Talking Brad (1114).

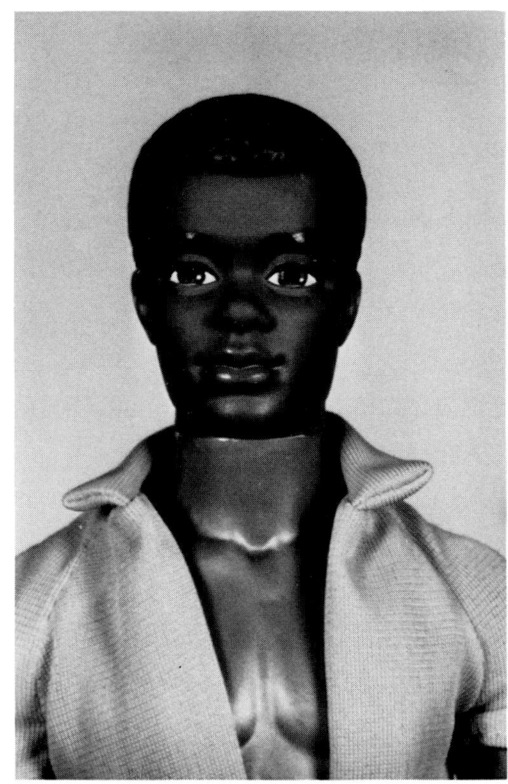

Bend leg Brad (1142).

The first model of a doll is made in the Orient with a hand carved head. If the company thinks the doll will sell, they make molds. As molds get older they wear away slightly. This makes successive head and body parts slightly larger in size. This can account for some minute differences in size or appearance. Worn molds are replaced as needed.

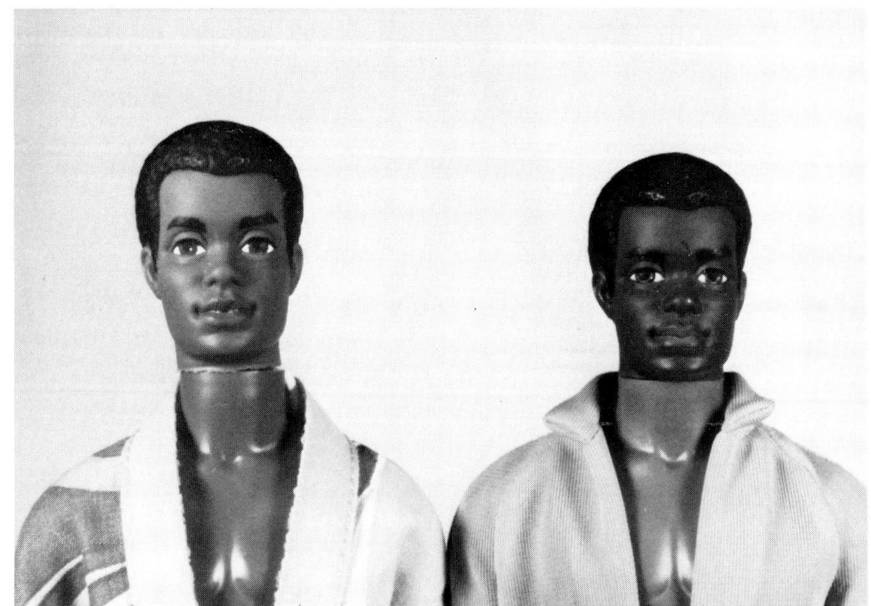

Talking Brad and bend leg Brad. Notice difference in head sizes.

First issue Twist Julia (1127).

First issue Talking Julia (1128).

#1199 Tiff. Made from the Fluff head mold.

Talking Truly Scrumptious (1107). Made from the Francie head mold.

1973—Brunette Quick Curl Miss America.

1975—Blonde Quick Curl Miss America.

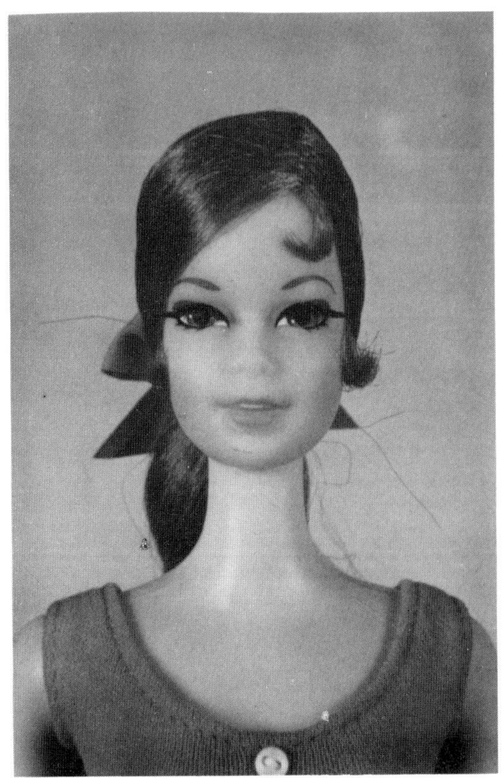

First issue Twist Stacey (1165).

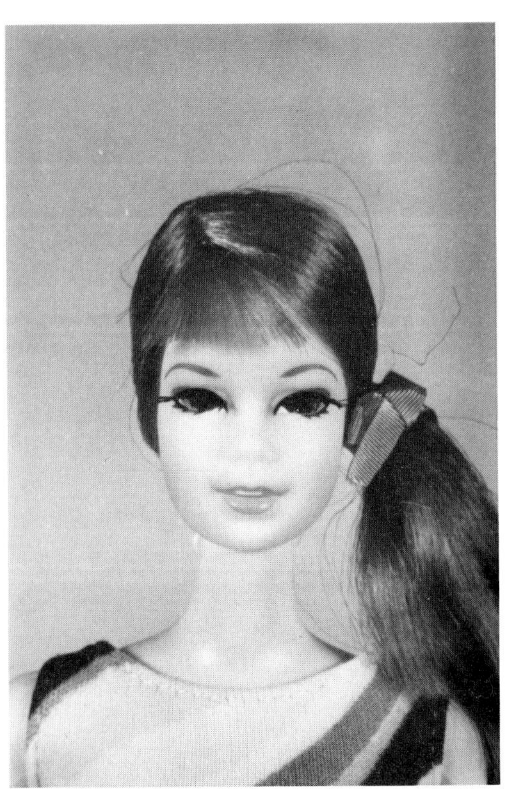

First issue Talking Stacey (1125).

#1113 Talking P.J. Made from the Midge head mold.

#1118 Twist P.J.

Malibu P.J. (1187) made from the Steffie head mold.

1975 Sears set.

#1129 Francie With Growin' Pretty Hair. First issue with original Barbie arms and hands. Second issue with "Mexico" Barbie arms and hands.

Francie With Growin' Pretty Hair (1129).

1970—Francie Hair Happenin's (1122). Thick hair. Dark pink lips.

1971—Francie Hair Happenin's (1122). Thinner hair. Pale lips.

1967—First Twist Francie (1170).

1971—First Malibu Francie (1068). Made from the Casey head mold.

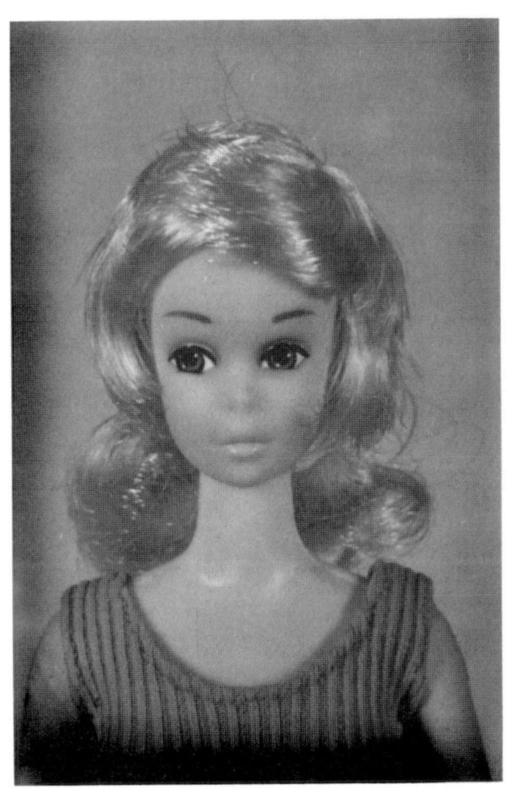

1972—#3313 Busy Francie.

1973—Quick Curl Francie (4222).

1972—#1179 Pose 'N Play Skipper with light titian hair.

A "Baggie" Pose 'N Play Skipper with blonde hair. Found in 1975.

A 1970 Twist Skipper (1105).

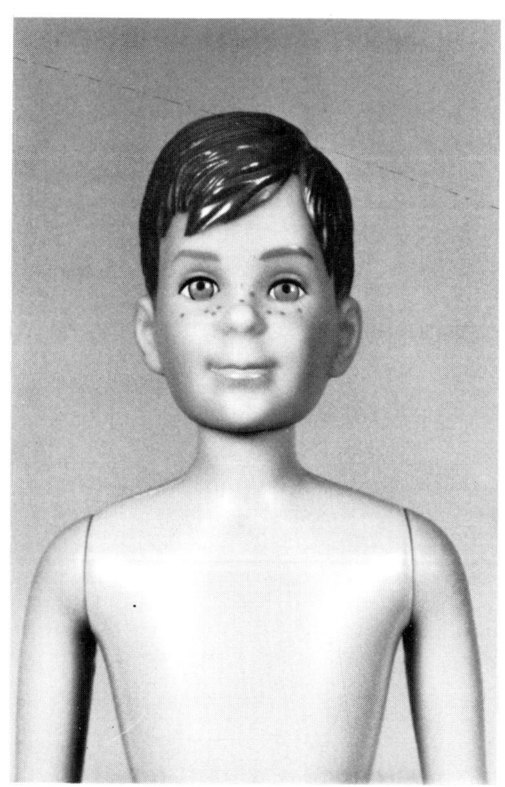

#1090 Ricky.

Malibu Skipper (1069).

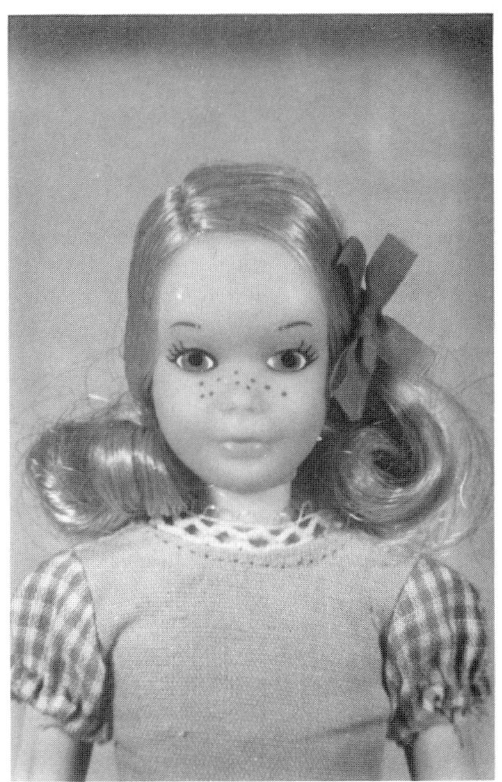

Quick Curl Skipper (4223).

First issue Growing Up Skipper (7259). Long pale blonde hair.

Second issue Growing Up Skipper. Shorter golden blonde hair.

Malibu Barbie (1067) made from the Stacey head mold.

#3311 Busy Barbie. Shown is the second issue made in Hong Kong (First issue made in U.S.A.).

Second issue Quick Curl Barbie (4220) with "silver" hair.

#9217 Deluxe Quick Curl Barbie.

1967—#1160 Twist Barbie. Rooted eyelashes.

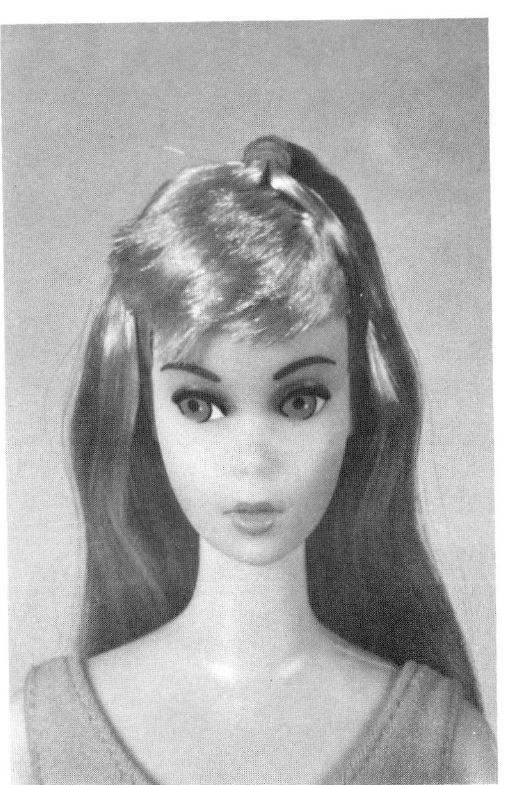

1967—#1190 standard Barbie. Painted eyelashes. Same hair style as #1160.

1968—First Spanish Talking Barbie (8348). Glossier hair than regular doll.

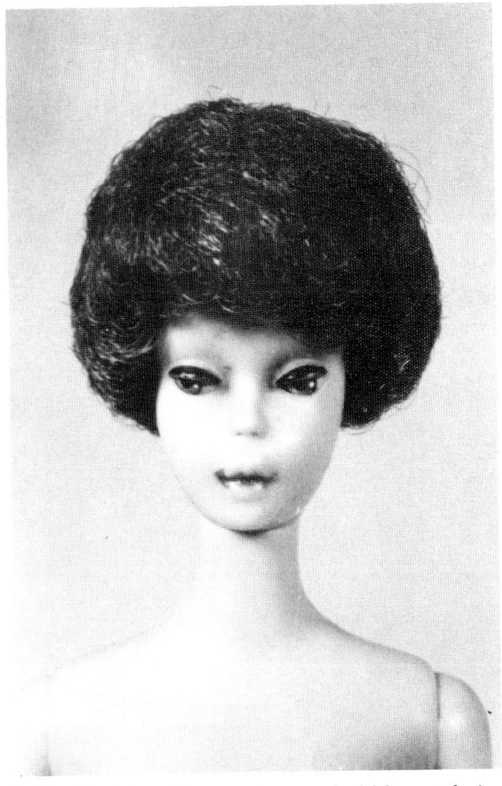

1961—Barbie with rare brown bubble cut hair. Original lips were bright red.

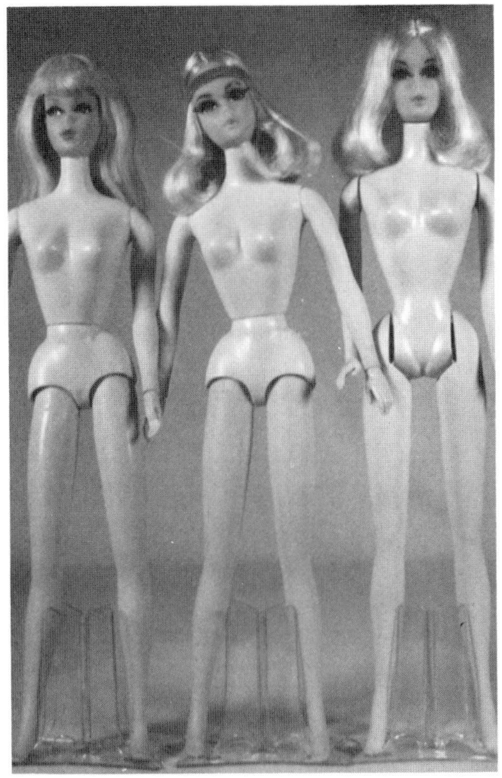

Living, Live Action and Walk Lively Barbies to show body construction.

Some collectors find Living, Live Action and Walk Lively Barbies confusing. Hopefully the following information will make identification of these dolls easier.

Living and Live Action bodies are alike, with one exception. Live Action has a different, looser waist construction.

Although the Live Action and Walk Lively heads are somewhat alike, there are some definite differences. Live Action has darker blonde hair and much longer eyelashes. The texture of the hair is also different. Walk Lively has softer, glossier hair.

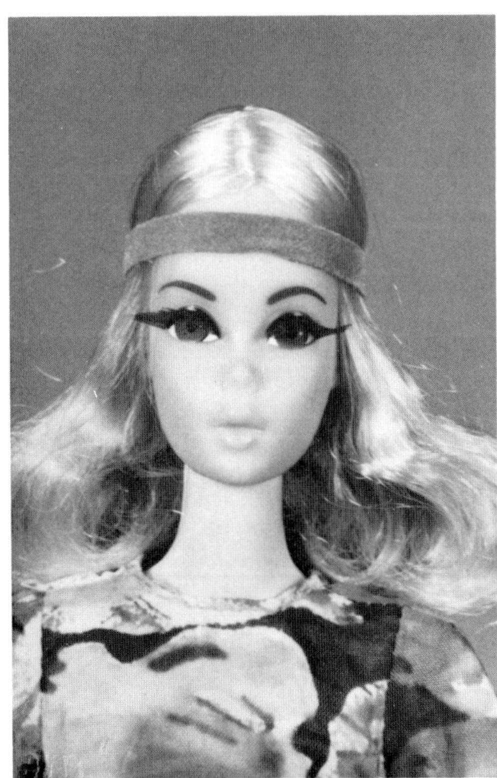

#1155 Live Action Barbie. Note the exaggerated eyelashes.

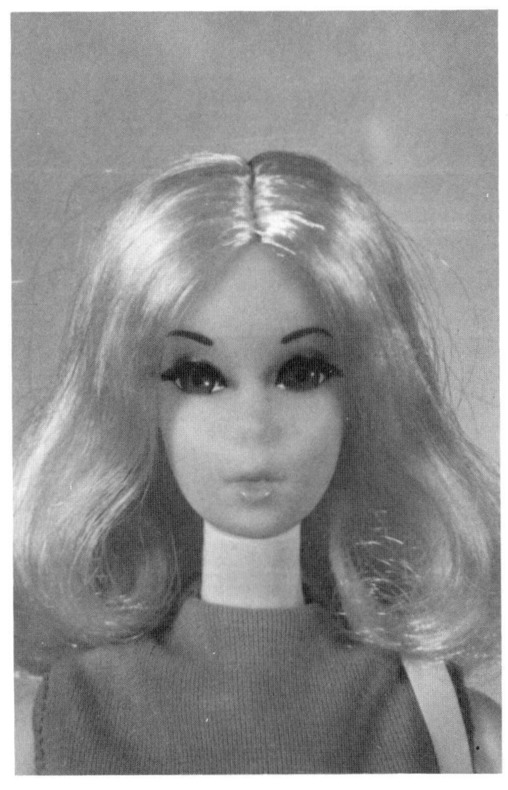

#1182 Walk Lively Barbie.

#4042 Hair Fair Barbie head.

#4043 Hair Fair Barbie head.

#4044 Hair Fair Barbie head. Centered eyes.

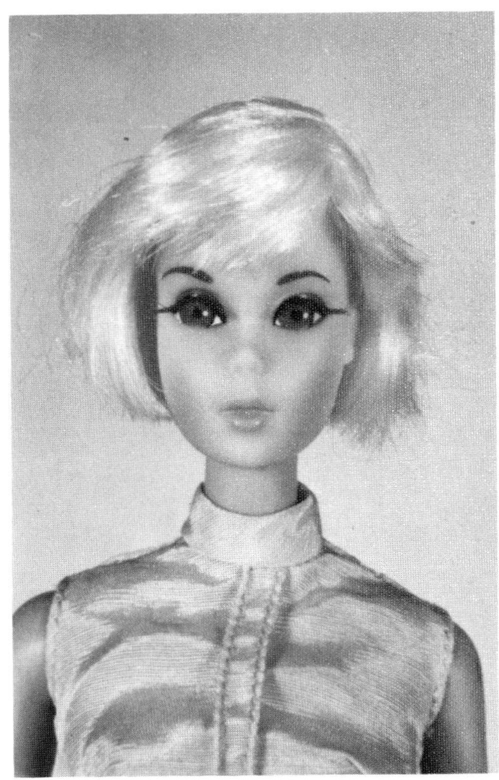
#4044 Hair Fair Barbie head in blonde.

1971 and 1972—Barbie With Growin' Pretty Hair. Different clothes, hair styles, coloring and eyelashes.

1971—#1144 Barbie With Growin' Pretty Hair.

1972—#1144 Barbie With Growin' Pretty Hair.

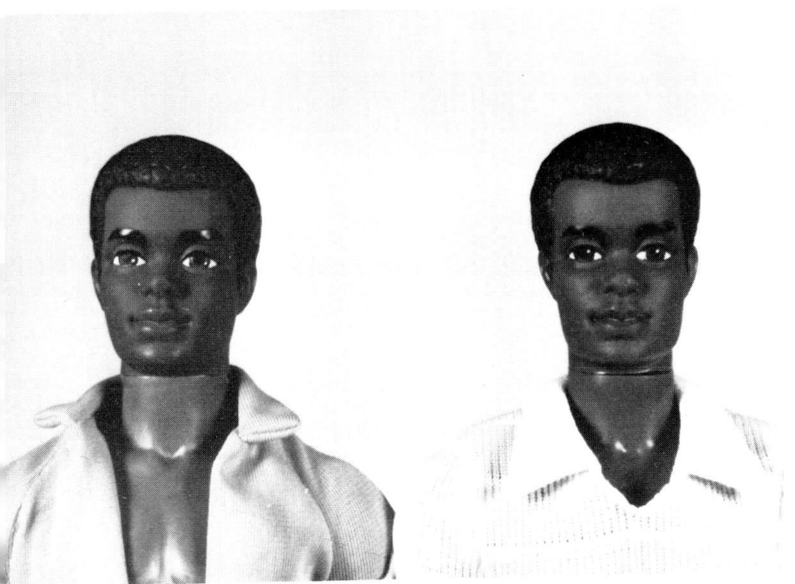

Bend leg Brad (1142) and Free Moving Curtis (7282). Made from same head mold.

#750 flocked hair Ken found dressed in "Tuxedo" in regular type of box. (Ashabraner collection)

Malibu Christies with four type hands—1973, "Mexico." 1974, Francie. 1975, "Korea." 1976, hard shiny "Mexico."

#7470 Hawaiian Barbies with three different hands—Original Barbie but not cut, Francie and hard shiny "Mexico."

#8128 Tutti. Pale blonde hair. Golden blonde hair.

#8129 Todd. Brown hair. Titian hair.

#8130 Chris. Titian hair. Brown hair.

#1080 Bendable leg Midge with odd hair-do.

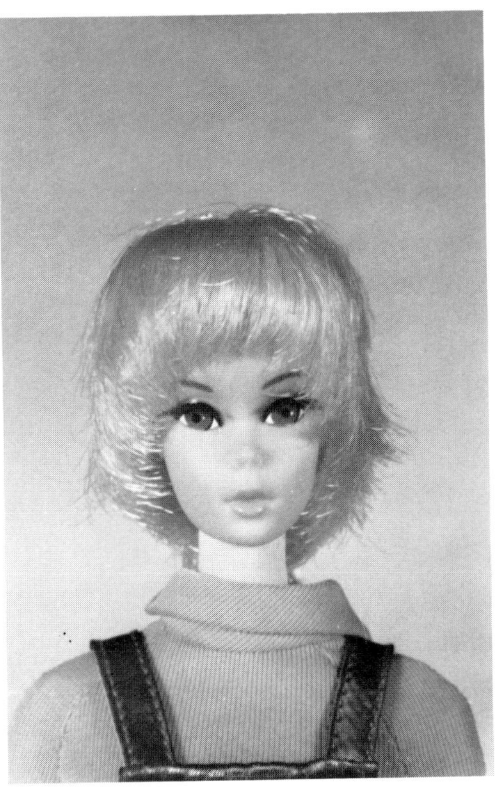

1972—Talking Busy Barbie (1195).

1973—Talking Busy Barbie (1195). Longer, thicker hair.

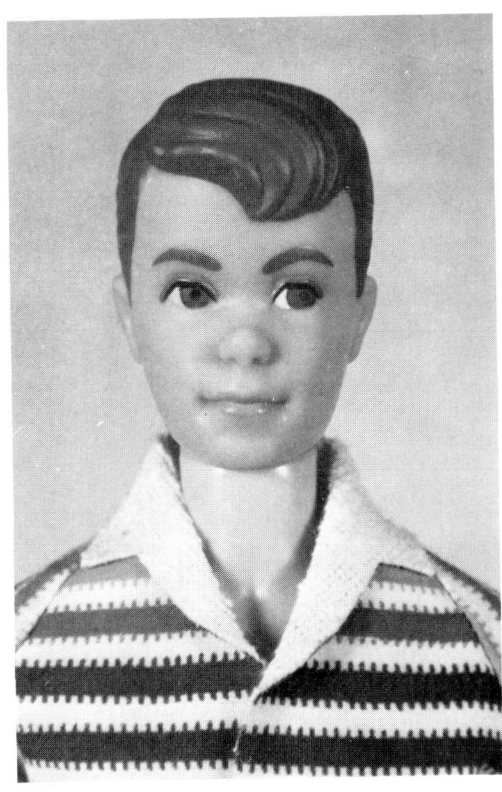

Straight leg Allan (1000).

Bendable leg Allan (1010).

This shows the second type of Quick Curl packaging.

This shows the third type of Quick Curl packaging.

This shows Sweet 16 without the free outfit.

Mod Hair Ken clothing and packaging varied considerably.

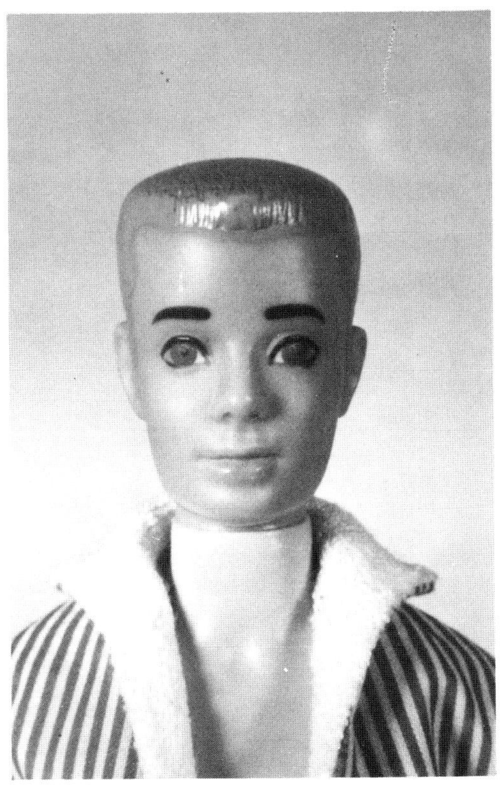
1963 Ken (750).

First Talking Ken (1111), 1969.

Bendable leg Ken (1124).

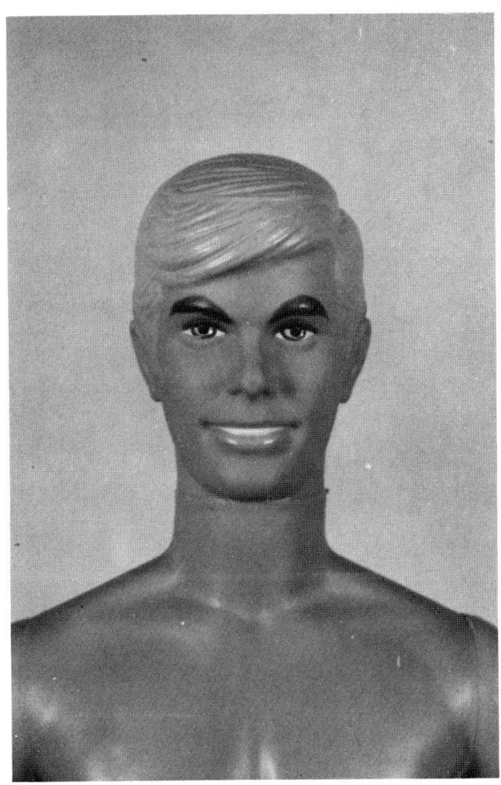
Malibu Ken (1088).

Live Action Ken (1159).

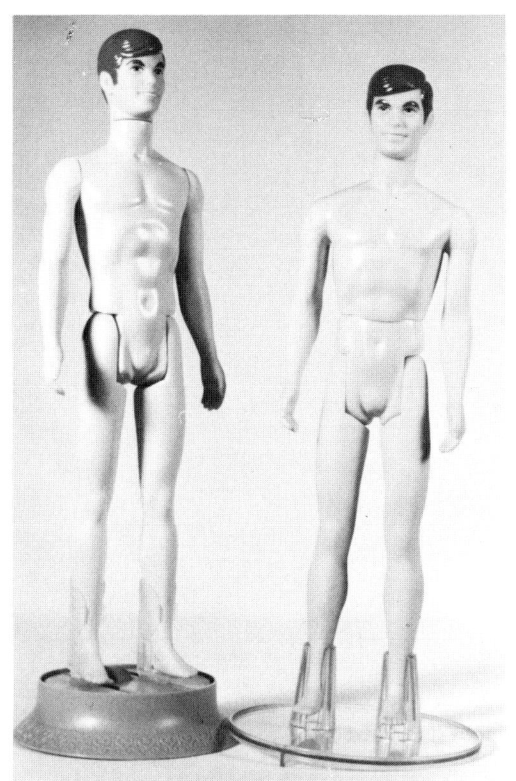

Walk Lively Ken and Live Action Ken. Notice different body construction.

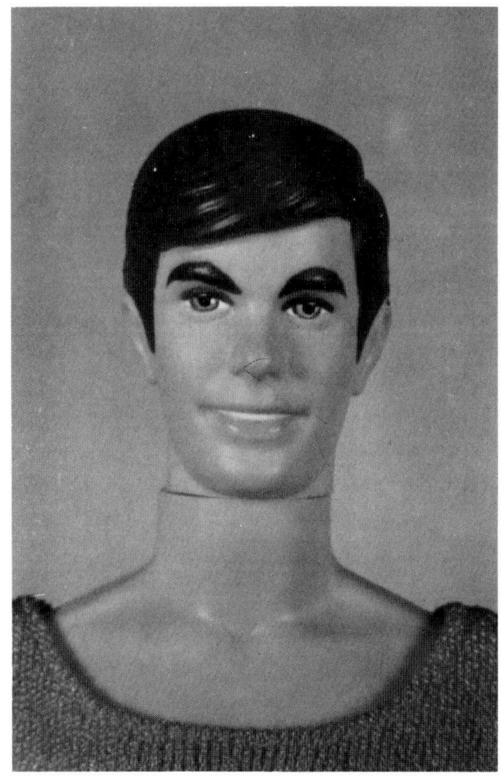

Busy Ken (3314), 1972.

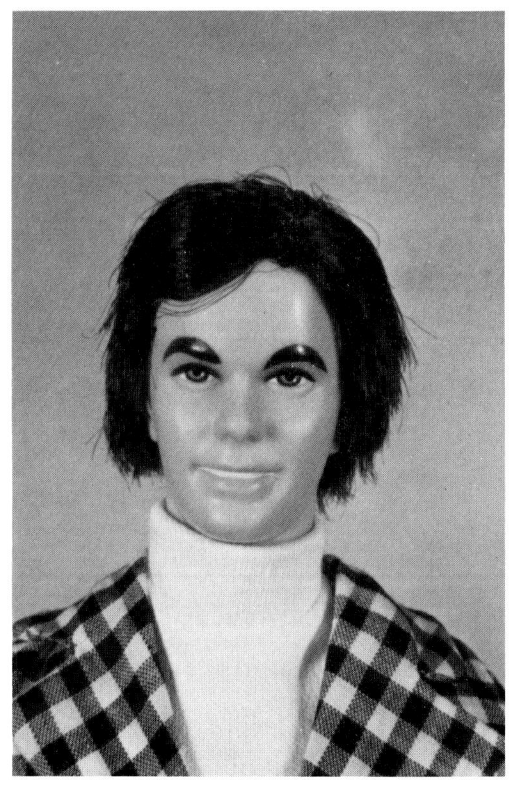

Mod Hair Ken (4224).

V. Chronological Lists for Quick Reference

The following lists will aid in identifying and dating dolls. They will also show the collector which dolls he already has in his collection and which he may need to complete his collection. Except for *markings* dates, all dates listed are the date the doll was on the market.

1. The Dolls, by the Year

1958

Barbie was tested and patented.

1959

850-Barbie (#1)—soft Saran ponytail with curly bangs in blonde or brunette, white irises, *pointed* eyebrows, bright red lips and nails, heavy partially solid torso marked: Barbie T.M./Pats. Pend./© MCMLVIII/by/Mattel/Inc., metal cylinders in legs with openings (holes) in feet to fit down on a pedestal stand with two prongs, wore a black and white striped one-piece swimsuit, high heeled shoes, sunglasses, and gold hoop earrings. Dolls are now ivory colored or whitish. Box shows ponytail dolls, © 1959, Barbie T.M., hair color.

850—Barbie (#2)—same as doll above except does not have the metal cylinders in feet and legs, because a different stand was used. Some dolls had new pearl earrings. Box similar to first one but now had Barbie "R" instead of "T.M."

1960

850—Barbie (#3)—new *blue* irises, new *curved* eyebrows, some dolls had brown eyeliner instead of the usual blue. The rest same as doll #2 above.

850—Barbie (#4)—now made of a new type of vinyl plastic that stayed tan colored—did not turn ivory or sickly white. Blue eyeliner only. Some gold hoops, some pearl earrings. The rest same as doll #3.

(Ken was patented in 1960.)

1961

850—Barbie (#5)—new type of body is now hard plastic and is hollow inside torso, but it has the same Pats. Pend. markings as the first four dolls. Some dolls had new firmer textured hair, some had the old soft hair and some had a combination of both. The box now gives hair style. Most dolls now have a new one-piece black wire stand. Sunglasses omitted. Pearl earrings. New arm tags. Several hair colors. Rest same as doll #4.

850—Barbie (#6)—new bubble cut hair-do in firm textured Saran. Rest same as doll #5.

750—Ken—blue eyes—flocked crew-cut hair (fuzzy headed) in blond, black and brown—hard plastic hollow torso marked: Ken ® /Pats. Pend./© MCMLX/by/Mattel/Inc.—wide stance—black wire stand—dressed in red trunks with a white stripe up the side and brown and red sandals—most had a yellow towel included—arm tags—first box pictures black and white striped trunks on front.

1962

850—Barbie—both *bubble cut* and *ponytail with curly bangs*—new red one-piece swimsuit—same bodies and markings as 1961—lip and nail colors varied from pale pink to bright red—new box shows both ponytail and bubble cut dolls and is undated. Rest same as preceding doll.

750—Ken—new head mold with painted crew-cut hair in blond or brunette—same hard hollow Pats. Pend. body and same stand—new red trunks and red and white striped jacket with stitched-in white terry cloth lining—same sandals—no towel—new box now pictures red trunks and striped jacket.

1963

860—Midge—freckles—blonde, brunette or titian hair—2 piece swimsuit—hard plastic body marked: Midge T.M./© 1962/Barbie® /© 1958/by/Mattel, Inc.—black wire stand.

870—Fashion Queen Barbie—molded head—blue band on head—3 wigs on wig stand (a platinum bubble on a bubble, brunette page boy and titian side part flip)—one-piece gold and white striped swimsuit and head scarf—black wire stand—on "Midge-Barbie" body—pearl earrings.

850—Barbie—both *bubble cut* and *ponytail* with curly bangs—same red swimsuit—new "Midge-Barbie" body—black wire stands—box same design as 1962 but is now dated © 1962.

750—Ken—same molded crew-cut blond or brunette hair—same clothes—new body ¼ inch shorter than other dolls, legs fit loosely where they join torso, slightly shorter and fatter arms, more pronounced kneecaps—new markings: Ken® /© 1960/by/Mattel, Inc./Hawthorne/Calif. U.S.A.

953—"Barbie Baby Sits"—baby with apron and other "sitter" items—also baby accessories—painted yellow hair—blue eyes—jointed at neck, shoulders and hips—no markings.

1964

0850—Barbie—new *no bangs*, side-swept ponytail called "Swirl" by collectors—same swimsuit, stand and box as 1963 dolls. First issue had the same markings as the 1963 dolls. Later issue had the word "Patented" added as a last line to markings.

1060—Miss Barbie—new—(Made in U.S.A.)—open and close eyes—first bendable knee doll—molded head with orange head band—3 wigs on stand (blonde, brunette, titian)—one-piece pink swimsuit and cap—gold colored wire stand—lawn swing and planter—torso had a different neck knob and new intaglio markings: ©1958/Mattel, Inc./U.S. Patented/U.S. Pat. Pend.—back of head marked: ©M.I.

0950—Skipper—Straight legs—long, straight hair in blonde, brunette or titian—"brass" band on hair—one-piece red and white swimsuit, red shoes—comb and brush—black wire stand—marked: Skipper/©1963/Mattel, Inc.

1000—Allan—molded red hair, brown eyes—straight legs—marked: ©1960/by/Mattel, Inc./Hawthorne/Calif. U.S.A.—blue trunks, multi-colored striped jacket with bonded on white terry cloth lining, brown and blue sandals—black wire stands.

0750—Ken—new markings same as Allan's: ©1960/by/Mattel, Inc./Hawthorne/Calif. U.S.A.—body now same height and similar to the 1962 doll—jacket now has bonded on lining—rest same.

0871—Barbie's Wig Wardrobe—1 molded Barbie head with blue band—3 wigs on stand.

0953—"Barbie Baby Sits"—baby has deeper yellow hair—rest same.

0850—Barbie—both *bubble cut* and *ponytail* with curly bangs—same swimsuit, stand and box as 1963. Same markings with the word "patented" added as last line.

0860—Midge—markings now have "patented" added as last line—rest fairly similar to 1963 dolls.

0870—Fashion Queen Barbie—markings now have "patented" added as last line—rest same as 1963.

1965

1040—Skooter—straight legs—freckles—brown eyes—twin ponytails hair-do in either blonde, brunette or titian—two-piece red and white swimsuit, red shoes—marked: ©1963/Mattel, Inc.—same size as Skipper—gold colored wire stand—comb and brush.

1090—Ricky—straight legs—molded red hair—blue eyes—same size as Skipper—blue trunks—multi-colored striped jacket and brown and red sandals—black wire stand—same markings as Skooter.

1070—Barbie—bendable legs—one-piece swimsuit, multi-colored striped top and solid teal bottom—most had a classic American Girl hair-do in four colors, but a rare few had a bubble cut or a side-part flip—gold colored wire stand—intaglio markings same as Miss Barbie.

1020—Ken—bendable legs—molded blond or brunette hair—red trunks, blue jacket with the letter "K", red and brown sandals—black wire stand—same markings as 1964 doll.

1010—Allan—bendable legs—same head—blue trunks, red jacket with letter "A", brown and blue sandals—black wire stand—same markings as 1964 doll.

1080—Midge—bendable legs—new casual hair-do in either blonde, titian or brownette—multi-colored striped one-piece swimsuit, shoes, blue hair band—gold colored wire stand—same intaglio markings as Miss Barbie.

1030—Skipper—bendable legs—same hair-do—one-piece blue and red swimsuit—gold colored wire stand—comb and brush—same markings as Skooter and Ricky.

4035—Color 'N Curl set—1 molded Barbie head with blue band and 1 molded Midge head with orange band—4 wigs—wig stand—dryer—color changer solution—other items for hair.

1009—Midge's Wig Wardrobe—1 molded Midge head with orange band—3 wigs and stand (titian Double Pony-Tail, blonde Swirl 'N Curl, brunette Topknot Pouf).

0953—"Barbie Baby Sits" set—the "sitter" items deleted—a layette added.

4038—Color 'N Curl set—1 molded Barbie head with blue band—2 wigs—wig stand—color changers—other hair items.

0950—Skipper—same as 1964 except has gold wire stand and different marking—now marking is same as Skooter and Ricky.

0850—Barbie—both *bubble cut* and *ponytail* in many colors—same clothes and markings as 1964.

0750—Ken—same as 1964.

0860—Midge—same as 1964.

1000—Allan—same as 1964.

0871—Barbie's Wig Wardrobe—same as 1964.

1060—Miss Barbie—during first part of year available from mail-order catalogues.

0870—Fashion Queen Barbie—during first part of year available from mail-order catalogues.

1966

1150—Color Magic Barbie—long straight hair without bangs—bendable legs—one-piece harlequin checked suit and head band—both hair and suit were color changeable—hair was either Midnight or Golden Blonde—color changer solution and other hair items—clear hard plastic "closet" box—first issue had same intaglio marking as Miss Barbie but with two additional lines in *raised* letters: Made In/Japan. Later issue had the same words as the first but now all letters were *raised*—a new mold was used. No posing stand.

1130—Francie—bend legs—brown eyes—brunette rooted eyelashes—blonde or brunette hair—greyish tan skin—one-piece swimsuit, patterned with an aqua background—shoes—eyelash brush—Skipper-size wire stand—marked: ©1965/Mattel, Inc./U.S. Patented/U.S. Pat. Pend./Made in Japan. (On some dolls the third line reads "U.S. Pat'd.")

1130—Francie—same as preceding doll except she has new

pink skin and new swimsuit—one-piece has solid green bottom with a patterned waist with white background.

1140—Francie—straight legs—pink skin—painted eyelashes—2 piece red and white suit—shoes—wire stand same size as Skipper's—marked: ©1965/Mattel, Inc./U.S. Patented/U.S. Pat. Pend./Made In Japan.

3550—Tutti—long straight hair and bangs in blonde or brunette—poseable—blue eyes—red and white checked gingham sunsuit and hat with white trim—shoes—comb and brush—no posing stand—marked: ©1965/Mattel, Inc./Japan.

3552—Tutti "Walkin My Dolly" playset—dress has solid red skirt and a red and white polka dot waist—wide brim straw hat—shoes and socks—panties—comb and brush—strawtone hair—same markings as #3550 Tutti—baby doll in a buggy.

3553—Tutti "Night-Night, Sleep Tight" playset—pink cambric nightgown, pink and white floral cambric robe, both lace trimmed—slippers—reddish hair—comb and brush—same markings—bed and spread.

3554—Tutti "Me and My Dog" playset—long brunette hair—red felt coat and bonnet with white plush trim, red leotards, shoes—comb and brush—same markings—has a big fuzzy white dog.

3555—Tutti "Melody in Pink" playset—blonde hair tied in two sections—pink nylon party dress with lace trim, panties, shoes and socks—same markings—piano and stool.

3556—Tutti & Todd "Sundae Treat" playset—twin sister and brother both have titian hair, matching outfits—Tutti wears red and white striped dress trimmed in blue and white, panties, shoes and socks—Todd's jacket matches Tutti's dress, blue shorts, white shirt, shoes and socks—2 swivel chairs, table, 2 parfait glasses, 2 spoons—comb and brush—same markings as preceding dolls.

No #—Tutti & Todd—same dolls, same clothes as Sundae Treat—sold in a small brown box—mail-order catalogues.

4039—Color 'N Curl set—1 molded Barbie head with blue band—4 wigs—wig stand—hair dryer—color changers—other hair accessories.

1120—Skooter—bendable legs—2 piece suit, navy shorts, red and white polka dot top—red shoes—comb and brush—same hair-do and markings as straight leg doll. The first issue had greyish tan skin. Later issue had pink skin.

1040—Skooter—straight legs—new pink skin—rest same as 1965.

1030—Skipper—bendable legs—new pink skin—rest same as 1965.

0950—Skipper—straight legs—new pink skin—rest same as 1965.

1090—Ricky—straight legs—new pink skin—rest same as 1965.

1070—Barbie—bendable legs—first part of year markings were the same intaglio as Miss Barbie but with two extra lines of raised letters: Made In/Japan. Later in year the *words* of the markings remained the same but now *all* letters are *raised*, a new mold was used. Rest same as 1965.

1080—Midge—bendable legs—markings same as Barbie's above.

4038—Color 'N Curl set—same as 1965.

0871—Barbie's Wig Wardrobe—same as 1965.

0850—Barbie—Bubble Cut—same as 1965.

0860—Midge—straight legs—same as 1965.

1020—Ken—bendable legs—same as 1965.

0750—Ken—straight legs—same as 1965.

1000—Allan—straight legs—available through mail-order catalogues first part of year.

1010—Allan—bendable legs—available through mail-order catalogues first part of year.

4035—Color 'N Curl set—available through mail-order catalogues first part of year.

0953—"Barbie Baby Sits" set—available through mail-order catalogues first part of year.

3580—Todd—This was listed in some Mattel publications but not in any booklets or catalogues. It is doubtful that this was ever on the market.

1967

1160—Barbie—Twist 'N Turn—new look, more youthful make-up—new twist waist—markings: ©1966/Mattel, Inc./U.S. Patented/U.S. Pat. Pend./Made In/Japan—rooted eyelashes—long hair, straight bangs, two strips of hair pulled together on top of head and tied with a ribbon—2 piece salmon bikini with a white net over-suit—new clear plastic posing stand that doubles as a seat.

1162—Barbie (Trade-in doll)—same as #1160 above—different box. Some dolls had "Made In Japan" on one line.

1180—Casey—Francie-size doll—twist waist—bend knees—rooted eyelashes—molded teeth—one-piece gold and white lame swimsuit—one earring in left ear—short hair parted on left in blonde or brunette—brunette turns reddish with time—same markings as #1160 Barbie above—clear plastic posing stand.

1100—Colored Francie—made from the Francie mold—bend knees—twist waist—rooted eyelashes—"rust" brown eyes—dark brown hair that turns reddish with time—clear plastic posing stand—bright colored print swimsuit with a sheer net waist—same markings as #1160 Barbie above.

1170—Francie — twist waist — bend knees — rooted eyelashes—long hair with *slight* flip in blonde or brunette—one-piece swimsuit, solid pink bottom, multi-colored striped waist—same markings as #1160 Barbie above—clear plastic posing stand.

1185—Twiggy (London's top teen model)—made from the Casey mold—short straight blonde hair—rooted eyelashes, heavy painted lower lashes—heavy eye make-up—blue eyes—clear plastic posing stand—yellow, blue and green striped cotton jersey mini dress, panties, yellow boots. Same markings as #1160 Barbie above.

1190—Barbie (standard doll)—straight legs, non-twist waist—pink skin—painted eyelashes—head and hair just like #1160 Barbie except for the painted eyelashes—2 piece pink swimsuit—Midge/Barbie markings with "patented."

4042—Barbie Hair Fair—1 Barbie head with short rooted hair in blonde or brunette—wig in 3 colors, wiglet, fall and braided crownette—earrings—barrettes.

3570—Chris—same size as Tutti—brown eyes—long blonde or brunette hair with 2 green bows and a green barrette—multi-colored dress, panties, shoes—same markings as Tutti: ©1965/Mattel, Inc./Japan.

3550—Tutti—new dress with solid rose waist, floral printed skirt—panties—shoes—comb and brush. Same markings.

3580—Tutti—new stock number but rest same as #3550 Tutti above.

3590—Todd—red, white and blue checked shorts and cap—red shoes, blue socks, blue short sleeve shirt. Same markings as Tutti: ©1965/Mattel, Inc./Japan.

3559—Tutti "Cookin Goodies" playset—brunette up-swept hair-do—yellow and orange dress, white apron, panties, shoes, socks—stove, pot, comb and brush. Same markings as #3550 Tutti.

3560—Tutti "Swing-A-Ling" playset—blonde hair—yellow, lace trimmed dress, panties, shoes, socks—swing, comb, brush—same markings as #3550 Tutti.

3556—Tutti & Todd playset "Sundae Treat"—same as 1966.

3552 through 3555—4 Tutti playsets—same as 1966.

1150—Color Magic Barbie—now in an open faced cardboard box—same markings as in later part of 1966—posing stand—rest same as 1966.

0750—Ken—straight legs—same as 1966.

1030—Skipper—bendable legs—new open faced box—new plastic posing stand—rest same as 1966.

0860—Midge—straight legs—same as 1966.

0950—Skipper—straight legs—same as 1966.

0850—Barbie—straight legs—bubble cut—same as 1966.

1040—Skooter—straight legs—same as 1966.

1090—Ricky—straight legs—same as 1966.

4039—Color 'N Curl set—same as 1966.

1130—Francie—bend legs—same as second issue of 1966.

1140—Francie—straight legs—same as 1966.

1120—Skooter—bend legs—during first part of year available through mail-order catalogues.

0871—Barbie's Wig Wardrobe—during first part of year available through mail-order catalogues.

1070—Barbie—bend legs—during first part of year available through mail-order catalogues.

1020—Ken—bend legs—during first part of year available through mail-order catalogues.

1080—Midge—bend legs—during first part of year available through mail-order catalogues.

No #—Tutti & Todd (brown box)—during first part of year available through mail-order catalogues.

1968

1115—Barbie—Talking—(Made in Mexico—neck rim marked Japan)—bend knees—rooted eyelashes—twist ponytail to side—new hand mold of undivided fingers—mentions Stacey—rose knit top over rose vinyl shorts—clear plastic box—rose colored box top and clear posing stand make a seat: Marked: ©1967/Mattel, Inc./U.S. & Foreign/Pats. Pend./Mexico.

8348—Barbie—Spanish Talking—has the original divided fingers—rest same as #1115 above. (Wrist tag says "Made in U.S.A.")

1125—Stacey—Talking (British accent) (Mexico)—molded teeth—bend knees—new undivided fingers—rooted eyelashes—diagonally striped pink and lavender two-piece swimsuit—long straight hair parted on right and tied in the back on left side in blonde or titian—same markings as #1115 Barbie. Same type box as Barbie's but with green top.

1126—Christie—Talking (black)—(Mexico—neck rim marked Japan)—bend knees—new undivided fingers—brown curly hair with slight part—rooted eyelashes—green knit top over rose vinyl shorts—clear plastic box with orange top to make seat. Same markings as #1115 Barbie: ©1967/Mattel, Inc./U.S. & Foreign/Pats. Pend./Mexico.

1105—Skipper—twist waist (Japan)—rooted eyelashes—bend knees—same hair as preceding doll but now has a blue elastic hair band—new one-piece swimsuit of solid blue and blue and pink striped cotton. Marked: ©1967 Mattel, Inc./U.S. Pat'd/U.S. Pats. Pend./Made in Japan—clear plastic posing stand. Late in year the doll was made in Taiwan and was so marked—same hair style and clothes.

1165—Stacey—twist waist (Japan)—molded teeth—bend knees—long straight hair tied in back with ribbon—rooted eyelashes—one-piece red swimsuit, white button trim, cut-out midriff—same markings as #1160 Barbie: ©1966/Mattel, Inc./U.S. Patented/U.S. Pat. Pend./Made in/Japan. Clear plastic posing stand.

3577—Buffy & Mrs. Beasley (Japan)—same size as Tutti—blonde hair, two long curls as double ponytail—dress, solid red skirt, red and white polka dot waist (same as #3552 dress), shoes, socks, panties—same markings as Tutti: © 1965/Mattel, Inc./Japan.

1160—Barbie (Japan)—new swimsuit, a pink with green knitted top over rose vinyl shorts, green belt—rest same as 1967.

3580—Tutti (Japan)—most had the same dress as 1967 but some had the skirt and waist material reversed—a print waist and solid rose skirt. Rest same as 1967.

1100—Colored Francie (Japan)—eyes a different, darker brown—hair of different material, does not turn reddish—rest same as 1967.

1185—Twiggy—twist (Japan)—same as 1967.

0950—Skipper—straight legs (Japan)—same as 1967.

1190—Barbie—straight legs (Japan)—same as 1967.

1170—Francie—twist (Japan)—same as 1967.

1140—Francie—straight legs (Japan)—same as 1967.

3570—Chris—(Japan)—same as 1967.

1180—Casey—twist (Japan)—brunette hair does not turn reddish—rest same as 1967.

4042—Hair Fair set (Japan)—same as 1967.

All 7 Tutti playsets (Japan)—same as 1967.

1030—Skipper—bend legs (Japan)—during first part of year available through mail-order catalogues.

1040—Skooter—straight legs (Japan)—during first part of year available thorugh mail-order catalogues.

0750—Ken—straight legs (Japan)—during first part of year available through mail-order catalogues.

3590—Todd (Japan)—available through one of the mail-order Christmas catalogues.

1969

1111—Ken—Talking (Mexico—neck rim Japan)—all new head and body—molded Edwardian hair style, brown—bend knees—blue eyes—red trunks, red jacket—marked: ©1968/ Mattel, Inc./U.S. & For. Pat'd/Other Pat's /Pending/Mexico

1128—Julia—Talking (Mexico—neck rim Japan)—made from the Christie head mold—undivided fingers—short straight dark brown hair—brown eyes—bend knees—rooted eyelashes—one-piece gold and silver jumpsuit—marked: © 1967/Mattel, Inc./U.S. & Foreign/Pats. Pend./Mexico.

1127—Julia—twist (Japan)—same hair and skin as #1128 above—hands made from the original Barbie mold but fingers not cut completely through—two-piece white nurse's uniform, cap, shoes, panties—marked: ©1966/Mattel, Inc./ U.S. Patented/U.S. Pat. Pend./Made in/Japan.

1107—Truly Scrumptious—Talking (Mexico)—made from the Francie head mold—undivided fingers—blonde hair brushed straight back—blue eyes—bend knees—rooted eyelashes—pink and rose satin and black net gown, fancy hat, shoes, panties—marked: ©1967/Mattel, Inc./U.S. & Foreign /Pats. Pend./Mexico.

1108—Truly Scrumptious—standard (Japan)—straight legs —original divided fingers—same head as #1107—pale pink net and satin gown, fancy hat, shoes, panties—marked: Midge T.M. / ©1962 / Barbie® / ©1958 / by / Mattel, Inc./ Patented.

1113—P.J.—Talking (Mexico—neck rim Japan)—made from Midge head mold—undivided fingers—blonde hair, short straight bangs, long hair in two sections held in place by beads—orangy mini dress with long sleeves, shoes, panties, sunglasses—brown eyes—bend knees—marked: ©1967/ Mattel, Inc./U.S. & Foreign/Pats. Pend./Mexico—plastic stand.

4043—Hair Fair (Japan)—Barbie head—new design—head has short rooted hair in blonde or brunette—wig, wiglet, twin ringlets, ponytail and hair accessories. The wig in this set was in blonde or brunette only.

1160—Barbie—twist (Japan)—new clothes and new hair-do—one-piece double diagonal stripes that cross—long flip hair in 4 colors—bend knees—same markings as 1968: © 1966/Mattel, Inc./U.S. Patented/U.S. Pat. Pend./Made in/ Japan.

1165—Stacey—twist (Japan)—new clothes and new hair-do—one-piece psychedelic print knit swimsuit—turned up curls in blonde or titian—same markings as 1968: ©1966/ Mattel, Inc./U.S. Patented/U.S. Pat. Pend./Made in/Japan. —plastic stand.

1105—Skipper—twist (Taiwan)—new hair style, new clothes —2 long curls—one-piece red and orange checked and solid orange swimsuit—marked: ©1967 Mattel, Inc./U.S. Pat'd./ U.S. Pats. Pend./Made in Taiwan.

1170—Francie—twist (Japan)—new clothes, new hair-do—short flip hair in blonde or brunette—ribbon hair band—one-piece swimsuit with solid pink top and pink and yellow striped bottom—plastic stand—same markings: ©1966/ Mattel, Inc./U.S. Patented/U.S. Pat. Pend./Made in/Japan.

3580—Tutti (Japan)—most are now in dress with printed yoke and solid rose skirt—same markings.

1115—Barbie—Talking (Mexico)—now in cardboard window box. During first part of year same style hair and clothes as 1968 and the neck rim still marked Japan—same markings as 1968. During later part of year the neck rim was marked Hong Kong—(Same side twist hair style as 1968)—same markings as 1968. The first of these wore the same outfit as 1968. Late in the year the side ponytail hair-do, neck rim Hong Kong doll wore a new outfit—the 2 piece reddish vinyl swimsuit with net jacket trimmed in the reddish vinyl. Undivided fingers.

8348—Barbie—Spanish Talking (Mexico)—new cardboard box—now has the undivided fingers—rest same as 1968.

1126—Christie—Talking (Mexico)—now in cardboard window box—neck rim still marked Japan—some hair turns red—rest same as 1968.

1125—Stacey—Talking (Mexico)—new cardboard box—rest same as 1968.

1190—Barbie—straight legs (Japan)—same as 1968.

1180—Casey (Japan)—same as 1968.

3577—Buffy & Mrs. Beasley (Japan)—same as 1968.

3590—Todd (Japan)—available through one of the mail-order Christmas catalogues.

3570—Chris (Japan)—available through mail-order catalogues during first part of year.

4042—Hair Fair set (Japan)—available through mail-order catalogues during first part of year.

8372—Spanish Talking Ken—This *may* have been on the market but this is unverified.

1116—Barbie—Living (Taiwan)—bend knees, elbows and ankels—swivel waist, neck, arms, hands and legs—medium long hair, straight bangs in blonde, brunette or titian—rooted eyelashes—gold and silver swimsuit with an orange net hooded jacket—plastic stand—marked: ©1968 Mattel, Inc./U.S. & For. Pat'd./Other Pats. Pend./Taiwan.

1585—Barbie—Living (Japan)—neck rim Japan. This doll was in a Sears exclusive gift set, "Action Accents." Marked: ©1968 Mattel, Inc./U.S. & For. Pat'd/Other Pats. Pend./Japan.

1117—Skipper—Living (Taiwan)—neck rim Taiwan—bend knees and elbows—swivel waist, neck, hands, arms and legs—blonde hair with curled ends divided into two sections and tied with rose colored ribbons—rooted eyelashes—one-piece blue, green and rose swimsuit—plastic stand—marked: ©1969 Mattel, Inc./Taiwan/U.S. & For. Patd./Other Pats. Pend./Patd. in Canada 1967.

1147—Skipper—Living (Taiwan)—Trade-in doll—same as #1117 above—different box.

1114—Brad—Talking (Mexico—later Hong Kong)—neck rim marked Hong Kong—dark brown skin—brown eyes—bend knees—bright Afro top and shorts—back of neck of both dolls marked: ©1969 Mattel, Inc. The early doll was marked: ©1968/Mattel, Inc./U.S. & For. Pat'd/Other Pat's/Pending/Mexico. The later doll was marked: ©1968 Mattel, Inc./U.S. & For. Pat'd/Other Pats./Pending/Hong Kong.

1142—Brad—bend knees (Hong Kong)—neck rim Hong Kong—hair and skin similar to talking Brad above—orange shirt over multi-colored cotton shorts—plastic stand—head marked: ©1969 Mattel, Inc.—hip marked: ©1968/Mattel, Inc./U.S. & For. Pat'd/Other Pats/Pending/Hong Kong.

1124—Ken—bend legs (Mexico, until fire)—hair and head similar to talking Ken of 1969—solid mustard shirt with multi-colored shorts—marked: ©1968/Mattel, Inc./U.S. & For. Pat'd./Other Pat's/Pending/Mexico. Plastic stand.

1122—Francie Hair Happenin's (Japan)—twist—bend knees—short blonde hair, bangs—four extra hair pieces—blue mini dress with white lace trim with attached panties, shoes—plastic stand—marked: ©1966/Mattel, Inc./U.S. Patented/U.S. Pat. Pend./Made in/Japan. Blue ribbon head band.

1129—Francie Growin' Pretty Hair (Japan)—no extra hairpieces—rooted eyelashes—blonde hair with a section that could be lengthened or shortened—bend knees—short pink satin and net party dress, shoes, panties—hard plastic stand—markings: ©1966/Mattel, Inc./U.S. Pat. Other/Pats. Pend./Pat. Canada/1967/Japan. This first issue had arms and hands made from the original Barbie mold with the divided fingers.

1119—Christie—twist (Japan)—brown curly hair parted on right side—light brown skin—rooted eyelashes—brown eyes—bend knees—one-piece multi-colored tricot swimsuit—plastic stand—marked: ©1966/Mattel, Inc./U.S. Patented/U.S. Pat. Pend./Made in/Japan. Hands made from the original Barbie mold but fingers are not cut completely through.

1118—P.J.—twist (Japan)—same head and hair as talking P.J.—divided fingers—rooted eyelashes—bend knees—one-piece rose colored swimsuit—plastic stand—marked: ©1966/Mattel, Inc./U.S. Patented/U.S. Pat. Pend./Made in/Japan.

0950—Skipper—re-issue of straight leg doll (Japan)—pinker skin—box pictures 1969 and 1970 clothes—markings same as 1965: ©1963/Mattel, Inc.—gold wire stand.

1132—Jamie—Walking (Japan)—made for Sears—made from Barbie head mold—divided fingers—rooted eyelashes—brown eyes—hair parted on right side in a medium length flip in blonde, brunette, titian—bend knees—plastic stand—has a plate on back that when pressed causes her arms and legs to move back and forth and her head to turn. Marked: ©1967Mattel, Inc./U.S. Patented/Pat'd Canada 1967/Other Pat's Pend./Japan.

1133—Lori 'N Rori—"Pretty Pairs"—Tutti size—blonde doll, brown teddy bear—blue and white dress trimmed in deep pink, shoes, socks—marked: ©1965/Mattel, Inc./Japan.

1134—Nan 'N Fran—"Pretty Pairs"—same size and markings as #1133 above—black doll holding small black doll—white with rose and green flowers flannel nightgown and pink mobcap—small doll in pink sleepers.

1135—Angie 'N Tangie—"Pretty Pairs"—same size and markings as #1133 above—long waisted red dress, white trim—small doll in matching dress—brunette doll, small doll with yellow string hair.

1115—Barbie—Talking (Mexico—Hong Kong)—new hair-do, curls on nape of neck—two piece red vinyl swimsuit with net jacket introduced in 1969—some dolls have the old voice box, some have new words mentioning P.J.—early dolls had the same markings as 1969—late in year dolls were marked: ©1967/Mattel, Inc./U.S. & Foreign/Pats. Pend./Hong Kong.

1115—Barbie—Talking *(Stacey head mold)* (Mexico, before fire)—new voice box mentions P.J.—Neck rim Hong Kong—same outfit as above—Mexico markings—undivided fingers—plastic stand—rooted eyelashes.

8348—Barbie—Spanish Talking (Mexico, before fire)—same clothes, same hair, same markings as regular doll.

8348—Barbie—Spanish Talking *(Stacey head mold)* (Hong Kong)—same clothes, hair-do and markings as regular doll.

1160—Barbie—twist (Japan)—new clothes, one-piece deep rose and white patterned swimsuit—same hair style as 1969—same markings.

1190—Barbie—straight legs (Japan)—new clothes, new box—one-piece rose and green swimsuit—plastic stand—same hair-do as 1969 and same markings: Midge T.M./ ©1962/Barbie® /1958/by/Mattel, Inc./Patented.

1111—Ken—Talking (Mexico, until fire)—new clothes—orange red shorts, blue jacket with orange red trim—plastic stand.

8372—Ken—Spanish Talking (Mexico, until fire)—same as regular Ken above.

1125—Stacey—Talking—first part of year same as 1969. Late in year new clothes, a blue and silver one-piece swimsuit—paler eyes, thinner bangs—now Hong Kong—marked: ©1967/Mattel, Inc./U.S. & Foreign/Pat. Pend/Hong Kong.

1165—Stacey—twist (Japan)—first part of year same as 1969. Late in year new clothes—one-piece rose and blue floral swimsuit—markings: ©1966/Mattel, Inc./U.S. Patented/U.S. Pat. Pend./Made in/Japan.

1126—Christie—Talking (Mexico, until fire)—same skin and hair as 1969—new clothes, a brightly colored Afro top over shorts (matches Brad's)—same markings as 1969.

1127—Julia—twist—new one-piece white uniform and cap. Rest same.

1105—Skipper—twist (Taiwan)—new clothes—orange vinyl jacket over shorts and "bra"—same hair and markings as 1969.

1170—Francie—twist (Japan)—new clothes—yellow, green and pink flowered side-closing top over rose shorts—same hair style as 1969—same markings.

4043—Hair Fair set (Japan)—same as 1969.

1180—Casey—twist (Japan)—same as 1969.

3580—Tutti (Japan)—same as 1969.

1128—Julia—Talking (Mexico, until fire)—same as 1969.

1113—P.J.—Talking (Mexico, until fire)—same as 1969.

3577—Buffy & Mrs. Beasley (Japan)—same as 1969.

3590—Todd (Japan)—still available through a mail-order catalogue during first part of year.

1971

1174—Barbie Hair Happenin's (Japan)—Department Store Exclusive Limited Edition—centered eyes—rooted eyelashes—bend knees—twist waist—original hand mold with divided fingers—short, straight rooted titian hair parted just left of center—no bangs—3 titian hair pieces, hair accessories—dress has cherry red skirt, white blouse and white attached panties, all in tricot—black shoes and a black waist cincher belt—marked: ©1966/Mattel, Inc./U.S. Patented/U.S. Pat. Pend./Made in/Japan.

1152—Barbie—Live Action on Stage (Taiwan)—long blonde hair almost straight, parted near center—rooted eyelashes—bend knees, ankles and elbows—swivel waist, neck, arms and legs (construction similar to Living Barbie except has different waist construction—waist is made to be looser)—motorized stage—bright purplish "tied-dyed" pants and long sleeve blouse with brown suede midriff, brown suede streamers at waist and on bracelets for each arm, brown suede head band—brown shoes—neck rim Taiwan—marked: ©1968 Mattel, Inc./U.S. & Foreign Patented/Patented in Canada 1967/Other Patents Pending/Taiwan.

1155—Barbie—Live Action (Taiwan)—neck rim Taiwan—clothes same as above doll—markings same as above—doll has long blonde hair in a loose page boy—extra long rooted eyelashes—touch 'n go posing stand.

1172—Ken—Live Action on Stage (Taiwan)—bend knees—brown hair—special loosely jointed waist—gold satin pants, brown shoes, multi-colored tricot shirt with long sleeves, a brown suede fringed vest—on a motorized stage—marked: ©1968/Mattel, Inc./Taiwan/U.S. & For. Pat'd./Patented In/Canada 1967/Other Pats./Pending. Head marked: ©1968 Mattel, Inc.. Neck rim Hong Kong.

1159—Ken—Live Action (Taiwan)—doll and clothes same as above but no stage. A plastic touch 'n go posing stand included instead.

1153—P.J.—Live Action on Stage (Taiwan)—one-piece orange and gold suit (gold "boots" stitched on to orange tights and the tights are stitched on to a long sleeved top), and a long fringed purple suede vest—rooted eyelashes—swivel waist, hands, neck, arms and legs—bend knees, ankles and elbows. Marked: ©1968 Mattel, Inc./U.S. & Foreign Patented/Patented in Canada 1967/Other Patents Pending/Taiwan. Has long blonde hair with two small sections of braided hair on each side. Gold colored beads encircle braids. Her face resembles the talking and the twist P.J.'s—Midge head mold—motorized stage included.

1156—P.J. Live Action (Taiwan)—doll and clothes same as above except the motorized stage has been replaced by a touch 'n go stand.

1175—Christie—Live Action (Taiwan)—Midge head mold used—long, straight black hair—rooted eyelashes—rust colored eyes—same body construction as Live Action Barbie and P.J.—same markings: ©1968 Mattel, Inc./U.S. & Foreign Patented/Patented in Canada 1967/Other Patents Pending/Taiwan. Dressed in a two-piece purple and orange figured tricot outfit—pants with a wide purple suede band at the waist, purple suede fringe at waist and edge of sleeves—top has divided sleeves that reach to the ankles—purple shoes—orange head band.

1067—Barbie--Malibu (Japan)—made from the Stacey head mold—suntan skin—long, straight blonde hair parted near the center—one-piece blue tricot swimsuit—sunglasses—yellow towel—in a new bubble type package—bend knees—twist waist—painted eyelashes—divided fingers—marked: ©1966/Mattel, Inc./U.S. Patented/U.S. Pat. Pend./Made in/Japan. No posing stand.

1068—Francie—Malibu (Japan)—made from the Casey head mold—blue eyes—painted eyelashes—long, straight blonde hair parted on the right—bend knees—twist waist—suntan skin—one-piece swimsuit with rose waist and red bottom—orange towel—sunglasses—marked: ©1966/Mattel, Inc./U.S. Patented/U.S. Pat. Pend./Made in/Japan. No posing stand.

1069—Skipper—Malibu (Japan)—suntan skin—long, straight blonde hair, parted in center—twist waist—bend legs—painted eyelashes—dark blue towel—sunglasses. Marked: © 1967 Mattel, Inc./U.S. Pat'd./U.S. Pats. Pend./Made in Japan. No posing stand.

1088—Ken—Malibu (Hong Kong)—suntan skin—yellow hair—bend knees—red trunks—medium blue towel—marked: © 1968/Mattel, Inc./U.S. & For. Pat'd./Other Pat's/Pending/Hong Kong. No posing stand.

4044—Hair Fair head (Japan)—new centered eyes--rest similar to #4043 set.

1143—Fluff—Living (Taiwan)—neck rim Taiwan—bend knees and elbows—swivel waist, neck, arms, hands and legs—brown eyes—rooted lashes—blonde hair in double ponytails—curly bangs—2 spit curls over ears, orange bows in hair—one-piece swimsuit with green, yellow and orange striped top and a solid orange bottom with short attached overskirt—marked: ©1969 Mattel, Inc./Taiwan/U.S. & For. Pat'd/Other Pats. Pend./patd. In Canada 1967. Yellow skateboard and a round plastic posing stand included.

1144—Barbie—Growin' Pretty Hair (Taiwan)—neck rim Taiwan—bend knees—undivided fingers—long rooted eyelashes—blonde upswept hair, small hanging curl at each ear, loose curl around face (this is parted on the right side) has the piece of hair that "grows"—short pink satin party dress with petal-skirt, stitched in panties, gold belt, pink shoes—2 extra hair pieces (four long curls attached to a barrette and a double loop braid attached to a barrette)—hair accessories—styling booklet—marked: ©1967 Mattel, Inc./U.S. Patented/Other Patents Pending/Patented in Canada 1967/Taiwan.

1190—Barbie (Japan)—new centered eyes—same clothes and markings as 1970. (This doll, plus an outfit, was available through a Chef Boy-ar-dee promotional offer.)

1074—Francie—Growin' Pretty Hair (Japan)—2 extra hair pieces included. Had arms and hands made from the talking Barbie mold, undivided fingers. Rest same as #1129 of 1970.

1129—Francie—Growin' Pretty Hair (Japan)—no extra hair pieces—now has the Barbie arms and hands with the undivided fingers—rest same as 1970—still avilable in 1971.

1116—Barbie—Living (Taiwan)—neck rim Taiwan—new centered eyes—new box—new clothes—pink, red and raspberry dotted tricot, a long side closing skirt over a one-piece swimsuit—new round plastic posing stand—rest same as 1970.

1585—Barbie—Living (Japan)—neck rim Japan. This doll was in a 1970 Sears' exclusive Gift Set still on the market in 1971.

1115—Barbie—Talking (Hong Kong)—neck rim Hong Kong—new centered eyes—new clothes, a two-piece white swimsuit with a long gold colored net jacket—same hair style as 1970, curls on nape of neck—many dolls have a hard plastic head. Marked: ©1967/Mattel, Inc./U.S. & Foreigh/Pats. Pend./Hong Kong. Undivided fingers—rooted eyelashes.

8348—Barbie—Spanish Talking—same as 1970.

1160—Barbie—twist (Japan)—new centered eyes—new clothes, a one-piece striped suit in red, yellow, purple—same hair-do as 1970—same markings.

1114—Brad—Talking (Hong Kong)—slightly darker skin—same suit as 1970—same markings as late 1970.

1117—Skipper—Living (Taiwan)—neck rim Taiwan—new clothes, a two-piece yellow swimsuit—same hair style—same body construction—same rooted eyelashes—now has a reddish skateboard and a new round plastic posing stand—same markings.

1170—Francie—twist (Japan)—new hair-do and new clothes—blonde or brunette hair brushed straight back with long flip ends—orange band on hair—orange pleated tricot mini dress with white trim, orange panties, white shoes—plastic stand—rest same as 1970.

1128—Julia—Talking (Hong Kong)—new hair-do and new skin—black modified Afro hair and darker skin—same clothes—marked: ©1967/Mattel, Inc./U.S. & Foreign/Pats. Pend./Hong Kong.

1127—Julia—twist ((Japan)—same as 1970.

1111—Ken—Talking (Hong Kong)—neck rim Japan—same clothes as 1970. Now marked: © 1968/Mattel, Inc./U.S. & For. Pat'd./Other Pat's/Pending/Hong Kong.

1124—Ken—bend legs—These are marked "Mexico." They must have been made before the fire but not sold until 1971.

1132—Jamie—Walking (Japan)—Sears'—same as 1970.

1113—P.J.—Talking (Hong Kong)—about the same as 1970, except now marked: ©1967/Mattel, Inc./U.S. & Foreign/Pats. Pend./Hong Kong.

1118—P.J.—twist (Japan)—same as 1970.

1126—Christie—Talking (Hong Kong)-new black modified Afro hair-do—darker skin—same clothes as 1970—now marked: ©1967/Mattel, Inc./U.S. & Foreign/Pats. Pend./Hong Kong.

1119—Christie—twist (Japan)—same as 1970.

1142—Brad—bend knees (Hong Kong)—slightly darker skin—rest same as 1970.

1105—Skipper—twist (Taiwan)—same as 1970.

1122—Francie Hair Happenin's (Japan)—paler lips than 1970. Rest about the same as 1970.

3580—Tutti (Japan)—same as 1970.

00950—Skipper (Japan)—same as 1970.

1125—Stacey—Talking (Hong Kong)—available until Fall through mail-order catalogues.

1165—Stacey—twist (Japan)—available until Fall through mail-order catalogues.

1972

1179—Skipper—Pose 'N Play and her Swing-A-Rounder Gym (Taiwan)—body construction similar to Living doll with one exception, the Pose 'N Play has "swing free" arms—painted eyelashes—short hair tied in two sections with blue bows, bangs—most dolls had light titian hair. (1975 a few were found with blonde hair.) Blue and white check with solid blue swimsuit—marked: ©1969 Mattel, Inc./Taiwan/U.S. & For. Pat'd/Other Pats. Pend./Pat'd. in Canada 1967.

1199—Tiff—Pose 'N Play—same construction and markings as Skipper above—long, straight titian hair—painted eyelashes—brown eyes—made from the Fluff head mold—blue jeans, white sleeveless shirt, white tennis shoes—red orange skateboard.

1182—Barbie—Walk Lively (Taiwan)—neck rim Taiwan—special "walking" body and turning head construction—undivided fingers—rooted eyelashes—head and hair similar to Live Action but hair is paler blonde and eyelashes are shorter—red tricot pants and top with double belt, yellow shoulder bag, red shoes—tan "walking" stand—marked: ©1967 Mattel, Inc./U.S. Pat. Pend./Taiwan.

1183—Steffie—Walk Lively (Taiwan)—same markings and construction as Barbie above—reddish print tricot jumpsuit, red shoes and scarf—tan "walking" stand—long flip brunette hair—brown eyes (the only Steffie with brown eyes)—undivided fingers—rooted eyelashes.

1184—Ken—Walk Lively (Taiwan)—same walking construction and stand as Barbie above—blue short sleeve shirt, tan and blue plaid pants, brown shoes—marked: ©1968 Mattel, Inc./U.S. Pat. Pend./Taiwan. Back of head marked: ©1968 Mattel, Inc.

1187—P.J.—Malibu—(Japan)—made from the Steffie head mold—blue eyes—divided fingers—painted eyelashes—blonde hair parted slightly to the left (no bangs) and divided into two sections decorated with multi-colored beads—one-piece lavender swimsuit, sunglasses, green towel. Marked: ©1966/Mattel, Inc./U.S. Patented/Other Pats. Pend./Made in/Japan. No posing stand.

3200—Miss America—Walk Lively (Taiwan)—made from the Steffie head mold—same walking construction as Barbie—white "walking" stand—rooted eyelashes—undivided fingers—brunette hair in end curls, medium length—blue eyes—evening dress has gathered white nylon over white taffeta skirt with a gold lame top, "silver" lacy crown, red cape with "ermine" trim, "Miss America" ribbon sash, white shoes, red rose bouquet—marked: ©1967 Mattel, Inc./U.S. Pat. Pend./Taiwan.

3194-9991—Miss America (Taiwan)—same as #3200 Miss America, minus the "walking" stand. This was a special promotional offer from the Kellogg Company. Laurie Lea Schaefer aided in the promotion.

3210—Barbie (Japan)—Ward's re-issue doll—brunette ponytail with curly bangs—curved eyebrows—blue eyes—painted eyelashes—divided fingers—tan skin tone—black and white striped swimsuit, white shoes—dolls sold in Ward's stores were in pink cardboard window boxes; the ones sold by mail were in brown cardboard mailing boxes—marked: Midge T.M./©1962/Barbie ®/©1958/by/Mattel, Inc./Patented.

3269—Barbie "Forget-Me-Nots" (Japan)—doll same as #1067 Malibu. This was a promotional offer from the Kellogg Company.

3311—Barbie—Busy (U.S.A.)—newly constructed hands with a movable thumb will grasp and hold items—some dolls have hard plastic heads—twist waist—bend knees—bend elbows—painted eyelashes—long, straight blonde hair parted on right with a "gold" barrette on the left—long patchwork skirt over a blue denim waist with attached white tricot panties—marked: ©1966/Mattel, Inc./U.S. & Foreign/Patented/Other Pat's/Pending/Made in/U.S.A. Included were a telephone, T.V., record player, travel case, tray with 2 glasses—all of brown plastic, and a clear plastic posing stand.

3312—Steffie—Busy (U.S.A.)—same construction as Busy Barbie above—painted eyelashes—blue eyes—long brunette hair, a small section of hair from each side of the face drawn to the back and held in place with a rubber band—long dress made of three different pieces of fabric, solid green, a dark print, a lighter print—green shoes—marked: ©1966/Mattel, Inc./U.S. & Foreign/Patented/Other Pat's/Pending/Made in/U.S.A. Same accessories as Barbie.

3313—Francie—Busy (Hong Kong)—same type hand and thumb construction as Busy Barbie above—long blonde hair parted on left, short sections of hair swirled around face, flip ends tied with green ribbon in the back—blue jeans, green tank top, green shoes, red belt—plastic stand—marked: ©1966/Mattel, Inc./Hong Kong/U.S. & Foreign/Patented/Other Pat's./Pending. Same accessories as Barbie.

3314—Ken—Busy (Hong Kong)—same hand and thumb construction as Barbie above—new bend elbows—bend knees—blue jeans, red tank top, brown belt, white tennis shoes—marked: ©1968/Mattel, Inc./U.S. & For. Pat'd/Other Pat's/Pending/Hong Kong. Same accessories as Barbie.

1195—Barbie—Talking Busy (Hong Kong)—same "busy" hand construction—bend elbows—bend knees—short blonde feather cut hair-do—rooted eyelashes—blue satin hot pants with a bib and attached long sleeve red tricot shirt, matching red half hat, green boots—marked: ©1967/Mattel, Inc./U.S. & Foreign/Pats. Pend./Hong Kong. Same accessories as Busy Barbie.

1196—Ken—Talking Busy (Hong Kong)—same construction as Busy Ken—red corduroy pants, red and blue plaid shirt, brown belt, brown shoes—same accessories as Busy Barbie—marked: ©1968/Mattel, Inc./U.S. & For. Pat'd./Other Pat's/Pending/Hong Kong. Back of head marked: ©1968 Mattel, Inc.

1186—Steffie—Talking Busy (Hong Kong)—same construction as Talking Busy Barbie—same accessories as Busy Barbie—blue shorts attached to pink and white checked long sleeve blouse, checked leggings, white shoes, black and white checked wide belt and half hat—marked: ©1967/Mattel, Inc./U.S. & Foreign/Pats. Pend./Hong Kong—long curly blonde hair—rooted eyelashes—blue eyes.

1144—Barbie Growin Pretty Hair (Taiwan)—new hair-do—new clothes—blonde hair brushed straight up from forehead and from back neck line, roll curls on each side of face, plus the strand of hair that "grows"—new hair pieces, a four-curl piece tied with blue ribbon and a long braided piece with blue ribbon on each end—undivided "Mexico" fingers—long dress had red, white and blue printed skirt, blue suede waist and attached panties and blue shoes—same markings as 1971.

1111—Ken—Talking (Hong Kong)—smaller head, ruddier complexion, lighter eyes.

1247—Jamie—available in a gift set, "Strollin in Style"

1067—Barbie—Malibu (Japan)—about the same as 1971.

1088—Ken—Malibu (Hong Kong)—about the same as 1971.

1069—Skipper—Malibu (Japan)—about the same as 1971.

1068—Francie—Malibu (Japan)—about the same as 1971.

1115—Barbie—Talking (Hong Kong)—about the same as 1971.

8348—Barbie—Spanish Talking—about the same as 1971.

1113—P.J.—Talking (Hong Kong)—about the same as 1971.

1126—Christie—Talking (Hong Kong)—about the same as 1971.

1114—Brad—Talking (Hong Kong)—about the same as 1971.

1128—Julia—Talking (Hong Kong)—about the same as 1971.

1155—Barbie—Live Action (Taiwan)—about the same as 1971.

1159—Ken—Live Action (Taiwan)—about the same as 1971.

1156—P.J.—Live Action (Taiwan)—about the same as 1971.

1175—Christie—Live Action (Taiwan)—about the same as 1971.

1119—Christie—twist (Japan)—about the same as 1971.

1142—Brad—bend legs (Hong Kong)—about the same as 1971.

1074—Francie—Growin Pretty Hair (Japan)—about the same as 1971.

4044—Barbie Hair Fair set (Japan)—available from the 1972 Sears' catalogue.

1132—Jamie—Walking (Japan)—available until Fall from mail-order catalogues.

1116—Barbie—Living (Taiwan)—available until Fall from mail-order catalogues.

1117—Skipper—Living (Taiwan)—available until Fall from mail-order catalogues.

1143—Fluff—Living (Taiwan)—available until Fall from mail-order catalogues.

1172—Ken—Live Action on Stage (Taiwan)—available until Fall from mail-order catalogues.

1152—Barbie—Live Action on Stage (Taiwan)—available until Fall from mail-order catalogues.

1153—P.J.—Live Action on Stage (Taiwan)—available until Fall from mail-order catalogues.

1122—Francie—Hair Happenin's (Japan)—available until Fall from mail-order catalogues.

1585—Barbie—Living—Sears' set (Japan)—available until Fall from mail-order catalogues.

1973

4220—Barbie—Quick Curl (Taiwan)—medium length blonde hair that could be styled without water or setting lotion—hair decorated with beads—painted eyebrows—twist waist—bend knees—undivided fingers—long pink and white checked dress with thin white sleeves, black ribbon trim, white shoes—comb, brush, curler, 4 ribbons, 4 rubber bands, bobby pins, booklet. Marked: ©1966/Mattel, Inc./U.S. & Foreign/Patented/Other Pat's/Pending/Made in/Taiwan. The first issue had the clear plastic posing stand. Later issues had a white plastic stand.

4221—Kelley—Quick Curl (Taiwan)—medium length red hair similar to Barbie's—painted eyelashes—brown eyes—twist waist—bend knees—undivided fingers—long green and white dress with thin white sleeves, black ribbon, white shoes—same accessories as Barbie above—marked: ©1966/Mattel, Inc./U.S. & Foreign/Patented/Other Pat's/Pending/Made in/Taiwan. Same two stands as Barbie.

4222—Francie—Quick Curl (Taiwan)—long brunette quick curl hair—painted eyelashes—twist waist—bend knees—arms and hands made from the Barbie "Mexico" mold—long yellow and white pin-dotted dress, short white sleeves, black ribbon trim, white shoes—same accessories as Barbie—marked: ©1966/Mattel, Inc./Taiwan/U.S. & Foreign/Patented/Other Pat's/Pending. Same 2 stands as Barbie.

4223—Skipper—Quick Curl (Taiwan)—long blonde quick curl hair — freckles — painted eyelashes — twist waist — bend knees—long blue and white check with solid blue waist dress, blue hair bow, white shoes—marked: ©1967 Mattel, Inc./U.S. Pat'd./U.S. Pats. Pend./Made in Taiwan. Same 2 stands as Barbie. Same accessories as Barbie.

8697—Miss America—Quick Curl (Taiwan)—long brunette quick curl hair — painted eyelashes — twist waist — bend knees— same accessories as Barbie—dressed same as the Walk Lively Miss America of 1972—marked: ©1966/Mattel, Inc./U.S. & Foreign/Patented/Other Pat's/Pending/Made in/Taiwan. Same 2 stands as Barbie.

4224—Ken—Mod Hair (Hong Kong)—rooted dark hair—extra beard, sideburns, 2 moustaches included—bend knees—brown and white checked jacket, lighter brown pants, white turtle neck dickey, brown shoes—marked: ©1968/Mattel, Inc./U.S. & For. Pat'd/Other Pat's/Pending/Hong Kong. Same 2 stands as Barbie.

7745—Christie—Malibu (Taiwan)—neck rim Taiwan—long straight black hair—brown eyes—twist waist—bend knees—one-piece red tricot swimsuit, white towel, no posing stand—sunglasses—"Mexico" arms and fingers—marked: ©1966/Mattel, Inc./U.S. & Foreign/Patented/Other Pats./Pending/Made in/Taiwan.

1067—Barbie—Malibu (now made in Taiwan)—now has the "Mexico" type fingers and arms—now marked: ©1966/Mattel, Inc./U.S. & Foreign/Patented/Other Pat's./Pending/Made in/Taiwan. Rest same as 1972.

3194-9991—Miss America (Taiwan)—Kellogg's promotional offer—Terry Ann Meeuwsen did the promoting—both the Walk Lively doll like 1972 and the new brunette Quick Curl doll were used this year.

3311—Barbie—Busy (now made in Hong Kong)—marked: ©1966/Mattel, Inc./U.S. & Foreign/Patented/Other Pat's/Pending/Made in/Hong Kong.—now has white plastic stand—rest about the same as 1972.

3312—Steffie—Busy (now made in Hong Kong)—marked: ©1966/Mattel, Inc./U.S. & Foreign/Patented/Other Pat's/Pending/Made in/Hong Kong—now has white plastic stand. Rest same as 1972.

3314—Ken—Busy (Hong Kong)—now has white plastic stand. Rest about the same as 1972.

1195—Barbie—Talking Busy (Hong Kong)—a different voice with slightly different words—now marked: ©1967/Mattel, Inc./U.S. & For./Pat'd Pat'd/In Canada/1967 Other/Pat's. Pend./Hong Kong—now has white plastic stand—rest about the same as 1972.

1179—Skipper—Pose 'N Play (Taiwan)—about the same as 1972.

1182—Barbie—Walk Lively (Taiwan)—about the same as 1972.

1183—Steffie—Walk Lively (Taiwan)—about the same as 1972.

1184—Ken—Walk Lively (Taiwan)—about the same as 1972.

1187—P.J.—Malibu (now made in Taiwan)—"Mexico" type fingers and arms—now marked: ©1966/Mattel, Inc./U.S. & Foreign/Patented/Other Pat's./Pending/Made in/Taiwan. Rest about the same as 1972.

1088—Ken—Malibu (Hong Kong)—about the same as 1972.

1069—Skipper—Malibu (Korea)—marked: ©1967 Mattel, Inc./U.S. Pat'd/U.S. Pats. Pend./Made In Korea. Rest same.

1068—Francie — Malibu (Korea) — marked: ©1966/Mattel, Inc./U.S. Patented/U.S. Pat. Pend./Made In/Korea. Rest same.

1117—Pose 'N Play Skipper (Taiwan)—in a plastic bag—same clothes as regular doll.

1115—non-talk Talking Barbie (Hong Kong)—in a plastic bag—same clothes as regular doll.

1111—non-talk Talking Ken (Hong Kong) in a plastic bag—same clothes as regular doll.

1113—non-talk Talking P.J. (Hong Kong)—in a plastic bag—same clothes as regular doll.

1155—Live Action Barbie (Taiwan)—in a plastic bag—same clothes as regular doll.

1159—Live Action Ken (Taiwan)—in a plastic bag—same clothes as regular doll.

1156—Live Action P.J. (Taiwan)—in a plastic bag—same clothes as regular doll.

4043—Hair Fair Head (Japan)—listed in the 1973 Sears' catalogue.

3210—Ward's re-issue Barbie (Japan)—available in early part of year.

1155—Barbie—Live Action (Taiwan)—available until Fall from mail-order catalogues.

1159—Ken—Live Action (Taiwan)—available until Fall from mail-order catalogues.

1156—P.J.—Live Action (Taiwan)—available until Fall from mail-order catalogues.

1175—Christie—Live Action (Taiwan)—available until Fall from mail-order catalogues.

1199—Tiff—Pose 'N Play (Taiwan)—available until Fall from mail-order catalogues.

3200—Miss America—Walk Lively (Taiwan)—available until Fall from mail-order catalogues.

1144—Barbie—Growin Pretty Hair (Taiwan)—available until Fall from mail-order catalogues.

1074—Francie—Growin Pretty Hair (Japan)—available until Fall from mail-order catalogues.

1115—Barbie—Talking (Hong Kong)—available until Fall from mail-order catalogues.

1111—Ken—Talking (Hong Kong)—available until Fall from mail-order catalogues.

1113—P.J.—Talking (Hong Kong)—available until Fall from mail-order catalogues.

1114—Brad—Talking (Hong Kong)—available until Fall from mail-order catalogues.

3313—Francie—Busy (Hong Kong)—available until Fall from mail-order catalogues.

8587—Barbie (Stacey head mold)—see Chapter III for complete description.

8588—Barbie—see Chapter III for complete description.

—Skipper—see Chapter III for complete description.

1974

7796—Barbie's Sweet 16 (Taiwan)—promotion set—blonde shag hair-do—twist waist—bend knees—painted eyelashes—"Mexico" arms and hands—long pink and white pin-dotted party dress, white shoes—make-up compact, applicators, comb, brush, 4 barrettes—a pair of fringed-leg short jeans and a yellow tank top with "Sweet 16" patch included—marked: ©1966/Mattel, Inc./U.S. & Foreign/Patented/ Other Pat's/Pending/Made in/Taiwan. No posing stand. First dolls had wrist tags, later ones did not.

7796—Barbie's Sweet 16 (Taiwan)—same as above but no jeans or tank top.

7806—Barbie—Sun Valley (Taiwan)—a Malibu doll like 1973 dressed in orange and yellow ski suit, yellow jacket, orange goggles, orange boots—yellow skis, orange poles—marked: ©1966/Mattel, Inc./U.S. & Foreign/Patented/Other Pat's./ Pending/Made in/Taiwan. No posing stand. First dolls had wrist tags, later ones did not.

7807—Barbie—Newport (Taiwan)—same Malibu doll as above—dressed in white pants, white blouse with sailor collar, red trim—a red and white striped tricot bikini and a white and red sailboat included. A few of the boats had a pink sail instead of red. No posing stand. First dolls had wrist tags, later ones did not.

7808—Kelley—Yellowstone (Taiwan)—new suntan skin—new long, straight red hair—"Mexico" hands—dressed in blue and white striped shorts, white knee socks, white tennis shoes, a red and white polka dotted long sleeve shirt—a pair of blue and white striped slacks, yellow sleeping bag, "mattress", pillow, camper stove, pots and pans and back pack included—markings: ©1966/Mattel, Inc./U.S. & Foreign/Patented/Other Pats./Pending/Made in/Taiwan. No posing stand. First dolls had wrist tags, later ones did not.

7809—Ken—Sun Valley (Taiwan)—suntan skin—early dolls had new orange colored hair—later dolls had mustard colored hair—light brown eyebrows—dressed in a 3 piece blue and red ski suit, red boots, goggles, red skis, blue poles—marked: ©1968/Mattel, Inc./U.S. & For. Patd/Other Pats./Pending/Taiwan. No posing stand. First dolls had wrist tags, later ones did not.

8697—Miss America—Quick Curl (Taiwan)—new blonde hair—no stand—first dolls had wrist tags, later ones did not.

3194-4—Miss America—Kellogg's offer—blonde Quick Curl same as above.

1187—P.J.—Malibu (Taiwan early part of year, Korea later)—the Taiwan doll wore a new green swimsuit, same style as 1973—same markings as 1973. The Korea doll wore the lavender suit, had the original Barbie divided fingers and arms. Early dolls had wrist tags, later ones did not.

7745—Christie—Malibu (Taiwan and Korea)—Taiwan doll about the same as 1973. Korea doll had new arms and hands made from the regular Francie mold. Same style suit but cut "skimpier."

1068—Francie—Malibu (Korea)—wrist tags discontinued later part of year.

1069—Skipper—Malibu (Korea)—wrist tags discontinued later part of year.

1067—Barbie—Malibu (Taiwan and Korea)—Taiwan doll the same as 1973. Korea doll has the original Barbie divided fingers—same swimsuit. Wrist tags discontinued later part of year.

1088—Ken—Malibu (Hong Kong)—about the same as 1973 except wrist tags discontinued later part of year.

1159—Ken in a plastic bag—had the talking body, second type talking doll clothes and a Live Action type head. #1159 is the regular stock number for Live Action Ken.

4234—Ken (Hong Kong)—Ward's Exclusive dressed doll. Came in red trunks with blue and black tuxedo outfit included.

7888—Babs—a regular Busy Steffie sold in a plastic bag.

8126—Skipper—see Chapter III for complete description.

8128—Tutti—see Chapter III for complete description.

8129—Todd—see Chapter III for complete description.

8130—Chris—see Chapter III for complete description.

8587—Barbie (Steffie head mold)—see Chapter III for complete description.

8588—Barbie—see Chapter III for complete description.

4220—Barbie—Quick Curl (Taiwan)—about the same as 1973 except wrist tags discontinued later part of year.

4221—Kelley—Quick Curl (Taiwan)—about the same as 1973 except wrist tags discontinued later part of year.

4222—Francie—Quick Curl (Taiwan)—about the same as 1973 except wrist tags discontinued later part of year.

4223—Skipper—Quick Curl (Taiwan)—about the same as 1973 except wrist tags discontinued later part of year.

4224—Ken—Mod Hair (Hong Kong)—about the same as 1973 except wrist tags discontinued later part of year.

7882—Barbie Baby Sits baby—Sears catalogue—baby same as Sunshine Family.

4043—Hair Fair head (Japan)—Sears' 1973 catalogue offer good until Fall 1974—eyes centered like the #4044 set.

3311—Barbie—Busy (Hong Kong)—available until Fall from mail-order catalogue.

3314—Ken—Busy (Hong Kong)—available until Fall from mail-order catalogue.

1975

7470—Barbie—Hawaiian (Korea)—a Department Store Special, not shown in U.S.A. catalogue—arms and hands made from the the Francie mold. (Hawaiian Barbie from Germany had different arms and hands. See Chapter III) Made from the Steffie head mold—suntan skin—long straight black hair parted on left with a flower in her hair—brown eyes—black painted eyebrows and lashes with brown eyeliner—twist—bend knees—multi-colored floral bikini, matching long wraparound skirt, lei—included was a grass skirt, panties, ukulele and sailboat.

7233—Barbie—Gold Medal (Taiwan)—a Malibu doll with the "Mexico" arms and hands—dressed in a one-piece red, white and blue swimsuit—an Olympic gold medal included.

7262—Barbie—Gold Medal Skater (Taiwan)—a Malibu doll with the "Mexico" arms and hands—dressed in a red, white and blue skating costume—special stand included—gold medal.

7264—Barbie—Gold Medal Skier—(Taiwan)—same as above except dressed for skiing—ski gear included.

7261—Ken—Gold Medal Skier (Taiwan)—Malibu doll dressed for skiing—ski gear included. Marked: ©1968 Mattel, Inc./Taiwan/U.S. & Foreign Patd./Patd. in Canada 1967.

7263—P.J.—Gold Medal Gymnast (Taiwan)—a Malibu doll with "Mexico" arms in a red, white and blue swimsuit—a warm-up jacket, booties and balance beam included. (The same doll was included in a Sears' set.)

7270—Barbie—Free Moving (Taiwan)—has a "Free Mover" tab on back—bend knees—hard, shiny "Mexico" arms and hands—painted eyelashes—long golden blonde hair with a red bow on side—dressed in a one-piece white playsuit with a red mid-section—a long red, white and black print skirt extra—white tennis shoes—a golf club, tennis racket and ball included. Marked: ©1967 Mattel, Inc./Taiwan/U.S. Pat. Pend.

7280—Ken—Free Moving (Taiwan)—same construction as Barbie above—brown hair—white shorts with an attached red and white striped shirt, white tennis shoes, white socks with colored stitching around top—same gear as Barbie. Marked: ©1968 Mattel, Inc./Taiwan/U.S. Patent/Pending. Head marked: ©1968 Mattel, Inc.

7282—Curtis—Free Moving (Taiwan)—a black doll—same as

Ken above except his shirt is orange instead of red. Made from the Brad head mold—black painted hair—brown eyes. Head marked: ©1969 Mattel, Inc. Other markings same as Ken's above.

7281—P.J.—Free Moving (Taiwan)—same construction and markings as Barbie above—same gear—same clothes except green where Barbie's are red—made from the Steffie head mold—long blonde hair divided into two sections and each tied with green ribbon—hair ends are fluffy. Marked: ©1967 Mattel, Inc./Taiwan/U.S. Pat. Pend.

7283—Cara—Free Moving (Taiwan)—a black doll—same construction and markings as Barbie—same gear—same clothes except orange instead of red—long curly dark brown hair with orange bows on each side—brown eyes—made from Steffie mold. Marked: ©1967 Mattel, Inc./Taiwan/U.S. Pat. Pend.

7291—Cara—Quick Curl (Taiwan)—long, dark brown "quick curl" hair—brown eyes—made from the Steffie head mold—"Mexico" hands—twist waist—bend knees—painted eyelashes—long wrap-around skirt in a multi-colored print tricot material, a matching short waisted blouse with long blue sleeves tied in front, white panties, blue shoes. Marked: ©1966/Mattel, Inc./U.S. and Foreign/Patented/Other Pat's /Pending/Made in Taiwan.

7259—Skipper—Growing Up (Hong Kong)—"two dolls in one"—by rotating her left arm she "grows" taller and develops a small bosom—long hair with red ribbon head band, first issue had platinum hair, second issue had golden blonde—hard, shiny plastic arms and hands—2 red and white checked skirts, one long and one short, red tricot bodysuit, blue scarf, blue collar, red knee socks, white platform shoes and red flats—marked: ©1967/Mattel, Inc./Hong Kong/ U.S. & For. Pat.

1067—Barbie—Malibu (Korea)—new styled red swimsuit—now in white cardboard window box—arms and hands could be called the "Korea type," meaning they were made from the original Barbie mold but fingers are not cut completely through—no towel—no sunglasses—marked: ©1966/Mattel, Inc./U.S. Patented/U.S. Pat. Pend./Made in/Korea—rest about the same as 1974.

1088—Ken—Malibu (Taiwan)—new green trunks—no towel —new white box—marked: ©1968/Mattel, Inc./U.S. & For. Patd./Other Pats./Pending/Taiwan.

7745—Christie—Malibu (Korea)—swimsuit now yellow—new white box—no sunglasses—no towel—"Korea hands" (arms and hands made from the original Barbie mold but fingers are not cut completely through)—marked: ©1966/ Mattel, Inc./U.S. Patented/U.S. Pat. Pend/Made in/Korea.

1069—Skipper—Malibu (Korea)—new white box—marked: ©1967 Mattel, Inc./U.S. Pat'd./U.S. Pats. Pend./Made in Korea. No sunglasses—no towel—rest same.

1187—P.J.—Malibu (Korea)—new white box—marked: © 1966/Mattel, Inc./U.S. Patented/U.S. Pat. Pend./Made In/ Korea. No towel—no sunglasses—"Korea hands"—rest same.

1068—Francie—Malibu (Korea)—new white box—no towel—no sunglasses—rest same.

7699—Francie—a baggie (Taiwan)—straight legs—non-twist waist—pink skin—painted eyelashes—brown eyes—long straight brunette hair—arms and hands made from the Barbie "Mexico" mold—2 piece yellow swimsuit—marked: ©1966/Mattel, Inc./Taiwan.

9000—Casey—a baggie (Taiwan)—made from the Francie head mold—same as #7699 Francie except has blonde hair and has a pink or red swimsuit.

7796—Barbie—Sweet 16 (Taiwan)—about the same as 1974.

4220—Barbie—Quick Curl (Taiwan)—about the same as 1974.

4221—Kelley—Quick Curl (Taiwan)—about the same as 1974.

4223—Skipper—Quick Curl (Taiwan)—about the same as 1974.

4224—Ken—Mod Hair (Hong Kong)—about the same as 1974.

4234—Ken (Hong Kong)—Ward's dressed doll—about the same as 1974.

8697—Miss America—Quick Curl (Taiwan)—about the same as 1974.

8697—Miss America—Kellogg's offer—same as doll above.

7807—Barbie—Newport (Taiwan)—about the same as 1974.

7882—Barbie Baby Sits baby—Sears—about the same as 1974.

9042—Barbie—Gold Medal (Taiwan)—Sears' set—doll marked: ©1966/Mattel, Inc./U.S. & Foreign/Patented/Other Pat's./Pending/Made in/Taiwan—"Mexico hands."

9044—Barbie—Gold Medal (Korea)—Sears' set—doll marked: ©1966/Mattel, Inc./U.S. Patented/U.S. Patented/ U.S. Pat. Pend./Made in/Korea—"Korea hands."

7806—Barbie—Sun Valley (Taiwan)—available until Fall through mail-order catalogues.

7809—Ken—Sun Valley (Taiwan)—available until Fall through mail-order catalogues.

7192—Funtime Barbie—see Chapter III for complete description.

7193—Funtime Skipper—see Chapter III for complete description.

7194—Funtime Ken—see Chapter III for complete description.

7453—Tutti "Swing-A-Ling"—see Chapter III for complete description.

7454—Tutti "Walkin' My Dolly"—see Chapter III for complete description.

7455—Tutti "Night Night"—see Chapter III for complete description.

8128—Tutti—see Chapter III for complete description.

8129—Todd—see Chapter III for complete description.

8130—Chris—see Chapter III for complete description.

8587—Barbie (Steffie head mold)—see Chapter III for complete description.

1976

9217—Barbie—Deluxe Quick Curl (Taiwan)—promotional set had free Jergen's beauty kit (bubble bath, soap) attached to side of box—free calendar—medium long blonde quick curl hair—extra long fall included—comb, brush, curler, accessories—painted eyelashes—bend knees—twist waist—"Mexico hands" — marked: ©1966/Mattel, Inc. U.S. & Foreign/Patented/Other Pat's./Pending/Made in/Taiwan—long blue dress, blue shoes, white beads, white fringed stole.

9217—Barbie—Deluxe Quick Curl (Taiwan)—same as above but no Jergen's beauty kit.

9218—P.J.—Deluxe Quick Curl (Taiwan)—medium length blonde hair—extra fall included—painted eyelashes—brown eyes—twist waist—bend knees—"Mexico" hands — long orange colored dress and shoes, white beads, white fringed stole—comb, brush, curler, accessories—same markings as Barbie.

9220—Cara—Deluxe Quick Curl (Taiwan)—medium length dark brown hair—extra fall included—painted eyelashes—brown eyes—twist waist—bend knees—"Mexico" hands—long yellow dress and shoes, white beads, white fringed stole—comb, brush, curler, accessories—same markings as Barbie.

9342—Ken—Now Look (Taiwan—Hong Kong)—new style rooted dark brown hair—new feathered eyebrows—beige pants and jacket, blue scarf, brown shoes—first dolls had deep pink skin, bend knees and were marked: ©1968/Mattel, Inc./U.S. & For. Patd./Other Pats./Pending/Taiwan. Later dolls had pale pink skin, longer hair, stiffer knees and were marked: 1088—0500 3/ ©Mattel/Inc. 1968/Hong Kong.

9093—Barbie—Ballerina (Taiwan)—blonde ponytail—painted eyebrows—swivel jointed head and arms—specially constructed legs for splits and kicks—new mold arms and hands of hard shiny plastic—new knees do not bend same as old ones—twist waist—white tutu and slippers, gold crown, red bouquet—marked: ©Mattel, Inc. 1966/U.S. Patent Pending/Taiwan. Round white posing stand.

9528—Cara—Ballerina (Taiwan)—made from the Steffie head mold—long black hair styled like Barbie's—brown eyes—same construction and markings as Barbie—pink tutu and slippers, gold crown, red bouquet—pink posing stand.

9222—Ginger—Growing Up (Hong Kong)—same construction as Growing Up Skipper—made from the Skipper head mold—long brunette hair—brown eyes—blue body suit, 2 blue and white dotted skirts, blue flats, white platforms, lavender scarf and collar—marked: ©1967/Mattel, Inc./Hong Kong/U.S. & For. Pat.

9599—Barbie—Beautiful Bride (Korea)—Department Store Special—new tan rooted eyelashes—greenish eyes—medium long blonde hair, flip ends—hard shiny "Mexico" arms and hands—twist waist—bend knees—dressed in #9149 wedding dress—marked: ©1966/Mattel, Inc./U.S. Patented/U.S. Pat. Pend./Made in/Korea.

9613—Barbie—Ballerina On Tour (Taiwan)—Department Store Special—doll same as #9093—has 2 extra costumes.

7194—Ken (Taiwan)—A few of the regular Malibu Kens in the green trunks were found in a box called "Funtime Ken." This box with a different Ken doll was available in Europe in 1975 and 1976. Apparently a mix-up occured at the factory in Taiwan. See Chapter III for more information.

1155—Barbie—Action (Taiwan)—came in a plastic bag. In 1973—1975 this doll sold in Europe as #8588 Barbie. She was made from the true Barbie mold—pink skin—blonde hair styled like Malibu P.J.'s—hard shiny torso—unjointed waist—bend knees—"Mexico" arms and hands—pink swimsuit styled like Malibu P.J.'s—marked: ©1967 Mattel, Inc./U.S. Patented/Other Patents Pending/Patented in Canada 1967/Taiwan.

7470—Barbie—Hawaiian (Korea)—some dolls had a third type of arm and hand, a hard shiny plastic "Mexico" mold—rest about the same as 1975.

7259—Skipper—Growing Up (Hong Kong)—golden blonde hair—rest about the same as 1975.

7882—Sears "Barbie Baby Sits" set—new pink box, new pink accessories.

9042—Gold Medal Barbie Winter Sports (Taiwan)—A Sears' set of 1975 now being sold in discount department stores.

9044—Gold Medal Barbie (Korea)—A Sears' set of 1975, now being sold in discount department stores.

1088—Ken—Malibu (Taiwan—Hong Kong)—new rose boxes—orangy blond hair—darker green trunks. First dolls had the same markings as 1975. Late in year the dolls were slightly darker and were made in Hong Kong. These were marked: 1088 0500 1 / ©Mattel/Inc. 1968/Hong Kong.

1067—Barbie—Malibu (Korea)—new hard shiny plastic arms and hands from the "Mexico" molds—new rose box—rest about the same as 1975.

1068—Francie—Malibu (Korea)—new rose box—rest about the same.

1069—Skipper—Malibu (Korea)—hard shiny plastic arms and hands—new rose box—rest about the same.

1187—P.J.—Malibu (Korea)—new hard shiny plastic arms and hands from the "Mexico" molds—new rose box—rest about the same as 1975.

7745—Christie—Malibu (Korea)—new hard shiny plastic arms and hands from the "Mexico" molds—new rose box—rest about the same as 1975.

8697—Miss America—Quick Curl (Taiwan)—about the same as 1975.

7261—Ken—Gold Medal Skier (Taiwan)—about the same as 1975.

7262—Barbie—Gold Medal Skater (Taiwan)—about the same as 1975.

7263—P.J.—Gold Medal Gymnast (Taiwan)—about the same as 1975.

7264—Barbie—Gold Medal Skier (Taiwan)—about the same as 1975.

4234—Ward's dressed Ken (Hong Kong)—about the same as 1975.

7699—Francie—a baggie (Taiwan)—about the same as 1975.

9000—Casey—a baggie (Taiwan)—about the same as 1975.

7377—Carla (black)—See Chapter III for description.

7381—Funtime Skooter—See Chapter III for description.

7382—Barbie—See Chapter III for description.

9428—Deluxe Quick Curl Skipper—See Chapter III for description.

7192—Funtime Barbie—See Chapter III for description.

7193—Funtime Skipper—See Chapter III for description.

7194—Funtime Ken—See Chapter III for description.

7453—Tutti "Swing-A-Ling"—See Chapter III for description.

7454—Tutti "Walkin' My Dolly"—See Chapter III for description.

7455—Tutti "Night-Night"—See Chapter III for description.

8128—Tutti—See Chapter III for description.

8129—Todd—See Chapter III for description.

8130—Chris—See Chapter III for description.

4220—Barbie—Quick Curl (Taiwan)—available until Fall from mail-order catalogues.

4221—Kelley—Quick Curl (Taiwan)—available until Fall from mail-order catalogues.

4224—Ken—Mod Hair (Hong Kong)—available until Fall from mail-order catalogues.

7270—Barbie—Free Moving (Taiwan)—available until Fall from mail-order catalogues.

7280—Ken—Free Moving (Taiwan)—available until Fall from mail-order catalogues.

7281—P.J.—Free Moving (Taiwan)—available until Fall from mail-order catalogues.

7283—Cara—Free Moving (Taiwan)—available until Fall from mail-order catalogues.

2. The Dolls, by the Doll

Barbie—11½″

1958

Patented

1959

850—#1 doll—white *irises—pointed* eyebrows—ponytail with curly bangs—holes in feet—bright red lips and nails—pale skin—heavy partially solid torso marked: Barbie T.M./Pat's. Pend./©MCMLVIII/by/Mattel/Inc.—black and white striped swimsuit.

850—#2 doll—does not have holes in feet—rest same as preceding doll.

1960

850—#3 doll—now has *blue* irises—*curved* eyebrows—some dolls have brown eyeliner, some have blue—rest same as preceding doll.

850—#4 doll—blue eyeliner—*tan* skin—rest same as preceding doll.

1961

850—New hard hollow torso—Barbie® /Pat's. Pend./©MCMLVIII/by/Mattel/Inc.—new wrist tag—rest same as preceding doll.

850—New bubble cut hair style—rest same as preceding doll.

1962

850—Bubble cut—new red swimsuit—various shades of lip and nail colors—rest same as preceding doll.

850—Ponytail with curly bangs—same as preceding doll.

1963

850—Bubble cut—new slightly taller body marked: Midge T.M./©1962/Barbie® /©1958/by/Mattel, Inc.—rest same as preceding doll.

850—Ponytail with bangs—same as preceding doll.

870—Fashion Queen—molded head, brown hair, blue head band—3 wigs—has the Midge/Barbie markings—wears gold and white striped swimsuit, matching head scarf.

1964

0850—New no-bangs, side-swept ponytail called "swirl" by collectors—same swimsuit as 1963 dolls. First issue had the same markings as the 1963 dolls. Later issue had the word "patented" added as a last line.

1060—Miss Barbie (Made in U.S.A.) open and close eyes—first bend legs—pink swimsuit and cap—intaglio mark: ©1958/Mattel, Inc./U.S. Patented/U.S. Pat. Pend.—back of head: ©M.I.

0871—Wig Wardrobe—1 molded head, brown hair, blue band—3 wigs.

0850—Bubble cut—same markings as 1963 with the word "patented" added as a last line—rest same as 1963.

0850—Ponytail with bangs—same as preceding doll.

0870—Fashion Queen—markings now has "patented" added as a last line—rest same as 1963.

1965

1070—Bendable legs—classic American Girl hair style (there were 2 other styles, both rare)—one-piece swimsuit had solid blue bottom and a multi-colored striped top—same intaglio markings as Miss Barbie.

4035—Color 'N Curl set—1 molded Barbie head and 1 molded Midge head—4 wigs—wig stand—hair dryer—color changers—accessories.

4038—Color 'N Curl set—1 molded Barbie head—2 wigs—color changers—accessories.

0871—Wig Wardrobe—same as 1964.

0850—"Swirl" ponytail—same as 1964 second issue.

0850—Bubble cut—same as 1964.

1060—Miss Barbie—available until Fall from mail-order catalogues.

0870—Fashion Queen—available until Fall from mail-order catalogues.

1966

1150—Color Magic—long straight hair, no bangs—bend legs—harlequin checked suit and head band—accessories. First issue had the same intaglio markings as Miss Barbie with two additional lines of *raised* letters: Made In/Japan. Later issue had the same words as the first but now all letters *raised* (new mold).

4039—Color 'N Curl set—1 molded Barbie head—4 wigs—wig stand—hair dryer—color changer—accessories.

1070—Bendable legs—first part of year markings were the same intaglio as Miss Barbie but with 2 extra lines of raised letters: Made In/Japan. Later in year the same words but all letters raised.

4038—Color 'N Curl set—same as 1965.

0871—Wig Wardrobe—same as 1965.

0850—Bubble Cut—same as 1965.

4035—Color 'N Curl set—available until Fall from mail-order catalogues.

1967

1160—Twist 'N Turn—twist waist—bend knees—long straight hair—straight bangs, red bow—rooted eyelashes—2 piece salmon vinyl swimsuit with a net over-suit—marked: ©1966/Mattel, Inc./U.S. Pat. Pend./Made In/Japan.

1162—Twist 'N Turn (Trade-In)—same as preceding doll exceptsome had "Made In Japan" on one line.

1190—New standard Barbie—straight legs—non-twist waist—painted eyelashes—same hair as #1160 above—two-piece pink swimsuit.

4042—Hair Fair set—1 Barbie head with short rooted hair in blonde or brunette—rooted eyelashes—hair pieces and accessories.

1150—Color Magic—new box—same markings as second issue of 1966—rest same as 1966.

0850—Bubble Cut—same as 1966.

4039—Color 'N Curl set—same as 1966.

0871—Wig Wardrobe—available until Fall of 1967 from mail-order catalogues.

1070—Bendable leg—available until Fall 1967 from mail-order catalogues.

1968

1115—Talking—(Mexico—neck rim Japan)—rooted eyelashes—twist ponytail to side, tied with 3 ribbons—new hand mold with slender undivided fingers (will refer to this type as the "Mexico hand")—rose knit top over rose vinyl shorts. (Full description in Year List).

8348—Spanish Talking—Wrist tag says "Made in U.S.A." Original divided fingers. Rest same as doll above.

1160—Twist 'N Turn (Japan)—new swimsuit, pink with green knit top over rose vinyl shorts—rest same as 1967.

1190—Standard straight leg (Japan)—same as 1967.

4042—Hair Fair set (Japan)—same as 1967.

1969

4043—Hair Fair set (Japan)—1 Barbie head—new design—short rooted hair—rooted eyelashes—new accessories.

1160—Twist 'N Turn (Japan)—new clothes and new hair style—double diagonal stripes that cross swimsuit—long flip hair—rest same as 1968.

1115—Talking (Mexico)—new box. First part of year same as 1968. Later the neck rim was marked Hong Kong—had the same hair-do as 1968. The first of these wore the same swimsuit as 1968, but later dolls wore a new 2 piece reddish vinyl swimsuit with a net jacket. All 3 versions had Mexico hands.

8348—Spanish Talking (Mexico)—new box—now has undivided fingers—rest same as 1968.

1190—Standard straight leg (Japan)—same as 1968.

4042—Hair Fair (Japan)—available until Fall from mail-order catalogues.

1116—Living (Taiwan)—bend knees, elbows and ankles—swivel, waist, neck, arms, hands and legs—medium long straight hair, straight bangs—rooted eyelashes—one-piece gold and silver swimsuit, orange net hooded jacket.

1585—Living (Japan)—neck rim marked Japan—body marked Japan. This doll was in a Sears exclusive set "Action Accents." See Chapter III for additional information.

1115—Talking (Mexico—Hong Kong)—neck rim Hong Kong—new hair-do, curls on nape of neck—2 piece reddish suit with net jacket—some had old voice box, some had new one mentioning P.J.—Mexico hands. Early dolls had the Mexico markings. Late in year they were marked Hong Kong.

1115—Talking (Stacey head mold) (Mexico—shortly before fire)—voice box mentions P.J.—neck rim Hong Kong—same clothes and hair as preceding doll.

8348—Spanish Talking (Mexico, until fire)—same as regular doll.

8348—Spanish Talking (Stacey head mold) (Hong Kong)—same as regular doll.

1160—Twist (Japan)—new one-piece rose and white patterned swimsuit—rest same as 1969.

1190—Standard straight legs (Japan)—new one-piece rose and green swimsuit—new box—rest same as 1969.

4043—Hair Fair set (Japan)—same as 1969.

1971

1174—Hair Happenin's (Japan)—Limited Edition—Department Store Exclusive—centered eyes—rooted eyelashes—original Barbie hands—short, straight, rooted titian hair, no bangs—3 titian hair pieces, accessories—dress has rose skirt and white waist, black shoes and wide black belt—marked: ©1966/Mattel, Inc./U.S. Patented/U.S. Pat. Pend./Made In/Japan.

1152—Live Action on Stage (Taiwan)—(See Year List for complete description.)

1155—Live Action (Taiwan)—same as preceding but no stage.

1067—Malibu (Japan)—made from the Stacey head mold—suntan skin—painted eyelashes—twist—bend knee—one-piece blue swimsuit—original divided fingers.

4044—Hair Fair set (Japan)—new centered eyes—rest similar to #4043 set.

1144—Growin Pretty Hair (Taiwan)—blonde—pink satin party dress—full description in Year List.

1190—Standard straight leg (Japan)—new centered eyes—same clothes and markings as 1970. (This doll, plus an outfit, was offered by the Chef Boy-Ar-dee Company as a promotional item.)

1116—Living (Taiwan)—new dotted swimsuit with matching long skirt—new centered eyes—rest same as 1970.

1585—Living (Japan)—Sears set still on market—about the same as 1970.

1115—Talking (Hong Kong)—new centered eyes—new white 2 piece bikini, long gold jacket—Mexico hands—many dolls have a hard plastic head.

8348—Spanish Talking—same as 1970.

1160—Twist (Japan)—new centered eyes—new one-piece striped suit in red, yellow and purple—same hair style as 1970.

1972

1182—Walk Lively (Taiwan)—blonde—Mexico hands—red pants and top—special "walking" construction.

3210—Ward's re-issue (Japan)—brunette ponytail—tan skin—blue eyes—painted lashes—Midge/Barbie markings—black and white striped swimsuit.

3269—"Forget-Me-Nots" (Japan)—doll same as #1067 Malibu—Kellogg Company promotional doll.

3311—Busy(U.S.A.)—new hand with movable thumb—painted lashes—long, straight blonde hair—long patchwork skirt, blue denim top attached to panties.

1195—Talking Busy (Hong Kong)—same hands as Busy above—short blonde hair—rooted eyelashes—blue hot pants with red top, red hat, green boots.

1144—Growin' Pretty Hair (Taiwan)—new hair style—new long dress with red printed skirt and a blue suede waist.

1067—Malibu (Japan)—about the same as 1971.

1115—Talking (Hong Kong)—about the same as 1971.

8348—Spanish Talking—same as 1971.

1155—Live Action (Taiwan)—about the same as 1971.

4044—Hair Fair set (Japan)—available from Sears catalogue.

1116—Living (Taiwan)—available until Fall from mail-order catalogues.

1152—Live Action on Stage (Taiwan)—available until Fall from mail-order catalogues.

1973

4220—Quick Curl (Taiwan)—painted eyelashes—blonde hair—Mexico hands—long pink and white checked dress.

1067—Malibu (now Taiwan)—Mexico hands—rest about the same.

8587—(Stacey head mold)—see Chapter III for complete description.

8588—See Chapter III for complete description.

3311—Busy (now Hong Kong)—new markings—rest about the same.

1195—Talking Busy (Hong Kong)—slightly different words and voice—new markings—rest about the same.

1182—Walk Lively (Taiwan)—about the same as 1972.

1115—A non-talk Talking (Hong Kong)—in plastic bag—similar to 1972 doll.

1155—Live Action (Taiwan)—plastic bag—similar to 1972 doll.

4043—Hair Fair (Japan)—listed in 1973 Sears catalogue.

3210—Ward's re-issue (Japan)—available early part of year from catalogue.

1155—Live Action (Taiwan)—available until Fall from mail-order catalogues.

1144—Growin Pretty Hair (Taiwan)—available until Fall from mail-order catalogues.

1115—Talking (Hong Kong)—available until Fall from mail-order catalogues.

1974

7796—Sweet 16 (Taiwan)—promotion doll with free jeans and yellow tank top—blonde shag hair—painted lashes—long pink dress—first dolls had wrist tags, later ones did not.

7796—Sweet 16 (Taiwan)—same as above but no extra free outfit.

8587—(Stacey head mold)—See Chapter III for description.

8588—See Chapter III for description.

7806—Sun Valley (Taiwan)—a Malibu doll dressed for skiing—ski gear included—no wrist tags late in year—Mexico hands.

7807—Newport (Taiwan)—a Malibu doll dressed for sailing—sailboat included—no wrist tags late in year—Mexico hands.

1067—Malibu (Taiwan—Korea)—Taiwan doll had the Mexico hands. Korea doll had the original Barbie divided fingers. No wrist tags late in year—same blue swimsuit.

4220—Quick Curl (Taiwan)—no wrist tags late in year—rest about the same as 1973.

4043—Hair Fair (Japan)—available from Sears catalogue until Fall—eyes centered like the #4044 set.

3311—Busy (Hong Kong)—available until Fall from mail-order catalogues.

1975

7470—Hawaiian (Korea)—Department Store Exclusive Limited Edition—made from the Steffie head mold—suntan skin—long, straight black hair—brown eyes—painted lashes—arms and hands made from the Francie mold. (Hawaiian Barbie from Germany had arms and hands made from the original Barbie mold, but the fingers were not cut quite through. These are known as the "Korean hands.")

7233—Gold Medal (Taiwan)—a Malibu doll—Mexico hands—dressed in red, white and blue swimsuit.

7262—Gold Medal Skater (Taiwan)—a Mailbu doll—Mexico hands—dressed in red, white and blue skating outfit.

7264—Gold Medal Skier (Taiwan)—same as above except dressed for skiing—ski gear included.

9042—A Malibu (Taiwan)—in a Sears set—same doll as above.

9044—A Malibu (Korea)—in a Sears set—has the "Korea hands."

7270—Free Moving (Taiwan)—See Year List for complete description—hard, shiny Mexico arms and hands—long golden blonde hair.

7192—Funtime—See Chapter III for complete description.

8587—(Steffie head mold)—See Chapter III for complete description.

1068—Malibu (Korea)—no sunglasses—no towel — new sytled red swimsuit — new white cardboard window box—Korea hands.

7796—Sweet 16 (Taiwan)—about the same as 1974.

4220—Quick Curl (Taiwan)—about the same as 1974.

7807—Newport (Taiwan)—about the same as 1974.

7806—Sun Valley (Taiwan)—available until Fall from mail-order catalogues.

1976

9217—Deluxe Quick Curl (Taiwan)—promotional set—had free Jergens beauty kit attached—blonde hair—long blue dress—painted lashes—Mexico hands—free calendar.

9217—Deluxe Quick Curl (Taiwan)—no free Jergens set—rest same as above.

9093—Ballerina (Taiwan)—blonde ponytail—painted eyelashes—see Year List for complete description.

7470—Hawaiian (Korea)—some dolls had a third type of arm and hand, a hard, shiny Mexico mold—rest about the same as 1975.

7264—Gold Medal Skier (Taiwan)—about the same as 1975.

7262—Gold Medal Skater (Taiwan)—about the same as 1975.

1067—Malibu (Korea)—new hard shiny arms and hands made from the Mexico mold—new rose box—rest about the same as 1975.

1155—Action Barbie in plastic bag—same as #8588 from Europe, 1974—see List by the Year for description.

7382—Straight leg—see Chapter III for description.

7192—Funtime—see Chapter III for description.

4220—Quick Curl (Taiwan)—available until Fall from mail-order catalogues.

7270—Free Moving (Taiwan)—available until Fall from mail-order catalogues.

9599—Beautiful Bride (Korea)—new rooted tan eyelashes—medium long blonde hair, flip ends—greenish eyes—dressed in a wedding outfit.

9613—Ballerina Barbie On Tour (Taiwan)—a limited edition Department Store Special—see List by Year for description.

9044—Barbie and her U.S. Olympic Wardrobe—now sold in Discount Department stores.

9042—Barbie Winter Sports set—now sold in Discount Department stores.

Ken — 12"

1960

Patented.

1961

750—Straight leg—flocked hair in blond, black or brown—hollow torso marked: Ken T.M./Pats. Pend./©MCMLX/by/Mattel/Inc.—red trunks with white stripe up side, sandals—most had a yellow towel.

1962

750—New painted hair—red trunks, red and white striped jacket with stitched terry cloth lining—no towel—same markings.

1963

750—New body ¼ inch shorter than previous dolls—loose legs, fatter arms and hands, more pronounced kneecaps—new markings: Ken®/©1960/by/Mattel, Inc./Hawthorne/Calif. U.S.A.

1964

750—New markings: ©1960/by/Mattel, Inc./Hawthorne/Calif. U.S.A.—body now same height as 1962 dolls—jacket lining now bonded on.

1965

1020—Bendable legs—same markings as preceding doll—red trunks, blue jacket.

0750—Straight legs—same as 1964.

1966

1020—Bendable legs—same as 1965.

0750—Straight legs—same as 1965.

1967

0750—Straight legs—same as 1966.

1020—Bendable legs—available until Fall from mail-order catalogues.

1968

0750—Straight legs—available until Fall from mail-order catalogues.

1969

1111—Talking (Mexico)—all new—molded Edwardian hair style in medium brown—bend knees—pink skin—blue eyes—red jacket and trunks—marked: ©1968/Mattel, Inc./U.S. & For. Pat'd/Other Pat's/Pending/Mexico.

8372—Spanish Talking—May have been on the market but this is unverified.

1970

1124—Bendable legs (Mexico, until fire)—head and hair similar to talking doll—same markings—mustard colored shirt, multi-colored shorts.

1111—Talking (Mexico, until fire)—new clothes, blue with orange jacket and orange shorts.

8372—Spanish Talking (Mexico, until fire)—same as regular doll above.

1971

1172—Live Action on Stage (Taiwan)—see Year List for description.

1159—Live Action (Taiwan)—same as preceding but no stage.

1088—Malibu (Hong Kong)—new suntan skin—new yellow hair—red trunks, blue towel—new markings.

1111—Talking (Hong Kong)—same clothes as 1970—new markings.

1124—Bendable legs (These are marked "Mexico". They must have been made before the fire but not sold until 1971.)

1972

1184—Walk Lively (Taiwan)—see Year List for description.

3314—Busy (Hong Kong)—see Year List for description.

1196—Talking Busy (Hong Kong)—see Year List for description.

1088—Malibu (Hong Kong)—about the same as 1971.

1111—Talking (Hong Kong) — smaller face, ruddier skin — rest same as 1971.

1159—Live Action (Taiwan)—about the same as 1971.

1172—Live Action on Stage (Taiwan) — available until Fall from mail-order catalogues.

1973

4224—Mod Hair (Hong Kong) — new rooted brunet hair — bend knees.

3314—Busy (Hong Kong)—about the same as 1972.

1184—Walk Lively (Taiwan)—about the same as 1972.

1088—Malibu (Hong Kong)—about the same as 1972.

1111—Non-talking Talking (Hong Kong) — in a plastic bag—same clothes as 1972.

1159—Live Action (Taiwan) — in a plastic bag — same as regular doll without the stand.

1159—Live Action (Taiwan)—available until Fall from mail-order catalogues.

1111—Talking (Hong Kong)—available until Fall from mail-order catalogues.

1974

7809—Sun Valley (Taiwan)—new orange colored hair and light brown eyebrows—suntan skin—dressed for skiing—ski gear included—no wrist tag late in year.

1088—Malibu (Hong Kong)—no wrist tag late in year—rest about the same as 1973.

1159—In a plastic bag—had the talking body dressed in the second talking clothes and a Live Action type head. #1159 is the stock number for the Live Action Ken.

4224—Mod Hair (Hong Kong)—no wrist tag late in year—rest about the same as 1973.

4234—Ward's exclusive dressed Mod Ken (Hong Kong)—wore red trunks—extra tuxedo included.

3314—Busy (Hong Kong)—available until Fall from mail-order catalogues.

1975

7261—Gold Medal Skier (Taiwan)—Malibu doll dressed for skiing.

7194—Funtime—see Chapter III for description.

7280—Free Moving (Taiwan)—tab on back releases for an "action" waist—brown hair—red and white sports clothes.

1088—Malibu (Taiwan)—no towel—new green trunks—new white box.

4224—Mod Hair (Hong Kong)—about the same as 1974.

4234—Ward's dressed doll (Hong Kong)—about the same as 1974.

7809—Sun Valley (Taiwan)—available until Fall from mail-order catalogues.

1976

9342—Now Look (Taiwan and Hong Kong)—new style rooted brunet hair—beige jacket and pants, blue scarf. See picture section for two different dolls.

7261—Gold Medal Skier (Taiwan)—about the same as 1975.

1088—Malibu (Taiwan and Hong Kong)—darker green trunks—new rose box. See picture section for differences in dolls.

4234—Ward's dress doll (Hong Kong)—about the same as 1975.

4224—Mod Hair (Hong Kong)—available until Fall from mail-order catalogues.

7280—Free Moving (Taiwan)—available until Fall from mail-order catalogues.

7194—Funtime—see Chapter III for description.

Midge — 11½″

1963

860—Straight legs—freckles—blue eyes—2 piece swimsuit—marked: Midge T.M./©1962/Barbie®/©1958/by/Mattel, Inc.

1964

0860—Straight legs—markings now has "patented" added as a last line.

1965

1080—Bendable legs—new hair style—one-piece striped suit — new intaglio markings: ©1958 / Mattel, Inc. / U.S. Patented/U.S. Pat. Pend.

0860—Straight legs—about the same as 1964.

4035—Color 'N Curl set—has 1 molded Midge head and 1 Barbie head—4 wigs—hair dryer—color changers—accessories.

1009—Wig Wardrobe—1 molded head—3 wigs.

1966

1080—Bendable legs—first part of year same intaglio markings with two lines of *raised* words added: Made In/Japan. Later in year, the same words but all letters raised.

0860—Straight legs—about the same as 1965.

4035—Color 'N Curl set—available until Fall from mail-order catalogues.

1967

0860—Straight legs—about the same as 1966.

1080—Bendable legs—available until Fall from mail-order catalogues.

"Barbie Baby Sits" baby — 3″

1963

953—Molded yellow hair—jointed at neck, shoulders and hips—apron—accessories.

1964

0953—Hair a deeper yellow.

1965

0953—Apron deleted—layette added.

1966

0953—Available until Fall from mail-order catalogues.

Skipper — 9¼″

1964

0950—Straight legs—long, straight hair—red and white one-piece swimsuit—marked: Skipper/©1963/Mattel, Inc.

1965

1030—Bendable legs—same straight hair style—one-piece blue and red swimsuit—marked: ©1963/Mattel, Inc.

0950—Straight legs—same as 1964 except now marked like preceding doll.

1966

1030—Bendable legs—new pink skin—rest same as 1965.

0950—Straight legs—new pink skin—rest same as 1965.

1967

1030—Bendable legs—new open face box—new plastic stand—rest about the same as 1966.

0950—Straight legs—about the same as 1966.

1968

1105—Twist 'N Turn (Japan)—twist waist—same hair as preceding dolls—new rooted eyelashes—one-piece blue and pink swimsuit—marked: ©1967 Mattel, Inc./U.S.Pat'd/U.S. Pats.Pend./Made in Japan. Late in year the doll was made in Taiwan and was so marked. Same hair-do and clothes.

0950—Straight legs—about the same as 1967.

1030—Bendable legs—available until Fall from mail-order catalogues.

1969

1105—Twist 'N Turn (Taiwan)—new hair-do and new clothes—2 long curls—one-piece red and orange checked and solid orange swimsuit.

1970

1117—Living (Taiwan)—bend knees and elbows—swivel waist, neck, hands, arms and legs—blonde hair tied in two sections—rooted eyelashes—marked: ©1969 Mattel, Inc./ Taiwan/U.S. & For. Patd./Other Pats. Pend./Patd. in Canada 1967.

1147—Living (Taiwan)—Trade-in doll—same as preceding doll.

0950—Re-issue of Straight legs (Japan)—pinker skin—new clothes (1969 & 1970) pictured on box—same markings as 1965: ©1963/Mattel, Inc.

1105—Twist 'N Turn (Taiwan)—new orange vinyl jacket over shorts and "bra"—same two long curls as 1969.

1971

1069—Malibu (Japan)—suntan skin—long straight blonde hair—twist—bend knees—painted eyelashes—2 piece orange swimsuit, blue towel, sunglasses.

1117—Living (Taiwan)—new yellow two-piece swimsuit—skateboard added.

1105—Twist 'N Turn (Taiwan)—about the same as 1970.

0950—Straight legs (Japan)—about the same as 1970.

1972

1179—Pose 'N Play (Taiwan)—gym included—"swing free" arms, rest similar to Living doll—painted eyelashes—short hair tied in two sections—most had light titian hair but in 1975 some were found with blonde hair—one-piece blue and blue and white checked swimsuit.

1069—Malibu (Japan)—about the same as 1971.

1117—Living (Taiwan)—available until Fall from mail-order catalogues.

1973

4223—Quick Curl (Taiwan) — long blonde hair — freckles — painted eyebrows—long blue and white checked dress—accessories.

1179—Pose 'N Play (Taiwan)—same as 1972.

1069—Malibu (Korea)—marked: ©1967 Mattel, Inc./U.S. Pat'd./U.S. Pats. Pend./Made in Korea. Rest same as 1972.

1117—Pose 'N Play—no gym (Taiwan)—sold in a plastic bag—doll and clothes same as regular doll. Wrong stock No.

—See Chapter III for description.

1974

1069—Malibu (Korea)—wrist tags discontinued later in year.

8126—See Chapter III for description.

4223—Quick Curl (Taiwan)—wrist tags discontinued later in year—rest about the same as in 1973.

1975

7259—Growing Up (Hong Kong)—"grows up" by rotating her arm—long pale or golden blonde hair—hard shiny plastic arms and hands.

7193—Funtime—See Chapter III for description.

1069—Malibu (Korea)—new white box—towel and glasses discontinued—rest same as 1974.

4223—Quick Curl (Taiwan)—about the same as 1974.

1976

7259—Growing Up (Hong Kong)—golden blonde hair—rest same as 1975.

1069—Malibu (Korea)—new rose box—hard shiny plastic arms and hands—rest about the same as 1975.

9428—Deluxe Quick Curl—See Chapter III for description.

7193—Funtime—See Chapter III for description.

Allan — 12"

1964

1000—Straight legs—molded red hair—brown eyes—blue shorts, striped jacket—marked: ©1960/by/Mattel, Inc./Hawthorne/Calif. U.S.A.

1965

1010—Bendable legs—same as preceding doll except has bendable legs.

1000—Straight legs—same as 1964.

1966

1000—Straight legs—available until Fall from mail-order catalogues.

1010—Bendable legs—available until Fall from mail-order catalogues.

Skooter — 9¼"

1965

1040—Straight legs—brown eyes—freckles—hair tied in two sections—marked: ©1963/Mattel, Inc.—2 piece red and white swimsuit.

1966

1120—Bendable legs—The first issue had the old tan skin. The next issue had the new pink skin. Dressed in two-piece swimsuit, navy shorts, red and white polka dot top.

1040—Straight legs—new pink skin—rest same as 1965.

1967

1040—Straight legs—same as 1966.

1120—Bendable legs—available until Fall from mail-order catalogues.

1968

1040—Straight legs—available until Fall from mail-order catalogues.

1976

7381—Funtime—See Chapter III for description.

Ricky — 9¼"

1965

1090—Straight legs—molded red hair—blue eyes—blue trunks, striped jacket—marked: ©1963/Mattel, Inc.

1966

1090—Straight legs—new pink skin—rest same as 1965.

1967

1090—Straight legs—same as 1966.

Francie — 11¼″

1966

1130—Bendable legs — old grayish tan skin — brown eyes—rooted eyelashes—one-piece swimsuit, patterned design on aqua background.

1130—Bendable legs—second issue had pink skin and a different swimsuit. The suit had a solid green bottom and a patterned top with a white background.

1140—Straight legs—pink skin—painted eyelashes—2 piece red and white swimsuit.

1967

1170—Twist 'N Turn—rooted eyelashes—twist waist—bend legs—one-piece swimsuit with solid pink bottom, striped top.

1140—Straight legs—same as 1966.

1130—Bendable legs—same as second issue of 1966.

1968

1170—Twist 'N Turn (Japan)—same as 1967.

1140—Straight legs (Japan)—same as 1967.

1969

1170—Twist 'N Turn (Japan)—new short flip hair—new one-piece swimsuit with solid pink top and yellow and pink striped bottom.

1970

1122—Hair Happenin's (Japan)—twist—bend knees—short blonde hair—blue dress.

1129—Growin' Pretty Hair (Japan)—First issue had arms and hands made from the original Barbie mold with the divided fingers — no extra hair pieces — rooted eyelashes—short pink party dress.

1170—Twist 'N Turn (Japan)—new yellow, pink and green print side-closing top over rose shorts—rest about the same as 1969.

1971

1068—Malibu (Japan) — made from the Casey head mold—suntan skin—long straight blonde hair—painted eyelashes—one-piece swimsuit with rose top and red bottom, orange towel and sunglasses.

1074—Growin' Pretty Hair (Japan)—two extra hair pieces—rooted eyelashes—arms and hands made from the "Mexico" Barbie molds—rest same as #1129 of 1970.

1129—Growin' Pretty Hair (Japan)—no extra hair pieces. Now has the "Mexico" Barbie arms and hands. Rest same as 1970.

1170—Twist 'N Turn (Japan)—new hair style—hair brushed straight back from forehead, orange head band, long flip ends—orange pleated mini dress—rest same as 1970.

1122—Hair Happenin's (Japan)—paler lips and fluffier hair than 1970. Rest about the same.

1972

3313—Busy (Hong Kong)—grasp hands—long blonde hair tied in back with green ribbon—green tank top, blue jeans, accessories—painted eyebrows.

1068—Malibu (Japan)—about the same as 1971.

1074—Growin' Pretty Hair (Japan)—about the same as 1971.

1122—Hair Happenin's (Japan)—available until Fall from mail-order catalogues.

1973

4222—Quick Curl (Taiwan)—brunette hair—painted eyelashes—Barbie "Mexico" arms and hands—long yellow dress.

1068—Malibu (Korea)—new green package—marked: © 1966/Mattel, Inc./U.S. Patented/U.S. Pat. Pend./Made In/Korea. Rest about the same.

1074—Growin' Pretty Hair (Japan)—available until Fall from mail-order catalogues.

3313—Busy (Hong Kong)—available until Fall from mail-order catalogues.

1974

1068—Malibu (Korea)—wrist tags discontinued later in year. Rest same.

4222—Quick Curl (Taiwan)—no wrist tags late in year—rest about the same as 1973.

1975

7699—A baggie (Taiwan)—straight legs—non-twist waist—painted eyelashes—brown eyes—long straight brunette hair—"Mexico" Barbie arms and hands—2 piece yellow swimsuit.

1068—Malibu (Korea)—new white box—no towel—no-sunglasses—rest same.

1976

1068—Malibu (Korea)—new rose box—rest same.

7699—A baggie (Taiwan)—same as 1975.

Tutti — 6¼″

1966

3550—Long, straight hair—blue eyes—red and white checked gingham play suit, matching hat with white brim—marked: ©1965/Mattel, Inc./Japan.

3552—"Walkin My Dolly" playset—doll and buggy with small doll inside.

3553—"Night Night-Sleep Tight" playset—doll with a bed.

3554—"Me And My Dog" playset—doll and a big white dog.

3555—"Melody In Pink" playset—doll, piano and stool.

3556—"Sundae Treat" playset—Todd included—ice cream table, seats, accessories.

No #—Same as Sundae Treat but in a small brown box—Todd included.

1967

3550—New dress with solid rose waist, floral skirt—same markings.

3580—New stock number but same as preceding.

3559—"Cookin Goodies" playset—doll, stove and pot.

3560—"Swing-A-Ling" playset—doll and swing.

3556—Playset—same as 1966.

3552 through 3555—same as 1966.

No #—same doll as Sundae Treat (brown box) available until Fall from mail-order catalogues.

1968

3580—(Japan)—most had the same dress as 1967. Some had the material reversed.

All 7 playsets.

1969

3580—(Japan)—most dresses have printed yoke, solid rose skirt.

1970

3580—(Japan)—same as 1969.

1971

3580—(Japan)—same as 1970.

1974

8128—See Chapter III for description.

1975

7453—"Swing-A-Ling"—see Chapter III for description.

7454—"Walkin' My Dolly"—see Chapter III for description.

7455—"Night Night"—see Chapter III for description.

8128—See Chapter III for description.

1976

7453—"Swing-A-Ling"—see Chapter III for description.

7454—"Walkin' My Dolly"—see Chapter III for description.

7455—"Night Night"—see Chapter III for description.

8128—See Chapter III for description.

Todd — 6¼″

1966

3556—"Sundae Treat"—with Tutti—ice cream table and seats, accessories. Rooted titian hair—brown eyes.

No #—Same doll as Sundae Treat but in a small brown box—Tutti included.

3580—This was listed in some Mattel publications but not in any booklets or catalogues. It is doubtful that this was ever on the market.

1967

3590—Red, white and blue checked shorts and cap, blue shirt and socks, red shoes—rooted titian hair—brown eyes.

3556—"Sundae Treat"—same as 1966.

No #—Same doll as Sundae Treat (brown box) available until Fall from mail-order catalogues.

1968

3556—"Sundae Treat"—same as 1967.

3590—Available from a mail-order catalogue. (Japan).

1969

3590—Available from a mail-order catalogue. (Japan).

1970

3590—Available until Fall from a mail-order catalogue.

1974

8129—See Chapter III for description.

1975

8129—See Chapter III for description.

1976

8129—See Chapter III for description.

Colored Francie — 11¼″

1967

1100—Twist—made from the Francie mold—brown skin—straight brown hair that turns red in time—rust brown eyes—rooted eyelashes—bend knees—bright printed swimsuit with a sheer top.

1968

1100—Twist—darker brown eyes—hair does not turn red—rest same as 1967.

Casey — 11¼″

1967

1180—Twist—molded teeth—short hair in blonde or brunette—the brunette turns reddish with time—rooted eyelashes—earring in left ear—one-piece gold and white swimsuit.

1968

1180—Twist (Japan)—hair does not turn reddish—rest same as 1967.

1969

1180—Twist (Japan)—same as 1968.

1970

1180—Twist (Japan)—same as 1969.

1975

9000—A baggie (Taiwan)—made from the Francie head mold—straight legs—non-twist waist—brown eyes—painted lashes—long blonde hair—has Barbie's Mexico arms and hands.

1976

9000—A baggie (Taiwan)—about the same as 1975.

Twiggy — 11¼″

1967

1185—Twist—made from the Casey head mold—short, straight blonde hair—rooted upper eyelashes and painted lower lashes—blue eyes—bend knees—yellow, blue and green striped mini dress—yellow boots.

1968

1185—Twist—same as 1967.

Chris — 6¼″

1967

3570—Long blonde or brunette hair with 2 green bows and a green barrette—brown eyes—multi-colored dress.

1968

3570—Same as 1967.

1969

3570—Available until Fall from mail-order catalogue.

1974

8130—See Chapter III for description.

1975

8130—See Chapter III for description.

1976

8130—See Chapter III for description.

Stacey — 11½″

1968

1125—Talking (Mexico)—British accent—Mexico hands—bend knees—rooted eyelashes—long straight hair tied in back and to the side, blonde or titian—2 piece striped swimsuit.

1165—Twist (Japan)—rooted eyelashes—long straight hair tied in back, blonde or titian—bend knees—one-piece red swimsuit trimmed with white buttons.

1969

1165—Twist (Japan)—new one piece psychedelic print swimsuit—new short turned up hair—rest same as 1968.

1125—Talking (Mexico)—new cardboard box—rest same as 1968.

1970

1125—Talking—First part of year same as 1969. Later in year new blue and silver swimsuit—now Hong Kong.

1165—Twist (Japan)—First part of year same as 1969. Later new blue and rose floral swimsuit.

1971

1125—Talking (Hong Kong)—available until Fall from mail-order catalogues.

1165—Twist (Japan)—available until Fall from mail-order catalogues.

Christie (Black) — 11½″

1968

1126—Talking (Mexico)—rooted eyelashes—short curly brown hair—brown eyes—bend knees—Mexico hands—brown skin—dressed in a knitted green top over rose vinyl shorts—clear plastic box.

1969

1126—Talking (Mexico)—new cardboard box—some hair turns red—rest same as 1968.

1970

1119—Twist (Japan)—rooted eyelashes—brown curly hair parted on right side—light brown skin—bend knees—one-piece pink and yellow swimsuit.

1126—Talking (Mexico, until fire)—same skin and hair as 1969—new clothes, a brightly colored Afro top over shorts (matches Brad's)—same markings as 1969.

1971

1175—Live Action (Taiwan)—made from the Midge head mold—long, straight black hair—rooted eyelashes—rust colored eyes.

1119—Twist (Japan)—same as 1970.

1126—Talking (Hong Kong)—darker skin—new modified Afro hair style—same clothes as 1970.

1972

1175—Live Action (Taiwan)—same as 1971.

1119—Twist (Japan)—same as 1971.

1126—Talking (Hong Kong)—same as 1971.

1973

7745—Malibu (Taiwan)—painted eyelashes—long, straight black hair — brown eyes — Mexico hands — bend knees — twist—one-piece red swimsuit, white towel, sunglasses.

1175—Live Action (Taiwan)—available until Fall from mail-order catalogues.

1974

7745—Malibu (Taiwan early—Korea later)—Taiwan doll about the same as 1973. The Korea doll had arms and hands made from the Francie mold.

1975

7745—Malibu (Korea)—new yellow swimsuit—new white box—no wrist tag—no towel—"Korea" arms and hands.

1976

7745—Malibu (Korea)—new rose box—new hard shiny plastic arms and hands made from the Mexico mold—rest about the same as 1975.

Buffy and Mrs. Beasley — 6¼″

1968

3577—(Japan)—blonde, double ponytail tied with red ribbons—dress—red skirt with red and white polka dot waist.

1969

3577—Same as 1968.

1970

3577—Same as 1969.

Truly Scrumptious — 11½″

1969

1107—Talking (Mexico)—made from the Francie head mold—Mexico hands—blonde hair brushed back—rooted eyelashes—blue eyes—bend knees.

1108—Standard (Japan)—straight legs—non-twist waist—head same as the #1107—original Barbie arms and hands.

Julia — 11½″

1969

1128—Talking (Mexico)—made from the Christie head mold—light brown skin—Mexico hands—brown eyes—short, straight dark brown hair—rooted eyelashes—bend knees—gold and silver jumpsuit.

1127—Twist (Japan)—same hair and skin as preceding doll—Korea hands—two-piece white nurse's uniform and cap.

1970

1128—Talking (Mexico, until fire)—same as 1969.

1127—Twist (Japan)—new one-piece white uniform and cap.

1971

1128—Talking (Hong Kong)—new darker skin—new black modified Afro hair style—same clothes.

1127—Twist—(Japan)—same as 1970.

1972

1128—Talking (Hong Kong)—same as 1971.

P. J. —11½″

1969

1113—Talking (Mexico)—made from the Midge head mold—Mexico hands—brown eyes—rooted eyelashes—bend knees.

1970

1118—Twist (Japan)—same head and hair as preceding doll — original divided fingers — rooted eyelashes — bend knees.

1113—Talking (Mexico, until fire)—same as 1969.

1971

1153—Live Action on Stage (Taiwan)—new hair style, long blonde with two sections of braided hair—neck rim marked Hong Kong—rooted eyelashes—brown eyes.

1156—Live Action (Taiwan)—same as preceding but no stage.

1113—Talking (Hong Kong)—about the same as 1970 except new markings.

1118—Twist (Japan)—about the same as 1970.

1972

1187—Malibu (Japan)—made from the Steffie head mold—original divided fingers—blue eyes—painted eyelashes—blonde hair tied in two sections and decorated with beads—lavender swimsuit, sunglasses, green towel.

1113—Talking (Hong Kong)—about the same as 1971.

1156—Live Action (Taiwan)—about the same as 1971.

1153—Live Action on Stage (Taiwan)—available until Fall from mail-order catalogues.

1973

1187—Malibu (Taiwan)—Mexico hands—rest about the same as 1972.

1113—Non-talk Talking (Hong Kong)—in a plastic bag—clothes same as regular doll.

1156—Live Action (Taiwan)—in a plastic bag—same as regular doll except no stand.

1156—Live Action (Taiwan)—available until Fall from mail-order catalogues.

1113—Talking (Hong Kong)—available until Fall from mail-order catalogues.

1974

1187—Malibu (Taiwan early—Korea later)—the Taiwan doll wore a new green swimsuit, same style as 1973. The Korea doll wore the old lavender suit. No wrist tags late in year.

1975

7263—Gold Medal Gymnast (Taiwan)—a Malibu doll with Mexico hands—dressed in a red, white and blue swimsuit—warm up jacket—balance beam.

7281—Free Moving (Taiwan)—has a "free mover" tab on back—hard, shiny Mexico arms and hands—new hair style—painted eyelashes—dark brown eyes—made from the Steffie head mold.

1187—Malibu (Korea)—new white box—sunglasses and towel discontinued.

1976

9218—Deluxe Quick Curl (Taiwan)—medium length blonde quick curl hair—painted eyelashes—Mexico hands.

7263—Gold Medal Gymnast (Taiwan)—same as 1975.

1187—Malibu (Korea)—new hard shiny Mexico arms and hands—new rose box—rest about the same as 1975.

7281—Free Moving (Taiwan)—available until Fall from mail-order catalogue.

Brad (Black) — 12″

1970

1114—Talking (Mexico—later Hong Kong)—neck rim marked Hong Kong—dark brown skin—brown eyes—bend knees—black painted hair—bright colored Afro top over shorts.

1142—Bendable legs (Hong Kong)—head and skin similar to preceding doll—orange shirt, print shorts.

1971

1114—Talking (Hong Kong)—slightly darker skin—same clothes—same markings as late 1970 doll.

1142—Bendable legs (Hong Kong)—slightly darker skin—rest same.

1972

1114—Talking (Hong Kong)—about the same as 1971.

1142—Bendable legs (Hong Kong)—about the same as 1971.

1973

1114—Talking (Hong Kong)—available until Fall from mail-order catalogues.

Jamie — 11½″

1970

1132—Walking (Japan)—made for Sears—made from the Barbie head mold—brown eyes—original divided fingers—rooted eyelashes.

1971

1132—Walking (Japan)—same as 1970.

1972

1132—Walking (Japan)—available until Fall from mail-order catalogues. Also available in a Gift Set.

Pretty Pairs — 6¼″

1970

1133—Lori 'N Rori—blonde doll, brown Teddy bear.

1134—Nan 'N Fran—black doll, small black doll.

1135—Angie 'N Tangie—brunette doll, small blonde doll.

Fluff — 9¼″

1971

1143—Living (Taiwan)—brown eyes—rooted eyelashes—double ponytail blonde hair—bend knees and elbows—swivel waist, neck, arms, hands and legs—one-piece swimsuit with a striped top and solid orange bottom—yellow skateboard.

1972

1143—Living (Taiwan)—available until Fall from mail-order catalogues.

Tiff — 9¼″

1972

1199—Pose 'N Play (Taiwan)—made from the Fluff head mold—swing free arms—brown eyes—painted lashes—long, straight titian hair—blue jeans and white sleeveless shirt.

1973

1199—Pose 'N Play (Taiwan)—available until Fall from mail-order catalogues.

Steffie—11½″

1972

1183—Walk Lively (Taiwan)—special walking mechanism—rooted eyelashes—long brunette hair—brown eyes—Mexico hands—red tricot jumpsuit.

3312—Busy (U.S.A.)—grasping hands—painted eyelashes—long brunette hair—blue eyes.

1186—Talking Busy (Hong Kong)—long curly blonde hair—blue eyes—grasping hands—rooted eyelashes.

1973

3312—Busy (Hong Kong)—new markings—rest about the same.

1183—Walk Lively (Taiwan)—about the same as 1972.

Babs—11½″

1974

7888—A regular Busy Steffie sold in a plastic bag.

Miss America—11½″

1972

3200—Walk Lively (Taiwan)—made from the Steffie head mold—rooted eyelashes—blue eyes—walking construction—Mexico hands—brunette hair with curled ends.

3194-9991—Kellogg's special (Taiwan)—same as preceding doll—no stand.

1973

8867—Quick Curl (Taiwan)—long brunette quick curl hair—painted eyelashes—twist waist—bend knees.

3194-9991—Kellogg's special (Taiwan)—both the Walk Lively and the Quick Curl were used this year.

3200—Walk Lively (Taiwan)—available until Fall from mail-order catalogues.

1974

8697—Quick Curl (Taiwan)—new blonde hair—rest about the same.

3194-4—Kellogg's offer (Taiwan)—the blond Quick Curl was used.

1975

8697—Quick Curl (Taiwan)—about the same as 1974.

8697—Kellogg's offer (Taiwan)—about the same as the doll above.

1976

8697—Quick Curl (Taiwan)—about the same as 1975.

Kelley—11½″

1973

4221—Quick Curl (Taiwan)—made from the Steffie head mold—medium length red hair—brown eyes—Mexico hands—painted eyelashes.

1974

7808—Yellowstone (Taiwan)—new suntan skin—new long, straight red hair—twist—bend knees.

4221—Quick Curl (Taiwan)—about the same as 1973.

1975

4221—Quick Curl (Taiwan)—about the same as 1974.

1976

4221—Quick Curl (Taiwan)—available until Fall from mail-order catalogues.

"Barbie Baby Sits" baby

1974

7882—Sears' catalogue offer—baby same as the Sunshine Family baby—wispy rooted blonde hair—blue glass eyes—accessories—unjointed.

1975

7882—About the same as 1974.

1976

7882—New accessories—new box—doll same as 1975.

Cara (Black)—11½″

1975

7283—Free Moving (Taiwan)—made from the Steffie head mold—hard shiny Mexico arms and hands—painted eyelashes—dark brown hair—brown eyes.

7291—Quick Curl (Taiwan)—made from the Steffie head mold—Painted eyelashes—Mexico hands—twist—bend knees—long, dark brown hair.

1976

9220—Deluxe Quick Curl (Taiwan)—medium length, dark brown hair—painted lashes—Mexico hands—twist—bend knees.

9528—Ballerina (Taiwan)—special leg construction to "dance"—a new model arms and hands—painted lashes—twist waist.

7283—Free Moving (Taiwan)—available until Fall from mail-order catalogues.

Curtis (Black)-12″

1975

7282—Free Moving (Taiwan)—made from the Brad head mold.

Ginger—9¼″

1976

9222—Growing Up (Hong Kong)—made from the Skipper mold—long brunette hair—rotate arm to "grow"—painted lashes—hard shiny arms and hands.

Carla—6¼″

1976

7377—See Chapter III for description.

3. Markings

The primary markings of a Barbie doll are found on the hip or the lower back. Some of the dolls do have less important markings on the rim of the neck and/or the back of the head.

Barbie T.M.
Pats. Pend.
©MCMLVIII
by
Mattel
Inc.

1959—Barbie T.M., #1 & 2 (850)
1960—Barbie T.M., #3 & 4 (850)
1961—Barbie®, #5 & 6 (850)
1962—Barbie®, #7 & 8 (850)

Ken T.M.
Pats. Pend.
©MCMLX
by
Mattel
Inc.

1961—Ken, flocked hair (750)
1962—Ken, painted hair (750)

Midge T.M.
©1962
Barbie®
© 1958
by
Mattel, Inc.

1963—Midge (860)
1963—Fashion Queen (870)
1963 Barbie, bubble (850)
1963—Barbie, ponytail (850)
1964—(Early)—Barbie, Swirl (850)

Ken®
©1960
by
Mattel, Inc.
Hawthorn
Calif. U.S.A.

1963—Ken (#750)

Midge T.M.
©1962
Barbie®
©1958
by
Mattel, Inc.
Patented

1964—(later)Swirl (0850)
1964—1965, Barbie, regular ponytail (0850)
1964—1967, Barbie bubble(0850)
1964—1967, Midge (0860)
1964—Fashion Queen (0870)
1967—1971, Barbie, standard (1190)
1969-Truly Scrumptious, straight leg (1108)
1972—Ward's Barbie (3210)

(intaglio)
©1958
Mattel, Inc.
U.S. Patented
U.S. Pat. Pend.

1964—Miss Barbie (1060)
1965—Barbie, bend leg (1070)
1965—Midge—bend leg (1080)

Skipper
©1963
Mattel, Inc.

1964—Skipper, straight leg (0950)

©1960
by
Mattel, Inc.
Hawthorn
Calif. U.S.A.

1964—1965, Allan, straight leg (1000)
1964—1967, Ken, straight leg (0750)
1965—1966, Ken, bend leg (1020)
1965—Allan, bend leg (1010)

©1963
Mattel, Inc.

1965—1967, Skooter, straight leg (1040)
1965—1967, Ricky (1090)
1965—1967 Skipper, bend leg (1030)
1965—1968, Skipper, straight leg (0950)
1966—1967, Skooter, bend leg (1120)
1970—1971, re-issue Skipper (0950)

(intaglio)
©1958
Mattel, Inc.
U.S. Patented
U.S. Pat. Pend.
(raised)
Made in
Japan

1966—Barbie, Color Magic (1150)
1966—Barbie, bend legs (1070)
1966—Midge, bend legs (1080)

(all raised)
©1958
Mattel, Inc.
U.S. Patented
U.S. Pat. Pend.
Made in
Japan

1966 (later) Barbie, Color Magic (1150)
1966 (later) Barbie, bend legs (1070)
1966 (later) Midge, bend legs (1080)
1967—Barbie, Color Magic (1150)

©1965
Mattel, Inc.
U.S. Patented
U.S. Pat. Pend.
Made in Japan

1966-1967, Francie bend leg (1130)
1966-1968, Francie, straight leg (1140)

©1965
Mattel, Inc.
U.S. Patd.
U.S. Pat. Pend.
Made in Japan

1966—Francie, bend leg (1130)
1966—Francie, straight leg (1140)

©1965
Mattel, Inc.
Japan

1966—1971, Tutti (all)
1966—-1968, Todd (all)
1967—1968, Chris (3570)
1968—1970, Buffy (3577)
1970—Lori (1133)
1970—Nan (1134)
1970—Angie (1135)

©1966
Mattel, Inc.
U.S. Patented
U.S. Pat. Pend.
Made in
Japan

67—1971, Barbie, twist (1160)
67—Barbie, Trade-in (1162)
67—1970, Casey (1180)
67—1968, Colored Francie (1100)
67—1971, Francie, twist (1170)
67—1968, Twiggy (1185)
68—1971, Stacey, twist (1165)
69—1971, Julia, twist (1127)
70-1971, Francie Hair Happenins (1122)
70—1972, Christie, twist (1119)
70—1971, P.J., twist (1118)
71—Barbie Hair Happenins (1174)
71—1972, Barbie, Malibu (1067)
71—1972, Francie, Malibu (1068)
72—Barbie, Forget-Me-Nots (3269)

1966
attel, Inc.
S. Patented
S. Pat. Pend.
ade in Japan

67—Barbie, Trade In (some) (1162)

1967
attel, Inc.
S. & Foreign
ts. Pend.
exico

68—1970, Barbie, talk (1115)
68—1970, Barbie, Spanish Talk (8348)
68-1970, Stacey, talk (1125)
68—1970, Christie, talk (1126)
69—1970, Julia, talk (1128)
69—Truly Scrumptious, talk (1107)
69—P.J., talk, (1113)
70—Barbie (Stacey mold), talk (1115)

1967 Mattel, Inc.
S. Pat'd
S. Pats. Pend.
ade in Japan

68—Skipper, twist (1105)
71—1972, Skipper, Malibu (1069)

1967 Mattel, Inc.
S. Pat'd.
S. Pats. Pend.
ade in Taiwan

68 (late)—1971, Skipper, twist (1105)
73—1975, Skipper, Quick Curl (4223)

1968
attel, Inc.
S. & For. Pat'd
ther Pat's
nding
exico

69—1970, Ken, talk (1111)
70—Ken, Spanish talk (8372)
70—Ken, bend legs (1124)
70—Brad, talk (1114)

©1968 Mattel, Inc.
U.S. & For. Pat'd
Other Pats. Pend.
Taiwan

1970—1971, Barbie, Living (1116)

©1968 Mattel, Inc.
U.S. & For. Pat'd
Other Pats. Pend
Japan

1970—1971, Barbie, Living in set (1585)

©1969 Mattel, Inc.
Taiwan
U.S. & For. Pat'd
Other Pats. Pend.
Patd. in Canada 1967

1970—1971, Skipper, Living (1117)
1970—Skipper, Trade-In (1147)
1971—Fluff, Living (1143)
1972—1973, Skipper, Pose 'N Play (1179)
1972—Tiff, Pose 'N Play (1199)

©1968
Mattel, Inc.
U.S. & For. Pat'd
Other Pats.
Pending
Hong Kong

1970 (late)—1972, Brad, talk (1114)
1970—1972, Brad, bend leg (1142)

©1966
Mattel, Inc.
U.S. Pat. Other
Pats. Pend.
Pat. Canada
1967
Japan

1970—1971, Francie Grow Pretty hair (1129)
1971—1972, Francie Grow Pretty hair (1074)

©1967 Mattel, Inc.
U.S. Patented
Pat'd Canada 1967
Other Pat's Pend.
Japan

1970—1971, Jamie, Walking (1132)

©1967
Mattel, Inc.
U.S. & Foreign
Pats. Pend.
Hong Kong

1970 (late)—Barbie (Stacey head), Spanish talk (8348)

1970 (late)—1972, Barbie, talk (1115)
1970 (late)—Stacey, talk (1125)
1971—1972, Barbie, Spanish talk (8348)
1971—1972, Julia, talk (1128)
1971—1972, P.J., talk (1113)
1971—1972, Christie, talk (1126)
1972—Barbie, Busy talk (1195)
1972—Steffie, Busy Talk (1186)

©1968 Mattel, Inc.
U.S. & Foreign Patented
Patented in Canada 1967
Other Patents Pending
Taiwan

1971—Barbie, Live Action on Stage (1152)
1971—P.J., Live Action on Stage (1153)
1971—1972, Barbie Live Action (1155)
1971—1972, P.J. Live Action (1156)
1971—1972, Christie, Live Action (1175)

©1968
Mattel, Inc.
Taiwan
U.S. & For. Pat'd
Patented in
Canada 1967
Other Pats
Pending

1971—Ken, Live Action on Stage (1172)
1971—1972, Ken, Live Action (1159)

©1968
Mattel, Inc.
U.S. & For. Pat'd
Other Pats
Pending
Hong Kong

1971—1974, Ken, Malibu (1088)
1971—1972, Ken, talk (1111)
1972—1973, Ken, Busy (3314)
1972—Ken, talk Busy (1196)
1973—1975, Ken, Mod Hair (4424)
1974-1976, Ken, Ward's dressed (4234)

©1967 Mattel, Inc.
U.S. Patented
Other Patents Pending
Patented in Canada 1967
Taiwan

1971—1972, Barbie, Grow Pretty Hair (1144)
1973, 1974, 1976—Barbie (8588)

©1967 Mattel, Inc.
U.S. Pat. pend.
Taiwan

1972-1973, Barbie, Walk Lively (1182)
1972—1973, Steffie, Walk Lively (1183)
1972-Miss America, Walk Lively (3200)
1972—1973, Miss America (Kellogg's 3194-9991)

©1968 Mattel, Inc.
U.S. Pat. Pend.
Taiwan

1972—1973, Ken, Walk Lively (1184)

©1966
Mattel, Inc.
U.S. Patented
Other Pats. Pend.
Made in
Japan

1972—P.J., Malibu (1187)

©1966
Mattel, Inc.
U.S. & Foreign
Patented
Other Pat's
Pending
Made in
U.S.A.

1972—Barbie, Busy (3311)
1972—Steffie, Busy (3312)

©1966
Mattel, Inc.
Hong Kong
U.S. & Foreign
Patented
Other Pat's
Pending

1972—Francie, Busy (3313)

©1966
Mattel, Inc.
U.S. & Foreign
Patented
Other Pat's
Pending
Made in
Taiwan

1973—1975, Barbie, Quick Curl (4220)
1973—1975, Kelley, Quick Curl (4221)
1973—1976, Miss America, Quick Curl (8697)
1973—Miss America (Kellogg's) (3194-9991)
1973—1974 (early)—Christie, Malibu (7745)
1973—1974 (early)—Barbie, Malibu (1067)
1973—1974 (early)—P.J., Malibu (1187)
1974—Miss America (Kellogg's) (3194-4)
1974—1975, Barbie, Sweet 16 (7796)
1974—Barbie, Sun Valley (7806)
1974—1975, Barbie, Newport (7807)
1974—Kelley, Yellowstone (7808)
1975—Barbie, Gold Medal (7233)
1975—1976, Baribe, Gold Medal Skater (7262)
1975—1976, Barbie, Gold Medal Skier (7264)
1975—1976, P.J., Gold Medal Gymnast (7263)
1975—Miss America (Kellogg's) (8697)
1975—1976—Barbie, Sears' set (9042)
1976—Barbie, Deluxe Quick Curl (9217)
1976—P.J., Deluxe Quick Curl (9218)
1976—Cara, Deluxe Quick Curl (9220)

©1966
Mattel, Inc.
Taiwan
U.S. & Foreign
Patented
Other Pat's
Pending

1973—1974, Francie, Quick Curl (4222)

©1966
Mattel, Inc.
U.S. & Foreign
Patented
Other Pat's
Pending
Made in
Hong Kong

1973—Barbie, Busy (3311)
1973—Steffie, Busy (3312)
1974—"Babs" Steffie (7888)

©1967
Mattel, Inc.
U.S. & For.
Pat'd Pat'd
In Canada
1967 Other
Pat's. Pend.
Hong Kong

1973—Barbie, talk Busy (1195)

©1967
Mattel, Inc.
U.S. & For. Pat'd.
Pat'd in Canada 1967
Other Pat's. Pend.
Hong Kong

1973—Barbie, talk Busy (Canada)

©1967 Mattel, Inc.
U.S. Pat'd
U.S. Pats. Pend.
Made in Korea

1973—1976, Skipper, Malibu (1069)
1975—1976, Skipper, Funtime (7193)
1976—Skooter, Funtime (7381)

©1966
Mattel, Inc.
U.S. Patented
U.S. Pat. Pend.
Made in
Korea

1973—1976, Francie, Malibu (1068)
1973—1975, Barbie (8587)
1974 (late)—1976, P.J., Malibu (1187)
1974 (late)—1976, Christie, Malibu (7745)
1974 (late)—1976, Barbie, Malibu (1067)
1975—1976—Barbie, Hawaiian (7470)
1975—1976—Barbie, Sears' set (9044)
1975—1976, Barbie, Funtime (7192)
1976—Barbie, Beautiful Bride (9599)

©1968
Mattel, Inc.
U.S. & For. Patd.
Other Pats.
Pending
Taiwan

1974—Ken, Sun Valley (7809)
1975—1976, Ken, Gold Medal Skier (7261)
1975—1976, Ken, Funtime (7194)
1975—1976 (early)—Ken, Malibu (1088)
1976 (early)—Ken, Now Look (9342)

©1967 Mattel, Inc.
Taiwan
U.S. Pat. Pend.

1975—Barbie, Free Moving (7270)
1975—P.J., Free Moving (7281)
1975—Cara, Free Moving (7283)

©1968 Mattel, Inc.
Taiwan
U.S. Patent
Pending

1975—Ken, Free Moving (7280)
1975—Curtis, Free Moving (7282)

©1966
Mattel, Inc.
U.S. and Foreign
Patented
Other Pat's
Pending
Made in Taiwan

1975—Cara, Quick Curl (7291)

©1967
Mattel, Inc.
Hong Kong
U.S. & For. Pat.

1975—1976, Skipper, Grow Up (7259)
1976—Ginger, Grow Up (9222)

©1968 Mattel, Inc.
Taiwan
U.S. & Foreign Patd.
Patd. in Canada 1967

1975—1976, Ken, Gold Medal Skier (7261)

©1966
Mattel, Inc.
Taiwan

1975—Francie (baggie) (7699)
1975—Casey (baggie) (9000)

©Mattel, Inc. 1966
U.S. Patent Pending
Taiwan

1976—Barbie, Ballerina (9093)
1976—Cara, Ballerina (9528)

©1965
Mattel, Inc.
Hong Kong

1976—Carla (7377)
1976—Tutti (8128)
1976—Todd (8129)
1976—Chris (8130)

©1959
Mattel, Inc.
U.S. Patented
U.S. Pat. Pend.
Made in
Korea

1976—Barbie (7283)

©1967 Mattel, Inc.
Taiwan
U.S. Patented
Other Patents Pending

1976—Skipper, Deluxe Quick Curl (9428)

1088 0500 1
©Mattel
Inc. 1968
Hong Kong

1976 (late)—Ken, Malibu (1088)

1088 0500 3
©Mattel
Inc. 1968
Hong Kong

1976 (late)—Ken, Now Look (9342)

4. Arm and Hand Molds

This list does not include the special arm and hand molds such as Living, Busy, Ballerina and so on. Only the molds needed to help identify or date a particular doll are listed.

Original Barbie arms and hands with divided fingers:
All Barbie-size dolls prior to 1968.
The first Spanish Talking Barbie, 1968.
Twist Stacey, 1968—1970.
Standard Truly Scrumptious, 1969.
First issue France With Growin' Pretty Hair (1129), 1970.
Twist P.J., 1970—1971.
Walking Jamie, 1970—1971.
Barbie Hair Happenin's, 1971.
Malibu Barbie, 1971—1972, and late 1974.
Malibu P.J., 1972, and late 1974.
Ward's Barbie, 1972.
#8587 Barbie (bubble box, Europe), 1974.
#8587 Barbie (bubble box, Canada), late 1974—1975.

Barbie arms and hands with slender undivided fingers:
(Called the "Mexico" hands by collectors)
Talking Barbie, 1968—1972.
Spanish Talking Barbie, 1969—1972.
Talking Stacey, 1968—1970.
Talking Christie, 1968—1972.
Talking Julia, 1969—1972.
Talking Truly Scrumptious, 1969.
Talking P.J., 1969—1972.
Barbie With Growin' Pretty Hair, 1971—1972.
Second issue Francie With Growin' Pretty Hair (1129), 1971.
Francie With Growin' Pretty Hair (1074), 1971—1972.
Walk Lively Barbie, 1972—1973.
Walk Lively Steffie, 1972—1973.
Walk Lively Miss America, 1972.
Quick Curl Barbie, 1973—1975.
Quick Curl Kelley, 1973—1975.
Quick Curl Francie, 1973—1975.
Quick Curl Miss America, 1973—1976.
Quick Curl Cara, 1975.
Malibu Christie, 1973.
Malibu Barbie, 1973—early 1974.
Malibu P.J., 1973—early 1974.
Barbie Sweet 16, 1974—1975.
Sun Valley Barbie, 1974.
Newport Barbie, 1974—1975.
Yellowstone Kelley, 1974.
Gold Medal Barbie, 1975.
Gold Medal Barbie Skater, 1975—1976.
Gold Medal Barbie Skier, 1975—1976.
Gold Medal P.J. Gymnast, 1975—1976.
#7699 "baggie" Francie, 1975.
#9000 "baggie" Casey, 1975.
#9042—Gold Medal Barbie, 1975—1976.
Deluxe Quick Curl Barbie, 1976.
Deluxe Quick Curl P.J., 1976.
Deluxe Quick Curl Cara, 1976.
#8588 Barbie, 1973—1976.

Hard, shiny "Mexico" arms and hands:
Free Moving Barbie, 1975.
Free Moving P.J., 1975.
Free Moving Cara, 1975.
Quick Curl Cara, 1975.
Beautiful Bride Barbie, 1976.
Hawaiian Barbie, 1976.
Malibu Barbie, 1976.
Malibu P.J., 1976.
Malibu Christie, 1976.
#7382 Barbie (Germany), 1976.
#8587 Barbie (Canada), 1976.

Original Francie arms and hands:
Malibu Christie, 1974.
Hawaiian Barbie (U.S.A.), 1975.
Funtime Barbie, 1975—1976.
#8587 Barbie (pink box, Canada), 1975.
#8587 Barbie (pink box, Italy), 1975.

Original Barbie divided fingers not cut completely through:
(Called the "Korea" hands by collectors)
Twist Julia, 1969.
Twist Christie, 1970.
Malibu Barbie, 1975.
Malibu Christie, 1975.
Malibu P.J., 1975.
#9044 Gold Medal Barbie, 1975—1976.
Hawaiian Barbie (Germany), 1975.
#8587 Barbie (Germany), 1975.

5. Head Molds

1. *Barbie*
2. *Ken, flocked*
3. *Ken, painted*
4. *Midge*
   P.J. (talking, twist and Live Action)
   Live Action Christy
5. *Barbie, molded*
6. *Midge, molded*
7. *Skipper*
   Ginger
   Funtime Skooter
8. *Allan*
9. *Skooter*
10. *Ricky*
11. *Tutti*
    Todd
    Chris
    Buffy
    Pretty Pairs
    Carla
12. *Francie* [*all except Malibu*]
    Truly Scrumptious
    1975 "baggie" Casey
13. *Barbie, new look*
    Walking Jamie
14. *Casey*
    Twiggy
    "Becky"
    Malibu Francie
15. *Stacey*
    one talk Barbie
    one Spanish talk Barbie
    Malibu Barbie
    #7382 Barbie
    one #8587 Barbie
16. *Christie* [*all except Live Action*]
    Julia
17. *Ken, new look*
18. *Brad*
    Curtis
19. *Steffie*
    Miss America
    Malibu P.J.
    Free Moving P.J.
    Cara
    Kelley
    #8587 Barbie (one exception)
    Hawaiian Barbie
    Gold Medal P.J.
    Deluxe Quick Curl P.J.
20. *Fluff*
    Tiff

VI. Accessory Dolls and Animals

Mattel made several small dolls, toy animals and "live" animals as accessories for the Barbie dolls. Serious Barbie collectors consider these little dolls and animals an important part of the Barbie collecting hobby. Often they become a "collection within a collection."

1. The Dolls

The first of these little dolls was a miniature Barbie. This doll came in two sizes, 1 7/8 inches and 2 inches. She wore a painted-on red one-piece swimsuit. All of the dolls found to date have blonde hair, but a redheaded doll was pictured in one of the View-Master slides in "Barbie's Around the World Trip." And *sketches* of the doll in several of the early booklets showed red hair.

These little Barbie dolls were included in three Skipper sets in 1965 and 1966. These were "Day at the Fair" (1911), "Me and My Doll" (1913) and "Just For Fun," one of the Fashion Paks. "Just For Fun" was still available in 1967.

—:—

In 1965 and 1966 "Skipper Dream Room" (4094) was on the market. Included was a flat cardboard "rag" doll, about 3 inches tall.

—:—

"Let's Play House" (1932), a Skipper set of 1966, included a tiny doll in a tiny cradle.

—:—

The Tutti playsetting, "Walkin My Dolly" (3552), of 1966, 1967 and 1968 included a little baby doll in a buggy.

This set was re-issued in 1975 in Germany with the same little baby doll, stock number 7454. It was still on the market in 1976.

The early version of the doll had painted features and a blue hair bow. The re-issued doll was left unpainted.

In 1967 a tiny Barbie doll and a Barbie case were part of a Tutti set, "Let's Play Barbie" (3608).

—:—

Tutti's set, "Clowning Around" (3606), of 1967 included a small clown made of material that matched Tutti's dress, a black and white checked skirt with a solid yellow waist.

In 1968 and 1969 Tutti's set, "Pink P.J.'s" (3616), included a tiny baby doll in a tiny lace-trimmed pink pillow-holder.

—:—

"Mrs. Beasley," Buffy's doll (3577), was on the market in 1968, 1969 and 1970. She had short blonde hair and blue eyes. She wore a blue with white dots dress that was trimmed in yellow. She also wore a pair of granny glasses.

—:—

In 1970 "Fran," Nan's doll (1134), and "Tangie," Angie's doll (1135), were on the market. They were called "Pretty Pairs."

Fran, a black doll, had short black curly hair and brown eyes. She wore a one-piece pink lace-trimmed sleeper.

Tangie had yellow yarn hair tied in two sections and big blue eyes. Her long-waisted pink dress with lace trim matched Angie's.

—:—

Two 1967 Kiddle sets, Peter Paniddle (3547) and Florence Niddle (3507), are pictured here with the Barbie accessory dolls—for a special reason.

A tiny Barbie doll was used to make Tinkerbell for the Peter Paniddle set. This doll had on a painted-on gold colored swimsuit instead of the usual red. Her nylon gauze and wire wings were red with gold glitter trim.

In the Florence Niddle set there was a tiny doll in a buggy. This doll was the same as the one in the Tutti set, "Pink P.J.'s."

—:—

Although not pictured here, a little baby doll like the one in "Walkin' My Dolly" was included in a sleeper set for one of Mattel's larger baby dolls.

Fluff wearing #1911 "Day at the Fair."

"Just For Fun" Pak with the miniature Barbie doll.

Twist Skipper wearing #1913 "Me 'N My Doll."

Cardboard "rag" doll from #4094 "Skipper Dream Room."

#3552 "Walkin' My Dolly"—U.S.A.

#7454 "Walkin' My Dolly"—re-issued in Germany in 1975.

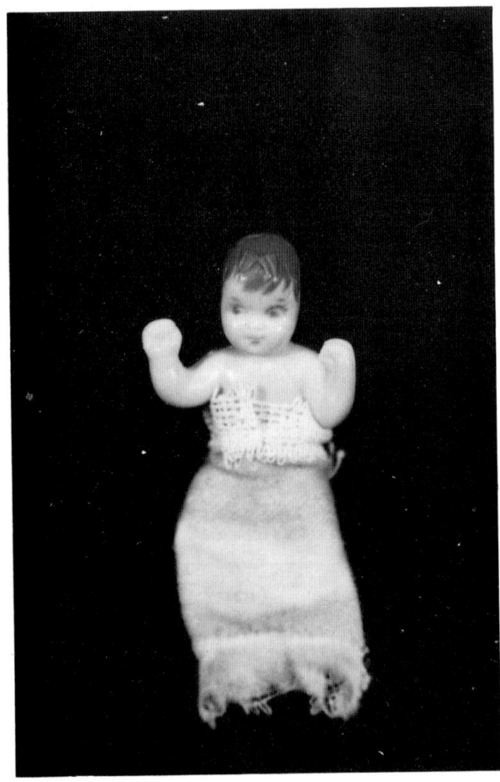

Baby from the original "Walkin' My Dolly." Painted features. Blue hair bow.

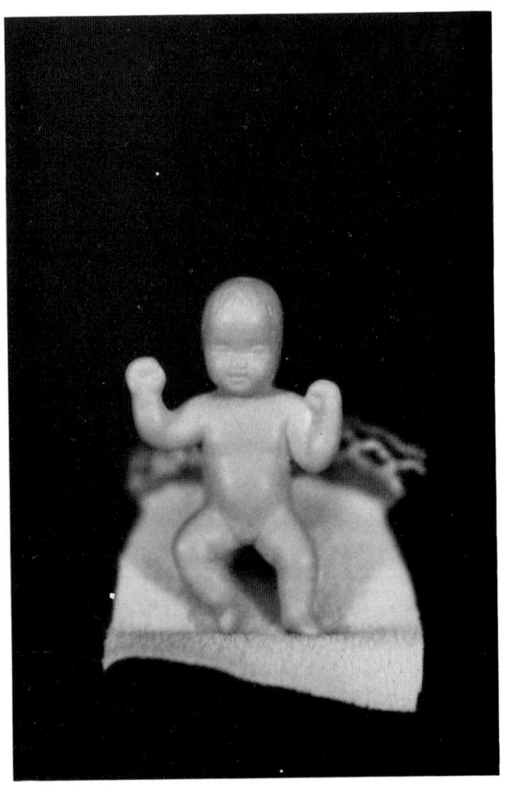

Baby from the re-issued "Walkin' My Dolly" set. Unpainted.

Bendable leg Skooter and #1932 "Let's Play House."

Tutti with the #3608 "Let's Play Barbie" set.

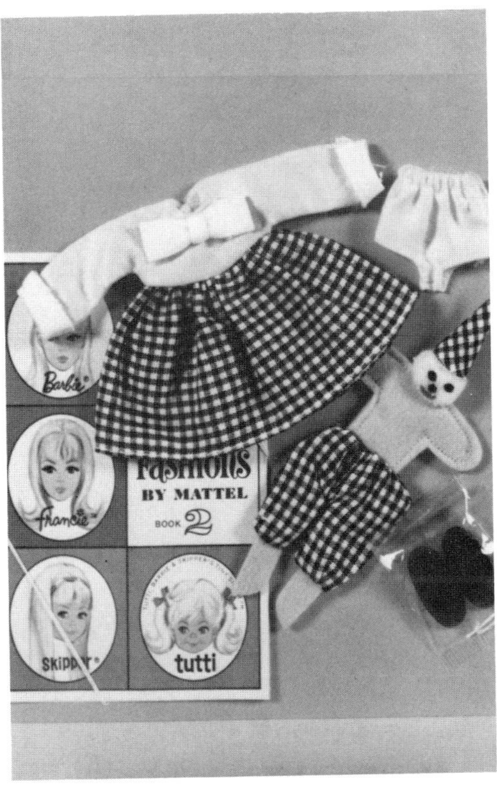

#3606 "Clowning Around," a Tutti set.

Tutti wearing #3616 "Pink P.J.'s." (This Tutti is only 5½" tall.)

Mrs. Beasley—From #3577 Buffy and Mrs. Beasley.

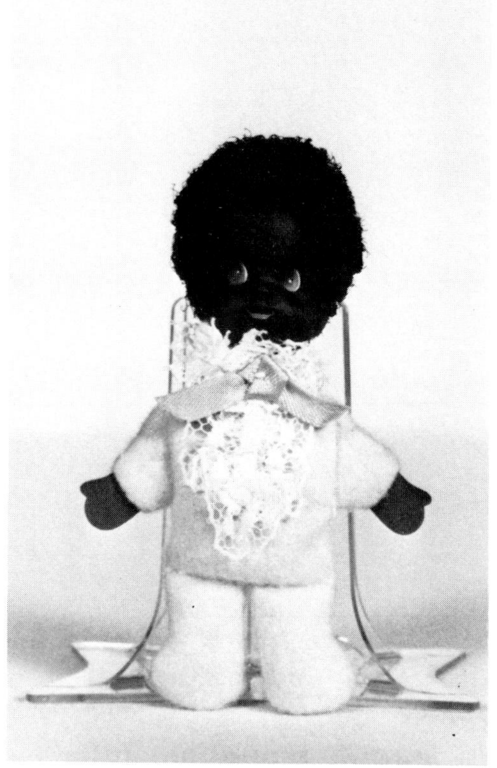

Fran—From #1134 Nan 'N Fran.

Tangie—From #1135 Angie 'N Tangie.

Tinkerbell—From #3547 Peter Paniddle, a Kiddle set. A tiny Barbie doll was used for Tinkerbell.

2. The Toy Animals

A little pink felt stuffed dog was included in Barbie's "Nighty-Negligee" set (965) on the market from 1959 through 1964. A little blue felt stuffed cat was included in Skipper's "Dreamtime" set (1909) of 1964, 1965 and 1966.

Since each little dog and cat was handmade in Japan, each one varied slightly. Each one reflected the talent and artistry of the individual worker who made it. The little dog seems to have varied more than the cat. They varied in size and in the color of the ears. Some of the ears were blue and some were purplish blue. It is believed that the first ones were blue and the later ones the purplish blue.

—:—

The wolf head mask from the little theatre costume "Red Riding Hood and the Wolf" (0880) is included here as one of the toy animals of 1964. It was made of grey plush with grey felt nose and ears. It had a red felt tongue and a pink felt mouth.

—:—

"Rori," Lori's Teddy bear (1133), was on the market in 1970. Lori 'N Rori was one of the Pretty Pairs group of dolls and toys.

The little Teddy bear was brown, about 2½ to 3 inches tall, and he resembeld the Kiddle type of toy, another Mattel product.

—:—

A white furry cat was a part of a Skipper "Get-Ups 'N Go" sleepwear set (7713) sold in 1973 and 1974. The neck ribbons on the cats were of various shades of rose.

—:—

Beginning in 1974 Sears catalogues offered a Barbie Baby Sits set (7882). In the set there was a tiny yellow plastic toy duck.

In September of 1976 this set was available in Sears retail stores as well as through the catalogue. The 1976 set had the same stock number but different accessories. It had a pink plastic duck and a pink plastic Teddy bear included.

—:—

In 1975 and 1976 Barbie's Room-Fulls (decorator-designed room backdrops with furniture and accessories) were on the market. One of these, "Studio Bedroom" (7405), contained a blue and white cotton print pillow in the shape of an elephant. These Room-Fulls were sold wherever toys were sold.

Barbie's Apartment (9188), a combination of the Studio Bedroom and the Country Kitchen Room-Fulls, was also on the market in 1975 but as a limited edition Department Store Special. The elephant pillow was included in this set too.

A 1962 ponytail Barbie wearing "Nighty-Negligee."

Pink and blue felt dogs from #965 "Nighty-Negligee." These varied in size and shade of colors.

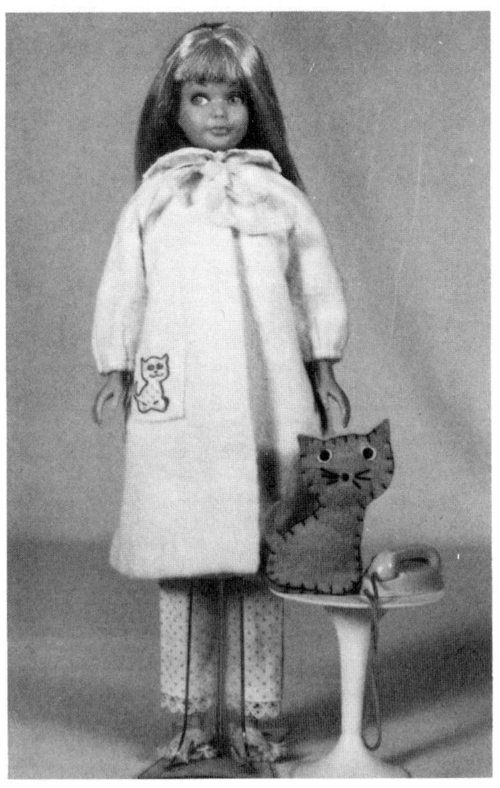

Skipper (950) wearing #1909 "Dreamtime."

Blue felt cats from #1909 "Dreamtime."

The wolf head mask from #0880 "Red Riding Hood and the Wolf," a Little Theatre costume.

Rori—From #1133 Lori 'N Rori.

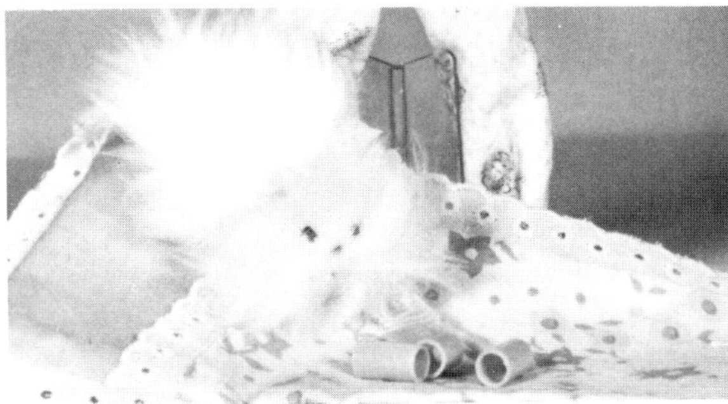

Fluff and #7713 Get-Ups 'N Go sleepwear set. Included was a furry white cat.

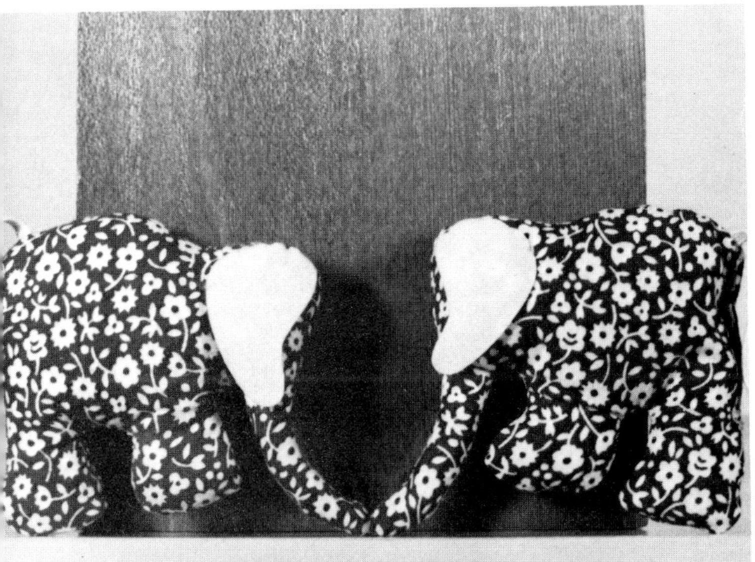

Blue and white printed material stuffed elephants. From the Studio Bedroom and Barbie's Apartment (9188).

Yellow duck, pink Teddy bear and pink duck from Sears' "Barbie Baby-sits" sets.

#7405 Studio Bedroom. Included was a stuffed elephant.

3. The "Live" Animals

The first Barbie "live" animal was a fish, a part of "Picnic Set" (967). Booklets for 1959—1961 showed a yellow and orange colored fish without fins. The 1962 booklet showed a different fish, a grey and blue one with fins. The hats and baskets from the two sets differed also.

Although not too plentiful, the second fish can be found by diligent searching. However, no amount of diligent searching has turned up one of the first fish! Several collectors are beginning to doubt that the fish was ever on the market. Others believe that it was. One argument in favor of its having been on the market is that at least one of the hats from the first set has been found.

The fish is pictured (a photograph of a real fish) in the 1959—1962 catalogues and on a cardboard store display set. This indicates that at least one fish was made.

Next came a grey, plush poodle in 1964 and 1965. This was in a set called "Dog 'N Duds" (1613).

The ©1963 Skipper booklet pictured a white Scotty in the "Dog 'N Duds" set, but this was never on the market in that particular set.

The white Scotty was used in 1966 as a part of "Dog Show" (1929), a Skipper set.

The Skipper Dream Room (4094) of 1965 and 1966 had in it a flat cardboard birdcage with two bluebirds inside.

Certainly the smallest of the Barbie "live" animals was the little butterfly from "Country Picnic" (1933), a Skipper set of 1966.

In 1966, 1967 and 1968 there was a Tutti playsetting, "Me and My Dog" (3554), on the market. The set included a large white fluffy dog.

The grey plush poodle was again on the market in 1970 and 1971 as a part of an exclusive Sears gift set. This was a Walking Jamie set called "Jamie Furry Friends" (1584).

In 1972 there was another Walking Jamie gift set. This one was called "Strollin In Style" (1247). It contained a white plush poodle.

"Dancer" (1157), Barbie's horse, was on the market in 1971—1972.

In 1976 the horse was re-issued in Germany with a new stock number (7385). Made from the original mold, the horse was a different shade of brown and the posing stand was omitted.

Three other Mattel horses made from the Dancer mold were available in Germany in 1976. They were Big Jim's horse and two for Karl May, a Wild West type of storyteller.

Put-ons & Pets was the name of three sets on the market in 1972. Each set contained a Barbie outfit and a pet.

"Poodle Doodles" (1061) had a black poodle, "Kitty Kapers" (1062) included a white cat and "Hot Togs" (1063) had a tan Afghan.

From 1973—1976 Sears offered an exclusive set called "Barbie Goin' Boating" (7738). A fish about 6 inches long was included. Over the years the color of the fish varied a little. The first ones were grey, white and chartreuse. Later ones were grey, white and bright green.

"Country Kitchen" (7407), one of the Room-Fulls mentioned earlier, had a brown fabric cat as part of the accessories.

Barbie's Apartment (9188), also mentioned earlier, had a brown fabric cat. This cat was a little darker brown than the first one.

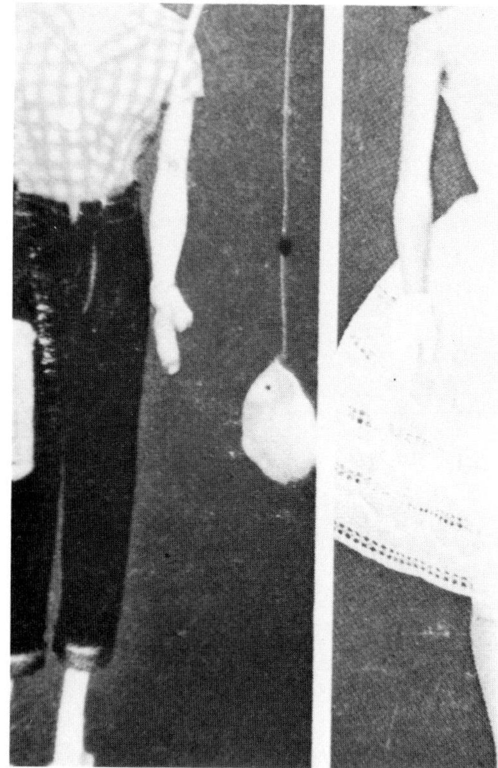

Barbie's first fish. This early poster shows the *actual* yellow and orange fish.

This shows a sketch of the first fish and hat from #967 "Picnic Set."

Blue and grey fish from the second "Picnic Set." Note the different hat, different shape of fish.

Grey poodle in #1613 "Dog 'N Duds."

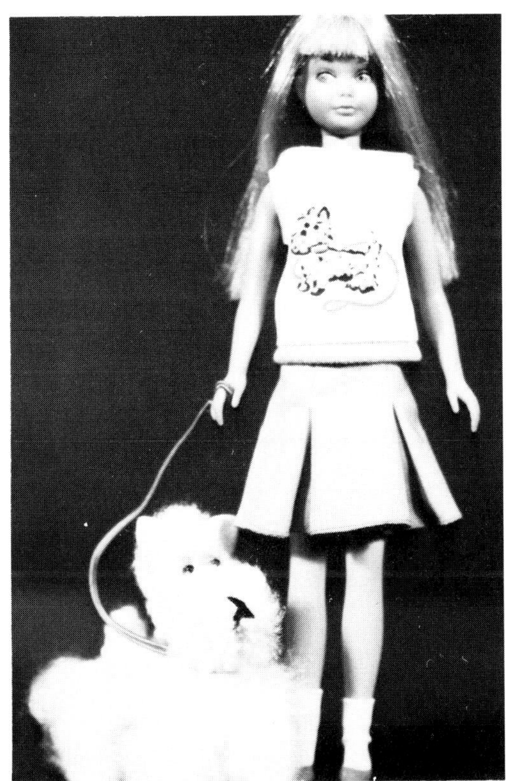

Re-issued Skipper (0950). White Scotty and outfit #1929 "Dog Show."

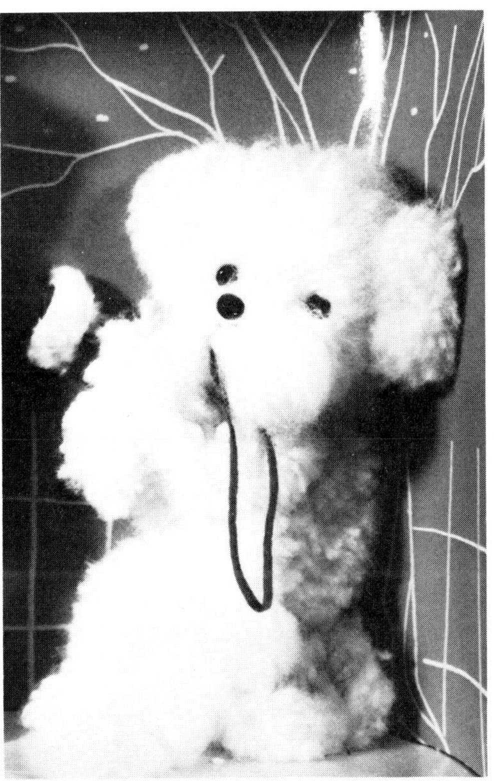

Tutti's white dog from "Me and My Dog" (3554).

Put-ons & Pets.
1. #1061 "Poodle Doodles."
2. #1062 "Kitty Kapers."
3. #1063 "Hot Togs."

Cardboard birdcage with two blue birds. From #4094 "Skipper Dream Room."

Fish from "Barbie Goin' Boating" (7738), a Sears exclusive.

An enlargement of the butterfly from #1933 "Country Picnic."

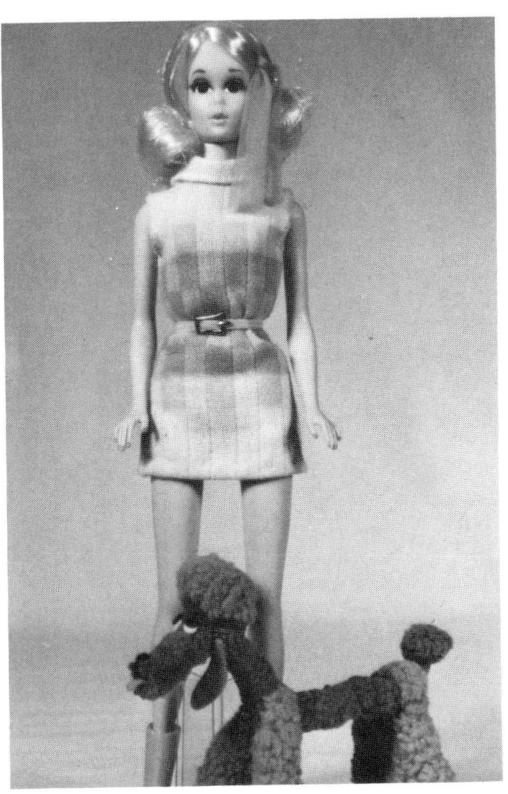

Walking Jamie and grey poodle from #1584 "Jamie Furry Friends," a Sears' Gift Set of 1970 and 1971.

The white poodle from #1247 "Strollin in Style," a Walking Jamie Gift Set of 1972. (Gift from Kathy Bennett)

Country Kitchen (7404)—Included was a brown fabric cat.

Cats from Barbie's Apartment (9188) and Country Kitchen. Note the different shades of brown, different ears.

"Dancer," Barbie's horse of 1971 and 1972.

"Dancer"—Re-issued in Europe in 1976. A lighter shade of brown. Posing stand omitted.

Found in Europe in 1976. Made from the "Dancer" molds. Cream colored.

"Hatatitla," made from the "Dancer" molds. Germany, 1976.

Sample black Skipper (never on the market) and
an imitation Skipper. (Ashabraner collection).

VII. Rarities in Barbie's World

The next few pages will feature the rare Barbie items that collectors hope to locate but hardly ever do. It is this searching and hoping (and occasionally finding) that makes this hobby such an interesting one.

The black doll on the opposite page is the only one of its kind known to exist. This doll is a sample doll that Mattel made and showed at one of the New York Toy Fairs. The exact date is unknown, but it was in the mid 1960's. Buyers at the fair must have responded unfavorably to the doll for Mattel did not produce it for the market.

Several toy buyers remember seeing the black doll at the Toy Fair. They also remember the lack of enthusiasm shown by the buyers. One buyer not only remembers seeing the doll, but he believes that the doll was not called a Black Skipper or a Colored Skipper. He believes that the doll had an entirely different name, a name of its own. Inquiries to Mattel have failed to confirm this.

This black doll is definitely a Mattel product. The body is a regular straight leg Skipper body, with the regular markings, that was stained brown. The head was made from a regular Skipper head mold using a brown plastic formula. The quality and styling of the hair is definitely Mattel's. The quality and styling of the swimsuit can be none other than Mattel's.

The freckle faced doll head on the right is on a regular straight leg Skipper body, but the head is not a Mattel product. It is an excellent Hong Kong copy of the real Skipper head. (It is marked "Hong Kong" on the back of the head.)

Perhaps a real Mattel mold was pirated and used, because the head looks very much like a real Skipper except for the freckles and the texture and coloring of the hair. Mattel hair has a different look and "feel" from this one, and none of the old Skippers had freckles. The first Skipper to have freckles was the Quick Curl (#4223) of 1973.

In this picture the doll is wearing a pantdress and coat from a 1969 Sears gift set, "Wow! What a Cool Outfit."

—:—

Most of the bendable leg Barbies (#1070) had a classic American Girl hair style—a center-parted short bob with bangs. A few of the dolls had a bubble cut hair-do.

A third hair-do was used on a very small number of the dolls. This was a side-parted medium length flip style with bangs. The doll was pictured modeling fashions in the 1966 Mattel catalogue and in the December 1966 issue of "Jack and Jill" magazine.

—:—

Another rare doll is a Miss Barbie with silver painted hair, black pointed eyebrows and no lip color. The regular Miss Barbie had brown painted hair, light brown curved eyebrows and deep pink lips. To date only one of these dolls has been found.

It is believed that this was a sample doll Mattel made for a special purpose. Just what that purpose was has not been established at the present time.

Miss Barbie with silver hair, black pointed eyebrows, no lip color.

Almost all Midge dolls had eyes looking straight ahead. A rare few had side-glancing eyes.

—:—

One of the hard-to-find dolls is the Living Barbie from an exclusive Sears gift set, "Action Accents" (#1585) shown in the 1970 and 1971 catalogues. This Living Barbie was made in Japan and is so marked. All other Living Barbies were made in Taiwan and are marked Taiwan.

—:—

Most Caseys had short straight hair. Some of the dolls used in store display sets had slightly fluffier hair. One doll has been found with curly hair. Another doll with a short flip hair-do was found in Canada in 1976.

—:—

Although shown in the 1971 list of dolls, the Barbie Hair Happenins (#1174) is such a scarce doll that it belongs here too. This doll was never shown in any booklet or catalogue.

—:—

Other items mentioned elsewhere that belong in this chapter are Tutti's white dog, the first two Barbie posing stands and Barbie's first fish. The first two Barbies are extremely hard to find. The Barbie Baby's layette is also rare.

The Midge Wig Wardrobe wigs are not very plentiful. Neither are the accessories from the Color 'N Curl sets and the first Hair Fair set. Colored Francie, Miss Barbie, Color Magic Barbie, straight leg Francie, Truly Scrumptious and Todd seem to be hard to find to some collectors.

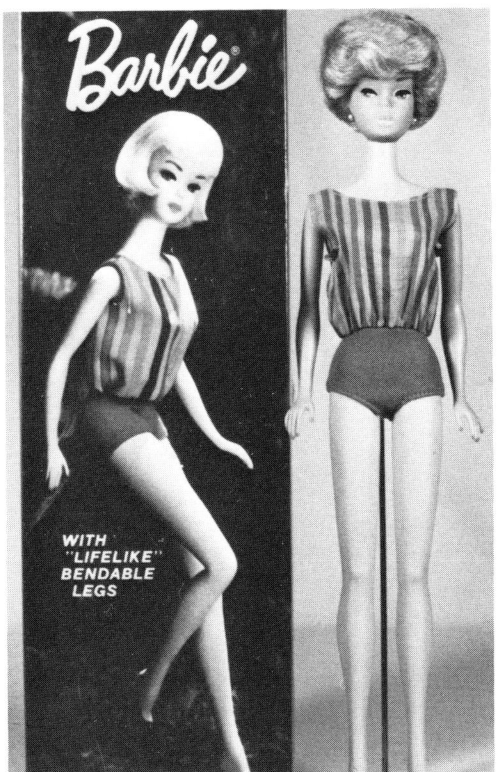

Bendable leg Barbie (1070) with a bubble cut hair-do. Original platinum hair has turned brassy bronze.

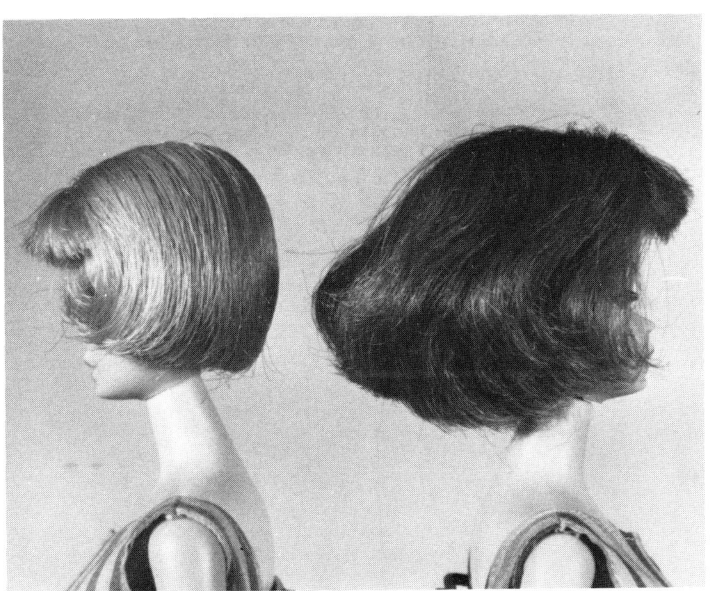

Two bendable leg Barbies (1070). On left, a regular hair-do. On right, a thicker and longer hair style in the rare shade of brown.

Extremely rare side-parted hair bendable leg Barbie (1070).

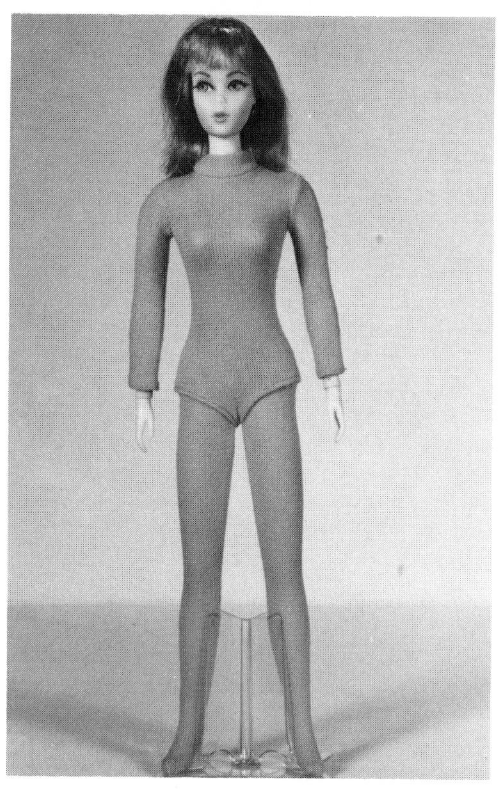

Living Barbie made in Japan. From #1585 "Action Accents," a Sears' exclusive Gift Set.

Japanese booklet featuring the Living Barbie made in Japan. (Gift from Viki Lyn Paulson)

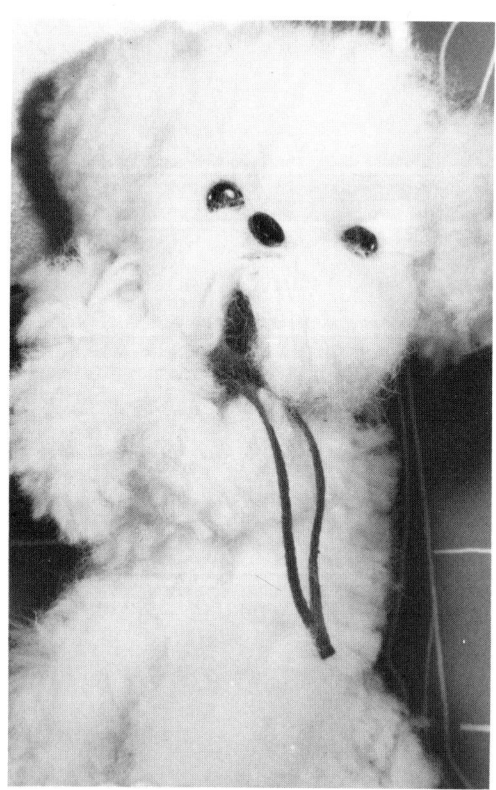

Tutti's large white dog is extremely rare. (Gift from Janice Kaderly)

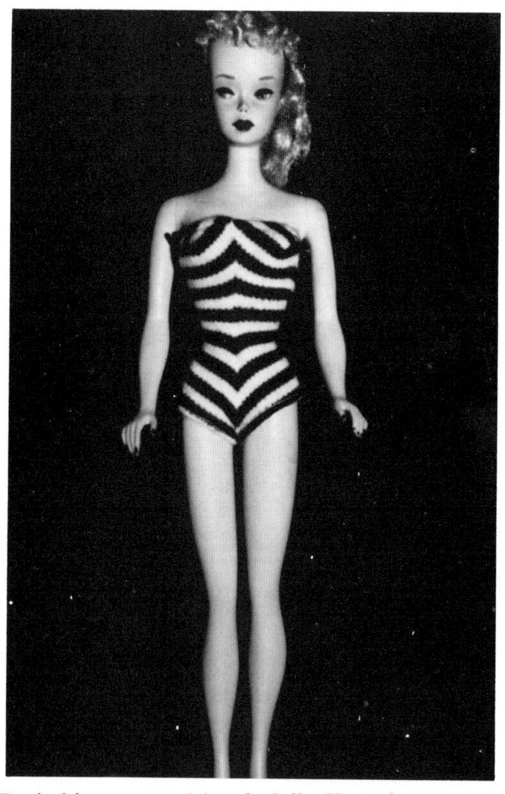

Probably a transitional doll—Has the second type head on the first type body. (Courtesy Bernice Lieb)

Casey with curly hair—From a store display.

Casey with turned-up hair. (Courtesy Bernice Lieb)

A store display P.J.—Note the different hair style and different placement of the beads.

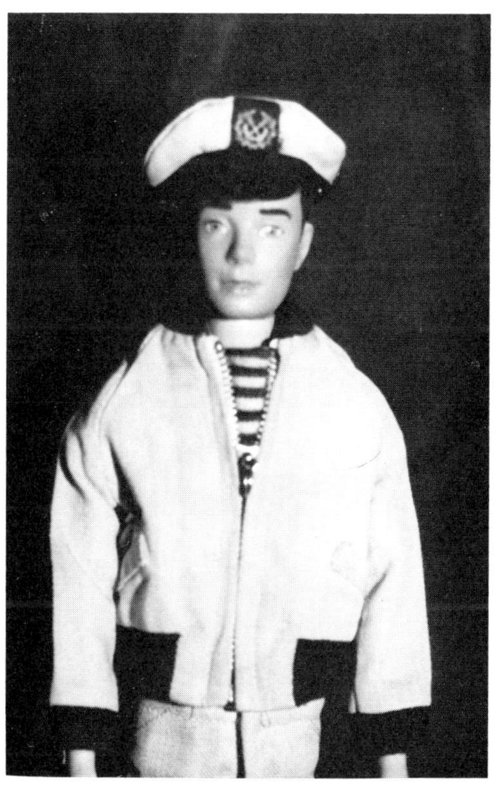

Ken wearing #0789 "The Yachtsman," the rare set with the cap. (Courtesy Bernice Lieb)

Although shown elsewhere, Barbie's first fish is so rare that it must be included in this section.

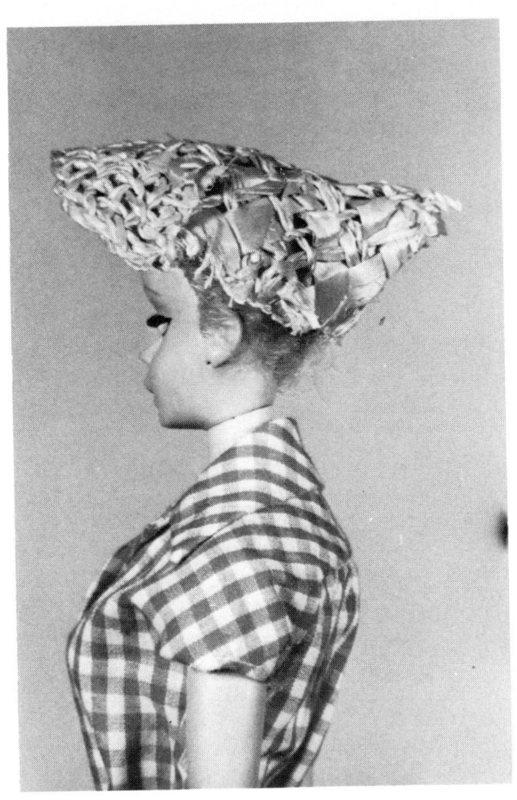

A side-view of the hat from the first "Picnic Set."

A 1962 ponytail Barbie wearing one of the rarest outfits. #964 "Gay Parisienne." Shown only in the first fashion booklet. (Ashabraner collection)

"Dressed Dolls" in their special "dressed doll" boxes are rare. Notice the two bands on the front and sides of the box. The doll is a 1964 ponytail Barbie wearing #984 "American Airlines Stewardess." (Ashabraner collection)

Barbie Hair Happenin's (1174)—a rare Department Store Special.

Close-up of Barbie Hair Happenin's. Titian hair, centered eyes.

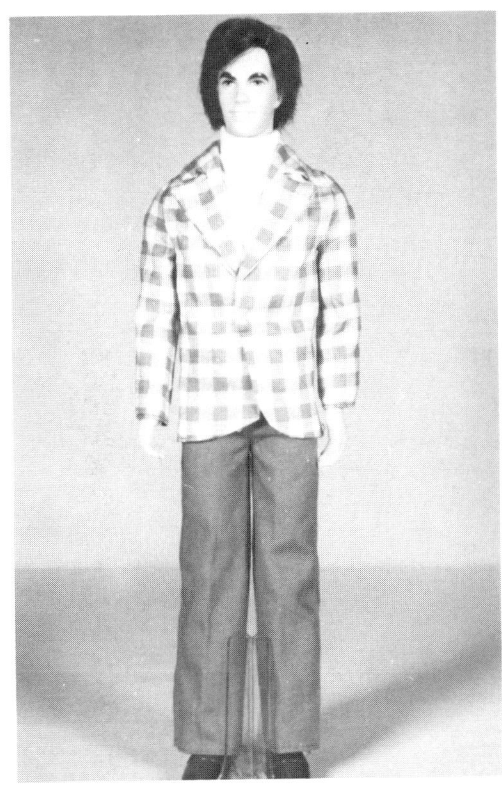

Mod Ken jacket in large checks. Most had small checks.

A rare brown haired Todd from Germany. Most had titian hair.

Left: A moldĕd Barbie head with brown eyes. Possibly re-painted. (Found by Pat Smith) Right: This doll has a molded head so small she appears to be deformed! (Found by Mary Partridge)

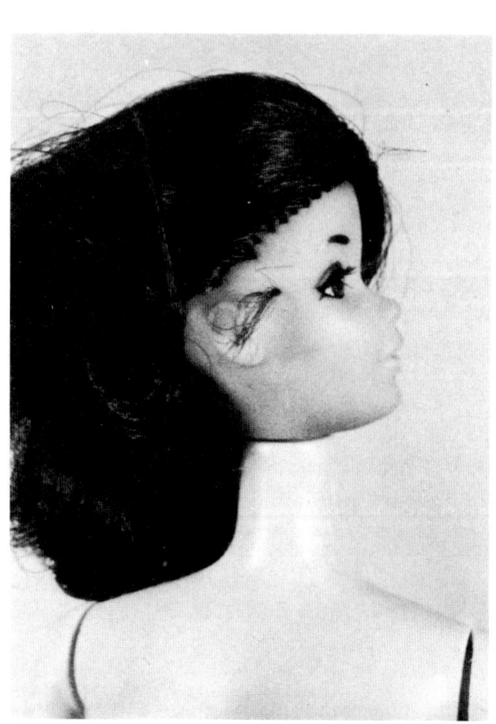

At one time Mattel allowed employees to buy at a nominal fee sample dolls, used dolls and "seconds" such as this Walking Miss America with the hair growing out her temple! Avid collectors consider these great "finds."

Mystery Barbie. doll—A "Swirl" ponytail head with black skin that appears to have been made that way at the factory. (Gift from Virginia Slade)

Probably an experimental Barbie doll. Has a heavy tan Pats. Pend. torso, soft hair with firmer textured bangs and white lips. These different features were on the market at different times. (Ashabraner collection)

This is the rare misprinted family portrait from the Barbie Fan Club pack of 1970. Casey and P.J. are reversed. Julia and Christy are reversed.

A Mod Hair Ken (4224) with weird hair! The avid collector is always on the lookout for freaks like this.

This freakish Malibu Barbie was found late in 1976 at a Sears store.

VIII. A Little Confusion in Barbieland

Copy for the Mattel toy catalogues, fashion booklets, packaging for the dolls, clothes and accessory items, and all related publications must be prepared far in advance of the actual date the items are on the toy store shelf.

Over the years a few items pictured in the fashion booklets and toy catalogues were early samples that differed slightly from the actual article that was marketed.

A few items on the market were never pictured, and a few items pictured were never on the market. From time to time there were a few misprints in these publications. Considering the large number of Mattel publications, it is remarkable that these were so few.

Although few in number, these differences have caused a little confusion especially to new collectors. Hopefully this chapter will alleviate some of the confusion.

1. "Beckyland"

About 1971 there appeared on the market packages of doll clothes for "Francie and her new friend Becky." Collectors began searching for Becky but could not find her. Mattel was besieged with inquiries.

The company explained that at one time they intended to made such a doll. Some costume packaging was printed and shipped before this idea was dropped. Mattel also stated that they did not make any of the dolls. But they must have made a sample or two, because the doll (or at least a doll different from any on the market) was pictured in the 1971 booklet wearing costumes Nos. 3444, 3446, 3449 and 3450. The same doll was also pictured on page 40 of the 1973 catalogue wearing one of the Sew Magic Costumes.

The doll's head was made from the Casey head mold. Her shoulder-length flip hair-do was dark blonde, parted on the left side and held in place with a deep rose colored head band.

Now whenever an item is pictured in a publication but is not put on the market, collectors say that it is in "Beckyland."

—:—

The first ©1968 booklet pictured twist Julia (#1127) wearing a short pink dress with silver trim around the neckline, and pink shoes. (A small close-up of the head and neckline was also shown on the covers of the ©1968 booklets.) Julia was never sold wearing this dress. Instead, she wore a nurse's white uniform.

—:—

The ©1968 booklet covers showed another item that was never on the market—the doll pictured in the lower left corner. At least that particular hair-do was never on the market. The head seems to be a Stacey with a sample hair style.

—:—

On two of the Tutti Playsetting boxes, "Cookin Goodies" (#3559) and "Swing-A-Ling" (#3560), the Todd doll pictured in the "Sundae Treat" set (#3556) had brunet hair. Since no brunet Todds have been found, the one pictured must have been a sample doll that was never marketed.

This is "Becky," a sample doll that was never produced for the market. Notice the hair-do and the Casey mold used for the head.

"Goodies Galore" (#1521), a plastic bag of accessories, was on the market in 1970 and later. The cardboard heading on the package pictured a Barbie doll and a bathing dress that were never on the market.

The doll had long blonde hair with flip ends and long straight bangs. The hair behind the bangs was brushed straight back and tied with a ribbon.

She wore a multi-colored, short-skirted tricot bathing outfit. Tiny bits of this same bathing dress can be seen on the Living Barbie on pages 2 and 3 of the ©1969 booklets.

—:—

Another Barbie hair style that was never on the market was pictured in the 1972 catalogue. This was a shoulder-length, fluffy and curly blonde hair style a little like the one worn by Talking Steffie.

The doll is shown on page 38 wearing "Party Lines" and on page 40 dressed in "Glowin Gold."

—:—

The Mattel catalogue, Spring Introductions '74, pictured "Francie and Her Ten Speeder" (#7803). The set contained a Francie doll and a bicycle. The bicycle was pink and had the name "Francie" on the basket. (Barbie's bicycle was yellow and had her name on the basket.)

The later regular 1974 catalogue did not list this set and none was ever on the market.

—:—

Booklets dated 1966 and 1967 showed sketches of Casey (#1180) without an earring and with a blue band on her head. The actual doll that reached the market had an earring in her left ear and no band on her head.

—:—

In 1969 twist Stacey (#1165) was shown in a two-piece psychedelic print swimsuit. This suit was never on the market. Instead, a one-piece suit was used.

—:—

The swimsuit on twist Skipper (#1105) shown in the 1969 catalogue and the ©1968 booklets was never on the market. This was a one-piece rose and red checked suit made from a fuzzy knitted material.

The actual suit was made from a smooth cotton fabric. It had a rose, red and purple checked waist stitched to a solid red flounce and red shorts.

The doll pictured in the catalogue and booklets was the first twist Skipper, the one with the long straight hair with a blue head band. The actual doll on the market had a new hair style—two long curls held in place with rubber bands and tied with ribbons.

The actual doll and suit were pictured in "For Kids Only," a November 21, 1969 newspaper supplement.

—:—

The green Country Camper (#4994) pictured in 1971 was never on the market. The one on the market was yellow.

—:—

One of Mattel's sample dolls, or perhaps a better term would be experimental dolls, was pictured in the 1973 catalogue. This was the Skipper doll wearing "Get-Ups 'N Go" outfits Nos. 7713 and 7714.

The doll had the new blonde Quick Curl type of hair-do on an older twist head, the head without freckles and with rooted eyelashes. (The Quick Curl Skipper had freckles and painted eyelashes.)

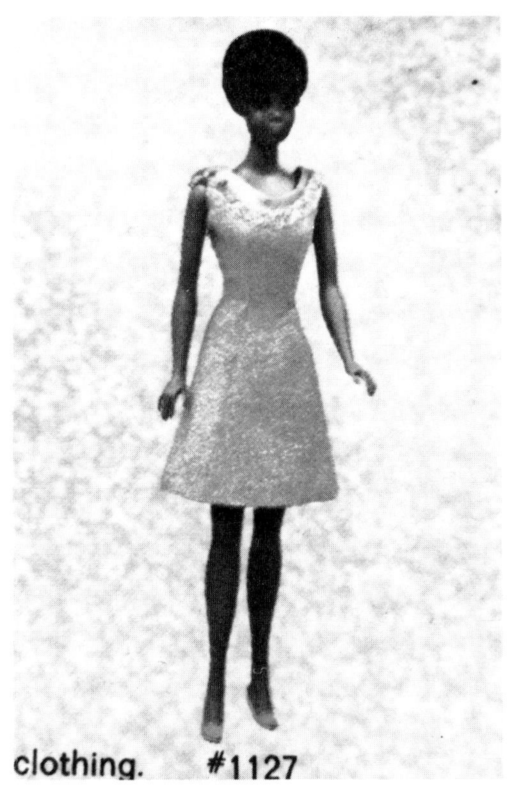

Julia was never sold wearing this short pink party dress. Instead a nurse's white uniform was used.

The hair-do shown on the doll in the lower left side was never on the market.

This hair style and bathing dress were never on the market. (Ashabraner collection)

The Todd shown here has brown hair. This doll was never produced for the market. (In 1976 a re-issued Todd from Germany was found with brown hair.)

The Barbie doll shown wearing "Party Lines" was never produced for the market.

Another view of the Barbie doll that was not produced for the market.

"Francie and Her Ten Speeder" was never on the market.

This Casey with the blue head band was never on the market.

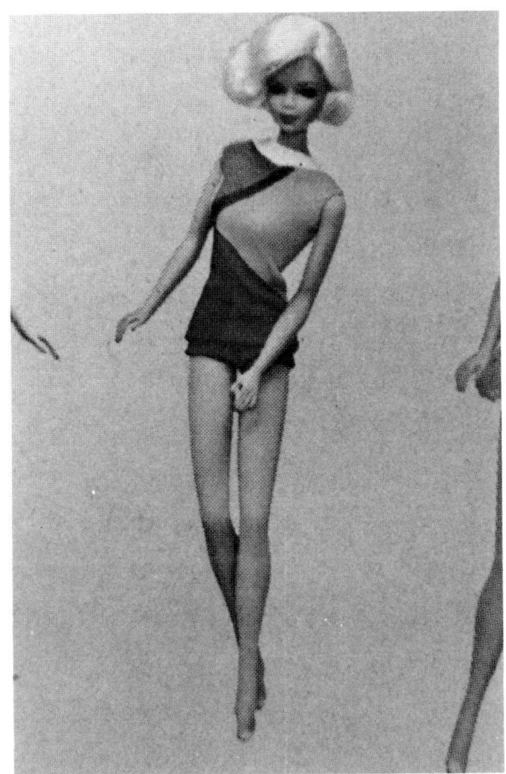

This two-piece Stacey swimsuit was not produced for the market. A one-piece suit was used instead.

The fish that was pictured in the 1973 Sears catalogue as a part of "Barbie Goin' Boating Set" (#7738) was not quite like the one that was on the market. The one shown had a much bigger stomach area. Later catalogues (1974, 1975) pictured the actual fish.

—:—

The ©1963 Skipper booklet pictured a white Scotty in the "Dog 'N Duds" set (#1613). A Scotty was never on the market as a "Dog 'N Duds" item.

However, the Scotty emerged from "Beckyland" in 1966 and became a part of "Dog Show" (#1929), a Skipper set.

—:—

Since all of the miniature Barbie dolls found to date have blonde hair, collectors believe that the red headed doll shown in one of the View-Master slides in "Barbie's Around the World Trip" was a sample that was never on the market. In the same scene there are some miniature packages of clothes for the tiny Barbie doll. None of these were ever on the market. They were probably made by someone at the GAF Corporation especially for the scene.

They also took regular Mattel dolls and re-did their features to make characters for the story. Of course this was done with Mattel's approval. Some of these characters were Barbie's father, a London bobby, a French fashion designer and a Greek Evzone.

—:—

All of the ©1965 booklets showed sketches of Color Magic Barbie (#1150) with curly hair and bangs. Two of the booklets showed the doll in a floral swimsuit. This swimsuit and hair style were never on the market. Instead, the doll had long straight hair parted on the left side and no bangs. She wore a diamond patterned suit with matching head band. This doll and suit were shown in the 1966 and 1967 catalogues and the ©1966 booklet.

This knit-like swimsuit shown on Twist Skipper was never on the market. (Note the old hair style; the actual doll had two long curls.)

#1613 "Dog 'N Duds" had a grey poodle, not a white Scotty as shown here. The white Scotty was used later as a part of "Dog Show," another Skipper set.

Color Magic Barbie (1150) had straight hair and no bangs. She wore the diamond check swimsuit shown on the left, not the floral one on the right.

This sample wolf suit was never on the market.

"Beckyland" Trivia

The following bits of information are added for the enjoyment of the avid Barbie collector known as "a real Barbie nut!"

Twist Skipper's bathing suit is shown with a pink and blue striped bottom in the ©1966 booklet and on the box the doll came in. The actual suit had a solid blue bottom.

—:—

The dress pictured on the Quick Curl Cara (#7291) in the 1975 catalogue was not quite like the one on the market. The design of the dress was the same but a different type of fabric with a different print was used.

—:—

The Free Moving P.J. (#7281) skirt pictured hanging inside two Barbie cases in the 1975 Sears catalogue was not on the market.

—:—

The actual two-piece pink swimsuit that the first #1190 standard Barbie wore was made of a smooth double knit material. The suit pictured on the box the doll came in was made of a different material, a material something like a fuzzy Orlon sock.

—:—

The pants pictured on Mod Hair Ken in the booklets and catalogues was of a different material from those on the market.

—:—

The 1966 and 1967 booklets showed white trim on the twist Barbie (#1160) suit. The actual trim was salmon or reddish.

—:—

Now Look Ken's jacket did not have pockets but the sample jacket pictured on the 1976 promotional calendar had pockets.

—:—

The 1974 Sears catalogue showed a pink and white striped apron in the Barbie Baby Sits set (#7882). The real apron was a pink and white check.

—:—

There has been some confusion about the jackets that the straight leg Ken and Allan came in. The catalogue referred to these as "terrycloth" jackets, but none of the jackets on the market were all terry cloth. The first Ken jackets had a stitched-on white terry cloth lining that formed a collar and a lapel. Later the terry cloth lining was bonded on. Both types of jackets were pictured in the booklets and catalogues and both were on the market.

In the 1964 catalogue there was pictured an Allan jacket with the stitched-on lining. Since none of these have been found, it is believed that this was a sample only, and the jacket with the bonded-on lining was the only one that reached the market.

—:—

The "Fashion Queen Barbie & Her Friends" gift set (#0863) shown in the 1964 catalogue has an unusual Fashion Queen Barbie. The doll pictured has hair showing beneath her bandana. The actual Fashion Queen doll had molded and painted hair. Perhaps the real doll was not completed in time for this picture and another doll was substituted.

—:—

The hair dryer and wig stand in the #4035 Color 'N Curl set were pictured as brown colored in the ®1964 booklet. The ones on the market were aqua and pink.

—:—

"Slightly Summery" Pak was pictured as pink in the booklets. The actual dress was Green.

—:—

The 1969 catalogue pictures two slightly different green tops on Talking Christie. One of the tops was on the market but the other one is in "Beckyland."

The Sweet 16 dolls pictured in the catalogues had the new heads on old style bodies. These bodies had the old divided fingers—one with pale pink nail polish and one with red polish. The doll that reached the market had the newer undivided fingers. The complete new doll must not have been ready by the time the photograph had to be made for the publications.

—:—

An old-fashioned phonograph was shown in #3445 "Zig-Zag Zoom" in the ©1971 booklet and the 1971 catalogues. This phonograph was not used in the set. A walkie-talkie was used instead.

—:—

The 1975 catalogue pictured an all white skate stand with the #7262 Barbie Skater set. The stand that reached the market had a blue base.

—:—

Four of the Free Moving dolls were pictured with white golf clubs. Grey clubs were used instead.

—:—

Barbie's Town & Country Market (#4984), shown in the 1971 Mattel catalogue, was not produced for the market.

—:—

Quick Curl Barbie and Kelley are pictured in the catalogues with the original Barbie divided fingers and Quick Curl Francie is pictured with the regular Francie arms and hands. All three dolls reached the market with the arms and undivided fingers collectors call "Mexico" hands.

—:—

Busy Francie's belt and hair ribbon differed from the ones pictured in the 1972 catalogue.

—:—

The wand in the "Snowflake Fairy" set was slightly different from the one pictured in the catalogue and on the calendar. The crowns of the three Ballerina costumes pictured on the calendar differed slightly from the ones on the market.

—:—

Several items were made especially to help illustrate articles in a 1964 publication called "The Barbie Magazine Annual." These items were not produced for sale. One was a plush "wolf" suit for the character in Little Red Riding Hood. Others were a Japanese kimono for Ken and Halloween costumes for Allan and Midge.

In one scene Barbie and Ken are shown in a two-seater plane with an open cockpit. This plane differed from the one made for Mattel by the Irwin Corporation. Barbie's helmet and Ken's goggles and flowing scarf were never on the market.

On pages 52 and 53 there were six Barbie and Skipper outfits that were never on the market.

In one scene several of the regular bassinets from the "Barbie Baby Sits" set were up on special stands. These stands were never on the market. This same scene showed a regular blonde baby, a brunette, a red head and a black baby. The regular baby doll had been altered to make these three different-seeming baby dolls. Since these dolls were made up just for this special photograph, none were ever on the market.

—:—

The following is not strictly a "Beckyland" item but there does not seem to be any other place to put it. Children are not the only people who switched doll heads and bodies. Several dolls used to illustrate stories in the "Barbie Talk" magazines had heads from one doll on the body of a different doll.

2. Misprints

Several of the ©1965 booklets reversed the stock numbers on the bendable leg Skipper and the bendable leg Skooter. New collectors are often confused by this.

The correct numbers are 1030 for Skipper and 1120 for Skooter.

—:—

The ©1965 booklets pictured #3550 Tutti with the wrong hair-do. The hair-do pictured was the one used for the doll in "Me and My Dog" set (#3554).

—:—

The hair pictured on the dolls in "Sundae Treat" (#3556) in the same booklets was also incorrect. Todd's hair was pictured as blond. He really had titian hair. Tutti's was also titian.

The hair-do shown on Tutti was the style used on the doll in "Melody In Pink" (#3555).

The 1966 catalogue lists the "Sundae Treat" dolls' hair color as brown.

—:—

The #4035 "Barbie's Color 'N Curl" set as pictured in the ©1964 booklet is not exactly a misprint. The actual set must not have been ready in time for the photographer so a staged set was used. This staged set included a molded Barbie head and a Miss Barbie head.

The actual set contained a molded Barbie head and a molded Midge head.

This ©1965 booklet shows bendable leg Skipper and bendable leg Skooter with reversed stock numbers. Skipper's number was 1030; Skooter's was 1120.

#3550 Tutti had a different hair style from this one shown in the ©1965 booklets. This style was used for #3554 Tutti.

The hair style shown on this Tutti was used on the doll in #3555 "Melody in Pink." The "Sundae Treat" Tutti had a different hair style.

The ©1969 booklets and the 1967, 1968 and 1969 catalogues described Tutti (#3580) as being 7 5/8 inches tall. Chris (#3570) and Todd (#3590) were also described as being 7 5/8 inches tall in some of the catalogues.

None of these dolls were 7 5/8 inches tall. The height of the dolls may have varied slightly, but only slightly. Most were about 6 1/4 inches tall.

—:—

All #1190 Barbies had painted eyelashes, not "real" ones, and the first boxes and booklets pictured the doll with painted lashes. In 1970 when the #1190 doll was presented in a new style swimsuit and new box, the box pictured a doll with rooted eyelashes. The ©1969 booklet described her as having "long real eyelashes." The doll pictured in the ©1969 and ©1970 booklets had real eyelashes.

It is possible that Mattel intended to market the doll with real eyelashes but changed its mind after the copy had gone to press. The doll head used for the photographs was probably one of the first twist Barbie heads from 1967.

—:—

Pretty Pairs were listed in the booklets and catalogues as being 5 inches tall. They were actually Tutti size—about 6¼ inches tall.

—:—

Although mentioned elsewhere, the shipping carton with the misprinted name certainly belongs in this chapter too.

The carton is marked "Malibu Steffie—Stock No. 1187." Malibu P.J.'s stock number is 1187, and the box contained Malibu P.J.'s.

As mentioned before, the Steffie head mold was used to make Malibu P.J. Perhaps that accounts for the name on the carton.

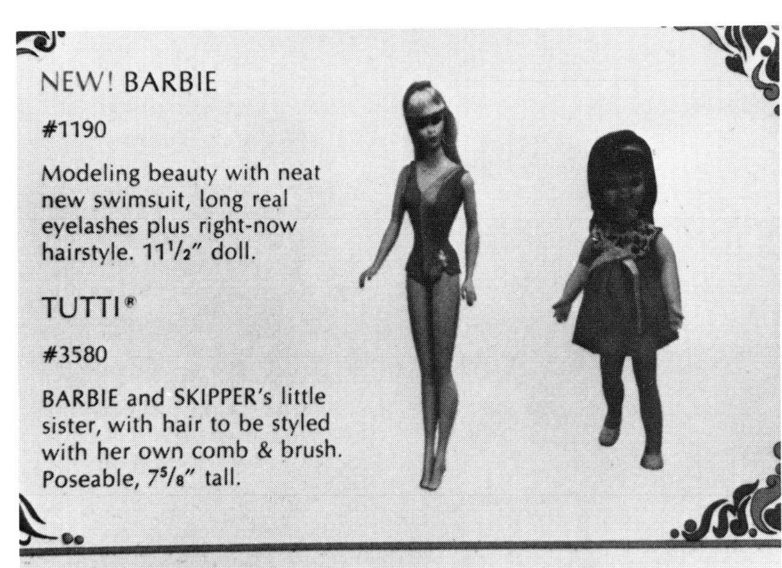

#1190 Barbie had painted eyelashes, not "real" lashes. #3580 Tutti was about 6¼" tall, not 7 5/8".

The actual #4035 Color 'N Curl set had a molded Barbie head and a molded Midge head, not a Miss Barbie head as shown in this picture.

The primary dolls in "Pretty Pairs" were 6¼" tall, not 5" as shown in the ©1969 and ©1970 booklets.

Twist 'N Turn Skipper's stock number was #1105, not #1030 as shown in one of the ©1966 booklets. (#1030 was the number of bendable leg Skipper.)

A Malibu Barbie was used in the picture depicting Yellowstone Kelley (7808) in the 1974 catalogue.

In one of the ©1966 booklets, twist Skipper was introduced with the stock number listed as 1030. The number should have been 1105, the 1030 being bendable leg Skipper's number.

The doll was pictured with the old brass headband instead of the blue band worn by the first twist dolls.

—:—

Evidently the 1974 catalogue went to print before the Yellowstone Kelley doll (#7808) was ready to be photographed.

A photograph of a Malibu Barbie doll dressed in the Yellowstone Kelley clothing was used in the catalogues to indicate the Yellowstone Kelley.

An interesting footnote—a photograph of the same doll and clothing was used in later catalogues to denote Barbie's High Sierra Adventure set (#7408). It was also used on the box the set came in.

—:—

The ©1970 booklet listed the re-issued straight leg Skipper as #095. The correct number was 950.

—:—

Talking Ken's number was 1111. In the ©1971 booklet and catalogue his number was incorrectly listed as 1117-7.

Misprint Trivia

Here are a few more tidbits for the avid insatiable collector.

—:—

Most early publications listed Ken and Allan as being 12½ inches tall. The dolls were 12 inches.

—:—

The 1968 booklet says standard Truly Scrumptious (#1108) has legs that bend. The doll had straight legs.

—:—

The 1966 catalogue says that a terry cloth blanket was included in the "Walkin My Dolly" set (#3552). All blankets found to date have been flannel.

—:—

The ©1963 booklets list #0490 as the stock number for Barbie & Ken Little Theatre. The number was 4090.

—:—

#1066 was the stock number for "World of Barbie Family House." One of the ©1968 booklets listed it as #1006.

—:—

In the 1976 catalogue the pictures of Growing Up Skipper fashions #9512 and #9513 showed the accessories reversed.

—:—

One of the ©1966 booklets reversed "Change-Abouts" and "Add-Ons" and "Cool-It" and "Slightly Summery."

—:—

The ©1965 booklets list #1000 straight leg Allan but picture the bend leg doll and clothes.

—:—

The 1972 and 1974 catalogues reversed the identity captions under Malibu P.J. and Francie.

—:—

The 1968 catalogue listed Skipper's height as 9½ inches and the talking dolls as 11¾ inches. The dolls were the same height as the year before—9¼ inches and 11½ inches.

—:—

The Francie-size dolls were sometimes listed as being 11 inches tall. Sometimes they were listed as being 11¼ inches.

IX. Accessories! Accessories! Accessories!

No other doll in history ever had the accessories that the Barbie doll has had—houses, furniture, shops, boats, planes, cars, bicycles, cases, trunks and so on.

These items were colorful, imaginative, well-made and designed for the pleasure and enjoyment of children. Many items were made by Mattel. Some items were made by other companies with Mattel's approval. Some of these companies were the Irwin Corp. of New York, Standard Plastic Products of New Jersey, Merry Manufacturing Co. of Ohio, Dynamic Toy, Inc. of New York and Susy Goose Toys of Michigan.

1. Houses And Shops

16—Barbie's Dream House, 1962—1965
17—Barbie's Fashion Shop, 1962—1964
90—Barbie & Ken Little Theatre, 1964
92—new Barbie's Dream House, 1964—1966
93—Barbie Goes to College
"Barbie's Campus," 1964—1965 Sears
"Barbie & Francie's Campus," 1966 Sears
94—Skipper's Dream Room, 1965—1966
95—Barbie's Dream Kitchen & Dinette, 1965—1966
—Travel Vanity Case for Barbie & Skipper, 1965 Sears
—Skipper's Schoolroom, 1965—1966 Sears exclusive
—Barbie & Skipper's Deluxe Dream House, 1965 Sears exclusive
—Barbie Family Deluxe House, 1966—1967 (2 different designs)
06—Tutti Playhouse with doll, 1966
00—Tutti Playhouse—no doll, 1967
02—Francie House, 1966
—Tutti & Todd Playhouse (Sears exclusive, 1966) one with 2 dolls; one without dolls
—Skipper's Deluxe Dream House, 1966 Sears exclusive
05—Barbie Family House, 1967—1970
24—Barbie & Francie Dressing Room Case, 1967—1968
26—Francie & Casey Studio House, 1967
63—Tutti Ice Cream Stand, 1967
38—Tutti & Chris Sleep & Play House, 1967
17—Tutti's Summer House, 1967
—Sears exclusive 3-house group (Barbie-Francie-Tutti), 1967—1968
—Sears exclusive Tutti & Chris Patio Picnic House, 1968—one with 2 dolls; one without dolls
—Sears double doll Sleep 'N Keep Case, 1968 to present time—these have varied in design over the years
48—The World of Barbie House, 1968
66—World of Barbie Family House, 1969—1972
61—Barbie Lively Livin' House, 1970—1971
1148—Barbie Fashion Stage, 1971
4983—Barbie Cafe Today, 1971
—Jamie's Penthouse, 1971 Sears
—Jamie's Room Case, 1971 Sears—(1972 says "1-doll case.")
—Barbie Boutique, 1971—1972
4282—Barbie's Surprise House, 1972—1974
4283—Barbie's Mountain Ski Cabin, Sears 1972 and 1974—none in 1973
8662—Country Living House, 1973 to present
8665—Quick Curl Boutique, 1973
7825—Barbie Townhouse, 1974 to present
7412—Barbie's Olympic Ski Village, 1975
9525—Fashion Plaza, 1976
9651—Ballerina Barbie Stage, 1976

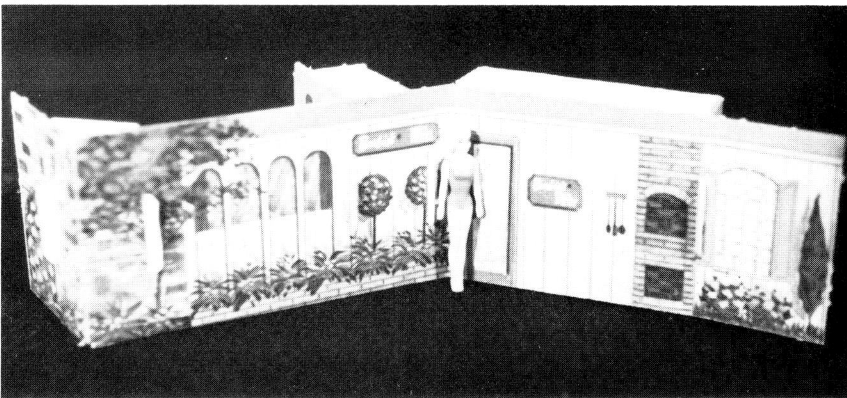

Skipper's "Barbie doll house"—From #4094 Skipper's Dream Room, 1965 and 1966.

#817 Barbie's Fashion Shop—1962-1964. (Gift from Ginger Kendrick)

Interior of Barbie's Fashion Shop.

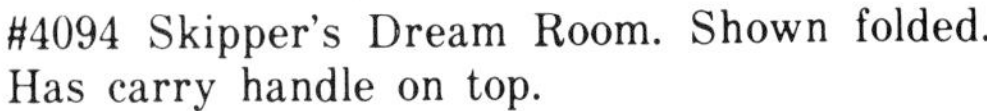

#4094 Skipper's Dream Room. Shown folded. Has carry handle on top.

#4090 Barbie & Ken Little Theatre, 1964. Shown folded up.

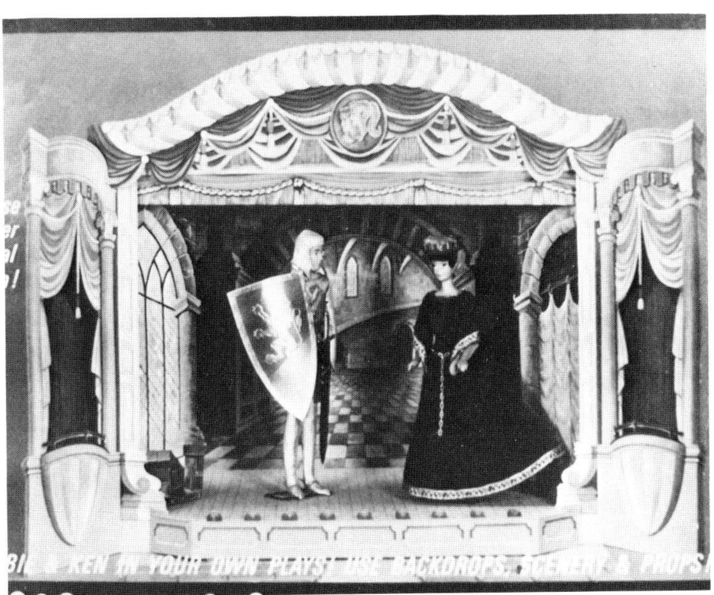

Opened view of Little Theatre.

#4983 Barbie's Cafe Today, 1971, shown closed. (Gift from Viki Lyn Paulson)

Opened view of Cafe Today.

#3300 Tutti Playhouse (no doll), 1967. (#3306 Tutti Playhouse with a doll same design as this one.)

Interior view of #8662 Country Living Home, 1973 to present.

#9651 Ballerina Barbie Stage, 1976.

#9525 Barbie Fashion Plaza, 1976.

#7412 Barbie's Olympic Ski Village, 1975.

#1148 Barbie Fashion Stage, 1971.

2. Vehicles

\# —Barbie Convertible, 1962—1963 (made by Irwin Corp. for Mattel)
—Racy Hot Rod, 1963—1964 (made by Irwin Corp. for Mattel)
—Barbie's Sport Plane, 1964
—Speedboat, 1964—1965
—Skipper's Sports Car, 1965 Wards (looks like Barbie's convertible)
1158—Sun 'N Fun Buggy, 1971—1972
4994—Country Camper—1971 to present
—Red Boat by Irwin Corp., 1972 Wards
8669—Barbie Goin' Camping Set, with Breeze Buggy, tent & trailer, 1973—1975
7738—Barbie Going Boating Set, 1973—1976 Sears
8639—Barbie's Friend Ship, 1973 to present
7777—Barbie's Ten Speeder, 1974 to present
7805—Beach Bus, 1974 to present
7232—Barbie's Dream Boat, 1975 to present
9106—Barbie's Sunsailor-Catamaran, 1976
9612—Barbie's "Classy Corvette" car, 1976 Department Store Special.

#9106 Barbie's Sunsailer—Catamaran, 1976.

#1158 Sun 'N Fun Buggy, 1971—1972. (The one pictured is from England—a gift from Bill St. John.)

#4994 Country Camper, 1971 to present.

#8639 Barbie's Friend Ship, 1973 to present.

Barbie's Sport Plane, 1964. Made by Irwin Corp. for Mattel. (Ashabraner collection)

#7805 Beach Bus, 1974 to present. (Courtesy Allison Dunn)

#7777 Barbie's Ten Speeder, 1974 to present.

#8669 Barbie Goin' Camping Set, 1973—1975.

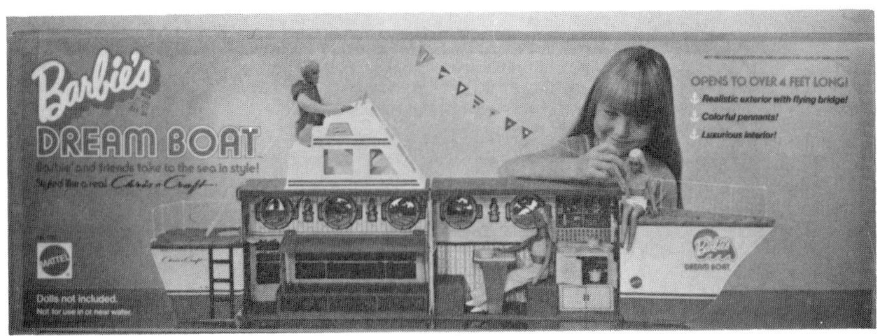

#7232 Barbie's Dream Boat, 1975 to present.

#9612 Barbie's "Classy Corvette" car—Dept. Store Special, 1976.

#7738 Barbie Going Boating Set, 1973—1976. Sears' exclusive.

3. Furniture

—Barbie Fourposter Outfit & Chest (Suzy Goose), 1961—1965
—Barbie Wardrobe (Suzy Goose), 1962—1964
—Barbie Vanity & Bench (Suzy Goose), 1963—1965
—Ken Wardrobe, 1964
—"Queen" Size Chifferobe, 1964
"Queen" Size Bed, 1964
—Go-Together Furniture, 1964—1965
0408 couch, 0409 chair, 0410 chair, 0411 swing
—Barbie's Music Box Piano, 1964—1966
—Miss Barbie's swing set, 1964
4010—Barbie & Skipper Dining Room Furniture, 1965
4011—Skipper & Skooter Bunk Beds, 1965—1967
4012—Barbie 'N Skipper Living Room furniture group, 1965
—Chifferobe, 1965—1966
—Skipper's Bed, 1965
—Skipper's Vanity & stool, 1965
—Skipper's Wardrobe, 1965
—Francie's Mod-A-Go-Go bedroom furniture, 1966
—Tutti & Todd "Dutch" bedroom (bed & rocker) 1966
4963—Living Room, 1970—may not have been on market
4962—Dinette, 1970—may not have been on market
4971—Bedroom, 1970—may not have been on market
4987—Kitchen—Barbie's Place Setting, 1971
4985—Bedroom—Barbie's Place Setting, 1971
4986—Living Room—Barbie's Place Setting, 1971
1016—Action Beauty Scene, 1971
4026—Action Sewing Center, 1972
7404—Country Kitchen—Barbie's Room-Fulls, 1975—1976
7405—Studio Bedroom—Barbie's Room-Fulls, 1975—1976
7406—Firelight Living Room—Barbie's Room-Fulls 1975—1976
9188—Barbie's Apartment ©1975 (a combination of Country Kitchen & Studio Bedroom)—a Department Store Special, 1975
9056—Vanity & Shower, 1975 Sears special
9223—Beauty Bath, 1976
9282—Growing Up Skipper Bedroom, 1976

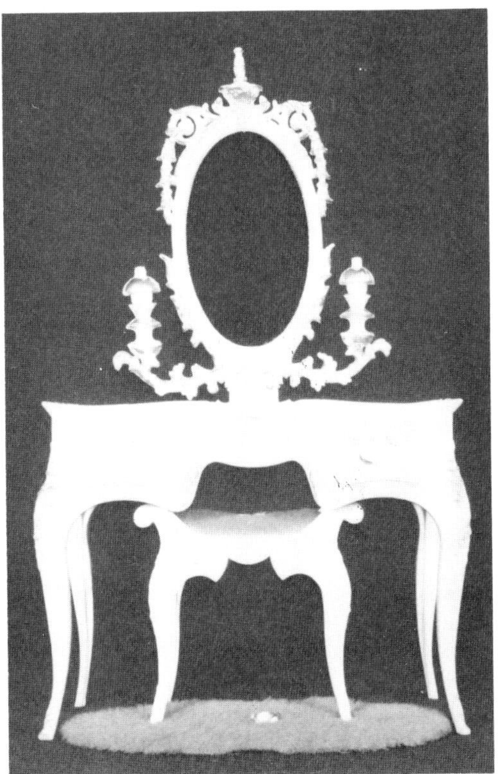

Barbie's Vanity, Bench & Rug (Suzy Goose), 1963—1965.

Barbie's Music Box Piano (Suzy Goose), 1964—1966.

Barbie's Wardrobe (Suzy Goose), 1962—1964.

Barbie's Fourposter & Chest (Suzy Goose), 1961—1965.

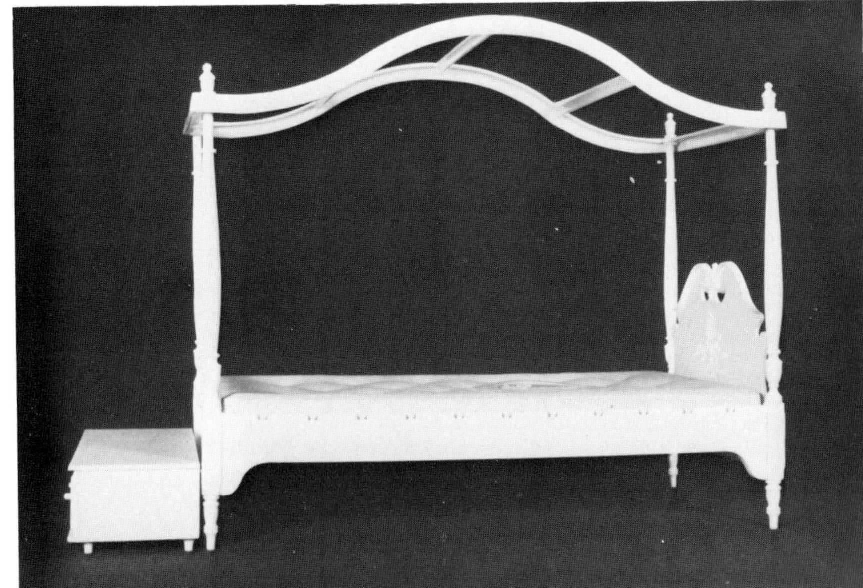

Skipper's Bed (Suzy Goose), 1965.

Skipper's Wardrobe, Vanity & Stool (Suzy Goose), 1965.

#7404 Country Kitchen, 1975—1976.

#7405 Studio Bedroom, 1975—1976.

#7406 Firelight Living Room, 1975—1976.

#9188 Barbie's Apartment. A 1975 Dept. Store Special.

#4011 Skipper & Skooter Bunk Beds, 1965–1967.

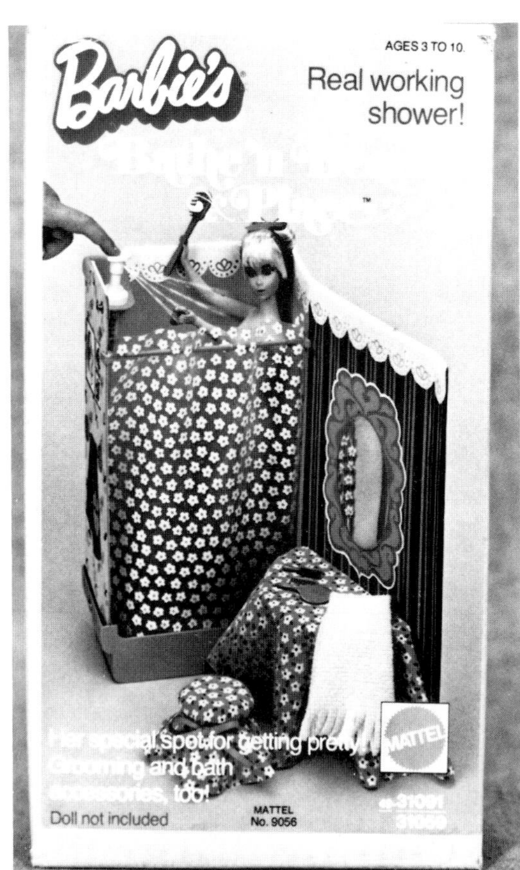

#9056 Bathe'n Beauty Place, 1975. Sears Special.

#9282 Growing Up Skipper Bedroom, 1976.

Mattel Go-Together Furniture, 1964—1965.
#0408 Couch.

Mattel Go-Together Furniture, 1964—1965.
#0409 Chair.

Mattel Go-Together Furniture, 1964—1965.
#0410 Chair.

4. Gift Sets

#856—Party Set, 1960
857—Mix 'N Match Set, 1960
857—Mix 'N Match Set, 1962—slightly different from 1960 set
858—Trousseau Set, 1960
—Barbie Mix 'N Match Gift Set, 1962—1963 Wards
—Barbie & Ken Mix'N Match Gift Set. 1962—1964 Wards, Spiegel
863—Fashion Queen Barbie & Her Friends, 1964
864—Fashion Queen Barbie & Ken Trousseau, 1964
892—Barbie & Ken (tennis o/f)
1011—Barbie's Sparkling Pink Gift Set, 1964
1012—Midge's Ensemble Gift Set, 1964
1013—Barbie's Round the Clock Gift Set, 1964—1965
1014—Barbie, Ken & Midge on Parade Gift Set, 1964
1017—Barbie's Wedding Party Gift Set, 1964—1965
1018—Baribe & Ken Little Theatre Gift Set, 1964
4005—Furniture Gift Set, 1964 Mattel
1021—Skipper Party Time Set, 1964—1965
1022—Barbie, Ken, Midge Pep Rally Gift Set, 1964—1965
1032—Skipper On Wheels, 1965—1966
1034—Barbie Hostess Set, 1965
4012—Living Room Furniture Gift Set, 1965 Mattel
—Skooter Cut 'n Button Gift Set, 1965—1967 Sears
—Color Magic Barbie Gift Set, 1966 Sears
1042—"Francie and Her Swingin' Separates" Gift Set, 1966 Sears
—Skipper Gift Set—doll and Skipper on Wheels items, 1966 Sears
—Francie's Sportin' Set, 1966 Penney's
—Bendable Barbie & "Sew-Free" Wardrobe, 1966 Ward's
—Chris Gift Set—doll and 5 outfits, 1967 Sears
—Skipper & Skooter Gift Set—bend Skipper and st. leg Skooter & double doll case—1967 Sears exclusive
—Skipper & Skooter Gift Set—bunk beds, dolls, sleepwear—1967 Ward's
3303—7-piece twist Barbie Gift Set—"Beautiful Blue" evening dress—1967 Sears exclusive
—7-piece Casey Goes Casual, 1967 Sears
—Braniff outfits by Emilio Pucci for Barbie, 1967 Wards
1552—"New Talking Barbie Silver 'N Satin" Gift Set, 1968 Penney's exclusive
—Skipper Lace 'N Velveteen, 1968 Sears
—8-piece Talking Barbie gift set—fur trimmed lame dinner suit, 1968 Sears
1544—10-piece #1190 Barbie "Barbie Travel In Style Set," 1968 Sears
—Stripes Are Happening Twist Stacey gift set, 1968 Sears
—8-piece #1190 Barbie gift set with "Movie Groovy" outfit, 1969 Sears
1591—Twist (flip) Stacey "Nite Lightning" set ©1969, 1969 Sears
1593—Twist Skipper "Wow! What a 'cool' outfit," 1969 Sears
1595—Barbie & Ken "Fabulous Formal Set"—talking dolls—1969 Sears
—8-piece Talking Julia Gift Set, 1969 Sears
—8-piece Talking Barbie gift set—fur trimmed brocade suit, hip boots—1969 Sears
1596—Talking Barbie "Pink Premiere" gift set, 1969—1970 Penney's exclusive
—Living Skipper Gift Set, 1970-1971 Sears
1585—"Action Accents" Living Barbie gift set, 1970—1971 Sears
—Bend Leg Ken Gift Set, 1970 Sears
1584—Walking Jamie "Furry Friends" gift set, 1970—1971 Sears
—Twist 'N Turn P.J. gift set, 1970 Sears
—Talking Barbie gift set—short plaid coat and dress—1970 Sears
1193—Talking Barbie gift set "Perfectly Plaid"—long plaid pants, short plaid coat with fur collar, 1971—1972 Sears
1194—Francie "Rise 'N Shine"—pink peignoir gift set—1971 Sears
1248—Malibu Ken "Surf's Up" gift set, 1971—1972 Sears
1249—Living Fluff "Sunshine Special" gift set, 1971 Sears
1508—Live Action 'P.J. "Fashion 'N Motion" 1971—1972 Sears
1247—Walking Jamie "Strollin In Style," 1972

#1014 Barbie, Ken & Midge "On Parade Gift Set," 1964. (Courtesy Bernice Lieb)

Box top to above set.

#1021 Skipper Party Time Set, 1964—1965. (Courtesy Bernice Lieb)

#1012 Midge's Ensemble Gift Set, 1964.

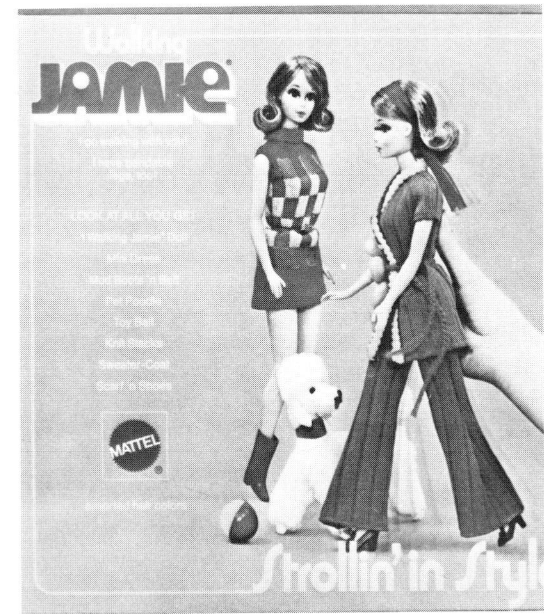

#1247 Walking Jamie "Strollin' In Style" Gift Set, 1972.

#864 Fashion Queen Barbie & Ken Trousseau Set, 1964. (Courtesy Bernice Lieb)

5. Cases

Barbie case ("Easter Parade"), 1961—1962
2 doll trunk, 1962
Ken case ("Rally Day"), 1963
Barbie case ("Enchanted Evening"), 1963
Barbie trunk ("Solo in the Spotlight"), 1963
Barbie & Midge case ("Lunch Date"), 1963
Midge case—red ©1963
Barbie & Ken trunk ("Tuxedo"), 1963
Ken case ("Campus Hero"), 1964
Barbie case ("Red Flair"), 1964—1965
Midge case ("Movie Date"), 1964
Barbie & Ken truck ("Orange Blossum"), 1964—1965
Skipper case ("School Days"), 1964—1965
Barbie "plane-car" case, 1965
Barbie & Skipper case, 1965
4 doll trunk (wedding party), 1965
Travel Vanity case, 1965
3 doll trunk (several varieties)
Skipper & Skooter case, 1965
360—Skipper case
390—Barbie case
1002—Single doll case (scenes varied)
1004—Four doll trunk (scenes varied)
1007—Double doll case (scenes varied)
1023—Francie case
1024—Barbie & Francie Dressing Room case
1025—Francie & Casey double case
1027—Francie & Casey case
1045—Skipper case
1046—Stacey case
2000—Barbie case with doll
2001—Skipper case with doll
2002—Skooter case with doll
3001—Tutti Play case
3002—Francie case
3003—Barbie & Francie case
3023—Tutti case
3561—Tutti case
4289—Barbie Travel trunk
4295—Overnight Case
4296—Tote Bag
4297—"Carry-All"
4966—Skipper case
5016—Tutti Hatbox
5017—Tutti Train Case
5018—Tutti Overnighter
5020—Barbie & Francie Hatbox
5021—Barbie & Francie Train Case
5022—Barbie & Francie Overnighter
5023—Ballet box
Sears 2-doll Sleep 'N Keep case (several varieties), 1968-1976
Sears 1-doll room case (2 varieties), 1971-1972

#5016 Tutti Hatbox.

#3001 Tutti Playcase.

Shown here are a few samples of the many different cases and trunks on the market over the years.

6. Display Sets For Stores (Partial List)

#851—display set, 1959
852—display set, 1959
854—7-piece display set plus Barbie 3-D Wheel of Fashion Display set, 1960
903—Barbie & Ken Fashion Bar—a revolving, permanent display set with three 4-color cards—6 slides of fashions, 1962
1084—Barbie Permanent Counter Catalogue, 1964
1085—Barbie Permanent Counter Catalogue, 1965
1092—The Wonderful World of Barbie Merchandiser, 1965
1093—World of Barbie Activity Display, 1965
1095—World of Barbie Activity Display, 1965
4009—Barbie & Skipper display house for furniture, 1965
1077—Tutti & Todd merchandiser
—Barbie and Stacey Fashion Boutique
—Francie and Casey Fashion Boutique
—Francie and Casey Fashion Boutique
—The World of Barbie
—The Wonderful World of Barbie
—The World of Barbie Fashion
—Skipper Fashion Boutique

McCall's pattern display poster of 1964. (Gift from Grace Otto)

Barbie and Stacey Fashion Boutique—Fashions of 1969. (Courtesy Bernice Lieb)

Francie and Casey Fashion Boutique—Fashions of 1969.

#903 Barbie & Ken Fashion Bar display poster, 1962.

Second view of #903. (There's that F-I-S-H again!)

Third view of #903.

Fourth view of #903.

Fifth view of #903.

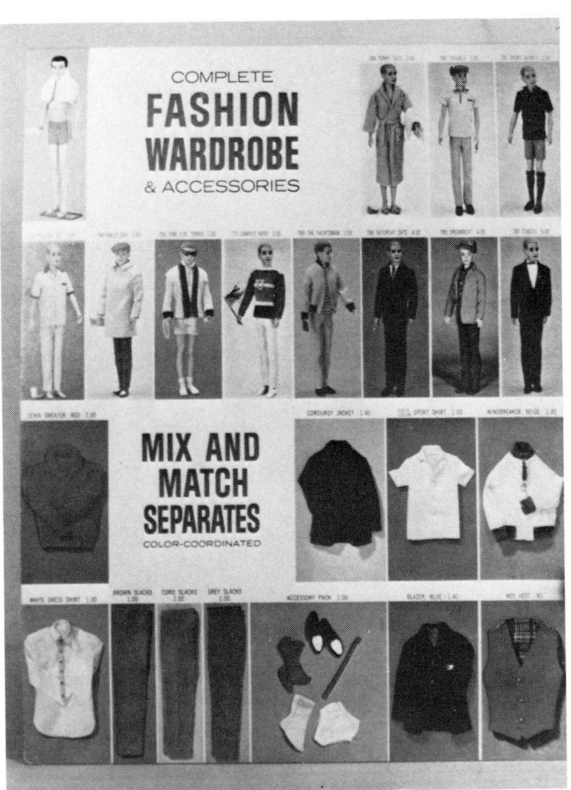

Sixth view of #903.

After a poster or display set is outdated, a store manager is usually happy to give it to a good customer!

7. Miscellaneous Items

#834—Ken pattern
836—Pattern assortment—Barbie, Ken & Chatty Cathy
837—4 sets of Barbie patterns
1703—Barbie & Ken Jumbo Trading Cards ©1962
4040—Barbie & Francie Color Magic Designer Set, 1966—1967
4041—Barbie & Francie Color Magic Fashion Fun, 1966
1006—World of Barbie Hangers (old style) 1967—1968
1065—Hangers (new style), 1969—1974 (2 dif. pkg. designs)
1159—Dancer (horse), 1971—1972
4027—Barbie Beauty Center, 1972—1974
1179—Skipper's gym, 1972—1973
4288—Barbie's Camping Out Tent, 1972—1975
4284—Barbie's Garden Patio with Real Growin' Plants, 1972—1973
7734—Christie Beauty Center, 1973—1974
8640—Hair Originals, 1973 to present
8670—Barbie Sew Magic Fashion Set, 1973—1975
7723—Deluxe Sew Magic Set, 1973
7726—Barbie & Ken Sew Magic Add-Ons, 1974—1975
7727—Francie & Skipper Sew Magic Add-Ons, 1974—1975
7800—Carry Case for Sew Magic machine and accessories, 1974
7850—Barbie Sweet 16 Fur Fashion, Sew Magic, 1974—1975
7277—Barbie & Ken Sportswear, Sew Magic, 1975
7795—Barbie's Pool Party, 1974 to present
7893—Miss America Beauty Center, 1974 Sears
7240—Olympic Gymnast Set, 1975 to present
7408—Barbie's High Sierra Adventure, 1975 to present
4027—Quick Curl Barbie Beauty Center, 1975 to present
7734—Quick Curl Christie Beauty Center, 1975 to present
—Quick Curl Miss America Beauty Center, 1975 to present
Official Barbie 4-speed Phonograph, 1961 Spiegel exclusive
Barbie sings—album, 6 songs, ©1961, 1961 Spiegel, others
Barbie Model Hat Box, 1961 Spiegel
Barbie Wallet, 1961 Spiegel
Barbie's Tea Set, 1962 Wards
Barbie Craft Set, 1962 Wards
Barbie Records, Phonograph, 1962 Wards
Barbie Dresser Set, 1962 Wards
Train Case, 1962 Wards
Play Costume, 1962 Wards
Jewelry, 1962 Wards
Barbie Story Books, 1962 Wards
Barbie Make-Believe Cosmetics—3 sets, 1963 (Glamour Cosmetics—Manicure—Make-up)
Barbie Electric Drawing Set, 1963
524—Barbie Ge-Tar, 1964
Barbie & Her Friends records—0501 through 0506
Barbie Fashions for children—size 7-14, 1965
4859—Barbie Mattel-O-Phone, 1968—1969
3 records in "Fashion 'N Sounds"—1055, 56 & 57, 1971—1972
7735—Barbie Vanity Case, 1973—1974
4296—Tote Bag
4295—Overnight Case
4297—"Carry-All" case
Barbie's Beauty Set—Jergens, 1975 Wards
Barbie Sweet 16 jewelry, 1975
Valentines
Jewelry Box
Sheets, pillow cases
Curtains, bedspread
Charm Bracelet for joining Fan Club
Charm Necklace from Barbie Sweet 16 promotion set
Clock

450—©1961 Queen of the Prom game, 1961—1962 ©MCMLX
0450—Queen of the Prom (new box cover) game, 1964 ©1963
5410—Barbie's Key to Fame Game, 1964, ©1963
5415—Skipper Game, 1965, ©1964
5452—Barbie World of Fashion Game, 1968, ©1967
5481—Barbie "Miss Lively Livin'" game ©1970, ©1970

#7408 Barbie's High Sierra Adventure, 1975 to present.

#4027 Barbie Beauty Center, 1972—1974. (Quick Curl Beauty Center, 1975 to present.)

#7734 Christie Beauty Center, 1973—1974. (Quick Curl Beauty Center, 1975 to present.)

#7893 Miss America Beauty Center, 1974, Sears. (Quick Curl Beauty Center, 1975 to present.)

One of the many items made by other companies under license from Mattel. This was made by Standard Toycraft.

#7240 Olympic Gymnast Set, 1975 to present.

#7795 Barbie's Pool Party, 1974 to present.

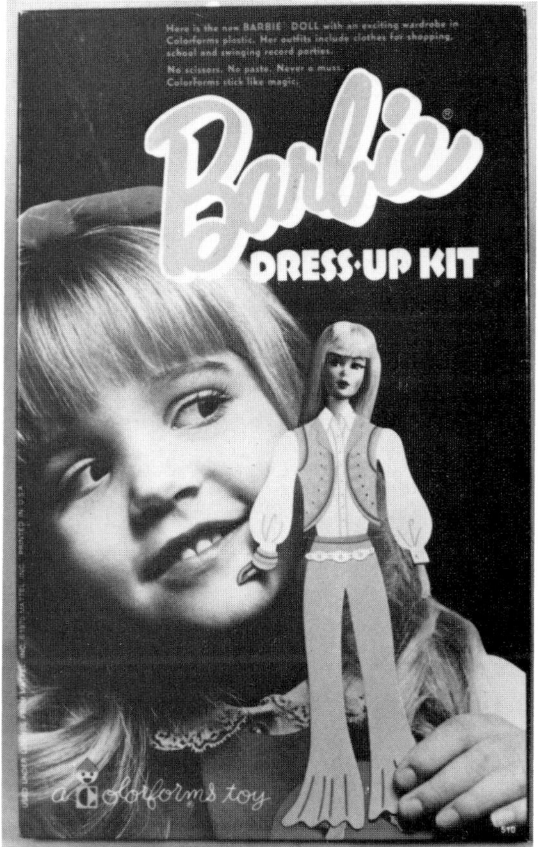

Barbie Dress-Up Kit by Colorforms.

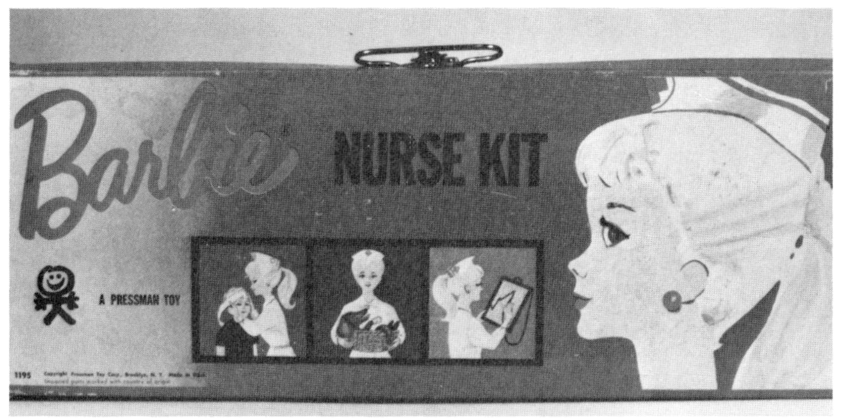

Barbie Nurse Kit made by Pressman.

Barbie necklace from the Sweet 16 promoti
set of 1974.

#450 "Queen of the Prom" game, 1961—1962.
(Gift from Pat Smith)

One of the many items made by Whitman.

A Forget-Me-Nots Valentine made under lic
from Mattel. (Gift from Elizabeth Michael)

#8640 Barbie Hair Originals, 1973 to present. Three colors.

Bed sheet printed with Barbie dolls.

#1065 Barbie Fashion Hangers, 1969—1974.

Barbie Sings. 3 records, 6 songs. 1961.

#1703 Jumbo Trading Cards, ©1962. (Gift from Beverly Gardner)

Stamp Pad Set made by Nasta Industries, 1976.

A small sample of the many paper dolls, coloring books, etc. on the market. Made by Whitman.

Jigsaw Puzzle made by Whitman, 1972.

#7726 SewMagic add-ons. To be used with the Sew Magic machine.

Fashion booklets. Pink cover. Barbie only. Dated MCMLVIII. Three different. (Third one a gift from Phyllis Houston)

Fashion booklets. Pink. Barbie & Ken. One undated, one dated 1961.

Fashion booklets. Light blue. One undated, one dated 1962.

Fashion booklet. White cover. Dated 1962.

Fashion booklets (two of these). Yellow cover. Dated 1962.

Fashion booklets (two of these). Bright blue cover. Dated 1962.

Fashion booklets (four of these). Dated 1963.

Fashion booklets (two of these). White cover. Dated 1963.

Fashion booklets (four of these). Dated 1964.

Fashion booklet. Yellow cover. Dated 1964.

Fashion booklets (four of these). Red cover. Dated 1965.

Fashion booklet. Dated 1965.

Fashion booklet. Dated 1965.

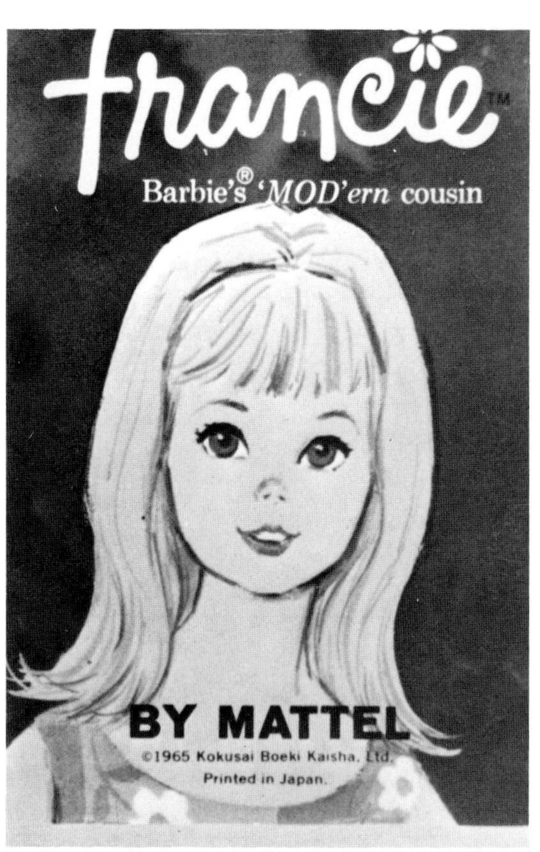

Fashion booklet. Dated 1965.

Fashion booklet. Dated 1966.

Fashion booklets (three of these). Dated 1966.

Fashion booklets (three of these). Dated 1967.

hion booklets (four of these). Dated 1968.

Fashion booklets (two of these). Dated 1969.

Fashion booklets (five of these). Dated 1970.

Fashion booklet. Dated 1972.

Fashion booklet. Dated 1971.

These little magazines were included in Barbie's Go-Together Furniture of 1964—1965.

Fashion booklet. Dated 1973.

X. Barbie, The World's Best Dressed Doll

If the doll world had a "Ten Best Dressed List," Barbie and her friends would win all ten places. At least that is what Barbie collectors believe!

From the beginning, the dolls were supplied with lovely clothes and accessories for all occasions. These were not doll clothes; they were true miniature fashions. They were made with great detail and skill, and fashion trends of the times were followed.

Mattel's fashion design department is headed by Charlotte Johnson, a former designer of women's sportswear. Although the fashions are designed in California, they are manufactured elsewhere.

The first clothes, made in Japan, were of superior workmanship and quality. As labor costs in Japan became prohibitively higher and higher, Mattel had to find less costly labor. Hong Kong, Taiwan and Korea produced the clothes in later years.

Present day fashions still have style and flair, but they are not quite as nice as the early ones. If the same skilled handwork, the same costly fabrics and the same minute details of the early fashions were utilized today, the products would be far too expensive for the mass market. In order to keep production costs at reasonable levels, some of the handwork and some of the detail have had to be eliminated.

—:—

Two new lines of clothing were offered in 1972, "Fashion Originals" and "Best Buys." "Fashion Originals" were the more expensive outfits with all needed accessories included. "Best Buys" were good clothes sold at budget prices.

1972 was the year color-coded packaging was introduced in the clothing line. And 1972 was the last year for clothing labels and names or titles for the outfits.

—:—

On the following page begins a list of clothes known to have been on the market in this country. See Chapter III for clothes available in other countries.

Barbie-size Clothes

911—Golden Girl, 1959—1962
912—Cotton Casual, 1959—1961
915—"Peach-Fleecy" Coat, 1959—1961
Pak—"Peach-Fleecy" Coat, 1963
916—Commuter Set, 1959—1960
917—Apple Print Sheath, 1959—1960
918—Cruise Stripe Dress, 1959—1961
919—Fashion Undergarments, 1959—1961
921—Floral Petticoat, 1959—1963
961—Evening Splendour, 1959—1964
962—Barbie-Q Outfit, 1959—1961
963—Resort Set, 1959—1962
964—Gay Parisienne, 1959
965—Nighty-Negligee Set, 1959—1964
966—"Plantation Bell" Dress Set, 1959—1961
967—Picnic Set, 1959—1961
967—Picnic Set (new hat, basket, fish), 1962
968—Roman Holiday Separates, 1959
969—Surburban Shopper, 1959—1964
971—Easter Parade, 1959
972—Barbie "Wedding Day" Set, 1959—1962
973—"Sweet Dreams," 1959—1963
Pak—"Sweet Dreams," 1964—1965
975—Winter Holiday, 1959—1963
976—Sweater Girl (apricot sweater, grey skirt), 1959—1962
977—Silken Flame, 1960—1964
978—Let's Dance, 1960—1962
979—Friday Nite Date, 1960—1964
981—Busy Gal, 1960—1961
982—Solo in the Spotlight, 1960—1964
983—Enchanted Evening, 1960—1963
923—Barbie Accessories, 1961
984—American Airlines Stewardess, 1961—1964
985—Open Road, 1961—1962
986—Sheath Sensation, 1961—1964
987—Orange Blossom, 1961—1964
988—Singing in the Shower, 1961—1962
Pak—Singing in the Shower, 1962
989—Ballerina, 1961—1965
991—Registered Nurse, 1961—1964
931—Garden Party, 1962—1963
933—Movie Date, 1962—1963
934—After 5, 1962—1964
937—Sorority Meeting, 1962—1963
939—Red Flair, 1962—1965
940—Mood For Music, 1962—1963
941—Tennis, Anyone, 1962—1964
942—Icebreaker, 1962—1964
Pak—Gathered Skirt, 1962—1963
Pak—Two Piece Pajamas, 1962—1963
Pak—Tee Shirt and Shorts, 1962—1963
Pak—Accessory Pack, 1962—1963
Pak—Square Neck Sweater, 1962—1963
Pak—Plain Blouse & Purse, 1962—1963
Pak—Cardigan, 1962—1963
Pak—Bell Dress, 1962—1963
Pak—Slacks, 1962—1963
Pak—Helanca Swimsuit, 1962—1963
Pak—Lingerie Pack, 1962—1963
Pak—Purse Pack, 1962—1963
Pak—Fur Stole With Bag, 1962—1963
Pak—Sheath with gold buttons, 1962—1963
Pak—Silk Sheath, 1962—1963
Pak—Sheath Skirt & telephone, 1962—1963
Pak—Apron and Utensils, 1962—1963
Pak—Slip-Pant-Bra, 1962—1963
Pak—Scoop Neck Playsuit, 1962—1963
943—Fancy Free, 1963—1964
944—Masquerade, 1963—1964
945—Graduation, 1963—1964
946—Dinner at Eight, 1963—1964
947—Bride's Dream, 1963—1965
948—Ski Queen, 1963—1964
949—Raincoat, 1963
0949—Stormy Weather, 1964—1965
951—Senior Prom, 1963—1964
953—Barbie Baby-Sits (apron), 1963—1964
0953—Barbie Baby-Sits (layette), 1965
954—Career Girl, 1963—1964
955—Swingin' Easy, 1963
956—Busy Morning, 1963
957—Knitting Pretty (blue), 1963
0957—Knitting Pretty (pink), 1964
958—Party Date, 1963
959—Theatre Date, 1963
1612—Theatre Date (no hat), 1964
0961—Evening Splendour, 1964
992—Golden Elegance, 1963
993—Sophisticated Lady, 1963—1964
Pak—Knit Shorts and Top, 1963
Pak—Knit Blouse, 1963
Pak—Knit Full Evening Skirt, 1963
Pak—Knit Slacks, 1963
Pak—Knit Sheath Dress With Fringed Collar, 1963
Pak—Knit Sheath Skirt and Sash, 1963
Pak—Jeans, 1963
Pak—Fur Hat/Bag, 1963
Pak—Square Neck Sweater & Scarf, 1963
Pak—Satin Slacks, 1963
Pak—Satin Sheath Skirt, 1963
Pak—Satin Coat, 1963
Pak—Satin Evening Top, 1963
Pak—Satin Bolero & Hat, 1963
Pak—Full Satin Evening Skirt, 1963
Pak—Gold Lame Sheath, 1963
Pak—Shoe Pack, 1963
Pak—Straw Hat, Purse, Shoes, 1963
0819—It's Cold Outside, 1964—1966
0820—Barbie In Mexico, 1964
0821—Barbie In Japan, 1964
0822—Barbie In Switzerland, 1964
0823—Barbie In Holland, 1964
0872—Cinderella, 1964—1965
0873—Guinevere, 1964—1965
0874—Barbie Arabian Nights, 1964—1965
0875—Drum Majorette, 1964—1965
0876—Cheerleader, 1964—1965
0880—Red Riding Hood and the Wolf, 1964
0889—Candy Striper Volunteer, 1964
1600—Lunch Date, 1964
1601—Pajama Party, 1964—1965
1602—Knit Separates, 1964
1603—Country Fair, 1964
1604—Crisp 'N Cool, 1964—1965
1605—Barbie in Hawaii, 1964
1606—Garden Tea Party, 1964
1607—White Magic, 1964
1608—Barbie Skin Diver, 1964—1965
1609—Black Magic Ensemble, 1964—1965
1610—Golden Evening, 1964
1611—Satin 'N Rose, 1964
1613—Dog 'N Duds, 1964—1965

1616—Campus Sweetheart, 1964—1965
1617—Midnight Blue, 1964—1965
Pak—For Rink & Court, 1964—1965
Pak—Fashion Feet, 1964—1965
Pak—Ruffles 'N Lace, 1964—1965
Pak—Go Everywhere, 1964—1965
Pak—For Barbie Dressmakers, 1964—1967
Pak—Color Coordinates, 1964—1965
Pak—Going To The Ball, 1964—1965
Pak—Lovely Lingerie, 1964—1967
Pak—On The Go, 1964—1965
Pak—Barbie's Boudoir, 1964—1965
Pak—Costume Completers, 1964—1965
Pak—Jumpin' Jeans, 1964—1965
Pak—Dress-Up Hats, 1964—1965
Pak—Campus Bell, 1964—1965
Pak—Shoe Wardrobe, 1964—1965
Pak—Spectator Sport, 1964—1965
Pak—What's Cookin, 1964—1965
Pak—Fashion Accents, 1964—1965
Pak—Leisure Hours, 1964—1965
Pak—In the Swim, 1964—1965
Sears Natual Mink Jacket, 1964—1965
1034—Barbie Hostess Set, 1965
1614—Junior Prom, 1965
1615—Saturday Matinee, 1965
1619—Fun 'N Games, 1965—1966
1620—Junior Designer, 1965—1967
1621—Knit Hit, 1965
1622—Student Teacher, 1965—1966
1623—Vacation Time, 1965
1624—Fun at the Fair, 1965
1625—Modern Art, 1965
1626—Dancing Doll, 1965
1627—Country Club Dance, 1965
1628—Brunch Time, 1965
1629—Skater's Waltz, 1965—1966
1631—Aboard Ship, 1965
1632—Invitation to Tea, 1965
1633—Disco Date, 1965
1634—Barbie Learns to Cook, 1965
1635—Fashion Editor, 1965
1636—Sleeping Pretty, 1965
1637—Outdoor Life, 1965
1638—Fraternity Dance, 1965
1639—Holiday Dance, 1965—1966
1640—Matinee Fashion, 1965
1641—Miss Astronaut, 1965
1642—Slumber Party, 1965
1643—Poodle Parade, 1965
1644—On The Avenue, 1965
1645—Golden Glory, 1965—1966
1646—Magnificience, 1965
1647—Gold 'N Glamour, 1965
1671—Sporting Casuals, 1965—1967
1701—Nine to Five, 1965—1966
1703—Sorority Tea, 1965—1966
1706—Pretty Travelers, 1965—1966
1707—Hootenanny, 1965—1966
1708—Patio Party, 1965—1966
1711—Debutante Party, 1965—1966
1712—Day in Town, 1965—1966
1713—Sightseeing, 1965—1966
1721—Moonlight 'N Roses, 1965—1966
1722—Stardust, 1965—1966
1723—Day 'N Night, 1965—1966
1724—Golden Ball, 1965—1966
1649—Lunch on the Terrace, 1966—1967
1650—Outdoor Art Show, 1966—1967
1651—Beau Time, 1966—1967
1652—Pretty as a Picture, 1966—1967
1653—International Fair, 1966—1967
1654—Reception Line, 1966—1967
1655—Underfashions, 1966—1967
1656—Fashion Luncheon, 1966—1967
1658—Garden Wedding, 1966—1967
1660—Evening Gala, 1966—1967
1661—London Tour, 1966—1967
1663—Music Center Matinee, 1966—1967
1664—Shimmering Magic, 1966—1967
1665—Here Comes The Bride, 1966—1967
1666—Debutante Ball, 1966—1967
1667—Benefit Performance, 1966—1967
1668—Riding in the Park, 1966—1967
1669—Dreamland, 1966—1967
1670—Coffee's On (similar to #1628), 1966—1967
1672—Club Meeting (similar to #1635), 1966—1967
1673—Lunchtime (similar to #1634), 1966—1967
1674—Sleepytime Gal (similar to #1642), 1966—1967
1675—Sunday Visit (similar to #1644), 1966—1967
1676—Fabulous Fashion (similar to #1646), 1966
1678—Pan American Airways Stewardess, 1966
4040—Barbie & Francie Color Magic Set, 1966—1967
4041—Barbie & Francie Color Magic Fashion Fun, 1966
Pak—Have Fun, 1966—1967
Pak—Set 'N Serve, 1966—1967
Pak—Lunch Date, 1966-1967
Pak—Pert Skirts, 1966—1967
Pak—Kitchen Magic, 1966—1967
Pak—Tailored Tops, 1966—1967
Pak—Red Delight, 1966—1967
Pak—Flats 'N Heels, 1966—1967
Pak—Glamour Hats, 1966—1967
Pak—Match-mates, 1966—1967
—(Sears) Pink Formal, 1966
1440—Pink Sparkle, 1967
1460—Tropicana, 1967—1968
1470—Intrigue, 1967—1968
1683—Sunflower, 1967—1968
1685—Underprints, 1967—1968
1686—Print Aplenty, 1967—1968
1687—Caribbean Cruise, 1967
1688—Travel Togethers, 1967
1690—Studio Tour, 1967
1691—Fashion Shiner, 1967—1968
1692—Patio Party, 1967—1968
1694—Pink Moonbeams, 1967—1968
1695—Evening Enchantment, 1967
1696—Floating Gardens, 1967
1697—Formal Occasion, 1967
1698—Beautiful Bride, 1967
1775—Stripes Away, 1967
1776—Smart Switch, 1967
1777—Pretty Wild!, 1967
1778—Bloom Bursts, 1967
1779—Mix 'N Matchers (same as #4041), 1967
Pak—Flats 'N Heels, 1967—1968
Pak—Cook-Ups, 1967
Pak—Best Bow, 1967
Pak—Fancy Trimmins, 1967
Pak—Skirt Styles, 1967
Pak—Top Twosome, 1967
—(Wards) Barbie Goes Braniff (Emilio Pucci outfits) 1967
3303—(Sears) "Beautiful Blue" gift set, 1967
1805—Bouncy Flouncy, 1967—1968
1807—Disco Dater, 1967—1968
1808—Drizzle Dash, 1967—1968

1809—Mini Prints, 1967—1968
—Red Fantastic, 1967
—Weekenders, 1967
—The Yellow Go, 1967
1818—Velvet-Teens, 1967
1804—Knit Hit, 1968—1969
1813—Snug Fuzz, 1968—1969
1814—Sparkle Squares, 1968—1969
1820—Zokka!, 1968—1969
1821—Under-Liners, 1968—1969
1822—Swirly-Que, 1968—1969
1823—Jump Into Lace, 1968
1824—Snap-Dash, 1968
1841—Night Clouds, 1968
1842—Togetherness, 1968
1843—Dancing Stripes, 1968
1844—Extravaganza, 1968
1845—Scene-Stealers, 1968
1846—Trail-Blazer, 1968
1848—All That Jazz, 1968—1969
1849—Wedding Wonder, 1968—1969
Pak—Dressed-Up, 1968
Pak—Extra-Casuals, 1968
Pak—Pedal Pushers, 1968
Pak—Change-Abouts, 1968
Pak—Add-Ons, 1968
—Pajama-Pow!, 1968
—Bermuda Holiday, 1968
—(Sears) Talking Barbie gift set, 1968
1544—(Sears) "Travel in Style" gift set, 1968
—(Sears) "Glimmer Glamour," 1968
—(Sears) Stacey "Stripes Are Happening," 1968
1552—(Penney's) "Silver 'N Satin" set, 1968
1862—Country Capers, 1969
1863—Pretty Power, 1969
1864—Close-Ups, 1969
1865—Glo-Go, 1969
1866—Movie Groovie, 1969
1867—Dream-Ins, 1969
1868—Happy Go Pink! 1969
1869—Midi Magic, 1969
1870—Midi-Marvelous, 1969
1871—Romantic Ruffles, 1969
1872—Sea-Worthy, 1969
1873—Plush Pony, 1969
1874—Fab City, 1969
1879—Let's Have a Ball, 1969
1880—Winter Wedding, 1969—1970
1881—Made for Each Other, 1969
1885—Silver Sparkle, 1969
—Salute to Silver (same as #1885), 1969—1970
1476—Dream Wrap, 1969—1970
1477—Hurray for Leather, 1969—1970
1478—Shift into Knit, 1969—1970
1479—Leisure Leopard, 1969—1970
1481—Firelights, 1969—1970
1482—Important In-Vestment, 1969—1970
1483—Little Bow-Pink, 1969—1970
1484—Yellow-Mellow, 1969—1970
1486—Winter Wow, 1969—1970
1487—Shirtdressy, 1969—1970
1488—Velvet Venture, 1969—1970
1489—Cloud 9, 1969—1970
1491—Red, White 'N Warm, 1969—1970
1492—Silver Polish, 1969—1970
1493—Fab Fur, 1969—1970
1494—Goldswinger, 1969—1970
1751—(Julia) Leather Weather, 1969—1970
1752—(Julia) Brrr-Furrr, 1969—1970
1753—(Julia) Candlelight Capers, 1969—1970
1754—(Julia) Pink Fantasy, 1969—1970
—Now-Wow!, 1969
—Twinkle Togs, 1969
—Team Ups, 1969
—Wild 'N Wonderful, 1969
—Dreamy Pink, 1969
—Fancy-Dancy, 1969
—Tunic 'N Tights, 1969
—Smasheroo, 1969
1591—(Sears) "Nite Lightning," 1969
1595—(Sears) "Fabulous Formal Set," 1969
—(Sears) 8 pc. Julia set, 1969
—(Sears) 8 pc. Barbie set, 1969
1596—(Penney's) "Pink Premiere" set, 1969—1970
Pak—Flats 'N Heels, 1969
Pak—Tour-Ins, 1969
Pak—Finishing Touches, 1969
Pak—Petti-Pinks, 1969
Pak—Terrific Twosome, 1969
Pak—Sun-Shiner, 1969
1451—Tangerine Scene, 1970
1452—Now Knit, 1970
1453—Flower Wower, 1970
1454—Loop Scoop, 1970
1456—Dreamy Blues, 1970
1457—City Sparklers, 1970
1458—Gypsy Spirit, 1970
1459—Great Coat, 1970
1462—Rare Pair, 1970
1463—Lovely Sleep-Ins, 1970
1464—Anti-Freezers, 1970
1465—Lemon Kick, 1970
1467—Lamb 'N Leather, 1970
1468—Special Sparkler, 1970
1469—Blue Royalty, 1970
1781—Tennis Team, 1970—1971
1782—Shape-Ups, 1970—1971
1783—Ruffles 'N Swirls, 1970—1971
1784—Harem-M-M's, 1970—1971
1786—Bright 'N Brocade, 1970-1971
1787—Prima Ballerina, 1970—1971
1788—Scuba-Do's, 1970—1971
1789—Fiery Felt, 1970—1971
1791—The Lace Caper, 1970—1971
1792—Mood Matchers, 1970—1971
1783—Skate Mates, 1970—1971
1794—Check the Suit, 1970—1971
1796—Fur Sighted, 1970
1797—The Ski Scene, 1970
1798—Rainbow Wraps, 1970
1799—Maxi 'N Mini, 1970
Pak—Soft 'N Snug, 1970—1971
Pak—Walking Pretty, 1970—1971
Pak—Plush 'N Warm, 1970—1971
Pak—Fashion Firsts, 1970—1971
Pak—Cool 'N Casual, 1970—1971
Pak—The Sew-In, 1970—1971
—(Penney's) 64 pc. accessory set, 1970—1971
—(Sears) "Glamour Group," 1970—1973
—(Sears) "Fashion Bouquet," 1970—1973
—(Sears) Accessory Pack, 1970—1974
—(Sears) Goodies Galore, 1970—1973
1584—(Sears) "Furry Friends," 1970—1971
1585—(Sears) "Action Accents," 1970—1971
—(Sears) Twist P.J. set, 1970
—(Sears) Talking Barbie set, 1970

Fashions 'N Sounds

1055—Country Music, 1971—1972

1056—Festival Fashion, 1971—1972
1057—Groovin' Gauchos, 1971—1972
3401—Fringe Benefits, 1971—1972
3402—Two-Way Tiger, 1971—1972
3403—Baby Doll Pink, 1971—1972
3404—Glowin' Out, 1971—1972
3406—Evening In, 1971—1972
3407—Midi Mood, 1971—1972
3408—Super Scarf, 1971—1972
3409—Red for Rain, 1971—1972
3411—Poncho Put-On, 1971—1972
3412—Fun Flakes, 1971—1972
3413—Golfing Greats, 1971—1972
3414—Satin Slumber, 1971—1972
3416—Wild 'N Wintery, 1971—1972
3417—Bridal Brocade, 1971—1972
3418—Magnificient Midi, 1971—1972
3419—Silver Serenade, 1971—1972
3421—Bubbles 'N Boots, 1971—1972
3422—The Color Kick, 1971—1972
3423—Night Lighter, 1971—1972
3424—In Blooms, 1971—1972
3426—Turtle 'N Tights, 1971—1972
3427—The Dream Team, 1971—1972
3428—The Zig-Zag Bag, 1971—1972
3429—Cold Snap, 1971—1972
3431—Victorian Velvet, 1971—1972
3432—In Stitches, 1971—1972
3433—All About Plaid, 1971—1972
3434—Fun Fur, 1971—1972
3436—Gaucho Gear, 1971—1972
3437—Dancing Lights, 1971—1972
3438—Peasant Dressy, 1971—1972
3439—Wild Things, 1971—1972
1193—(Sears) "Perfectly Plaid" set, 1971—1972
1508—(Sears) "Fashion 'N Motion" P.J. set, 1971—1972
—(Penney's) Sun Set Accessories, 1971
1247—"Strollin In Style," 1972

Put-Ons 'N Pets

1061—Poodle Doodles, 1972
1062—Kitty Kapers, 1972
1063—Hot Togs, 1972

Miss America Costumes

—Majestic Blue, 1972—1973
—Miss America red gown, 1972—1973
—Miss America rose gown, 1972—1973
3382—Shoes, 1972—1976
3480—Fun Shine, 1972
3481—The Short Set, 1972
3482—Peasant Pleasant, 1972
3483—Purple Pleasers, 1972
3485—Madras Mad, 1972
3486—O-Boy Corduroy, 1972
3487—Sleepy Set, 1972
3488—Overall Denim, 1972
3490—Party Lines, 1972
3491—Suede 'N Fur, 1972
3492—Flying Colors, 1972
3493—Satin 'N Shine, 1972

Best Buys

3336—Furry 'N Fun, 1972
3337—All American Girl, 1972
3338—Mainly for Rain, 1972
3339—Light 'N Lazy, 1972
3340—Golden Glitter, 1972
3341—Long 'N Fringy, 1972
—Good Sports, 1972
—Sweet Dreams, 1972
—White 'N With It, 1972
—Sport Star, 1972
—Glowin Gold, 1972
—Picture Me Pretty, 1972
—Silver Blues, 1972
—Lovely 'N Lavender, 1972
—Pants-Perfect Purple, 1972
—Pleasantly Peasanty, 1972
—Fancy That Purple, 1972
—Sweetheart Satin, 1972
3203—long skirt, blouse, red, white and black, 1973
3205—midi skirt, blouse—yellow and white, 1973
3206—long print tricot skirt and hat, green top, 1973
3208—orange slacks and jacket, 1973
3343—flowered midi skirt, white blouse, 1973
3346—navy middy dress, 1973
3347—short printed dress, 1973
3348—yellow sleep set, 1973
8620—long dark printed dress, 1973
8621—blue and white checked midi suit, 1973
8622—red pants, sheer over-skirt, white top, 1973
8623—wedding outfit, 1973
3347—Sears' solid red dress, 1973
—Sears' green and white nighty, 1973
8626—shoes, 1973—1974

Get-Ups 'N Go

7700—Doctor, 1973—1976
7701—Ballerina, 1973—1974
7702—Camping, 1973—1974
7703—United Airlines Stewardess, 1973—1975

Best Buys

8680—long tricot print, 1973
8681—tan skirt, red blouse, 1973
8682—tan coat, fur trimmed, 1973
8683—long printed skirt, yellow blouse, 1973
8684—long off-white dress, 1973
8685—printed pants, white blouse, yellow weskit, 1973
8687—pink pants suit, 1973
8688—long rose dress, black net coat, 1973
8689—long gold skirt, white blouse, 1973
8690—robe and nightgown, 1973
8691—pants, skirt, hat, blouse, 1973
8692—blue evening gown, 1973

Sew Free

8670—long printed skirt, rose blouse and bag, short yellow skirt, printed blouse, baby dolls and blue and white printed dress, 1973—1975

Get-Ups 'N Go

7839—Bride, 1974—1975
7840—Blue Party Dress, 1974
7841—Pink Party Separates, 1974—1975
7842—Tennis, 1974—1975
7843—Salmon Party Dress, 1974
7787—Skiing, 1974
7788—Beach, 1974—1975

Best Buys

7746—red palazzo pants, white top, 1974
7747—long pink skirt and top, 1974
7748—2-piece red print, white dickey, 1974
7749—long blue dress, white apron, 1974
7750—2-piece blue printed dress, 1974
7751—jeans, Hawaiian print halter, 1974
7752—3-piece blue suit, 1974
7753—long brown suit, 1974
7754—pink sleep set, 1974
7755—black, red, white peasant dress, 1974
7756—Pepsi outfit, 1974
7757—long red dress, 1974
7813—red and white dotted pants and top, 1974
7814—long salmon tricot dress, 1974
7815—plaid cotton suit, 1974
7816—red baby dolls, 1974
7817—short striped dress, red hat, 1974
7818—jeans, red top, 1974
7819—blue midi, dotted scarf, 1974
7820—long red gown, jacket, 1974
7821—red and beige outfit, 1974
7822—blue and orange outfit, 1974
7823—4 piece red, blue and white outfit, 1974
7824—long beige dress, lace apron, 1974
—(Sears), long red print and solid yellow peasant dress, denim pants and jacket, white halter, 3 piece knit suit, 1974
—(Sears), long green and red print peasant dress, nightgown and robe, brown coat and hat, 1974
—(Sears), red evening gown and jacket, 1974
—(Sears), Sweet 16, 11 piece Mix 'N Match set, 1974
7850—Sew Magic—3 red outfits, 1974—1975

Get-Ups 'N Go

7241—Indian Print Separates, 1975—1976
7242—Casuals, 1975—1976
7243—Olympic Warm-Ups, 1975
7244—Olympic Parade, 1975

Best Buys

7200—red printed skirt, white blouse, 1975
7202—printed pants and top, 1975
7203—red sleepers, 1975
7204—dark print 2 piece dress, 1975
7205—long red print 2 piece dress, 1975
7206—solid blue, red print 2 piece set, 1975
7208—beige and red print, apron, 1975
7209—red pants, red and white checked jacket, 1975
7210—long skirt, halter, hat, 1975
7211—long yellow dotted dress, 1975
7271—Olympic outfit, 1975
7272—Olympic Skating set, 1975
7413—Olympic outfit, 1975
7414—yellow top, patchwork skirt, 1975
7415—black and rose pants, red top, 1975
7416—long green and pink printed dress, 1975
7417—dress, white with red dots, 1975
7418—dress, blue top, red and white skirt, 1975
7419—Olympic outfit, 1975
7420—burnt orange dress, brown hat, 1975
7421—pants, shirt, cap, 1975
7422—skirt, striped top, cap, 1975
7423—bandana jumper, blouse, 1975
7424—yellow and blue set, 1975—1976

Fashion Originals

7931—red evening cape, 1975
7932—silver and red evening gown, 1975
7933—green separates set, 1975
7934—rose dress, stole, hat, 1975
—(Sears), rose evening gown and jacket, 1975
9078—(Sears), 9 piece red, white, blue outfit, 1975
9042—(Sears), long skirt, white blouse, 1975
9043—(Sears), regular Olympic outfit, 1975
9047—(Sears), pants, cape, cap, 1975
9046—printed skirt, white top, 1975
9048—"tweed" skirt, blue blouse, 1975

Sears' Best Buy Exclusives

9006—red print tricot, 1975
9007—blue denim dress and hat, 1975
9008—pink baby dolls, 1975
9009—yellow suit, printed halter, 1975
9010—red plaid pants and jacket, 1975
9011—yellow and print skirt, printed top, 1975

Ballerina Costumes

9326—Sugar Plum Fairy, 1976
9327—Snowflake Fairy, 1976
9329—Princess Aurora, 1976

Get-Ups 'N Go

7176—Bride, 1976
9151—Summer Gown, 1976
9152—Knit Ensemble, 1976
9594—Pink Evening Gown, 1976
9595—Coral Evening Gown, 1976

Best Buys

9153—orange checked skirt, top, 1976
9154—white pants, red shirt, 1976
9155—striped dress, 1976
9156—floral printed dress, 1976
9157—rose nightgown, 1976
9158—red, white, blue dress, 1976
9160—rose and white printed party dress, 1976
9161—blue pants, bandana blouse, 1976
9162—yellow jumper, blouse and scarf, 1976
9163—underwear, 1976
9164—red, white, blue print, 1976
9571—long red printed dress, 1976
9572—gaucho pants, boots, blouse, 1976
9573—dress, bag, 1976
9574—pants, shirt, socks, 1976
9575—long printed dress, yellow sleeves, 1976
9576—checked pants, solid shirt, 1976
9577—pink party dress, 1976
9578—"tweed" suit, 1976
9579—blue pants, checked top, 1976
9580—long yellow and red party dress, 1976
9581—pants, jacket and cap, 1976
9582—blue and lame short party dress, 1976

Sears' Best Buys Exclusives

9682—black and rose nightgown, 1976
9683—white with navy stripes dress, 1976
9684—yellow suit, 1976
9685—blue pants, yellow top, 1976

9686—long blue and white printed dress, 1976
9687—long red and white dress, 1976
9650—(Sears), Ballerina Costume, 1976
—(Sears), red evening gown and cape, 1976
—(Sears), red palazzo pants, gold halter, 1976
—(Sears), 8 piece Coordinated set, 1976
—(Sears), Mix 'N Match set, 1976

Ken-size Clothes

770—Campus Hero, 1961—1964
780—In Training, 1961—1962
781—Sleeper Set (short sleeves), 1961—1962
781—Sleeper Set (long sleeves), 1962—1963
0781—Sleeper Set—blue, 1964
782—Casuals (yellow shirt), 1962—1963
0782—Casuals (striped shirt), 1964
783—Sport Shorts, 1961—1963
784—Terry Togs, 1961—1964
785—Dreamboat, 1961—1963
786—Saturday Date, 1961—1963
787—Tuxedo, 1961—1965
788—Rally Day, 1962—1964
789—The Yachtsman (no cap), 1962—1963
0789—The Yachstman (has a cap), 1964
790—Time for Tennis, 1962—1965
Pak—Red Vest, 1962—1963
Pak—Sewn Sweater, 1962—1963
Pak—Corduroy Jacket, 1962—1963
Pak—Windbreaker, 1962—1963
Pak—Blazer, 1962—1963
Pak—White Dress Shirt, 1962—1963
Pak—Solid Colored Sport Shirt, 1962—1963
Pak—Pattern Printed Shirt, 1962—1963
Pak—Polo Shirt, 1962—1963
Pak—Accessory Pack, 1962—1963
Pak—Brown Slacks, 1962—1963
Pak—Cord Slacks, 1962—1963
Pak—Grey Slacks, 1962—1963
791—Fun on Ice, 1963—1964
792—Play Ball, 1963—1964
793—Dr. Ken, 1963—1965
794—Masquerade, 1963—1964
795—Graduation, 1963—1964
796—Sailor, 1963—1965
797—Army and Air Force, 1963—1965
798—Ski Champion, 1963—1964
799—Touchdown, 1963—1965
Pak—Skin Diver Outfit, 1963
Pak—Hunting Outfit, 1963
Pak—Boxing Outfit, 1963
Pak—Jeans, 1963
Pak—Cardigan Sweater, 1963
Pak—Sweat Shirt, 1963
0772—The Prince, 1964—1965
0773—King Arthur, 1964—1965
0774—Ken Arabian Nights, 1964—1965
0775—Drum Major, 1964—1965
0776—Ken in Switzerland, 1964
0777—Ken in Holland, 1964
0778—Ken in Mexico, 1964
0779—American Airlines Captain, 1964—1965
1400—Country Clubbin, 1964
1401—Special Date, 1964—1965
1403—Going Bowling, 1964—1965
1404—Ken in Hawaii, 1964
1405—Roller Skate Date, 1964
1405—Roller Skate Date (cap omitted, slacks added) 1965
1406—Ken Skin Diver, 1964—1965
1407—Fountain Boy, 1964—1965
1408—Fraternity Meeting, 1964
1409—Goin' Huntin, 1964—1965
1410—Campus Corduroys, 1964—1965
1411—Victory Dance, 1964
Pak—Cheerful Chef, 1964—1967
Pak—Lounging Around, 1964—1967
Pak—White Is Right, 1964—1967
Pak—Shoes For Sport, 1964—1967
Pak—Party Fun, 1964—1967
Pak—At Ease, 1964—1967
Pak—Morning Workout, 1964—1967
Pak—Top It Off, 1964—1967
Pak—Sportsman, 1964—1967
Pak—Dr. Ken's Kit, 1964—1967
Pak—Soda Date, 1964—1967
Pak—Best Foot Forward, 1964—1967
1412—Hiking Holiday, 1965
1413—Off to Bed, 1965
1414—Holiday, 1965
1415—Mr. Astronaut, 1965
1416—College Student, 1965
1417—Rovin' Reporter, 1965
1418—Time to Turn In, 1966
1419—Tv's Good Tonight, 1966
1420—Jazz Concert, 1966
1421—Seein' the Sights, 1966
1422—Summer Job, 1966
1423—Ken A Go Go, 1966
1424—Business Appointment, 1966
1425—Best Man, 1966
1426—Here Comes the Groom, 1966
1427—Mountain Hike, 1966
—(Wards) Pilot uniform, 1967
1428—Breakfast At 7, 1969—1970
1429—Rally Gear, 1969—1970
1430—Town Turtle, 1969—1970
1431—Guruvy Formal, 1969
1595—(Sears) "Fabulous Formal Set," 1969
Pak—Shoe Ins, 1970—1971
Pak—Golf Gear, 1970—1971
Pak—Slacks Are Back, 1970—1971
Pak—Sun Fun, 1970—1971
1433—Play It Cool!, 1970
1434—Big Business, 1970
1435—Shore Lines, 1970
1436—Bold Gold, 1970
—(Sears) Bend Leg Ken gift set, 1970
—(Sears) "Casual All-Stars," 1970—1973
1438—Skiing Scene, 1971—1972
1439—Suede Scene, 1971—1972
1449—Sea Scene, 1971—1972
1472—Casual Scene, 1971—1972
1473—V.I.P. Scene, 1971—1972
1496—Night Scene, 1971—1972
1248—(Sears) "Surf's Up," 1971—1972
3384—Beach Beat, 1972
1717—Casual Cords, 1972
1718—Brown on Brown, 1972
1719—Midnight Blues, 1972
1720—Way-Out West, 1972

1828—Mod Madras, 1972
1829—Red, White & Wild, 1972

Best Buys

—Denims for Fun, 1972
3377—Wide Awake Stripes, 1972
—Western Winner, 1972
—Cook 'N Casual, 1972
8615—white pants, red and white printed shirt, 1973
8616—navy slacks, yellow and navy sweater, #73 on sweater, 1973
8617—light brown pants and jacket, gold dickey, 1973
8618—denim suit with red plaid trim, 1973
8627—shoes, 1973—1974

Get-Ups 'N Go

7705—Doctor outfit, 1973
7706—Camping outfit, 1973—1974
7707—United Airlines Pilot outfit, 1973—1975
—(Sears stores)—red printed shirt, blue pants, 1974
—(Sears catalogue)—argyle pants, knit top, red and black plaid pants, red vest-shirt, denim pants and jacket, 1974

Best Buys

7758—brown pants, argyle shirt, 1974
7759—red pants, plaid shirt, 1974
7760—green pants, Hawaiian shirt, 1974
7761—Pepsi outfit, 1974
7762—red pants and jacket, 1974
7763—suit, blue pants, red and blue jacket, 1974

Get-Ups 'N Go

7836—Bridegroom (blue and black), 1974—1975
7837—Tennis, 1974—1975
7838—Brown Suit, 1974
7246—Business Suit, 1975—1976
7247—Olympic Hockey, 1975

Best Buys

7224—checked pants, red sweater, 1975
7225—jeans suit, red printed yoke, 1975
7226—red pants, beige shirt
7227—belted coat, 1975
7229—navy pants, plaid jacket, red dickey, 1975
7245—Olympic outfit, 1975
9046—(Sears) light pants, jacket with printed yoke, 1975
9047—(Sears) plaid pants, black jacket, 1975
9048—(Sears) "tweed" suit, 1975

Sears' Best Buys Exclusives

9001—dark pants, printed shirt, 1975
9002—black pants, polka dotted shirt, 1975
9003—red and white pajamas, 1975
9004—checked pants, denim jacket, 1975

Best Buys

9127—pants, jacket, shirt, 1976
9128—pants, jacket, scarf, 1976
9129—pants, tee shirt, cap, 1976
9130—yellow and blue set, 1976
9131—pants, shirt, cap, 1976
9132—pants, tee shirt, hat, 1976

Get-Ups 'N Go

9167—Casual Suit, 1976
9168—Baseball, 1976
9596—Groom, 1976

Sears' Best Buys Exclusives

9696—blue pants, printed shirt, 1976
9697—striped tank top, denims, 1976
9698—red pants, printed shirt, 1976
9699—red shirt, red and white pants, 1976

Skipper-size Clothes

1900—Under-Pretties, 1964—1965
1901—Red Sensation, 1964—1965
1902—Silk 'N Fancy, 1964—1965
1903—Masquerade, 1964—1965
1904—Flower Girl, 1964—1965
1905—Ballet Lessons (or Class), 1964—1965
1906—Dress Coat, 1964—1965
1907—School Days, 1964—1966
1908—Skating Fun, 1964—1966
1909—Dreamtime, 1964—1966
1910—Sunny Pastels, 1965—1966
1911—Day at the Fair, 1965—1966
1912—Cookie Time, 1965—1966
1913—Me 'N My Doll, 1965—1966
1914—Platter Party, 1965
1915—Outdoor Casuals, 1965—1966
1916—Rain or Shine, 1965—1966
1917—Land and Sea, 1965—1966
1918—Ship Ahoy, 1965—1966
1919—Happy Birthday, 1965
1920—Fun Time, 1965—1966
1921—School Girl, 1965—1966
1922—Town Togs, 1965—1966
Pak—Hats 'N Hats, 1965—1966
Pak—Beauty Bath, 1965—1966
Pak—Just For Fun, 1965—1967
Pak—Shoe Parade, 1965—1966
Pak—Wooly P.J.'s, 1965—1967
Pak—Party Pink, 1965—1967
—Cut 'N Button dress, coat, gown & cap, 1965—1967
1923—Can You Play?, 1966
1924—Tea Party, 1966
1925—What's New at the Zoo?, 1966
1926—Chill Chasers, 1966
1928—Rainy Day Checkers, 1966
1929—Dog Show, 1966
1930—Loungin' Lovelies, 1966
1932—Let's Play House, 1966
1933—Country Picnic, 1966
1934—Junior Bridesmaid, 1966
1935—Learning to Ride, 1966
1936—Sledding Fun, 1966
1938—Beachy-Peachy, 1967
1939—Flower Showers, 1967
1940—Rolla-Scoot, 1967
1941—All Spruced Up!, 1967

1942—Right In Style!, 1967
1943—Popover, 1967
1944—'Jamas 'N Jaunties, 1967
1945—Hearts 'N Fowers, 1967
1946—Glaid Plaids, 1967
1947—Lolapaloozas, 1967
1948—Velvet 'N Lace, 1967
1949—All Prettied Up, 1967
1955—Posy-Party, 1968
1956—Skimmy-Stripes, 1968
1957—Baby-Dolls, 1968
1958—Patent 'N Pants, 1968
1959—Warm 'N Wonderful, 1968
1960—Trim Twosome, 1968
1961—Real Sporty, 1968
1962—Quick Change, 1968
—(Sears) Perfectly Pretty Set, 1968
—(Sears) Confetti Cutie, 1968
1966—Jeepers Creepers, 1969—1970
1967—Jazzy Jamys, 1969—1970
1968—Hopscotching, 1969—1970
1969—Knit Bit, 1969—1970
1970—Ice Cream 'N Cake, 1969—1970
1971—Pants 'N Pinafore, 1969—1970
1972—Drizzle Sizzle, 1969—1970
1973—Chilly Chums, 1969—1970
1974—Eeny, Meeny, Midi, 1969—1970
1975—Sunny-Suity, 1969—1970
1976—School's Cool, 1969—1970
1977—Plaid City, 1969—1970
1593—(Sears) Wow! What a Cool Outfit, 1969
1730—Lots of Lace, 1970
1731—Budding Beauty, 1970
1732—Daisy Crazy, 1970
1733—Rik Rak Rah, 1970
1735—Twice as Nice, 1970—1971
1736—Super Slacks, 1970—1971
1737—Velvet Blush, 1970—1971
1738—Fancy Pants, 1970—1971
1746—Wooly Winner, 1970—1971
1747—Pink Princess, 1970—1971
1748—Triple Treat, 1970—1971
1749—Lemon Fluff, 1970—1971
Pak—The Slumber Party, 1970—1971
Pak—Skimmer 'N Scarf, 1970—1971
Pak—Some Shoes, 1970—1971
Pak—Action Fashions, 1970—1971
Pak—Sporty Shorty, 1970—1971
Pak—Check the Slacks, 1970—1971
—(Sears) "Young Ideas," 1970—1973
—(Sears) Living Skipper gift set, 1970—1971
3465—Sweet Orange, 1971—1972
3466—Tennis Time, 1971—1972
3467—Teeter Timers, 1971—1972
3468—Little Miss Midi, 1971—1972
3470—Ice-Skatin', 1971—1972
3471—Ballerina, 1971—1972
3472—Double Dashers, 1971—1972
3473—Lullaby Time, 1971—1972
3475—Goin' Sleddin,' 1971—1972
3476—All Over Felt, 1971—1972
3477—Dressed in Velvet, 1971—1972
3478—Long 'N Short of it, 1971—1972
1249—(Sears) "Sunshine Special" set, 1971
3291—Nifty Knickers, 1972
3292—Play Pants, 1972
3293—Dream-Ins, 1972
3295—Turn Abouts, 1972
3296—Red, White 'N Blues, 1972
3297—Party Pair, 1972

Best Buys

3371—Super Snoozers, 1972
3372—Fun Runners, 1972
3373—Flower Power, 1972
3374—White, Bright 'N Sparkling, 1972
8610—long yellow dress, 1973
8611—short red, black, white dress, 1973
8612—pink sleep set, 1973
8613—red coat, white trim, 1973
8624—shoes, 1973—1975

Get-Ups 'N Go

7713—Sleep Set, 1973—1974
7714—Ballerina, 1973—1974
7715—Camping, 1973

Best Buys

7770—Pepsi outfit, 1974
7771—Hawaiian print dress, 1974
7772—white pants, blue print blouse, 1974
7773—short dark print, white blouse, 1974
7774—long red print jumper, 1974
7775—long light print dress, 1974

Get-Ups 'Go

7847—Flower Girl, 1974—1976
7848—Beach, 1974—1975

Growing Up Fashions

9021—red, white, blue, 1975—1976
9022—solid red, floral print, 1975—1976
9023—bandana print, 1975—1976
9024—tan, yellow, orange, 1975—1976

Get-Ups 'N Go

7250—School clothes, 1975—1976
7251—Olympic Skating, 1975

Best Buys

7218—long red print dress, 1975
7220—pink sleepers, 1975
7221—4 piece red, blue set, 1975
7222—striped overalls, red blouse, 1975
7223—long dark print skirt, white waist, 1975
7274—Olympic outfit, 1975

Get-Ups 'N Go

9165—Bicentennial Fashions, 1976
9166—Weekend Wardrobe, 1976

Growing Up Fashions

9512—pink, blue, yellow, 1976
9513—orange, green, yellow, 1976

Best Buys

9121—red plaid coat, cap, 1976
9122—red plaid skirt, blouse, vest, 1976
9123—long blue and white dress, 1976
9124—white pants, red tee shirt, 1976
9125—long green and pink print dress, 1976
9126—red and white long skirt, white top, 1976

Francie-size Clothes

1250—Gad-About, 1966—1967
1251—It's A Date, 1966
1252—First Things First, 1966
1253—Tuckered Out, 1966—1967
1254—Fresh as a Daisy, 1966
1255—Polka Dots 'N Raindrops, 1966
1256—Concert in the Park, 1966
1257—Dance Party, 1966—1967
1258—Clam Diggers, 1966
1259—Checkmates, 1966
1260—First Formal, 1966—1967
1261—Shoppin' Spree, 1966
1263—Orange Cosy, 1966—1967
1264—Swingin' Skimmy, 1966—1967
1265—Hip Knits, 1966—1967
1266—Quick Shift, 1966—1967
1267—Go Granny, Go, 1966—1967
1268—Style Setters, 1966—1967
1269—Leather Limelight, 1966—1967
—Fur Out, 1966—1967
1042—(Sears) "Francie and Her Swingin' Separates" set, 1966
—(Penney's) Sportin' Set—9 pieces, 1966
1270—Groovy Get-Ups, 1967
1271—Slumber Number, 1967—1968
1272—Hi-Teen, 1967—1968
1273—Side-Kick!, 1967—1968
1274—Iced Blue, 1967—1968
1275—Bells, 1967
1276—Summer Frost, 1967
1277—Sun Spots, 1967
1279—The Bridge Bit, 1967
1280—Cool White, 1967
1281—Clear Out!, 1967
1283—Sweet 'N Swingin', 1967
1284—Miss Teenage Beauty, 1967
1286—Tweed-Somes, 1967
1287—Border-Line, 1967
1288—In-Print, 1967
1289—Note the Coat!, 1967
1290—Denims On!, 1967
1291—Check This, 1967
1292—Summer Coolers, 1967
Pak—Pleat-Neat, 1967
Pak—Undies, 1967
Pak—Mod-Hatters, 1967
Pak—Hair-Dos, 1967
Pak—Foot-Notes, 1967
Pak—For Francie Dressmakers, 1967—1968
—(Sears) Casey Goes Casual set, 1967
—Suits Me, 1967
—Prom Pinks, 1967
1294—Go Gold, 1967
—Furry-Go-Round, 1967
1207—Floating-In, 1968—1969
1208—The Silver Cage, 1968—1969
1209—Mini-Chex, 1968—1969
1210—Hill-Riders, 1968—1969
1211—Tenterrific, 1968—1969
1212—Night Blooms, 1968—1969
1213—Pazam!, 1968—1969
1214—Culotte-Wot?, 1968—1969
1215—The Combo, 1968
1216—The Lace-Pace, 1968
1217—Dreamy Wedding, 1968
1218—Wild 'N Wooly, 1968
1725—(Twiggy) Twiggy-Dos, 1968
1726—(Twiggy) Twiggy Turnouts, 1968
1727—(Twiggy) Twigster, 1968
1728—(Twiggy) Twiggy Gear, 1968
Pak—Cool-It!, 1968
Pak—Get-Readies, 1968
Pak—Slightly Summery, 1968
Pak—Hair-Dos, 1968
Pak—Foot-Notes, 1968
—(Sears) "Orange Zip," 1968
1219—Somethin' Else!, 1969—1970
1220—Land Ho!, 1969—1970
1221—Tennis Tunic, 1969—1970
1222—Gold Rush, 1969—1970
1223—The Yellow Bit, 1969
1224—Vested Interest, 1969
1225—Snazz, 1969
1226—Snooze News, 1969
1227—Long on Looks, 1969
1228—Sissy Suits, 1969
1229—Sugar Sheers, 1969
1230—Merry-Go-Rounders, 1969
1231—Pink Lightning, 1969—1970
1232—Two for the Ball, 1969—1970
1233—Victorian Wedding, 1969—1970
1234—The Combination, 1969—1970
1237—Satin Happenin,' 1970, 1971 & 1974
1238—Snappy Snoozers, 1970, 1971 & 1974
1239—Bloom Zoom, 1970, 1971 & 1974
1240—Pony Coat, 1970, 1971 & 1974
1242—Although Elegant, 1970, 1971 & 1974
1243—Striped Types, 1970, 1971 & 1974
1244—Wedding Whirl, 1970, 1971 & 1974
1245—Snake Charmers, 1970, 1971 & 1974
1761—Sunny Slacks, 1970—1971
1762—Pink Power, 1970—1971
1763—The Entertainer, 1970—1971
1764—Corduroy Cape, 1970—1971
1766—Wild Bunch, 1970—1971
1767—Plaid Plans, 1970—1971
1768—Waltz in Velvet, 1970—1971
1769—Long on Leather, 1970—1971
Pak—Slacks 'N Cap, 1970—1971
Pak—In Step, 1970—1971
Pak—Super Shirt, 1970—1971
Pak—Western Wild, 1970—1971
Pak—Nighty Brights, 1970—1971
Pak—Panco Bravo, 1970—1971
—(Sears) "Pretty Power," 1970—1973
3443—Satin Supper, 1971—1972
3444—Midi Plaid, 1971—1972
3445—Zig-Zag Zoom, 1971—1972
3446—Midi Bouquet, 1971—1972
3448—With-It Whites, 1971—1972 & 1974
3449—Buckeroo Blues, 1971—1972 & 1974
3450—Dreamy Duo, 1971—1972 & 1974
3451—Midi Duet, 1971—1972 & 1974
3453—Snooze News, 1971—1972 & 1974
3454—Summer Number, 1971—1972 & 1974
3455—Frosty Fur, 1971—1972 & 1974
3456—Wild Flowers, 1971—1972 & 1974
3458—Olde Look, 1971—1972
3459—Twilight Twinkle, 1971—1972
3460—Change-Offs, 1971—1972
3461—Peach Plush, 1971—1972
1194—(Sears) "Rise 'N Shine" set, 1971

3275—Little Knits, 1972
3276—The Slacks Suit, 1972
3277—Simply Super, 1972
3278—Checker Chums, 1972
3280—Totally Terrific, 1972
3281—Cool Coveralls, 1972
3282—The Long View, 1972
3283—Suited for Shorts, 1972
3285—Peach Treats, 1972
3286—Double Ups, 1972
3287—Smashin' Satin, 1972
3288—Bridal Beauty, 1972

Best Buys

3364—Sleepy Time Gal, 1972
3365—Ready! Set! Go! 1972
3366—Pretty Frilly, 1972
3367—Right For Stripes, 1972
3368—Red, White 'N Bright, 1972
3369—Pink 'N Pretty, 1972
8625—shoes, 1973—1974
8644—long red, white, blue halter dress, 1973
8645—short red print dress, 1973
8646—brown coat and hat, 1973
8647—brown skirt, plaid blouse, 1973
8648—red baby dolls, 1973
8649—red plaid pants, yellow & blue top, 1973

Get-Ups 'N Go

7709—Candystriper, 1973
7710—Beach outfit, 1973—1975
7711—Cheerleading outfit, 1973—1975

Best Buys

7764—lavender jumper, 1974
7765—lavender dress, 1974
7766—Pepsi outfit, 1974
7767—long white and black pin dot, 1974
7768—short red print dress, 1974
7769—long dark print dress, 1974

Get-Ups 'N Go

7485—Ice Skating, 1974—1975
7846—Camping, 1974—1975

Best Buys

7212—red skirt, white top, 1975
7214—red print skirt and vest, white top, 1975
7215—pink sleep suit, 1975
7216—plaid pants & jacket, 1975
7217—solid blue, red & white print, 1975
7273—Olympic outfit, 1975

Ricky-size Clothes

1501—Lights Out, 1965—1967
1502—Saturday Show, 1965
1503—Sunday Suit, 1965
1504—Little Leaguer, 1965—1967
1505—Skateboard Set, 1966—1967
1506—Let's Explore, 1966—1967

Tutti-size Clothes

3601—Puddle Jumpers, 1966—1967
3602—Ship-Shape, 1966
3603—Sand Castles, 1966
3604—Skippin' Rope, 1966—1967
3606—Clowning Around, 1967
3607—Come To My Party, 1967
3608—Let's Play Barbie, 1967
3609—Plantin' Posies, 1967
—(Sears) Chris set 1967
3614—Sea-Shore Shorties, 1968—1969
3615—Flower Girl, 1968—1969
3616—Pink P.J.'s, 1968—1969
3617—Birthday Beauties, 1968—1969

In 1963 Mattel introduced "Dressed Dolls." These were the regular dolls dressed in some of the regular fashions. These were packaged in individual boxes with acetate window covers or in cardboard boxes. The following are known to have been on the market.

Barbie in "After Five"
Barbie in "Ice Breaker"
Barbie in "Masquerade"
Barbie in "Dinner At Eight"
Barbie in "Career Girl"
Barbie in "Knitting Pretty"
Barbie in "Evening Splendor"
Barbie in "Nighty-Negligee"
Barbie in "Country Fair"
Barbie in "Garden Tea Party"
Barbie in "Black Magic Ensemble"
Barbie in "Theatre Date"
Barbie in "Barbie In Switzerland"
Barbie in "Barbie In Holland"
Barbie in "Barbie In Mexico"
Barbie in "Cinderella"
Barbie in "Guinevere"
Barbie in "Barbie, Arabian Nights"
Midge in "Fancy Free"
Midge in "Orange Blossom"
Midge in "Crisp 'N Cool"
Ken in "Dr. Ken"
Ken in "Touchdown"
Ken in "Fraternity Meeting"
Ken in "Ken In Switzerland"
Ken in "Ken In Holland"
Ken in "Ken In Mexico"
Ken in "The Prince"
Ken in "King Arthur"
Ken in "Ken, Arabian Nights"
Barbie in "Garden Party"
Ken in "Rovin' Reporter"
Skipper in "Happy Birthday"
Ken in "Holiday"

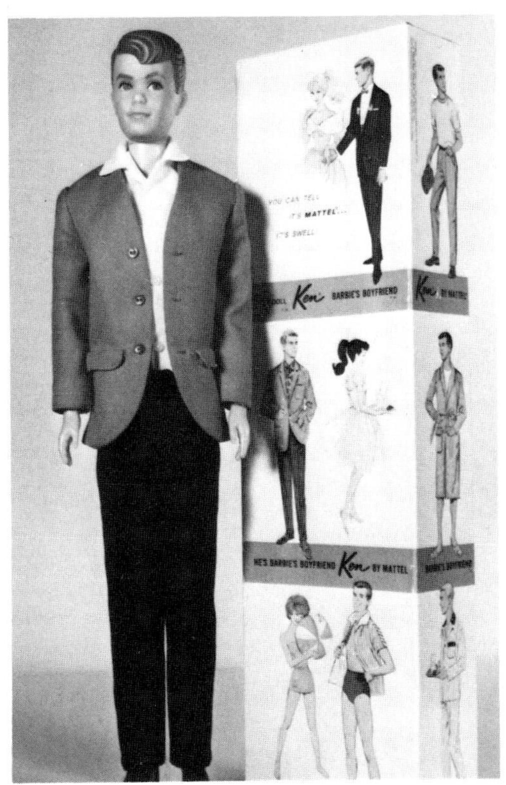

Allan, found in a Ken "Dressed Doll" box. #1417 "Rovin' Reporter." (Ashabraner collection)

Skipper "Dressed Doll" box and doll. #1919 "Happy Birthday." (Ashabraner collection).

Barbie "Dressed Doll" box and doll. Barbie in #984 "American Airlines Stewardess." (Ashabraner collection)

Ken "Dressed Doll" box and doll. Ken in #1414 "Holiday." (Ashabraner collection)

These three outfits were pictured in only one fashion booklet, the first one. They are:
1. #964 "Gay Parisienne" Costume
2. #968 Roman Holiday Separates
3. #971 "Easter Parade"
(Ashabraner collection)

Barbie in #987 "Orange Blossom," 1961—1964.

Barbie in #966 "Plantation Belle," 1959—1961.

en in #798 "Ski Champion," 1963—1964.

Ken in #770 "Campus Hero," 1961—1964.

Ken in #786 "Saturday Date," 1961—1963.

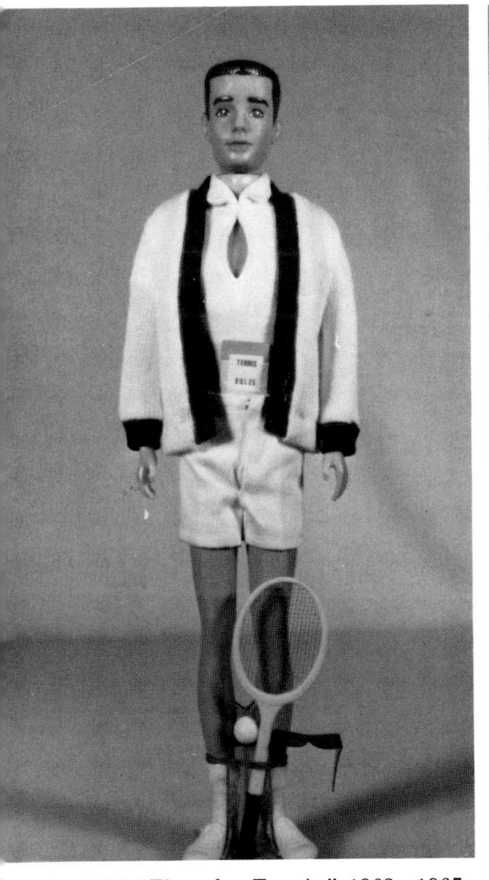

Ken in #790 "Time for Tennis," 1962—1965.

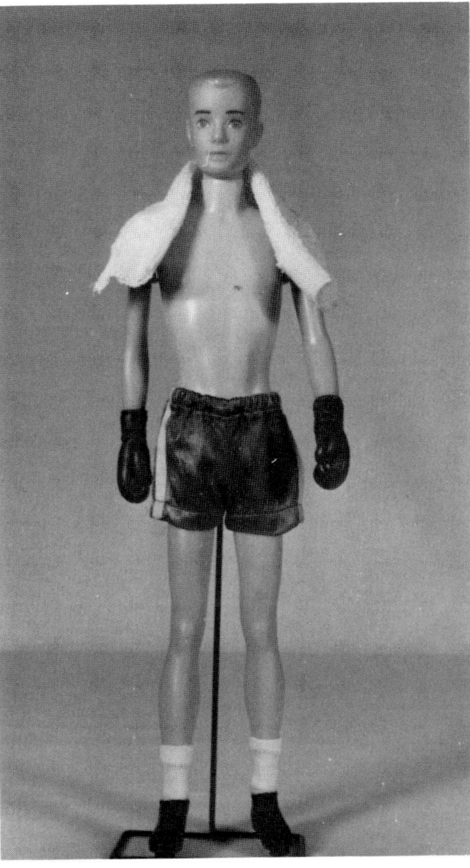

Ken in Pak "Boxing Outfit," 1963.

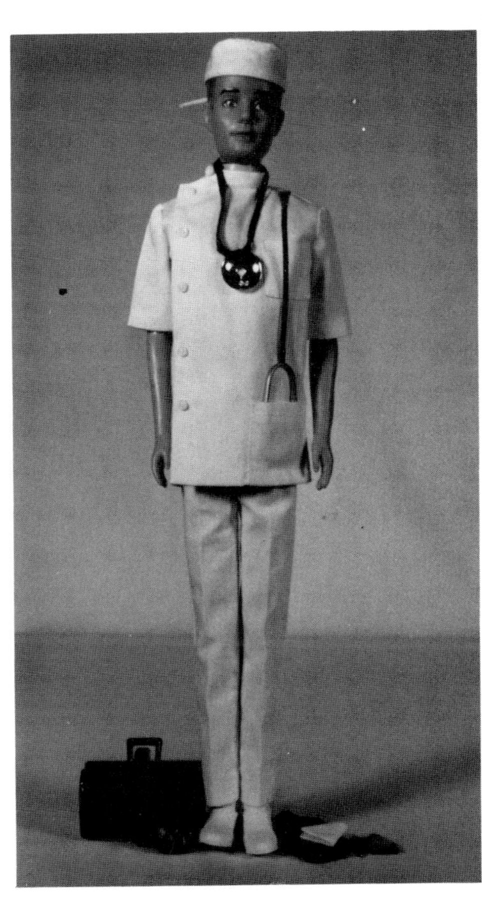

Ken in #793 "Dr. Ken," 1963—1965.

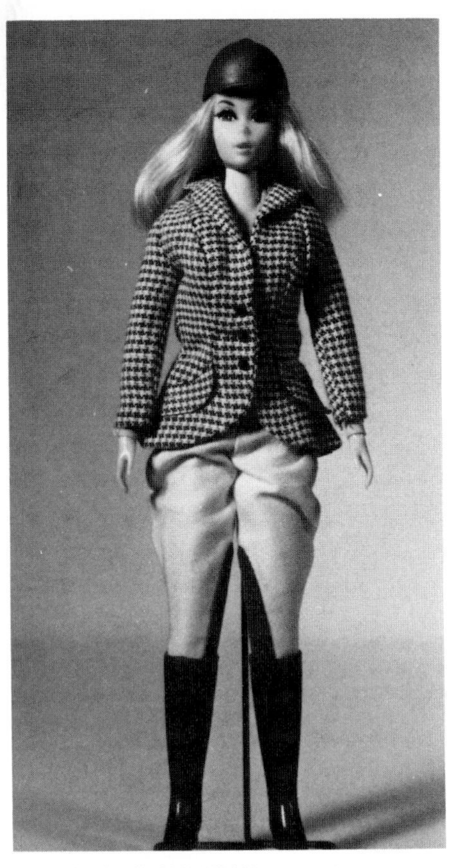
Barbie in #1668 "Riding in the Park," 1966—1967.

Barbie in #978 "Let's Dance," 1960—1962.

Barbie in #1624 "Fun at the Fair," 1965

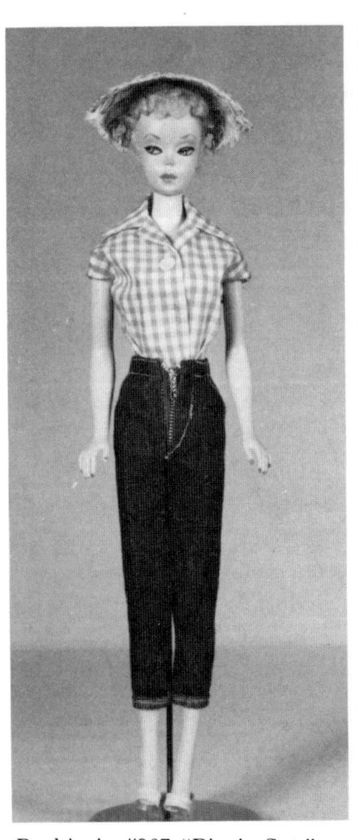
Barbie in #967 "Picnic Set," 1959—1961.

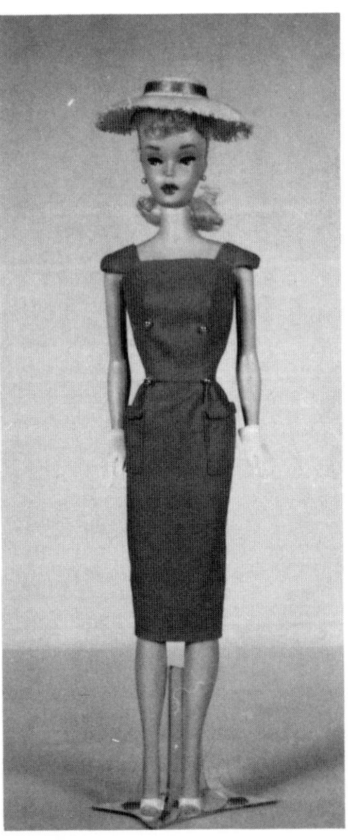
Barbie in #986 "Sheath Sensation," 1961—1964.

Barbie in Pak "Gold Lame Sheath," 1963.

Barbie in #918 "Cruise Stripe Dress," 1959—1961.

Ken in #789 "The Yachtsman," 1962—1964.

Ken with various Pak shirts, 1962—1963.

Allan in #794 "Masquerade," 1963—1964.

Allan in #1405 "Roller Skate Date," 1964—1965.

Allan in Pak "Corduroy Jacket," 1962—1963. (Allan's mustache courtesy Harold DeWein)

Ken in #0775 "Drum Major," 1964—1965.

Barbie in #912 "Cotton Casual," 1959—1961.

Barbie in #946 "Dinner at Eight," 1963—1964.

Barbie in #1603 "Country Fair," 1964.

Midge in #1606 "Garden Tea Party," 1964.

Barbie in #975 "Winter Holiday," 1959—1962.

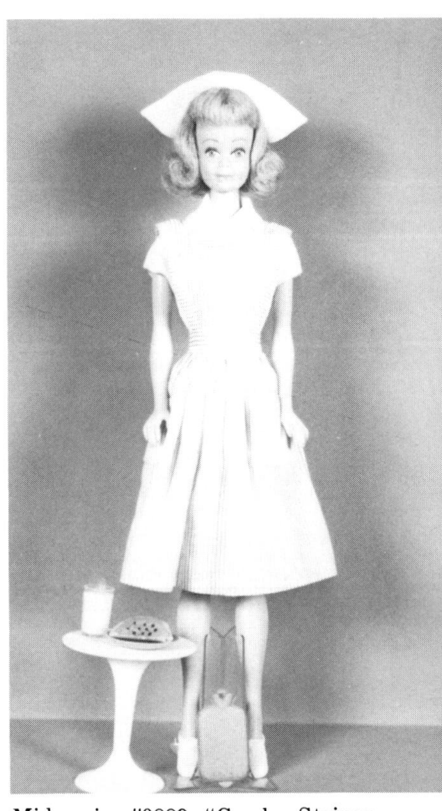
Midge in #0889 "Candy Striper Volunteer," 1964.

bie in #941 "Tennis, Anyone," 1962—1964.

Barbie in #955 "Swingin' Easy," 1963.

Midge in #991 "Registered Nurse," 1961—1964.

rbie in #934 "After 5," 1962—1964. (Gift
m Harold DeWein, Jr.)

Barbie in #956 "Busy Morning," 1963.

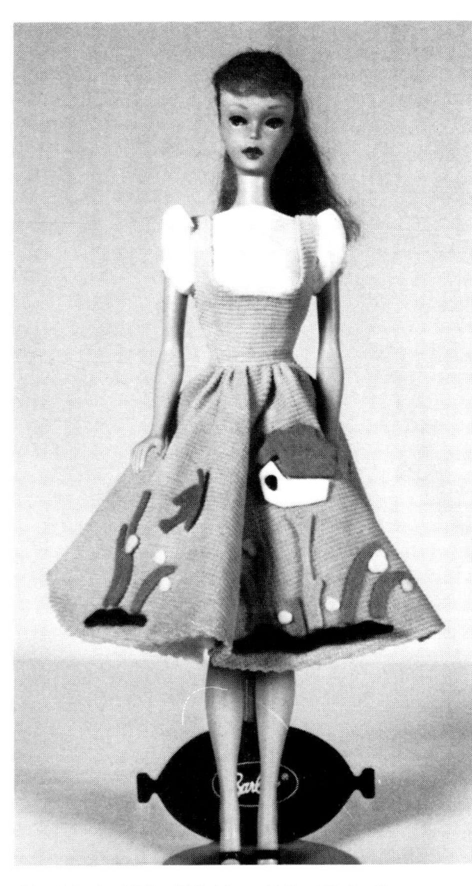

Barbie in #979 "Friday Nite Date,"
1960—1964.

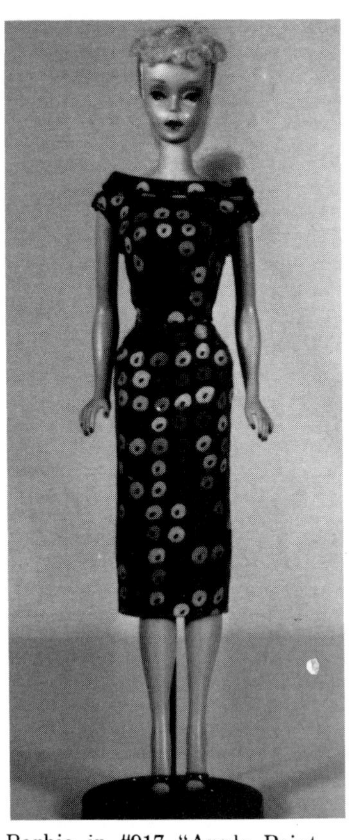
Barbie in #917 "Apple Print Sheath," 1959—1960.

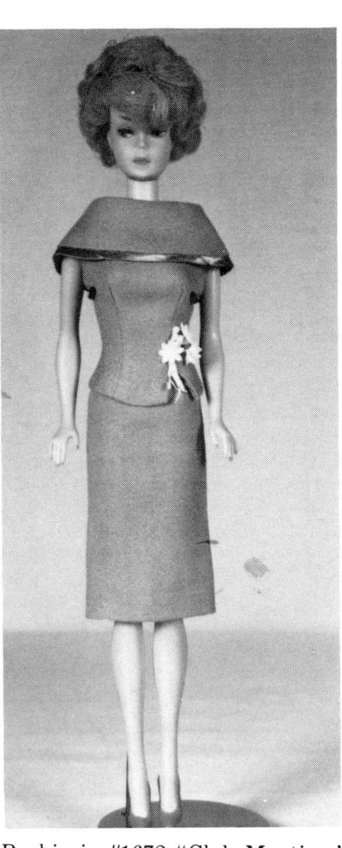
Barbie in #1672 "Club Meeting," 1966—1967.

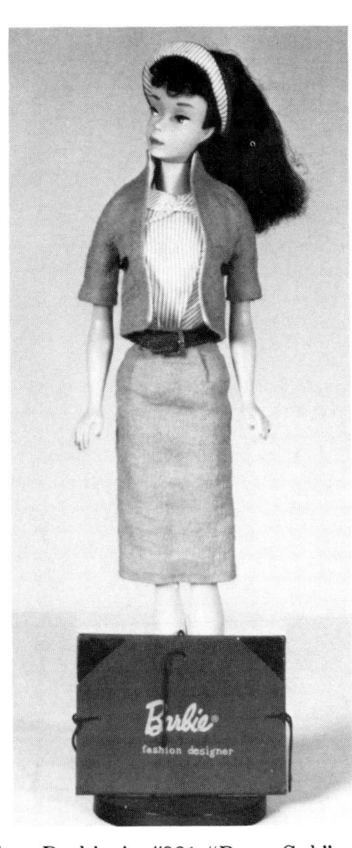

Barbie in #981 "Busy Gal," 1960—1961.

Barbie in #1653 "International Fair," 1966—1967.

Barbie in #1479 "Leisure Leopard," 1969—1970.

Barbie in #8620 Best Buy, 1973.

Barbie in #7272 Best Buy, 1975.

Julia in #1843 "Dancing Stripes," 1968.

Allan in #796 "Sailor," 1963—1965. (Gift from Harold John DeWein)

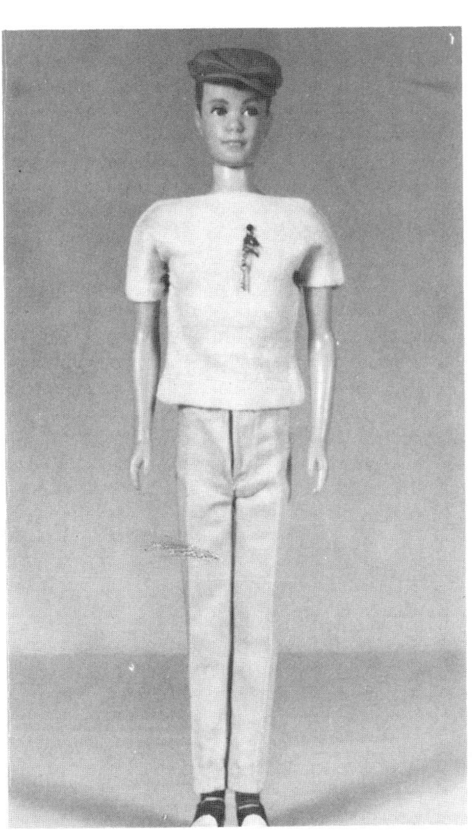

Allan in #782 "Casuals," 1961—1973.

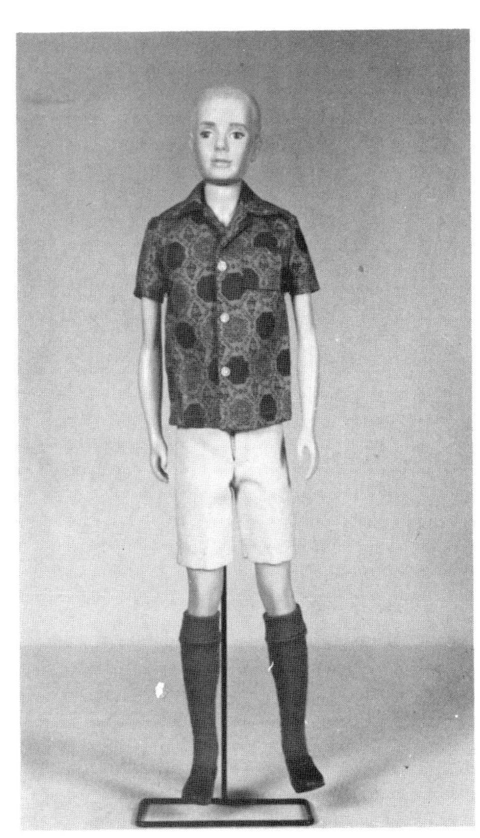

Ken in #783 "Sport Shorts," 1961—1963.

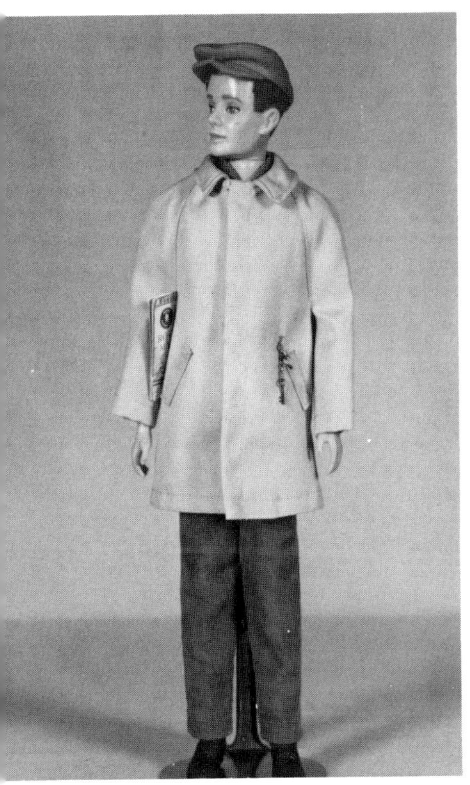

Ken in #788 "Rally Day," 1962—1964.

Ken in #795 "Graduation," 1963—1964.

Ken in Pak "Windbreaker," 1962—1963.

Barbie in Pak blouse and skirt, 1962—1963.

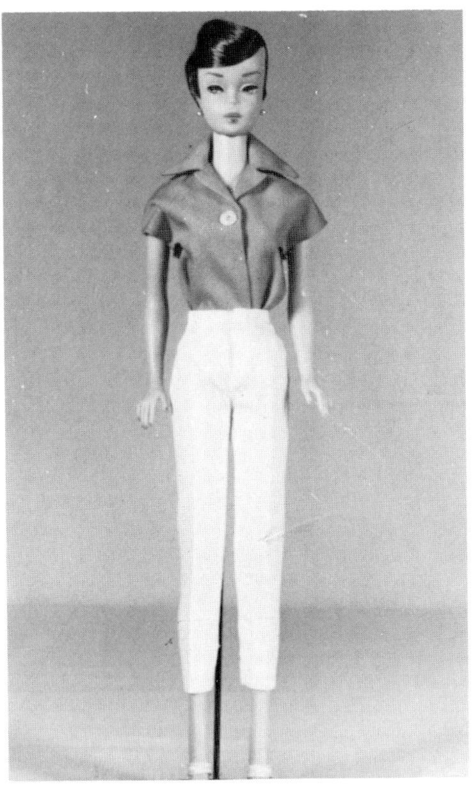

Barbie in Pak slacks and shirt, 1962—1963.

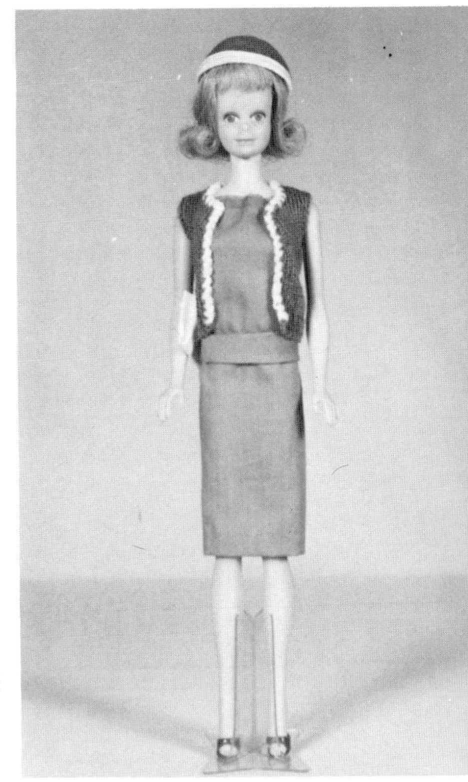

Midge in #937 "Sorority Meeting," 1962—1963.

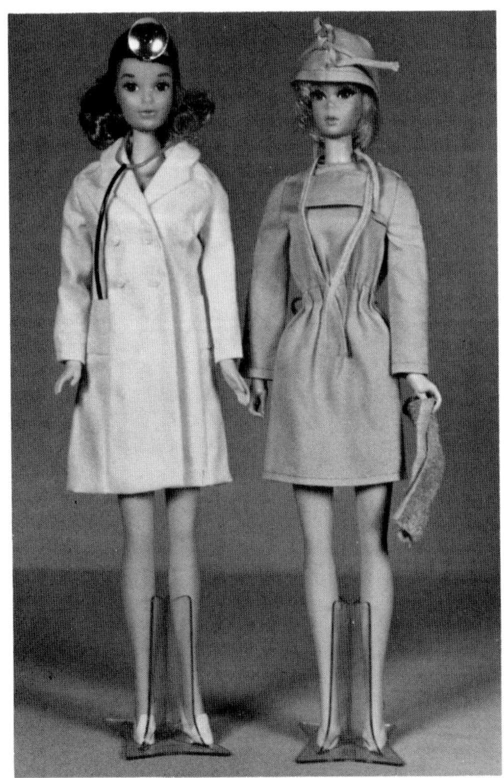

Kelley and Barbie in #7700 Get-Ups 'N Go, 1973—1976.

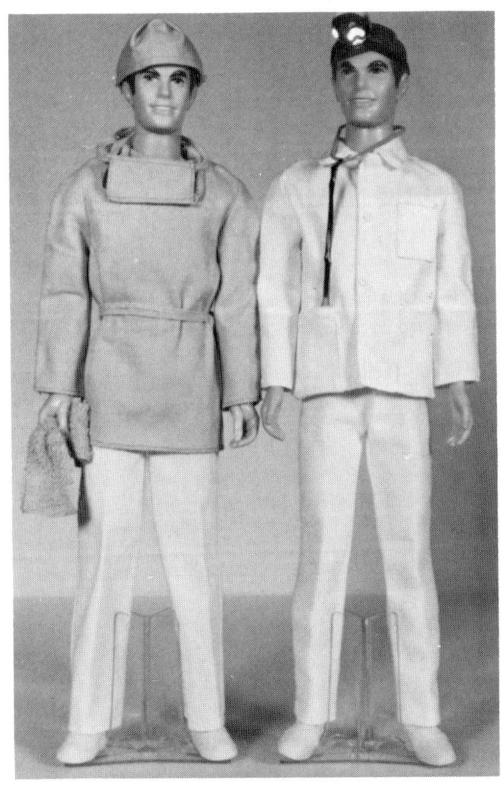

Ken and Ken in #7705 Get-Ups 'N Go, 1973.

en in #1433 "Play It Cool!" 1970.

Ken in #1434 "Big Business," 1970.

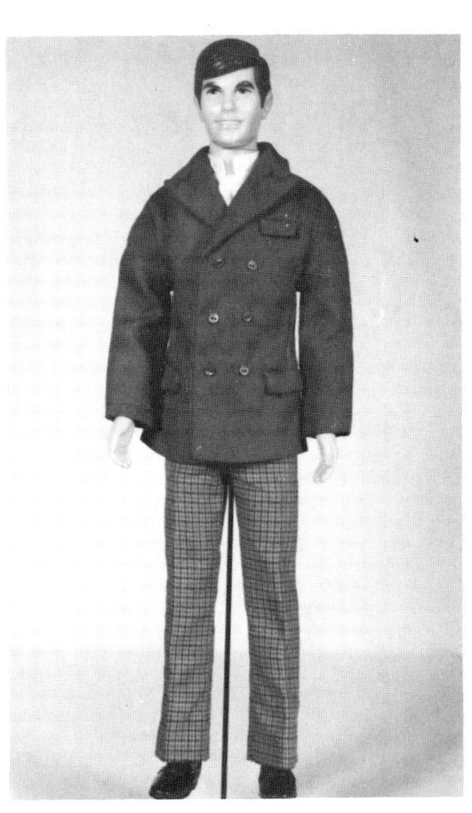
Ken in #1430 "Town Turtle," 1969—1970.

en in #1496 "Night Scene," 1971—1972.

Brad in #1473 "V.I.P. Scene," 1971—1972.

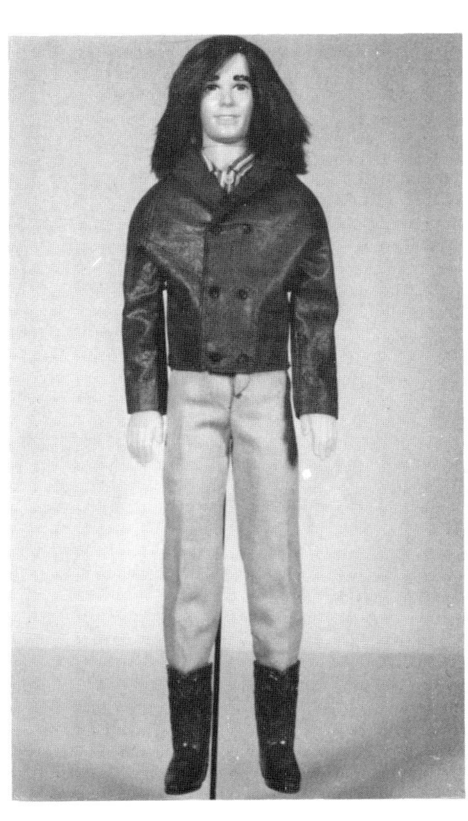
Ken in #1429 "Rally Gear," 1969—1970.

Stacey and Ken in #9047 Sears' outfits, 1975.

Steffie and Ken in #9048 Sears' outfits, 1975.

Kelley and Ken in #9046 Sears' outfits, 1975.

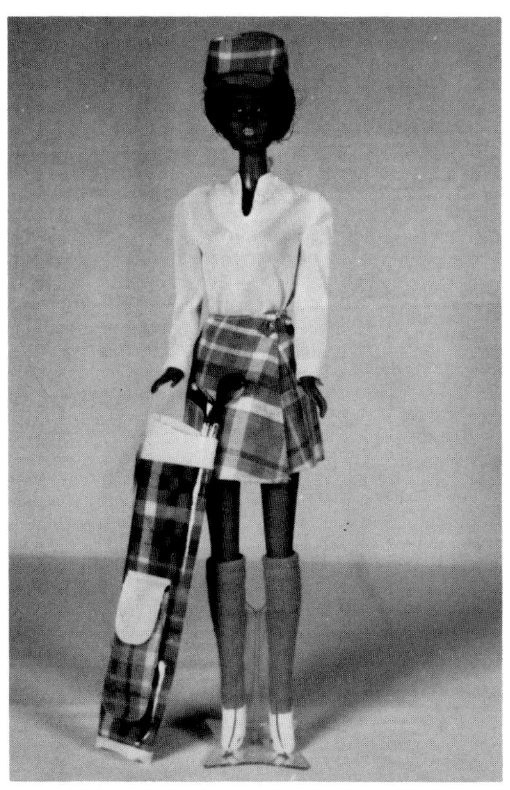

Christie in #3413 "Golfing Greats," 1971—1972.

Ken in #1449 "Sea Scene," 1971—1972.

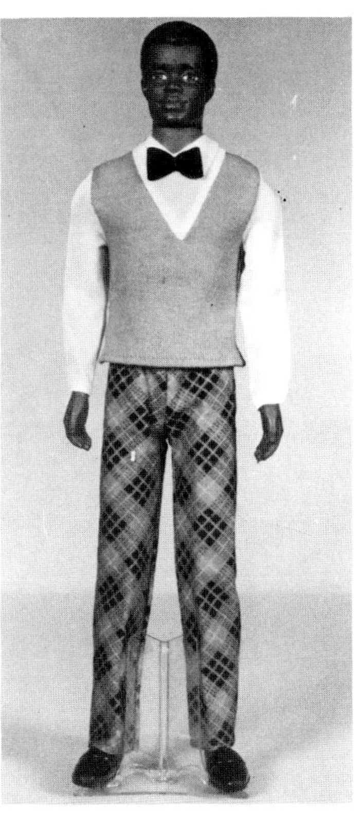

Brad in a 1974 Sears' exclusive Best Buy.

Ken in #7707 Get-Ups 'N Go, 1973—1975.

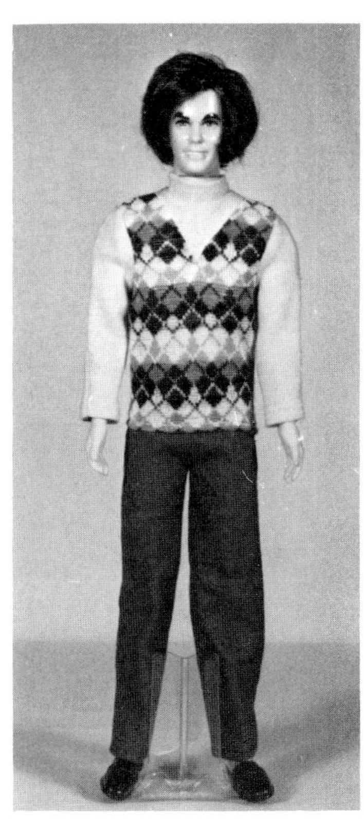

Ken in #7758 Best Buy, 1974.

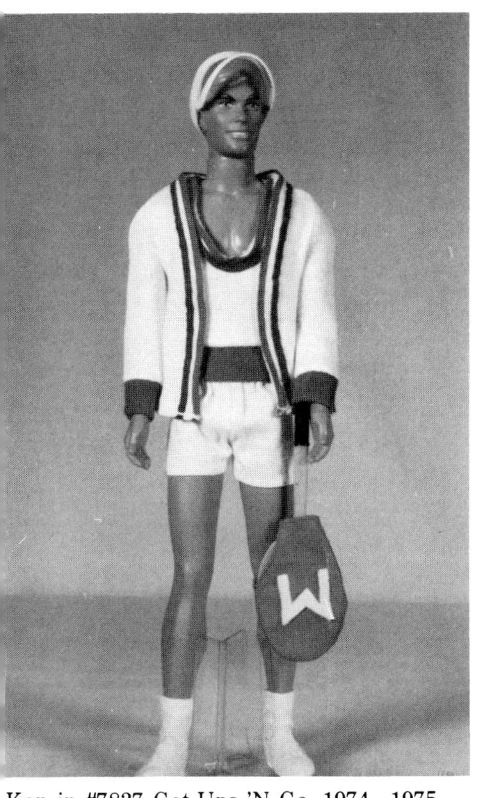

Ken in #7837 Get-Ups 'N Go, 1974—1975. (Gift from Norman DeWein)

Ken in #7224 Best Buy, 1975.

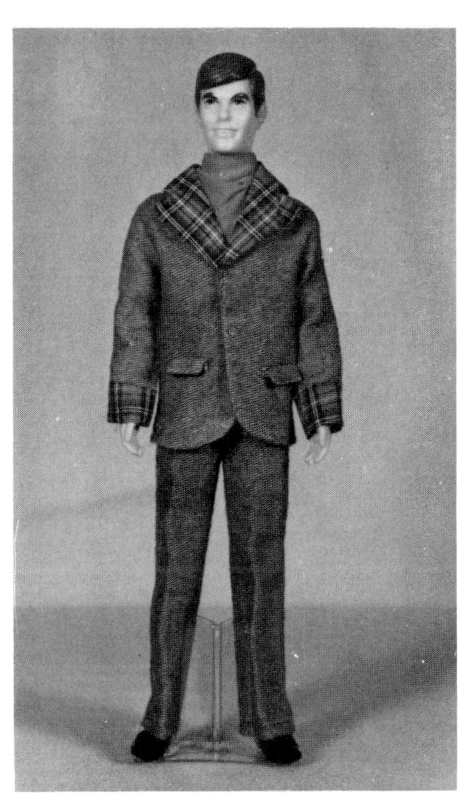

Ken in #8618 Best Buy, 1973.

1. Ken in #9596 Get-Ups 'N Go, 1976.
2. Beautiful Bride Barbie (9599), 1976.
3. Kelley in #9151 Get-Ups 'N Go, 1976.

#948 "Ski Queen," 1963—1964.

#3445 "Zig-Zag Zoom," 1971—1972.

1. Barbie in #9152 Get-Ups 'N Go, 1976.
2. Ken in #9168 Get-Ups 'N Go, 1976.
3. Ken in 1976 Sears' exclusive Best Buy.

#1457 "City Sparkler," 1970.

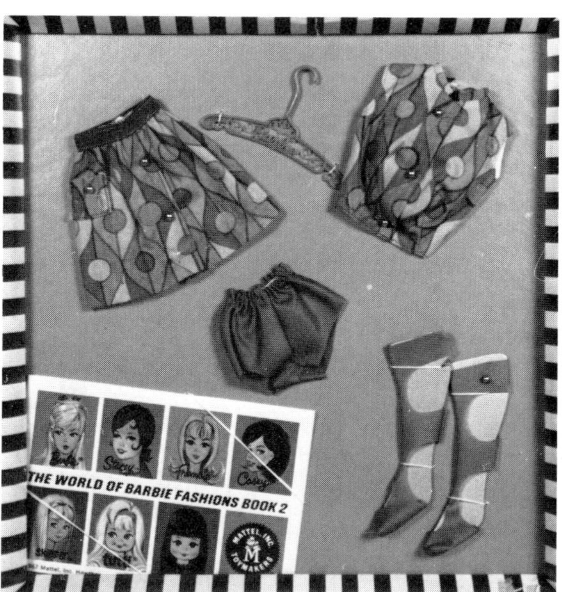

"Wild 'N Wonderful," 1969.

#3444 "Midi Plaid," 1971—1972.

Francie in #1230 "Merry-Go-Rounders," 1969.

Barbie in #1789 "Fiery Felt," 1971.

#1240 "Pony Coat," 1970, 1971 and 1974.

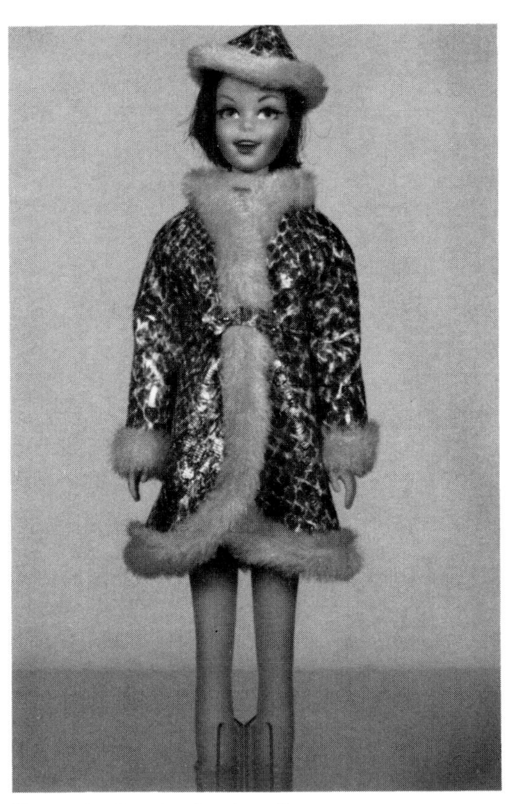

Casey in #1245 "Snake Charmers," 1970, 1971 and 1974.

Casey in #1227 "Long on Looks," 1969.

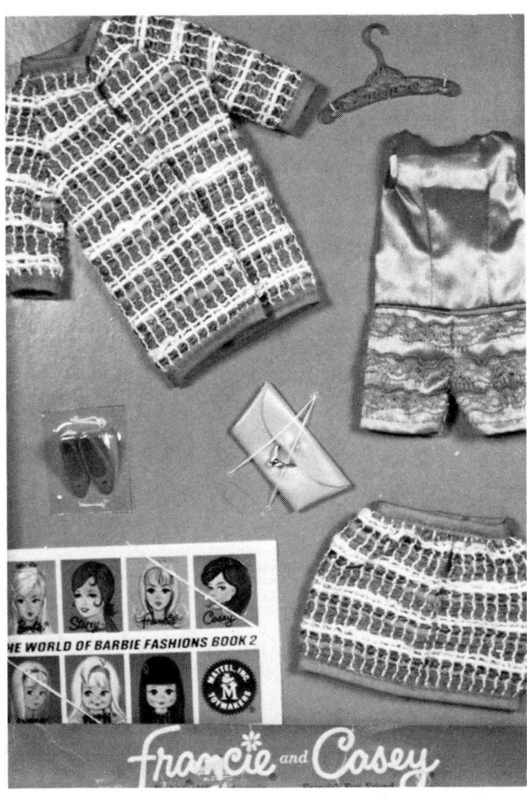

#1218 "Wild-'N Wooly," 1968.

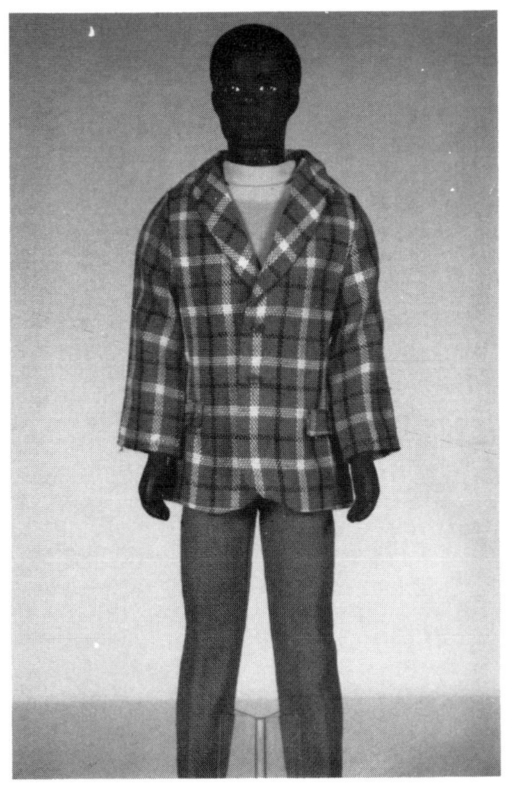

Brad in #1436 "Bold Gold," 1970.

#785 "Dreamboat," 1961—1963.

#786 "Saturday Date," 1961—1963.

#1407 "Fountain Boy," 1964—1965.

#1503 "Sunday Suit," 1965.

#1504 "Little Leaguer," 1965—1967.

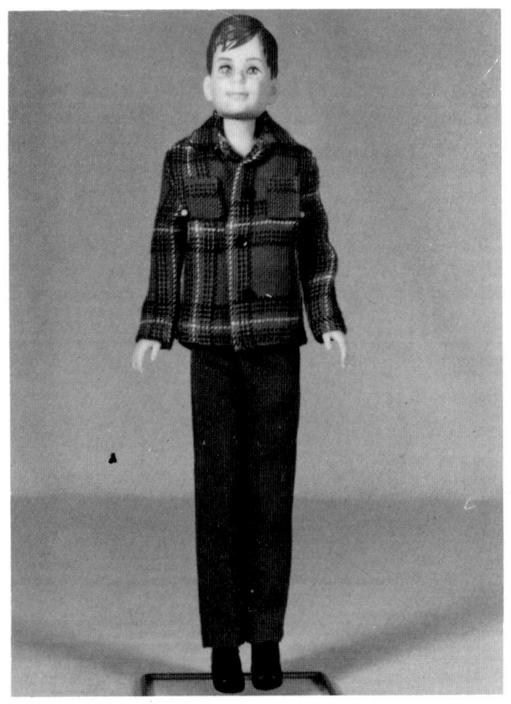

Ricky in #1506 "Let's Explore," 1966—1967.

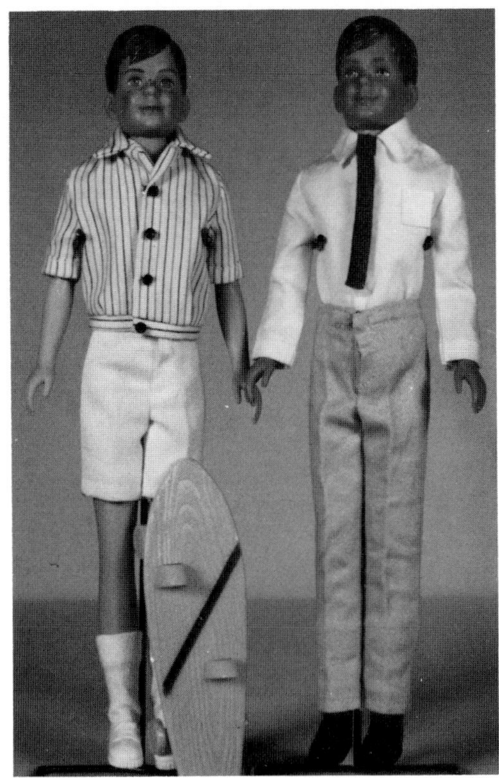

Ricky in #1505 "Skateboard Set," 1966—1967, and in #1502 "Saturday Show," 1965.

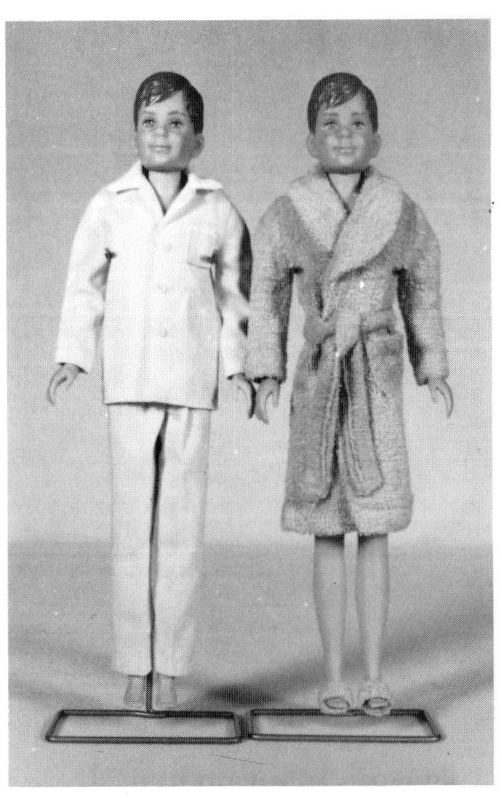

Ricky in #1501 "Lights Out," 1965—1967.

#3603 "Sand Castles," 1966.

Chris in #3615 "Flower Girl," 1968—1969.

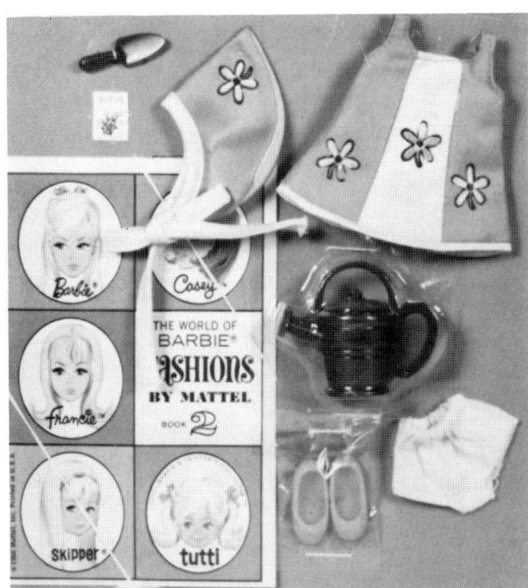

#3609 "Plantin' Posies," 1969.

#3601 "Puddle Jumpers," 1966—1967.

Skipper in #1736 "Super Slacks," 1970—1971.

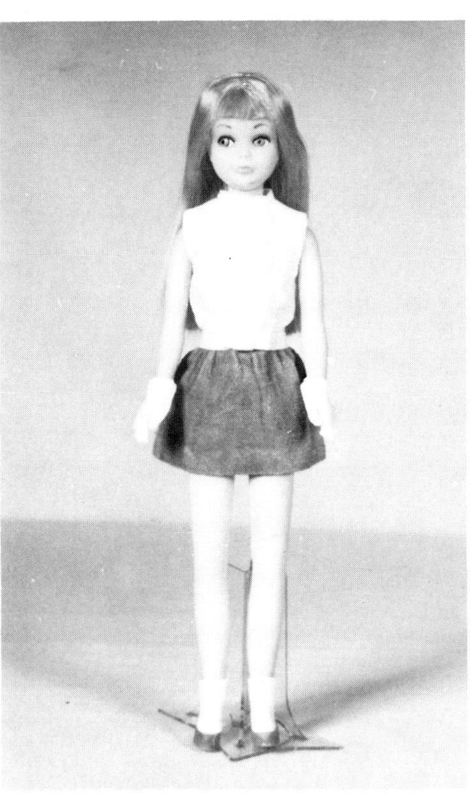

Skipper in "Perfectly Pretty," a 1968 Sears' exclusive.

#1912 "Cookie Time," 1965—1966.

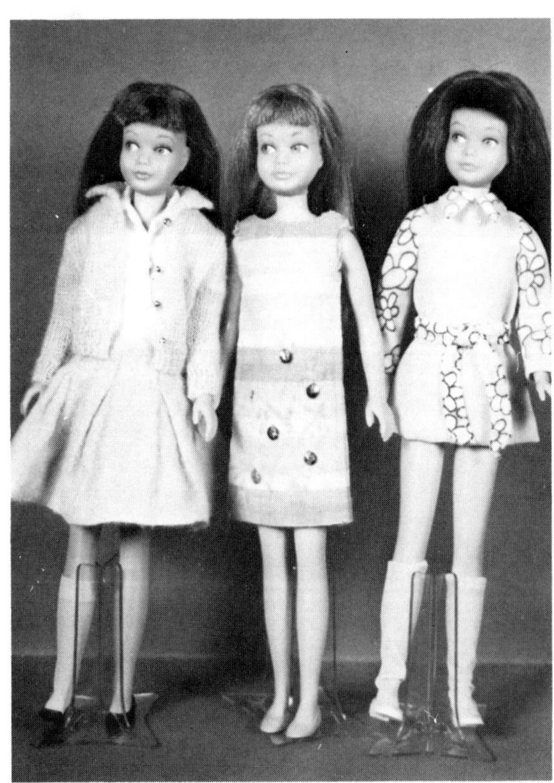

Skipper in "School Days," "Sunny Pastels" and "Daisy Crazy."

#3475 "Goin' Sleddin'," 1971—1972.

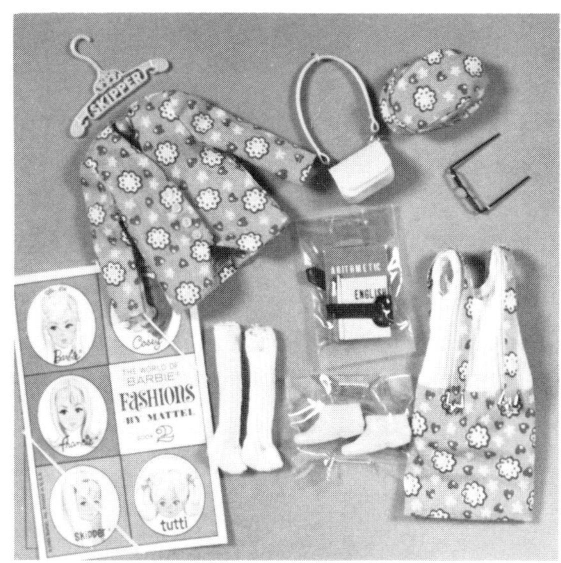

#1945 "Hearts 'N Flowers," 1967.

#1748 "Triple Treat," 1970—1971.

#1935 "Learning to Ride," 1966.

#1946 "Glad Plaids," 1967.

#1920 "Fun Time," 1965—1966.

#1747 "Pink Princess," 1970—1971.

Barbie in 1976 Sears' exclusive "Evening Gown Outfit."

Barbie in #1784 "Harem-M-M's," 1970—1971.

#4041 set of 1966.

#1775 "Stripes Away," 1967.

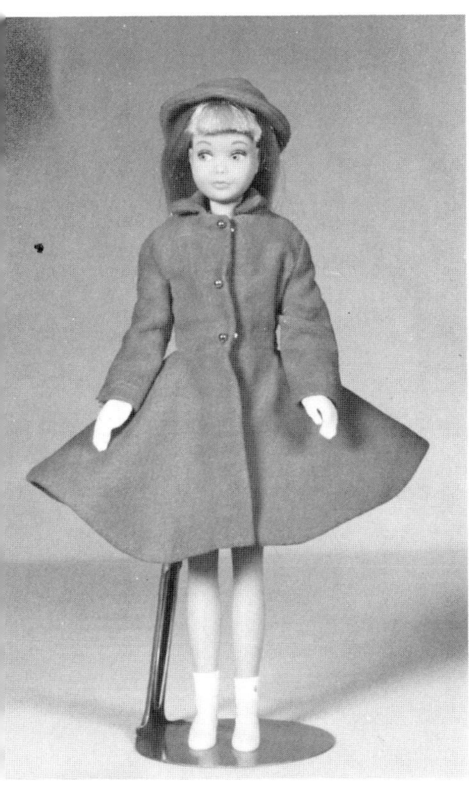

Skipper in #1906 "Dress Coat," 1964—1965.

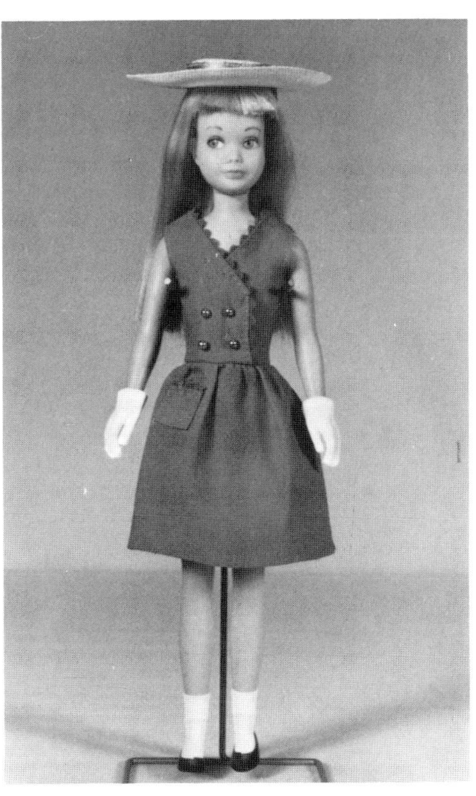

Skipper in #1901 "Red Sensation," 1964—1965.

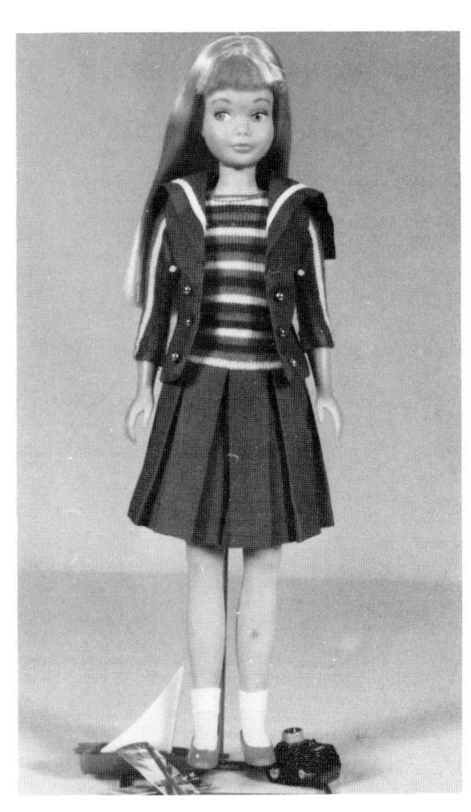

Skipper in #1918 "Ship Ahoy," 1965—1966.

Skooter in #7774 Best Buy, "Can You Play?" and #8613 Best Buy.

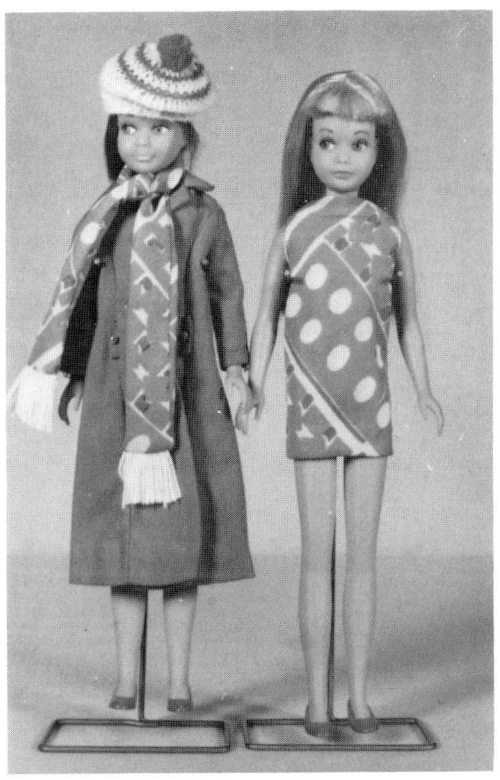

Skipper in #3478 "Long 'N Short of It," 1971—1972.

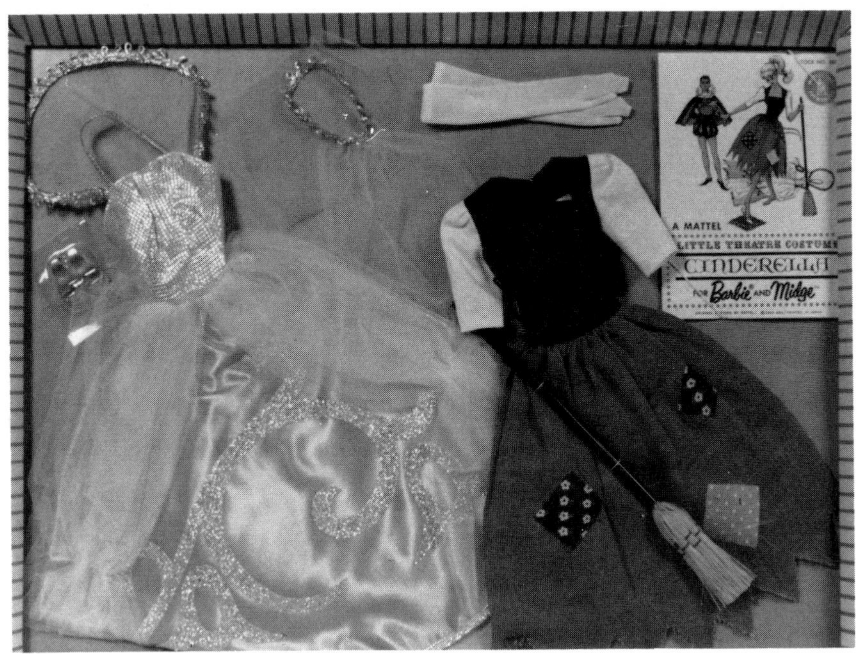

#0872 "Cinderella," 1964—1965. (Courtesy Connie McDonald)

Put-ons & Pets—Hot Togs (1063). Notice the attractive packaging. (Found by Bernice Lieb)

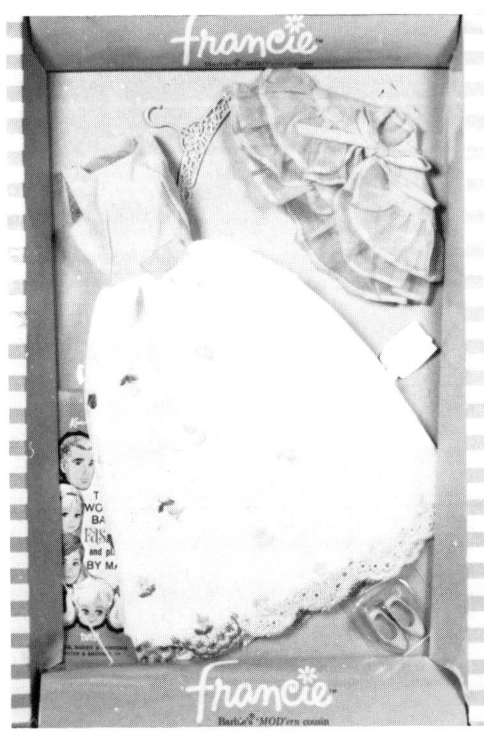

#1260 "First Formal," 1966—1967.

#0875 "Drum Majorette," 1964—1965. (Gift from Janice Kaderly).

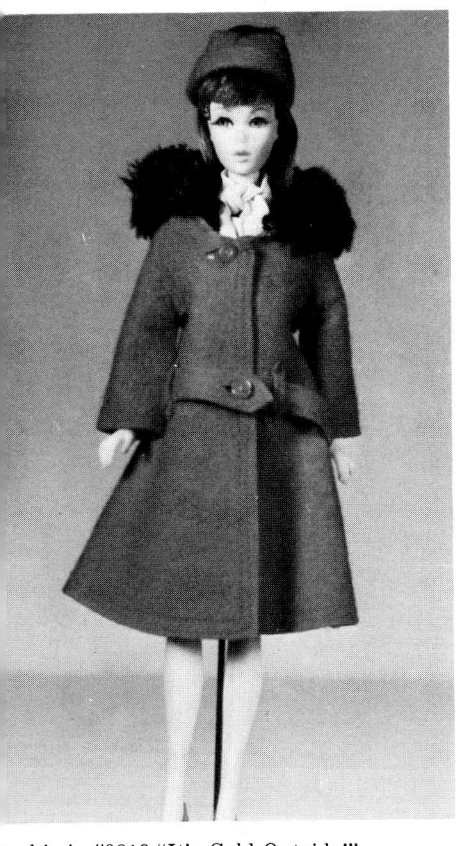

arbie in #0819 "It's Cold Outside!" 964—1966.

Barbie in 1974 Sears's exclusive Best Buy.

Kelley in #7416 Best Buy, 1975.

rancie in #8644 Best Buy, 1973.

Francie in #7212 Best Buy, 1975.

Francie in #7767 Best Buy, 1974.

#1292 "Summer Coolers," 1967.

#1214 "Culotte-Wot?" 1968—1969.

#1257 "Dance Party," 1966—1967.

#3461 "Peach Blush," 1971—1972.

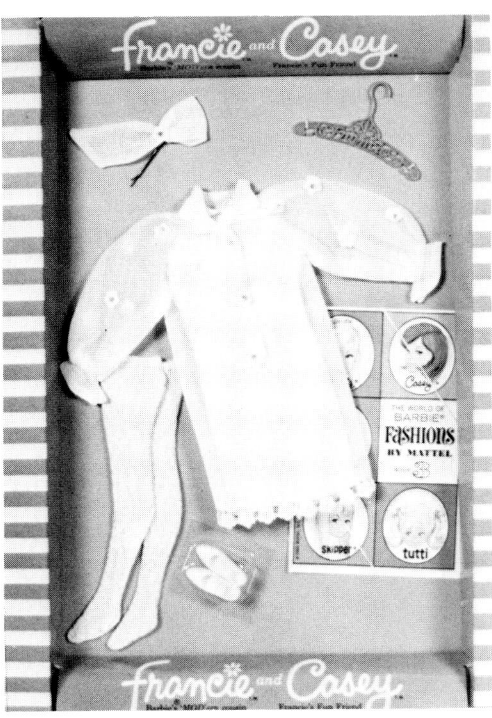

#1280 "Cool White," 1967.

#1723 "Day 'N Night," 1965.

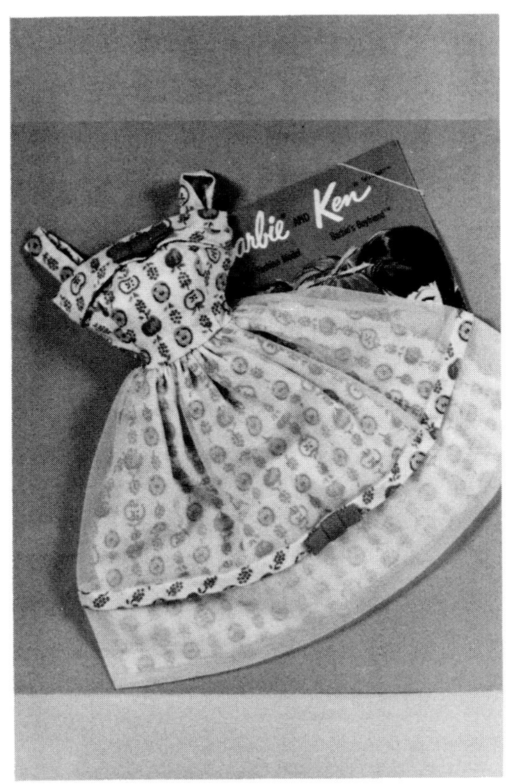

#1600 "Lunch Date," 1964.

"Fancy—Dancy," 1969.

Francie in Pak "Slightly Summery," 1968. (Ashabraner collection)

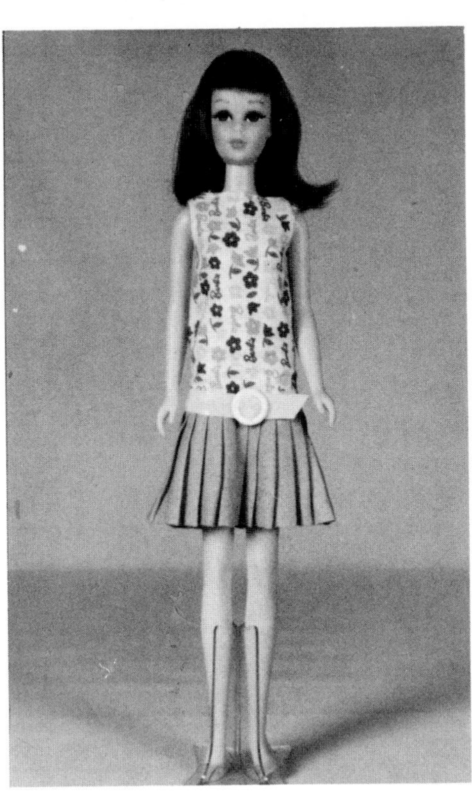

Another version of the "Slightly Summery" dress.

Francie in #3446 "Midi Bouquet," 1971—19

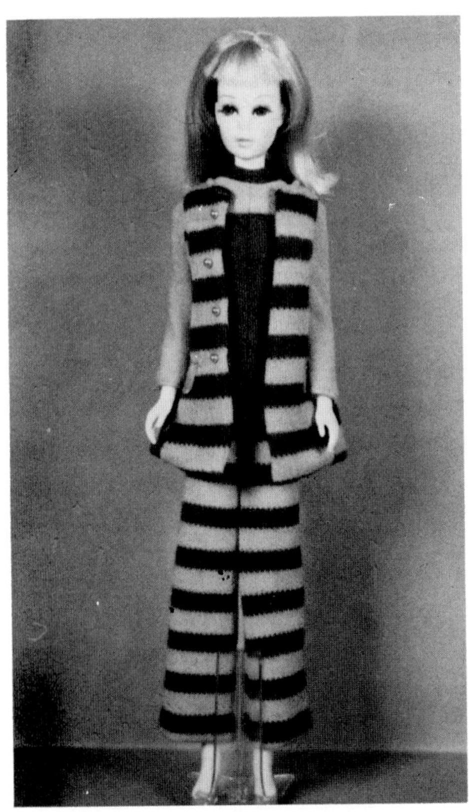

Francie in #1243 "Striped Types," 1970, 1971 and 1974.

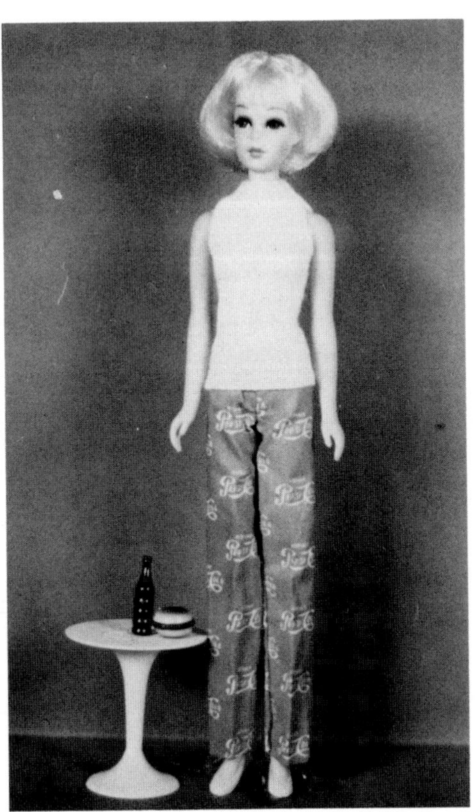

Francie in #7766 Best Buy, 1974.

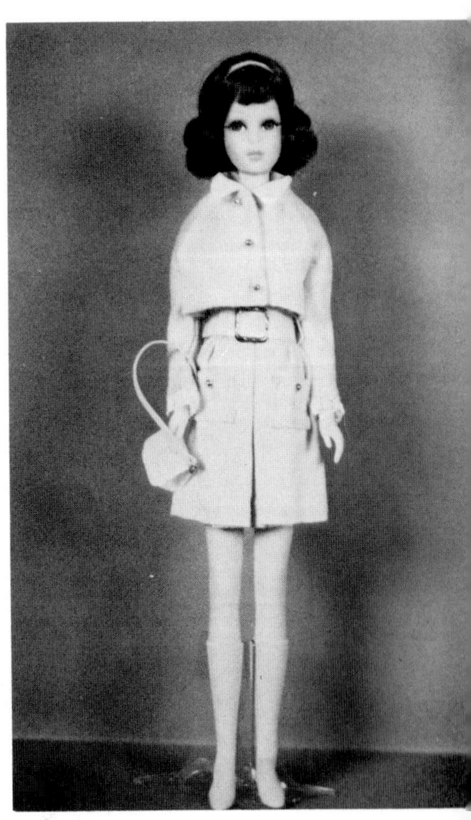

Francie in #1228 "Sissy Suits," 1969.

Bibliography

Mattel Toy Catalogues: 1959, 1960, 1961, 1962, 1964, 1965, 1966, 1967, 1968, 1969, Spring 1970, 1970, Spring 1971, 1971, 1972, 1973, Spring 1974, 1974, Spring 1975, 1975, 1976.
50 Mattel Fashion Booklets: 1959 through 1973.
Barbie Newsletters: 1959, 2 issues.
Barbie Club News: 1961, 2 issues.
Barbie magazines: September, 1961 through July, 1972.
"The Impossible Really is Possible"—The Story of Mattel by Elliot Handler.
Barbie's Sweet 16 Background Information.
The Barbie Era—A Chronology.
The Barbie Family Tree.
Mattel's Fashion Doll List.
Mattel's 1974 Christmas Shopping Basket.
Mattel's Gold Medal Spectacular—1974/1975.
Barbie, The World's Most Famous Doll—1975.
Mattel's 1975 Fall Ad-Stravaganza.
Mattel's Right on the Money 1975/1976.
The World of Barbie First Annual Magazine—1964.
Mattel Toy Catalogue (German): 1975 and 1976.
Mattel Fashion Booklets (German):1974, 1975.
Mattel Fashion Booklets (Italian): 1974, 1975.
Mattel Fashion Booklet (Spanish): 1966.
Mattel Fashion Booklet (Japanese): 1970.
"Years—Years of Dolls"— a Mattel publication.
"Matel's Spring Spectacular"—1976.
Sears Catalogues: 1961 through 1976.
Montgomery Ward Catalogues: 1962 through 1976.
Spiegel Catalogues: 1961, 1964, 1965, 1968, 1969, 1970, 1971, 1974, 1975.
Alden Catalogues: 1966, 1968, 1969, 1970, 1971, 1973.
Penney's Catalogues: 1965, 1966, 1968, 1969, 1970, 1971, 1974, 1975.
John Plain Catalogue: 1970.
Life Magazine: August 23, 1963.
Jack and Jill Magazines: 1966, 1967, 1968.
"For Kids Only"—November, 1969.
"The Greatest Toy Show on Earth"—November, 1971.
Hobbies Magazine: January, 1975.
Nashville Tennessean Newspaper: November 12, 1972.
"A Parent's Guide to Christmas Toys"—1973.
"Playthings"—1974, 1975.

Picture Index

PRICE GUIDE TO:
The Collector's Encyclopedia of
BARBIE DOLLS and Collectibles

The numbers in the first column are the pages in *The Collector's Encyclopedia of Barbie Dolls and Collectibles* where the item is pictured and/or described. The prices quoted in column A are for dolls in **THE SAME CONDITION THEY WERE IN WHEN THEY LEFT THE FACTORY---THE SAME HAIRDO, THE SAME CLOTHES, THE SAME ACCESSORIES AND THE SAME UNOPENED PACKAGING!** If the package has been opened and the doll or the other contents altered in any manner, then the price should be reduced accordingly.The prices quoted in column B are for **nude dolls in good condition.** Some of the things that would reduce the value of the doll are: missing fingers, cut or missing hair, chewed feet, ink marks, worn paint, broken knees, sprung legs, pin pricks and missing eyelashes. Some of the things that could increase the value of the doll are: new or excellent condition, original clothing, other Mattel clothes, any of the original accessories such as a wrist tag, booklet or posing stand and original box.

NAME OF DOLL	PAGE IN BOOK	A	B
Allan			
Bendable legs	18,19,161	300.00	75.00
"Dressed Doll", boxed	275	375.00	
Straight Legs	14,161	100.00	35.00
Angie 'N Tangie	62	200.00	
Angie (alone)	143		50.00
Tangie (alone)	204		50.00
"Babs"	92	200.00	
Barbie			
"Baggies"	88,89,110,111	35.00	
Ballerina	106,107	45.00	12.00
Ballerina on Tour	110	50.00	12.00
Beautiful Bride #9599	110,111	80.00	25.00
Bendable Legs	18	300.00	75.00
Bubble Cut (1961)	6,7,155	150.00	30.00
Bubble Cut (1962)	8,9	125.00	25.00
Bubble Cut (1963-1967)	10,11,140	100.00	15.00
Busy	82,154	100.00	25.00
Busy Talking	82,83,125,161	175.00	35.00
Color Magic	21,23	400.00	100.00
Color 'N Curl #4035	18,20	375.00	
Color 'N Curl #4038	18,20	300.00	
Color 'N Curl #4039	21,23	350.00	
Deluxe Quick Curl	105,106	45.00	10.00
"Dressed Doll", boxed	34	400.00	
Fashion Queen	10	250.00	20.00
Free Moving	98,126	50.00	10.00
Funtime	118,120,122	45.00	15.00
Gold Medal	96,127	35.00	6.00
Gold Medal Set #9042	96	40.00	6.00
Gold Medal Set #9044	96	40.00	6.00
Gold Medal Skater	96,97	60.00	6.00
Gold Medal Skier	96,97	60.00	6.00

NAME OF DOLL	PAGE IN BOOK	A	B
Growin' Pretty Hair (1971)	72,158	85.00	35.00
Growin' Pretty Hair (1972)	84,158	250.00	65.00
Hair Fair Set #4042	38,157	50.00	3.00
Hair Fair Set #4043	45,46,93,157	30.00	3.00
Hair Fair Set #4044	77,157	30.00	3.00
Hair Happenin's #1174	72	500.00	150.00
Hawaiian #7470	103,104,111,118,120,121,159	45.00	20.00
Live Action	70,71,156	75.00	20.00
Live Action On Stage	70	85.00	20.00
Living	50,59,77,78,156	75.00	15.00
Malibu (1971-1972)	72,73,85,154	20.00	6.00
Malibu (1973-1976)	102,103,109	15.00	6.00
Miniature Doll Sets	200,201,203,204	100.00	
Miniature Doll, alone	200,201,203,204		50.00
Molded head, alone	10,13,18,20,21,23		10.00
Newport	91,92	125.00	6.00
Number 1 (1959)	3,4	2,000.00	800.00
Number 2 (1959)	3,4	1,750.00	800.00
Number 3 (1960)	5,140	500.00	150.00
Number 4 (1960)	5,140	375.00	125.00
#7382 Promo	121,122,123	20.00	6.00
#8587	113,114,115,122	25.00	8.00
#8588	114,118,121,122	50.00	10.00
Ponytail (1961)	6,7	375.00	45.00
Ponytail (1962)	8,9	300.00	40.00
Ponytail (1963-1965)	10,11,140	250.00	40.00
Ponytail, "Swirl"	13,15	375.00	100.00
Quick Curl	86,87,154,162	45.00	10.00
Sleep-eyed	14,15	450.00	150.00
Standard #1190 (1967-1969)	26,155	150.00	20.00
Standard #1190 (1970-1971)	66,67,74,75	150.00	20.00
Sun Valley	91	50.00	6.00
Sweet 16, Promo	90,125	45.00	12.00
Sweet 16, Regular	90,162	40.00	12.00
Talking, plastic box (1968)	40,41	100.00	20.00
Talking (1969-1970)	46,49,68,69	75.00	20.00
Talking (1971-1972)	76	75.00	20.00
Talking, Spanish	40,46,68,155	100.00	20.00
Twist 'N Turn	26,42,43,47,64,76,155	125.00	25.00
Walk Lively	80,125,156	75.00	15.00
Ward's Anniversary	85	275.00	150.00
Wig Wardrobe	13	75.00	
"**Barbie Baby-sits**" set (1963-1965)	12,20	200.00	25.00
"**Barbie Baby-sits**" set (1974-1976)	93,95,112	35.00	15.00
Brad			
Bendable Legs	65,78,146,159	65.00	25.00
Talking	60,78,146	60.00	25.00
Buffy & Mrs. Beasley	30,42,43	250.00	
Buffy, alone	30,42,43		50.00
Mrs. Beasley, alone	204		50.00

NAME OF DOLL	PAGE IN BOOK	A	B
Cara			
Ballerina	107	50.00	10.00
Deluxe Quick Curl	105,106	35.00	10.00
Free Moving	98,99,100	50.00	12.00
Quick Curl	101,104,127	45.00	12.00
Carla	55,121,123,143	75.00	25.00
Casey			
"Baggie"	103,104	25.00	
Twist 'N Turn	35,39	100.00	30.00
Chris (1967-1968)	36,37	150.00	50.00
Chris, re-issued (1974-1976)	113,116,117,160	45.00	15.00
Christie			
Live Action	70,71,79	75.00	25.00
Malibu (1973-1976)	88,102,103,109,144	20.00	6.00
Talking, plastic box (1968)	40,41	100.00	20.00
Talking (1969-1972)	60,77,144	75.00	20.00
Twist 'N Turn	62,63,144	100.00	35.00
Colored Francie	29,35,144	400.00	150.00
Curtis, Free Moving	98,99,100,159	75.00	25.00
Fluff, Living	74,75	100.00	45.00
Francie			
"Baggie"	103,104	25.00	
Bendable Legs	22,23	100.00	25.00
Busy	82,83,151	100.00	35.00
Colored	29,35,144	400.00	150.00
Growin' Pretty Hair	61,74,150	75.00	25.00
Hair Happenin's	61,150	150.00	35.00
Malibu (1971-1972)	72,73,151	25.00	6.00
Malibu (1973-1976)	102,103,109	20.00	6.00
Quick Curl	86,87,151	45.00	10.00
Straight Legs	22,23	150.00	35.00
Twist 'N Turn (1967-1970)	35,46,47,151	100.00	15.00
Twist 'N Turn (1971)	63,75,76	500.00	200.00
Ginger, Growing Up	109,111	75.00	25.00
Jamie, Walking	60,61	375.00	100.00
Julia			
Talking	45,77,79,147	75.00	20.00
Twist 'N Turn (2-piece uniform)	45,147	100.00	20.00
Twist 'N Turn (1-piece uniform)	64,65	75.00	20.00
Kelley:			
Quick Curl	86,87,88	45.00	10.00
Yellowstone	91,95	200.00	75.00

NAME OF DOLL	PAGE IN BOOK	A	B
Ken			
"Baggies"	88,89,92	25.00	
Bendable Legs #1020	18,19,20	300.00	75.00
Bendable Legs #1124	65,163	75.00	15.00
Busy	82,164	85.00	25.00
Busy Talking	82,83	175.00	35.00
"Dressed Doll", boxed	58,275	350.00	
Flocked Hair #750	6	150.00	35.00
Free Moving	98,99,100,126	50.00	10.00
Funtime	112,118,120,124	45.00	15.00
Gold Medal Skier	96,97	65.00	4.00
Live Action	70,71,164	75.00	20.00
Live Action On Stage	70	85.00	20.00
Malibu (1971-1973)	72,73,163	20.00	6.00
Malibu (1974-1976)	102,103,109	15.00	6.00
Mod Hair	86,162,164	45.00	12.00
Now Look	107,108	45.00	12.00
Painted Hair #750	8,12,13,15,139,163	100.00	15.00
Sun Valley	91,95	50.00	6.00
Talking	45,66,79,163	75.00	20.00
Talking, Spanish	66	100.00	20.00
Walk Lively	80,164	75.00	15.00
Ward's Dressed	94	100.00	8.00
Lori 'N Rori	62	375.00	
Lori, alone	143		50.00
Rori, alone	206		175.00
Midge			
Bendable Legs	18,19,160	300.00	100.00
Color 'N Curl #4035	18,20	400.00	
"Dressed Doll", boxed		350.00	
Molded Head, alone	16,17,18,20		20.00
Straight Legs	10,11	75.00	15.00
Wig Wardrobe	16,17	150.00	
Miss America			
Kellogg's Blonde Quick Curl	93	50.00	5.00
Kellogg's Brunette Quick Curl	86	75.00	35.00
Kellogg's Walk Lively	80	75.00	35.00
Quick Curl, blonde (1974-1976)	93,94,95,148	45.00	5.00
Quick Curl, brunette	86,148	175.00	35.00
Walk Lively	80,81	150.00	35.00
Nan 'N Fran	62	200.00	
Nan, alone	143		50.00
Fran, alone	204		50.00
P.J.			
"Baggie"	88,89	25.00	
Deluxe Quick Curl	105,106	45.00	6.00
Free Moving	98,99,100,126	50.00	10.00
Gold Medal Gymnast	96,97	75.00	6.00
Live Action	70,71,79	75.00	20.00
Live Action On Stage	70	85.00	20.00
Malibu (1972)	80,81,149	20.00	6.00
Malibu (1973-1976)	102,103,109	15.00	6.00

NAME OF DOLL	PAGE IN BOOK	A	B
Talking	46,75,149	75.00	20.00
Twist 'N Turn	62,63,149	125.00	25.00
Ricky	16,152	100.00	35.00
Skipper			
"Baggie" Pose 'N Play	88,89,104,152	20.00	
Bendable Legs	18,20,39	150.00	35.00
Deluxe Quick Curl	29,121,123,124	50.00	
"Dressed Doll", boxed		350.00	
Funtime	118,120,124	45.00	15.00
Growing Up	101,112,126,153	45.00	8.00
Living	50,59,77,78,117	45.00	8.00
Malibu (1971-1972)	72,73,153	20.00	6.00
Malibu (1973-1976)	102,103,109	15.00	6.00
Pose 'N Play with gym #1179	84,152	200.00	20.00
Quick Curl	86,87,153	45.00	6.00
Straight Legs	14,15	50.00	8.00
Straight Legs, re-issue	66,67	100.00	20.00
Twist 'N Turn	42,48,63,152	75.00	15.00
Skooter			
Bendable Legs	21	200.00	20.00
Funtime	121,123,124	150.00	50.00
Straight Legs	16	75.00	20.00
Stacey			
Talking, plastic box (1968)	40,41,148	100.00	20.00
Talking (1969-1971)	46,49,66	75.00	20.00
Twist 'N Turn	42,46,48,64,148	125.00	25.00
Steffie			
"Babs"	92	200.00	
Busy	82,125,145	150.00	25.00
Busy Talking	82,83,145	250.00	50.00
Walk Lively	80,81,145	100.00	25.00
Tiff, Pose 'N Play	84,147	250.00	100.00
Todd			
Brown box, with Tutti	24	150.00	
#3590	36,37	100.00	30.00
#8129, re-issue	113,116,117,160	45.00	15.00
"Sundae Treat" Set with Tutti	24	350.00	30.00
Truly Scrumptious			
Straight Legs	44	400.00	150.00
Talking	44,147	400.00	150.00
Tutti			
Brown box, with Todd	24	150.00	
"Cookin' Goodies" Set	36,142	300.00	25.00
"Me and My Dog" Set	24,25,141	300.00	25.00
"Melody In Pink" Set	24,25,142	150.00	25.00
"Night-Night" Set, with top	24,25,141	100.00	25.00
#3550	24,36,27,141	75.00	15.00
#3580	36,37,46,141	75.00	15.00

NAME OF DOLL	PAGE IN BOOK	A	B
#8128, re-issue	113,116,117,160	45.00	10.00
Re-issue Playsettings	118,119,202	75.00	12.00
"Sundae Treat" Set with Todd	24,142	350.00	30.00
"Swing-A-Ling" Set	36,142	300.00	50.00
"Walkin' My Dolly" Set, with top	24,25,141,202	200.00	25.00
Twiggy	38,39	100.00	25.00

MISCELLANEOUS ITEMS	PAGE IN BOOK	MINT CONDITION
Airplane	237	300.00
Album, Record	255	20.00
Ballerina Stage	234	35.00
Bathe'n Beauty (Sears)	242	30.00
Beach Bus	237	25.00
Beauty Bath	242	25.00
Beauty Center	252	12.00
Bed, Barbie's Suzy Goose	240	15.00
Bed, Skipper's Suzy Goose	240	25.00
Bike	237	15.00
Boat, Dream	238	25.00
Boat, Sears	238	50.00
Boat, Sunsailor	236	45.00
Bunk Beds, Skipper's	33,242	100.00
Cafe Today	233	50.00
Cards, Trading	255	25.00
Cases	246,247	5.00
Classy Corvette	238	125.00
Colorforms	253	8.00
Country Camper	236	35.00
Country Living House	234	35.00
Dancer	130,212	60.00
Display Sets	248	400.00
Embroidery Set	253	25.00
Fashion Plaza	235	50.00
Fashion Shop	232	75.00
Fashion Stage	235	15.00
Friend Ship	237	45.00
Furniture, European	129	150.00
Furniture, Go-Together (each set)	243	75.00
Game, Queen of the Prom	254	10.00
Gift Set, "Fashion Queen Barbie & Her Friends"	245	400.00
Gift Set, "Fashion Queen Barbie & Ken Trousseau"	245	500.00
Gift Set, "Midge's Ensemble"	245	400.00
Gift Set, "On Parade"	244	400.00
Gift Set, "Party Time"	245	300.00
Gift Set, "Strollin' In Style"	245	475.00
Goin' Camping Set	238	50.00
Gym, Skipper's Swing-A-Rounder (without doll)	84	40.00
Hair Originals	255	8.00
Hangers	255	5.00
High Sierra Set	251	10.00
Jewelry Box	251	5.00
Magazines, miniature	263	5.00
Necklace	254	5.00

MISCELLANEOUS ITEMS	PAGE IN BOOK	MINT CONDITION
Nurse Kit	254	18.00
Piano, Barbie's Suzy Goose	239	150.00
Pool, Swimming	253	25.00
Posing Stand, First	3	75.00
Room-fulls	241	45.00
Room-fulls, Apartment	241	75.00
Skipper Bedroom, Growing up	242	40.00
Skipper Dream Room	232	100.00
Ski Village, Olympic	235	45.00
Sun 'N Fun Buggy	236	100.00
Theatre	233	200.00
Tutti's House	234	75.00
Vanity & Bench, Barbie's Suzy Goose	239	15.00
Vanity & Bench, Skipper's Suzy Goose	240	20.00
Wardrobe, Barbie's Suzy Goose	239	15.00
Wardrobe, Skipper's Suzy Goose	240	20.00